Representing the Irreparable:
The Shoah, the Bible, and the Art of
Samuel Bak

EDITED BY DANNA NOLAN FEWELL,
GARY A. PHILLIPS, AND YVONNE SHERWOOD

Acknowledgements

In his provocative *A Rabbi Reads the Bible,* Jonathan Magonet, citing Rav Shmuel Sperber, writes: "Religion offers you answers without obliterating the questions. They become blunted and will not attack you with as much ferocity, but without them the answers would dry up and wither away....The question is a great religious act. It helps you live great religious truths" (27). Like religion, the artwork of Samuel Bak privileges the question; however Bak's art invites questions about unspeakable, irreparable events whose answers elude grasp, escape comprehension. Bak insists that he offers only questions, not answers... but does he? Bak's question-raising art in its very materiality is response, indeed we might call it a provisional answer—his answer—to the most profound questions brought to mind by the useless suffering of the Shoah. Art as both question and answer. Are we permitted to think of Bak's painting, his concerns, as "religious?" Bak, a self-described "God-fearing atheist," might object to too close an identification of his art with religion although, as his self-description announces, his engagement with the great masters of Western art in general and the book of Genesis in particular would suggest a more complicated, even paradoxical, relationship. We suspect that he might not object to this recasting of the Rabbi's words: the question is the great artistic act that helps you struggle with great and painful existential truths. Religion and Bak's art are not so easily distinguishable in either content or function.

For those of us who engage religion and the Bible as teachers and scholars in religious studies or theology departments, Bak's art both complicates and clarifies the reading of Torah and Christian Scriptures in light of the Shoah. This book is an acknowledgment of that disturbance in different ways. As response, this book would not have been possible were it not for the labor, dedication, and generosity of many individuals committed to a wider discussion of the questions and answers which Bak's artwork elicits.

The editors wish to thank Linda Dietch and Grant Gieseke, Drew University graduate students, who prepared the bibliography and indices, respectively. We are greatly indebted to the talented Pucker Gallery staff and associates: Destiny McDonald Barletta and Kate Lincoln for their organizational and editorial skills; Maritza Medina for design; David Winkler for managing the exhibition at Drexel University in conjunction with the Society of Biblical Literature Annual meeting in November 2006 where many of the volume essays were first presented. We also express thanks to the Society of Biblical Literature for subvening Sam and Josée Bak's stay in Philadelphia. Our special thanks are reserved, however, for Sue and Bernie Pucker whose commitment to a greater public awareness of Sam's work and the questions he raises is matched only by a generosity of spirit and resources in subvening the full cost of this book's production. And, finally, it goes without saying, our thanks to Sam whose work and person continue to invite us to ponder and live with the questions in that elusive search for *Tikkun Olam.*

Representing the Irreparable:
The Shoah, the Bible, and the Art of
Samuel Bak

EDITED BY DANNA NOLAN FEWELL,
GARY A. PHILLIPS, AND YVONNE SHERWOOD

Texts by
Samuel Bak
Danna Nolan Fewell
Michael Fishbane
Lawrence L. Langer
Dan Mathewson
Alicia Ostriker
Gary A. Phillips
S. Brent Rodríguez Plate
Bernard H. Pucker
Charles Rix
Yvonne Sherwood

Introduction
Gary A. Phillips and Danna Nolan Fewell

Design: Maritza Medina
Editors: Destiny McDonald Barletta, Kate Lincoln

Published by Pucker Art Publications
Boston, Massachusetts 02116

Distributed by Syracuse University Press
Syracuse, New York 13244-5160

Printed in China by South China Printing Company Limited
New York, New York 10021

Library of Congress Cataloging-in-Publication Data

Representing the irreparable : the Shoah, the Bible, and the art of Samuel Bak / edited by Danna Nolan Fewell, Gary A. Phillips, and Yvonne Sherwood. -- 1st ed.

p. cm.

Includes bibliographical references and index.

ISBN 1-879985-18-7 (hardcover)

1. Bak, Samuel--Criticism and interpretation. 2. Holocaust, Jewish (1939-1945), in art. 3. Jewish art and symbolism. I. Fewell, Danna Nolan. II. Phillips, Gary Allen. III. Sherwood, Yvonne.

ND979.B27R47 2008

759.95694--dc22

2008000003

CONTENTS

Continued on page VI

CONTENTS, *continued*

List of Images

INTRODUCTION

Gary A. Phillips and Danna Nolan Fewell

The art of Samuel Bak entrances. It also disquiets. Dismembered human figures of flesh, metal, wood, and stone. Broken pottery and rusted keys, petrified teddy bears and discarded children's shoes, floating rocks, and uprooted trees. Broken chess pieces. Fractured rainbows. Books turned buildings, tablets turned tombstones, memorial candles turned crematoria. Soundless musical instruments, flightless doves, mechanized, immobile angels, crucified children. And yet: pears and paradise, new growth on broken branches, sunrises in sunsets. Color and catastrophe. Genesis and genocide. Exodus and expulsion. Ruins and remnants. Michelangelo, Rembrandt, Mantegna, Dürer, de Chirico echoed and subverted. Paradoxes. Contradictions. Ambiguities. Excesses. All ingredients of a survivor's post-Holocaust landscape.

"Like complex literary texts, Bak's works impose on his audience the responsibility of interpretation. The outcome of this venture is always uncertain, because more often than not we are left with the burden of afflicted consciousness rather than the satisfaction of having found easy meanings."[1] So comments Holocaust scholar Lawrence Langer on the visual and interpretive effects of Bak's images. The subject matter of Bak's painting is anything but easy. His still lives, people, and landscapes depict a world destroyed, and yet provisionally pieced back together. Although the broken world is never to be made whole again, Bak says "...we can still make something that looks as if it was whole and live with it."[2] This tension between destruction and construction,[3] a living on "as if," perfuses his work, leaving viewers to decide for themselves how the shattered Tablets of the Law and *Tikkun Olam* can be thought together. No easy either/or solution here to let the viewer—or Bak himself for that matter—off the interpretive hook.

A child survivor of the Vilna liquidation, a child prodigy whose first exhibition was held in the ghetto at age nine, Bak weaves together personal history and Jewish history to articulate an iconography of his Holocaust experience. Across nearly seven decades of artistic production, Sam Bak has explored and reworked a set of metaphors, a visual grammar and vocabulary that ultimately privileges questions: How does a fragmented, murdered world cohere? What does "covenant" mean in light of Auschwitz and the liquidation of the Vilna ghetto? In the face of such massive and meaningless suffering, how do traditional religious and cultural symbols, stories, and ceremonies retain past vitality and validity? How does one authentically preserve memory of personal loss and suffering? *Why* and *how* do we now face the loss of 1.5 million murdered children? In direct resistance to a Holocaust world where to ask "Why?" was forbidden and futile,[4] Bak's canvasses demand that we ask "Why?" and that we do so repeatedly.

What are we to *make* of these questions? What are we to *do* with them? Bak communicates no resolutions, only a steady resolve to press ahead in an interrogatory mode. We hear a similar antinomy in Rainer Maria Rilke's counsel to a young poet who has written for sage advice: "love the questions themselves as if they were locked rooms or books written in a very foreign language....Live the questions now."[5] Bak *lives* the questions, *loves* the questions, indeed *obsesses over* the questions, even as, precisely because, they disrupt. Images of keys, key holes, and broken locks; blindfolded chess pieces; mute and mangled musicians; blank canvasses; mirrors that double as windows; shifting metaphors of site, sight, and insight accentuate the elusiveness of answers, the imposition of interpretation. Bak shifts to us, his viewers, the onus of understanding the Holocaust re-visioned. We stand, afflicted in consciousness and conscience, on the doorsills of Bak's locked rooms just within reach of his foreign books. For, to borrow the imagery of Marcel Proust, Bak's works are not monuments, but *thresholds*: They "take us a certain way and then leave us, having shown us a road."[6]

Why is Samuel Bak's art and the questions he raises important for scholars of religion today? In other words, why create a book of collected essays that engages the landscapes of Bak's Holocaust experiences? First, and foremost, Bak is overtly concerned with matters religious and biblical. Creation, covenant, exodus, exile, Diaspora, Torah, Decalogue, theodicy, and midrash are recurring Jewish themes that emerge in his work. His re-visions of Genesis stories—the creation of Adam and the expulsion from the Garden, the Noahic flood, Jacob's dream, and the Akedah—as well as of New Testament motifs of crucifixion and apocalypse, defamiliarize these texts and our conventional ways of reading them. For readers of the Bible, whether scholar or lay, the juxtaposition of ancient sacred story with modern suffering story challenges us to see the biblical text in a different light, illumined both by the light of reason and the glow of crematoria furnaces. Bak's images, which often include plays upon words, invite those who read the Bible as literary work to confront the Bible as canvas work. Bak's pictorial readings invite a reconsideration of the Post-Reformation privileging of word over image, and of the post-Enlightenment privileging of reason over experience.

A second reason Bak's work is important for Jewish and Christian readers of the Bible is articulated best in Emil Fackenheim's call for interrupted reading. In *The Jewish Bible after the Holocaust: a Re-Reading*,[7] Fackenheim insists that the event of the Holocaust must shatter prior theological and exegetical thinking about the biblical text for both Jews and Christians, maybe especially for Christians. Exegetes are challenged with the moral responsibility to interrogate the ways in which Christianity historically has been and continues to be defined by a virulent contempt for Judaism, the ways in which Christianity has co-opted Jewish scriptures to produce meanings far removed from their original contexts, and the ways in which Christian doctrine and dogma have contributed to and remained immune to the deaths of 1.5 million children. Religion and religious traditions, in all forms, must now stand accountable for overt violence, passive neglect, and short-sighted naiveté.

Consequently, although preoccupied with matters biblical and religious, Bak does not simply reiterate or expand upon tradition. Rather, as a self-conscious artist, exegete, and critic, he "lives in doubt" before artistic and biblical images and seems compelled to critique the very image he constructs.[8] Bak's oft-repeated questioning of the permanence of God's covenant with Israel specifically and humankind more generally—cobbled-together rainbows, fractured Tablets of the Law—becomes a concern, too, for Christians as well as Jews as he disrupts conventional religious understandings and conventional modes of biblical representation in which suffering, whether on Mt. Moriah or Golgotha, can be given meaning. For instance, Bak's staging of the Akedah with death camp props, like Elie Wiesel's restaging of a *Din Torah* in the setting of an eighteen-century Eastern European pogrom in *The Trial of God,*[9] unhinges any theological imagination content to stand at a distance from history and the realities of shattered worlds. And when Bak joins and juxtaposes crucified child with fractured rainbow, both Christians and Jews have now to wonder what if any religious symbols and understanding are left intact after the destruction. A different, more rigorous, standard of judgment must now apply to any and all theological and exegetical statements, whether visual or verbal. One thinks of Irving Greenberg's unequivocal formulation: "No statement, theological or otherwise, should be made that would not be credible in the presence of burning children."[10] Bak is no less unequivocal. His renderings of broken child and world demand in visual terms what Greenberg stipulates verbally. But for Bak, the mode of communication is the question rather than the declaration. As question, Bak's work resists settling into a fixed understanding, statement, or assertion, but persistently interrupts every effort to resolve. It is as question that Bak attempts to do justice to his responsibility to the lost children by painting fragmented faces and bodies as repeated interruptions of the everyday world. Do you remember? Can we re-member? For the sake of the past? For the sake of the future?[11]

Through his style and subject matter Bak revisits and re-envisions his experience, continuously returning to and overturning earlier constructions. The numerous redrawings of the Warsaw ghetto boy, of Bak's own visage as child and adult, and of Dürer's melancholic angel, for example, effect an ethical interruption of moral complacencies and theological assurities. This visual returning is ever an undoing and redoing of what was earlier painted and questioned, a critique of past constructions that we might associate with Emmanuel Levinas's identification with the moment of ethics. For Levinas the ethical relation is a witnessing to the other person's suffering and a bearing responsibility for that suffering that is never satisfied or finished, only intensified. The other in his or her materiality perpetually imposes upon my world with its inclinations toward self-definition, self-containment, and self-absorption. Likened to insomnia, the ethical demand to bear witness agitates my consciousness and conscience, constantly aggravates my manner of interpreting and living, keeps me moving. There is no rest in the ethical relationship, no satisfying the demand for justice, no balancing of the moral ledger, no evasion. To respond is always to be kept off-balance, unhinged, interrupted by what is outside of me. Little wonder, then, before the paint on one canvas is dry Bak begins another, unsatisfied that he has said enough or that we have inquired sufficiently.

And finally, reflecting the survivor's experience where life for one came as death to another—Sam Bak's experience as a child writ large—we are left to rethink the very heart of religious questioning, namely, the connection between death and life. Langer refers to this as "deathlife" where death and life "are no longer opposites or alternatives, but co-exist with a painful intimacy that alters our way of seeing the self in relation to history."[12] Bak's redrawing of the relation between life and death reflects the deeper logic of his artistic vision, a paradoxical logic in which opposites cohere. More than the content of Bak's artistic compositions, the very act of artistic creation dramatizes the paradox of the living-inseparable-from-dying, creating in the midst of suffering, the urgency to survive, to live "as if," as Bak says.

Franz Rosenzweig captures the potency and paradox of such art in these terms:

> This Janus face of art, that it aggravates the suffering of life and at the same time helps people to bear it, allows it to accompany us through life. It teaches us to overcome without forgetting. Because a person is not to forget, but shall remember everything inside. A person shall bear suffering and shall be consoled.[13]

Bak preserves memory of the twentieth century ruination of Jewish life and culture by way of an artistic passion and precision that stubbornly announces the creativity of the human spirit. He fabricates visual monuments that maintain a tensive bond between the inhuman and the ingenious, confronting us with pain and suffering while at the same time helping us to bear loss through a re-minding, a re-membering, and a re-mending. It is "art for the Other," pointing us beyond ourselves to those murdered others who call for something from us—memory, accountability, the courage to continue to question.[14]

---

1 Lawrence Langer, "The Holocaust Theme in the Paintings of Samuel Bak" in *Samuel Bak Retrospektive 1946-97* at the Panorama Museum in Bad Frankenhausen in 1998, 135-36.

2 Cited in Langer, 1998. Originally Tape HVT-618 in the Fortunoff Video Archive for Holocaust Testimonies at Yale University.

3 See Yvonne Sherwood's work on "Iconoclash" in this volume.

4 One is reminded of Primo Levi's story of the concentration camp guard who refuses to let Levi grab an icicle to slake his thirst. Levi asks "Why?" And the guard replies: "There is no 'why' here *(Hier ist kein warum).*" *Survival in Auschwitz: The Nazi Assault on Humanity* (New York: Collier Books, 1986), 29.

5 Rainer Maria Rilke, *Letters to a Young Poet,* trans. Stephen Mitchell (New York: Random House, 1984), 34.

6 Gabriel Josopovici, discussing Proust and his own experience with the Bible in Jonathan Magonet, *A Rabbi Reads the Bible* (London: SCM, 1991, 2004), 40.

7 Manchester University Press, 1990.

8 See James Hatley, *Suffering Witness: The Quandary of Responsibility after the Irreparable* (State University of New York, 2000), 115-16. Emmanuel Levinas' comments about modern literature manifesting "a more and more clear awareness of [the] fundamental insufficiency of artistic idolatry" could well apply to Bak:

> [T]he artist refuses to be only an artist, not because he wants to defend a thesis or cause, but because he needs to interpret his myths himself. Perhaps the doubts that, since the renaissance, the alleged death of God has put in souls have compromised for the

> artist the reality of the henceforth inconsistent models, have imposed on him the onus of finding his models anew in the heart of his production itself, and made him believe he had a mission to be creator and revealer. The task of criticism remains essential, even if God was not dead, but only exiled. ("Reality and Its Shadow," in *Collected Philosophical Papers,* ed. Alphonso Lingis (Dordrecht: Martinus Nijhoff, 1987], 1-13, esp. 13)

9 *The Trial of God (as it was held on February 25, 1649, in Shamgorod: a Play by Elie Wiesel),* trans. Marion Wiesel (New York: Schocken Books, 1979, 1995).

10 Irving Greenberg, "Cloud of Smoke, Pillar of Fire," in *Auschwitz: Beginning of a New Era?,* ed. E. Fleischner (New York: KTAV, 1977), 7-55; 23.

11 In Bak's words,

> Sometimes I have the feeling that I would like to paint one million Jewish icons. One million of these Warsaw boys, for the number of children who were murdered. Perhaps as a way to deal with the enormous void left by all of them? I can see the boy's little figure over a flickering light in every Jewish home. A reminder of what has happened, and of what in some way has defined our contemporary Jewish identity. (Richard Raskin, "An Interview with Samuel Bak," in *A Child at Gunpoint: A Case Study in the Life of a Photo* [Gylling, Denmark: Aarhus University Press, 2004], 154.

12 Langer, 137.

13 In Barbara Galli's new translation of Rosenzweig's *The Star of Redemption* (University of Wisconsin, 2005), the discussion of art and suffering falls on pages 399-400. We, however, prefer Robert Gibbs's translation of this section (and the one below) that he includes in his helpful essay "Unjustifiable Suffering," in *Suffering Religion,* ed. Robert Gibbs and Elliott R. Wolfson. (London/New York: Routledge, 2002), 13-35.

14 As Rosenzweig writes,

> Art overcomes only by structuring suffering, not by denying it. The artist knows himself as he to whom it is given to say what he suffers. The muteness of the first human is also in his self. He tries neither to keep the suffering silent nor to scream it out: he represents it. In his representation he reconciles the contradiction, that he himself is there and the suffering also is there; he reconciles it, without doing the least debasement of it. (Gibbs, 30)

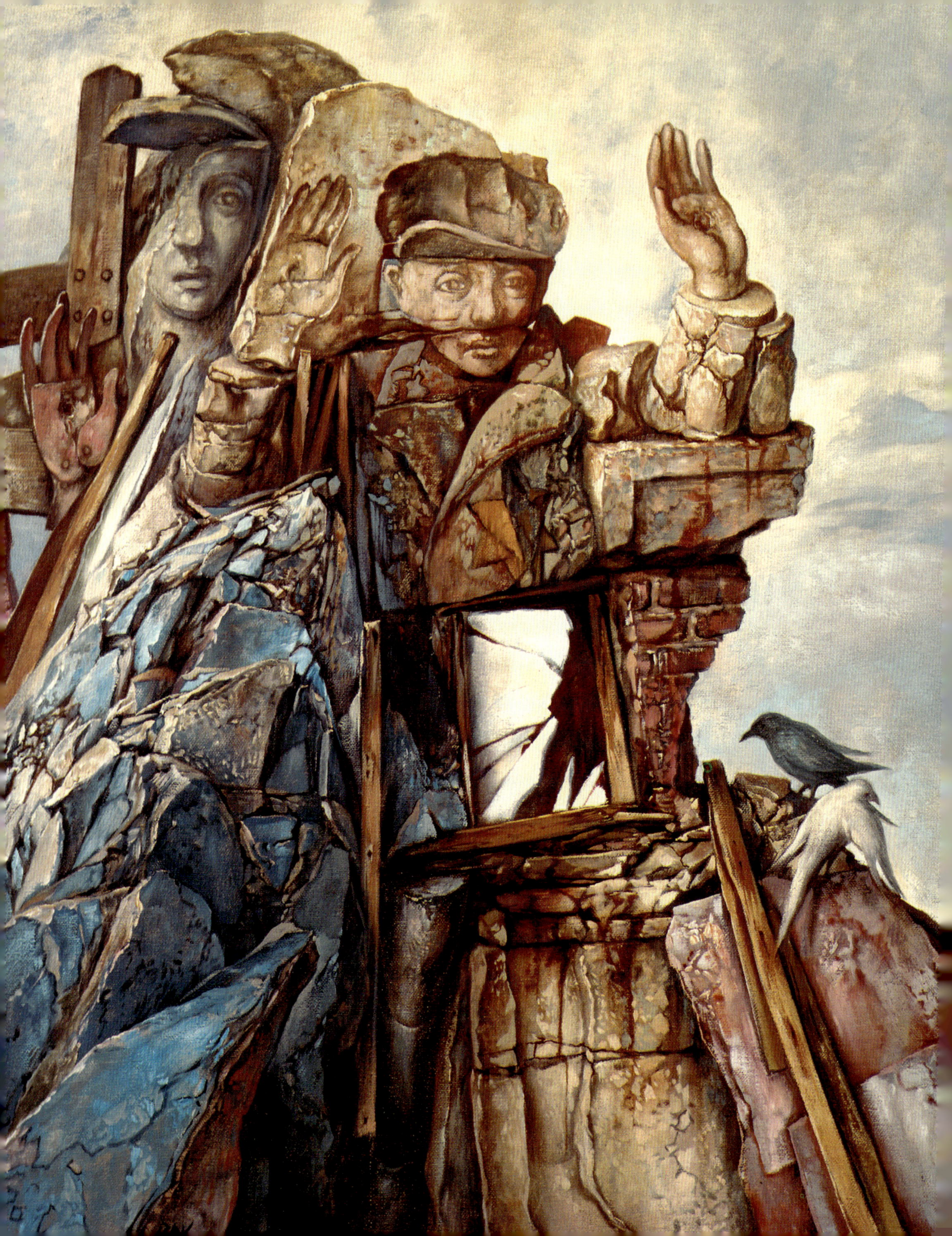

Where There is Still Life: Sketching the Life of Samuel Bak

BERNARD H. PUCKER

As I sat at the conference of the Society of Biblical Literature and the American Academy of Religion in Philadelphia on the afternoon of November 20, 2005, I was privileged to listen to the exceptional papers presented in this venue. Scholar after scholar provided personal, well-documented arguments inspired by a work or works by the artist Samuel Bak. He, too, was present and was transported ahead in time by one hundred and fifty years to a place and time when scholars will discuss, examine, explore, and interpret his work. It was a rare moment for a living artist. Each voice was stimulated by the fundamental questions ignited by his images.

Bak became excited by their interpretations and managed to continue his search, his journey, and his need to ask questions of the most profound nature. What is the meaning of life in our day? How can there be such inhumanity in our world? How can humankind allow such bestiality and wanton disregard for human rights and life? What can we learn from our recent past? How can we continue to read holy texts without regard for the powerful destruction of humankind in World War II and beyond?

Through visual metaphors meticulously rendered, Bak enables and challenges us to be alert to the profound brokenness in our universe that stands in need of a *tikkun*—a repair. Only through an honest acknowledgement of what was and what has transpired can we begin to correct, modify, and repair our world.

Samuel Bak was born in August 1933 in Vilna, an important center of Jewish life in Central Europe. Vilna was referred to as "The Jerusalem of Lithuania." Bak's childhood was secure, loving, and well-protected. Both sets of grandparents and parents doted on their only offspring and his remarkable artistic talent that was recognized when he was three years old. Within three more years his perfect world was to develop cracks with the Russian occupation, and by the summer of

Double Reflection, 1997
Oil on Linen, 20 1/2 x 20"

1941 the fissures had swallowed both sets of grandparents as the Nazis moved ahead with their program of murdering all Jews.

By decisive actions, good fortune, and the good will of specific "guardian angels," Sam and his mother survived the destruction of the Vilna Jewish community. Of nearly eighty thousand Jews only a mere 250 survived. The odds were not good.

Throughout the war his mother protected and nourished his artistic gift. Remarkable works survived and are now located in the National Jewish Museum of Vilnius. Post-war survival was difficult and eventually mother and son arrived at the Landsberg Displaced Persons Camp en route to Palestine. From 1946 their brief stopover in Landsberg was extended to 1948. Eventually they arrived in Israel, and Sam's formal education began. High school, Hebrew language, new contemporaries, the struggle with being a survivor, one of the very few not slaughtered, all defined his persona. His artistic ability and sensibilities enabled him to develop responses to the present and to his memories of the past.

Art school was followed by a fellowship to Paris, which launched his journey as an adult artist. All the while Bak created his art in the style of the day with a specific Bak optic; gradually his own distinctive voice emerged. Enigmatic images appeared; all were both clear and markedly unclear. Pears littered landscapes; they were presented as being assaulted, as housing for factories of death, as stone monuments to a life that was. Fragile fruit signified the fragility of the human condition. The pear became Bak's personal metaphor and a symbol for questioning all basic notions of moral and ethical behavior.

The works were irresistible, and the artist's need to express was overwhelming. For five decades his intense search for a kind of truth and a collection of questions and answers has motivated and caused each new body of work. Each motif was explored in depth, each image continued to ask questions. Chess as metaphor: game pieces were dispersed across a fractured, fragmented board. Pawns were sacrificed; knights became hobby horses; kings and queens were deposed—a world of chaos was portrayed. Birds appeared as vehicles for hope, for flight, for rescue, and yet none could fly. Clocks arose from a barren landscape; time stood still and did not fly.

An entire lexicon of Jewish experience appears. Broken tablets; towns buried with walls in the shape of the six-pointed star; wooden synagogues reconstructed out of the books, and Torah scrolls used within those spaces.

The tales of Genesis as portrayed by Michelangelo, Mantegna and Rembrandt were reconceived through Bak's optic—raising again and again questions of the presence/absence of God and the presence/absence of humanity in the midst of devastation beyond our ken. All of these different images were followed upon by the reappearance of his pears as a persistent search for answers. These works echoed in the midst of his return to his birthplace, Vilna, and its remarkable resurrection on his canvases. It is a world of loss, memory, and brokenness, yet it is our world.

For Bak, there is no calm, no peace of mind, no respite from his search. The questions seem to expand out of each new body of work. His most recent canvases, *Still, Life,* presents a spectacular collection of works that explore the words "Still Life;" Nature Morte in lush landscape. Each work emphasizes the fragility of the middle two letters "IF" in the word "Life." Again, Bak has fabricated another way to ask his unanswered and maybe unanswerable questions.

Each scholarly paper delivered in Philadelphia served to underscore the remarkable resource of the art of Samuel Bak for thinking about the Bible and religion, about the questions human beings must face. This journey of the spirit via Bak's art informs his imagination and challenges us. We are fortunate to have him and his art as part of our lives.

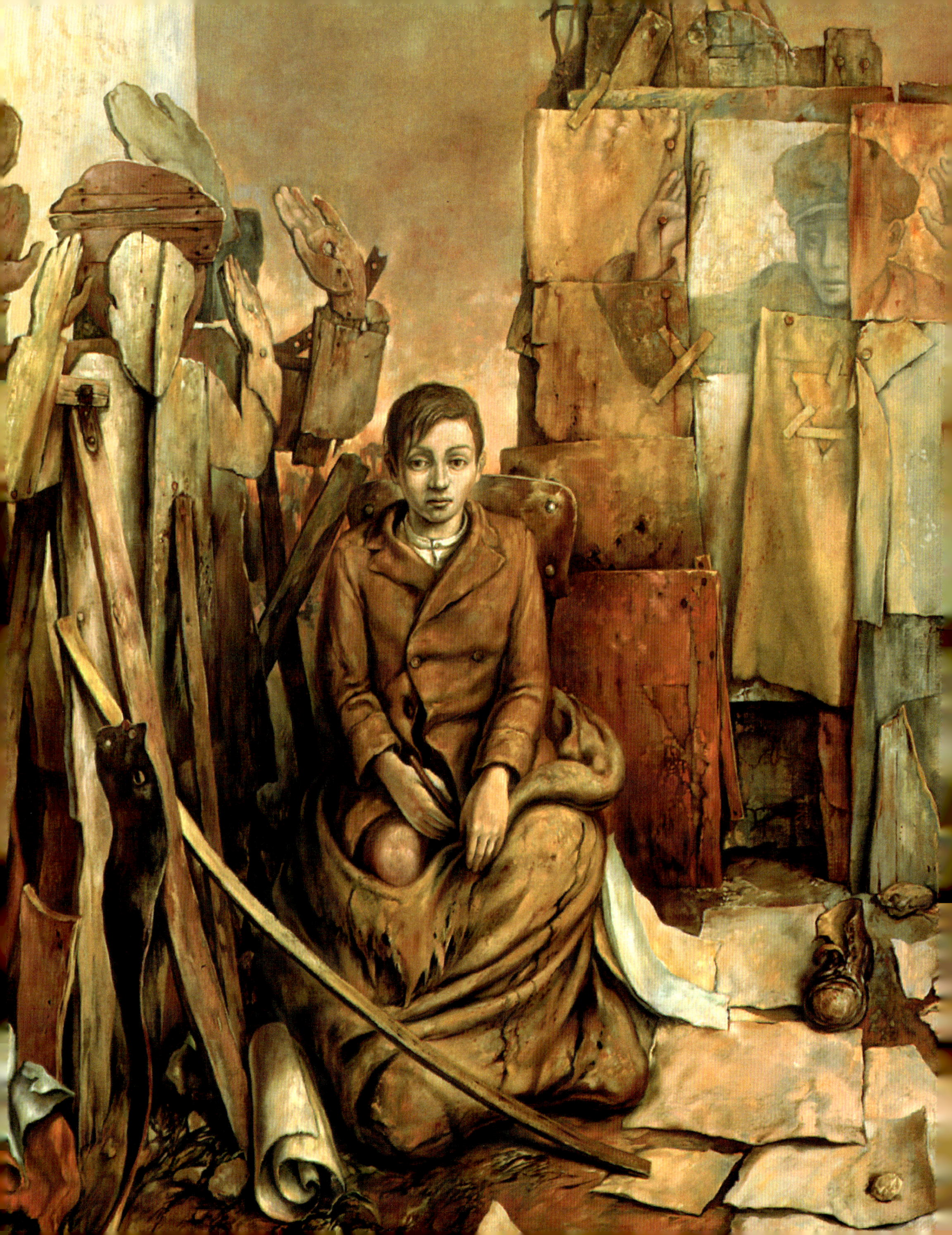

What, How, and When: On My Art and Myself

SAMUEL BAK

As a student and young artist I believed that the evolution of art was summed up by three words: *What, How,* and *When.*

The *What* had to do with subject matter. Ancient cave paintings spoke of magic. Roman sculpture celebrated power. Old masters served the needs of religion, portraiture, and historical documentation. Subject matter was the very essence of these works.

My student years of the early fifties seemed to have rejected subject matter in favor of "abstraction." The *How* had become most important. What counted was the way the colors were chosen and applied, the way shapes were formed and defined, and the manner in which the paint was laid on the canvas.

And then there is the *When,* which really means, "What's happening now? What is kosher in terms of historical correctness?" God help the young artist whose work is not perceived as avant-garde!

In 1959 I left Paris and settled in Rome. I was in my twenties and my shows of semi-abstract and abstract canvases were doing very well. I was invited to international shows. The museums of Tel Aviv and Jerusalem considered me a legitimate modernist and gave me large exhibits. My greatest achievement had been an invitation to contribute several large paintings to the Carnegie International of Pittsburgh. The show was then a major event in the world of art.

Four years later I turned thirty and began to question my current mode of painting. In spite of my successes, something in me was starting to change. The bubbling world of contemporary art encouraged such reconsideration. The early sixties saw the triumph of American Pop Art in Europe, legitimizing the return of subject matter. By using popular icons and glorifying them, artists were permitted to comment on the world, its culture, and its art. One was allowed to go beyond the seductions of abstract art and explore the actual. Thus, a new feeling began to unfold in me, telling me that I had been functioning in a world of too much certitude and that my work until then had been only a preparation for something else to come. My dealer was contented and

Detail of *Self-Portrait,* 1995
Oil on Canvas, 63 x 78 3/4"

the critics praised me, but I sensed that I was moving towards a dead end. It became imperative to delve deeper into my self and ask the most important of all questions: *Why paint?*

I realized that I had a special story to tell. There was a past that had been lying dormant in me. Indeed, my abstract canvases were letting it emerge, and as a result they were becoming more and more somber. To me their language seemed understandable, but was it understandable to others? I had a feeling that instead of unfolding my story, the abstract paintings were suppressing it. Now this past that was stirring and searching for expression made me ask myself how to let it speak.

These were years in which, theoretically, every possible artistic option was defensible. But I did not care to search for justification. It was to be expected that my shifting to another mode of expression would raise many eyebrows. I decided to let my paintings tell me what to do, to let my story (or was it their story?) come without forcing. I observed the ongoing change in my work, and little by little it became clearer to me what it was that I was doing. Mine was a story of a humanity that had survived two great wars and whose world now lay in shambles. Survivors were trying to repair the damage, to reconstruct what had been lost, to recreate something that would resemble in their eyes what was gone forever—and if possible to prevent additional or future suffering. A survivor myself, I observed and understood their need to reinvent life. Their story was my story. And in me it was also a story about a trauma that had been silenced for too many years. Now, its emergence could be seen as a sign of resilience. These were the elements of my inner self that were asking to be communicated through my art.

There was more to it. Circumstances have made me absorb a complex Jewish culture. Since I am not personally religious, I am able to experience my Jewish heritage unhampered by traditional reverence. This freedom has always been an asset to me. Moreover, for better or worse, I have been a Wandering Jew. From time to time, I carefully extracted my newly established roots from their soil and folded them into a suitcase. I had to preserve them for new journeys and new transplants. I have lived in Poland, Israel, France, Germany, Italy, Switzerland, and finally the United States. Different languages, cultures, and geographies have become an intrinsic part of my psyche. All these riches demanded to be integrated and to function as components of my art, to enlarge its perspective, or so I hoped.

What I was trying to achieve in my painting was a sense of both immediacy and estrangement. The idea of speaking about a human need for restoration in a language that restored old-fashioned, illusionary vision, a vision made of light and shade and verisimilitude, seemed to me the right venue. My painted images were to be sharp and clear, immediately and unavoidably present to the viewer. Yet, in the context of modern art this technique also provided the estrangement that I sought, a means of forcing viewers to see freshly those painful matters that have been dulled by habits of denial. But it came with the risk of being misunderstood. In our time, when the artist's personal style is the logo of his merchandise, I felt my painting had to be impersonal, painted in a style that would echo the traditions of paintings as representation, as in the Renaissance, the Baroque, or the nineteenth century. At the same time, my work could not be some exercise in reviving ancient mannerisms: that was certainly not the point of my endeavor.

Stereotypes plague the best of us. I knew that I could be mistaken for a latter-day Surrealist or an old-fashioned neo-post-Modernist. I had to keep telling myself that if I trusted the inner sources of my art, my work would acquire with time its own form or individuality. As I said before, the defining moment that brought me to the present form of my art happened some thirty-five years ago. It has been no intellectual journey, not the kind of search that many self-aware artists, conscious of their place in the evolving story of art, go through before reaching their characteristic style. Rather, I was responding to something that was pushing out from the inside, something visceral, something that takes a long time for the mind to comprehend.

The world of images that populated my paintings thirty-five years ago was very close to what it still is today. I know how my present art is perceived, and I feel comfortable about it. But at that time I had no intention of producing work that would automatically identify me with the experience of the Holocaust. Being a survivor, I was familiar with the world's reluctance to listen to our harrowing stories. This reluctance to expose ancient wounds might also come from a fear of being thought to solicit commiseration. We live in a society that hungers for sentiment. Thus, my fragile inner images, ready to be transferred onto canvas, had to be protected from exploitation. And so my antiquated style of painting also served to shield their meaning from too-easy access. I guess that I was looking for a place "far from the madding crowd," for an art that would exude an aura of timelessness.

These representational paintings of mine depicted devastated landscapes of ancient cities, urban constructions that seem to have been made of a child's building blocks. I painted figures that were half alive, and half contrived of bizarre prostheses. I imagined helpless and abused angels. Chess pieces were involved in games without rules. Huge fruit, mostly pears in various stages of reinvention, pears giving birth to other pears, pears made of stone, pears in the form of hovering planets, metaphors of a world without explanation. My paintings carried no answers, only questions.

Although I resisted making the connection explicit, these were questions that for me, personally, returned always to the experience of the Holocaust. Chimneys, sprouting heavy smoke and made of clusters of stones that reminded me of cemeteries, had already been hiding in my earlier paintings. Yet I still named such paintings *Ancient Industries,* hoping that no one would guess what they meant to me. In 1974, a contract with a New York gallery disconnected me from the "old world" that had given me a sense of identity and brought me for a few years to Manhattan. It was there that the Jewish symbols began to enter directly into my work: the Star of David that I had to wear stitched to my clothes as a young boy in the ghetto; the Tablets of the Law, which adorned most synagogues; the extinguished candles of Sabbath. Two decades later I added to them the figure of the Warsaw ghetto boy with his lifted arms, that most iconic of all Holocaust images.

From the beginning I have believed that specifically Holocaust-related interpretation would narrow the meaning of my work. After all, I am trying to express a universal malaise about our human condition. The experience of the Holocaust shed such a cruel light on the vast catalogue of human behavior that its lesson had to be hard to absorb; people needed time to study it and to grasp all its implications. Moreover, thirty-five years ago the Holocaust was considered mainly a calamity only of the Jewish people.

There were several other reasons why I shied away from a direct connection with the Holocaust. First, I did not like the term. In its biblical origin it meant a burnt offering that was proposed to God Almighty by a high priest. I felt it thus carried a notion of self-sacrifice that did not respect the desire for life to which millions of victims had clung desperately though in vain. It belittled the magnitude of their tragedy. Second, most of the art that I then encountered on this theme, art produced in the sixties and seventies, was to my eyes less than acceptable. Some powerful works must already have existed, but I was unfamiliar with them. It often felt as if the overpowering importance of the subject was expected to compensate for the lack of artistic imagination and force. A few decades ago many serious and creative artists refrained from touching the theme of the Holocaust. Fortunately, this situation has evolved. At present, the challenge of anchoring art in meaningful themes does not scare away talented artists. On the contrary, subject now matters.

As for the problematic denomination of the Jewish genocide, the word *Holocaust* has become so familiar that it has transcended its etymology. But there was another reason I hesitated to connect my work exclusively to that portentous event. I suspected that my art was being used improperly. Perhaps for the purpose of whitewashing a disturbed conscience. Perhaps for placing it into a space that was temporarily "fashionable." I feared that, unwillingly, I was being launched on an ambiguous trajectory that exploited my grievous personal losses for what could be seen as an advancement of career.

In 1978 a retrospective of my work was planned that would last several years and travel through ten German museums. I was torn between two opposing forces: my willingness to grant permission to show the work, and my reluctance, or rather my total unwillingness, to bring myself to revisit Germany. I never made it to Heidelberg's museum to attend the show's first official debut.

It took me months to put aside the hampering feelings of guilt that were blocking me. I had to extract myself from what is commonly called "the survivor's syndrome," take my courage in both hands, and assume the role of an exhibiting artist whom the public wishes to meet. Thus, due to the patient insistence of dedicated people who were later to become personal friends, I agreed to participate in a subsequent festive opening of my exhibition, this time in the German National Museum in Nuremberg. The opening took on the proportions of a state event. I stayed in a hotel not too far from the museum. To get to the exhibition I chose to go on foot. Was this a form of penitence? Perhaps.

I had to walk along the notorious Nazi stadium that was now partly destroyed. I knew it from old films of the Führer with the legions of his perfectly ordered men and his enthusiastic crowds. All of them continued to project themselves onto the screen of my mind. But also the faces of my murdered grandparents, uncles, aunts, and father accompanied me on my way. I walked, and I wept. When I finally arrived, I had to explain to my hosts that a sudden allergic attack had caused the reddening of my eyes.

It was on the day after the opening, when revisiting my show and stumbling on a visit of high school youngsters, that I learned something of value. Listening to a well-informed instructor and to the young people's interaction with him, I understood how important it had been to bring my art to that place. I was witness to a process of their coming to terms with a terrible past, a courageous process. Not too many people in other European countries have been up to it. Suddenly, letting my work be seen explicitly in the context of the Holocaust made a lot of sense. To my personal view, my paintings became transformed by the walls of the German National Museum.

My works have always refrained from overly explicit imagery. Everything in them is transposed to an imaginary realm. This transposition must have worked well, because I heard it echoing in the souls of these young Germans, giving them access to a horrendous, and until then, unmentionable past, and stimulating their sensitive minds to new excursions of thought.

I have previously implied that my process of painting was not "intellectual." Actually it resembles a sensual love affair, an affair with tubes of paint, bottles of oils, brushes, palette knives, and the odor of turpentine. Dealing with all the paraphernalia of an artist's imaginary world, the world of shapes, compositions, brushstrokes, colors, and hues is a voluptuous pleasure. Moreover, my countless hours in the studio fulfill yet another desire. They allow me to discover the many realities that emerge on the surfaces of the paintings I am making. Bridging the gap between the inner projection of a mental vision and the final, physical result of the completed canvas is the essence of my craft and passion.

At times I think this struggle must be similar to Jacob's wrestling with the Angel, whether one thinks of the Angel as God or as one's yet undiscovered self. After so many years in my profession I have learned to recognize what this wrestling means for me. The process of painting has an inner logic. The way a wrestler knows how to profit from an opponent's energy, so a painter realizes that paintings have a life of their own and knows how to open their door and get out of the way.

And this is how it happens. I am in front of my easel. The radio plays music, the speaker announces a change in the weather, and a part of my mind is busy with all sorts of mysterious creative systems. I feel like an obedient servant who is doing what the painting demands. At the end of the day I may feel satisfied, or I may wonder. I may also decide that everything went wrong. Contradictions are part of the game.

Paintings are never finished, yet I myself must finish with them. Sometimes when I revisit them, there are works I like and some others that ask for modification. On another visit my perceptions may well be different. Luckily, since once they are done the paintings no longer "belong" to me, I never touch them. It has taken me thirty-five years to recognize that if I choose the subject, the *What,* and let the artist in me release it in all its force, it will find its own voice, its own *How* and *When.*

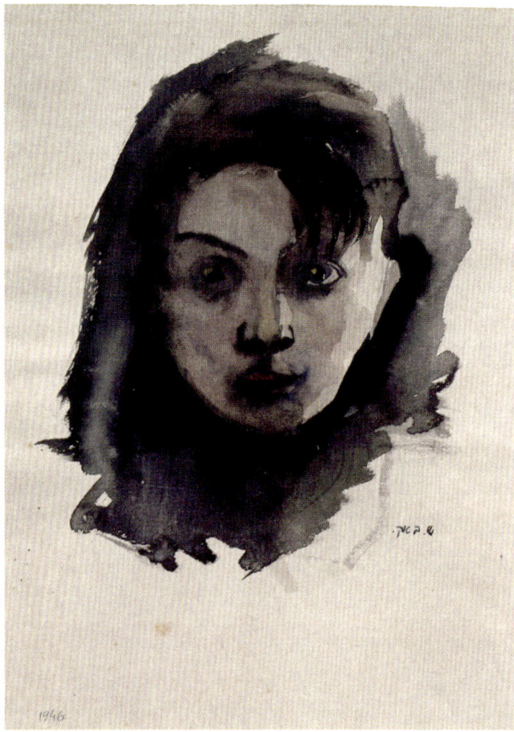

Self-Portrait, 1946
Watercolor, 15 x 12 1/4"

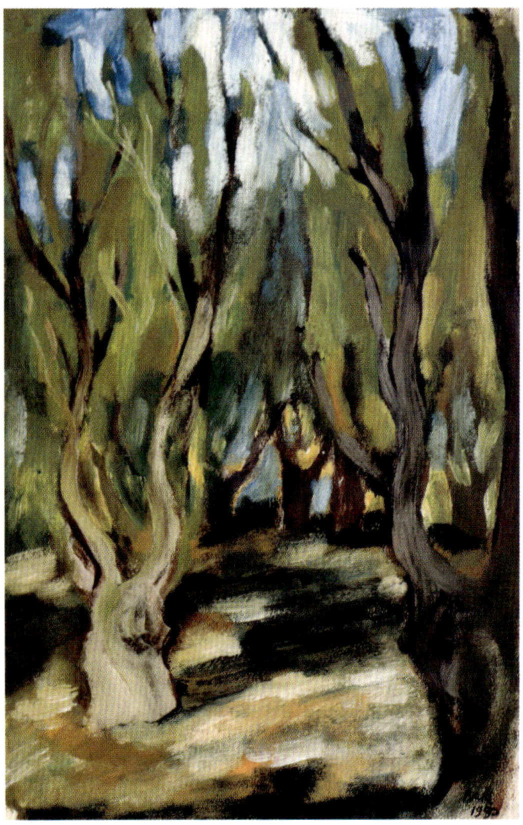

Gallil, 1950
Oil on Paper, 17 1/4 x 11 3/4"

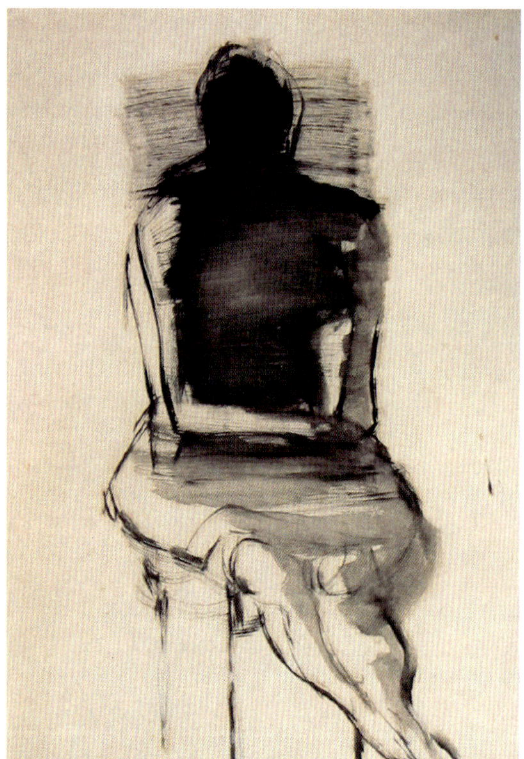

Seated Figure, 1956
Ink on Paper, 19 3/4 x 11 3/4"

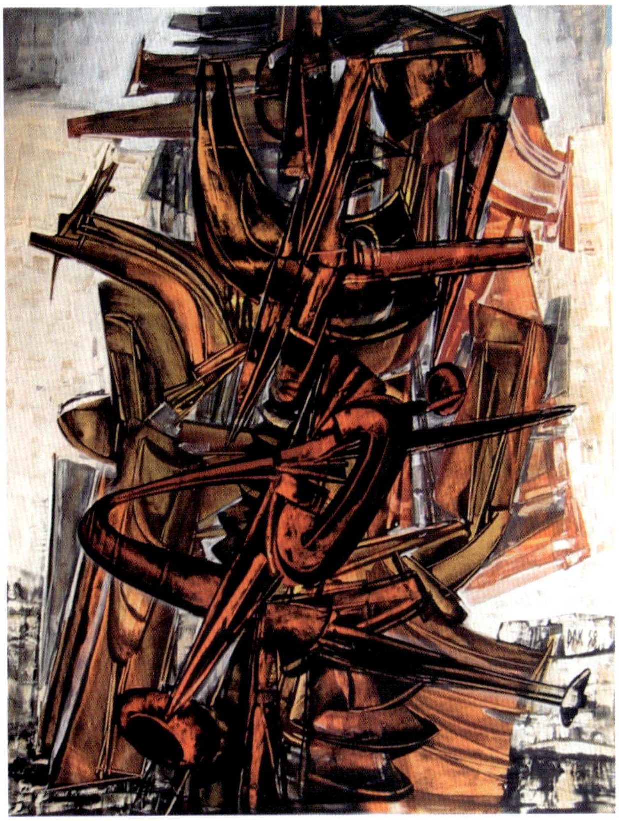

Totem, 1958
Gouache, 27 1/2 x 19 3/4"

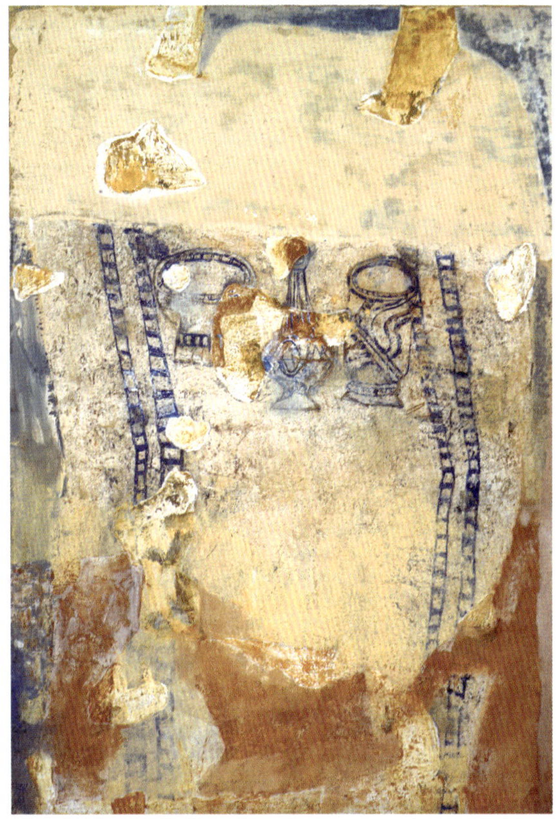

Etruscan, 1963
Acrylic on Canvas, 38 1/2 x 25 1/2"

To the Memory of R.K., 1968
Oil on Canvas, 51 1/4 x 35"

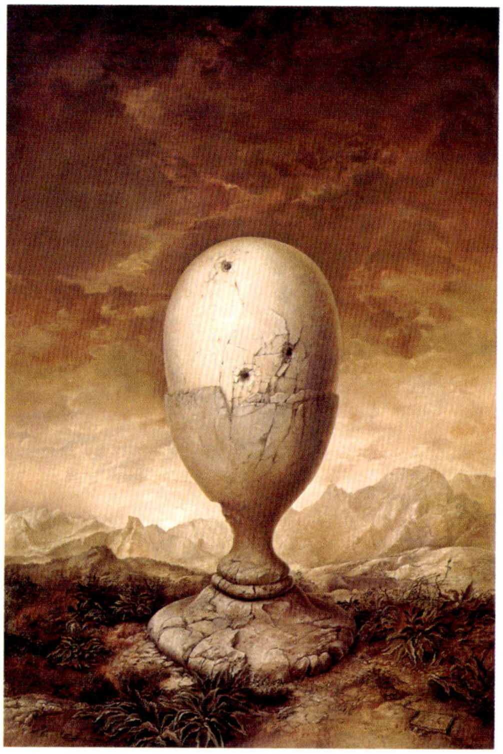

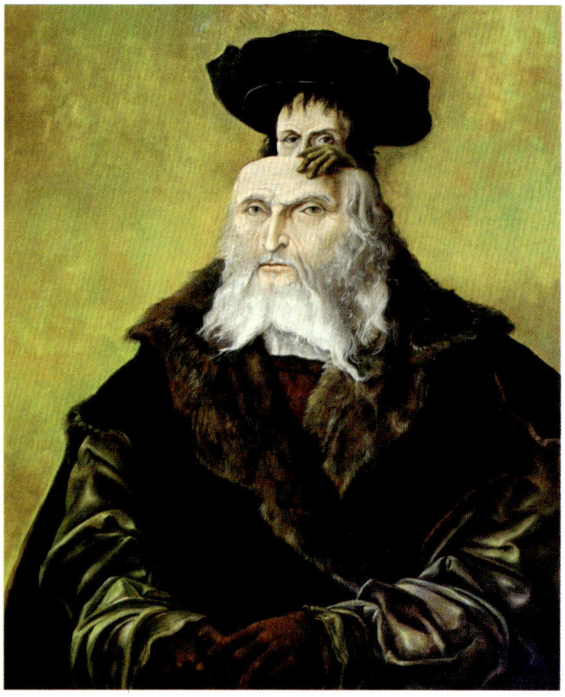

Portrait with Own Inner Self, 1967
Oil on Canvas, 24 x 19 3/4"

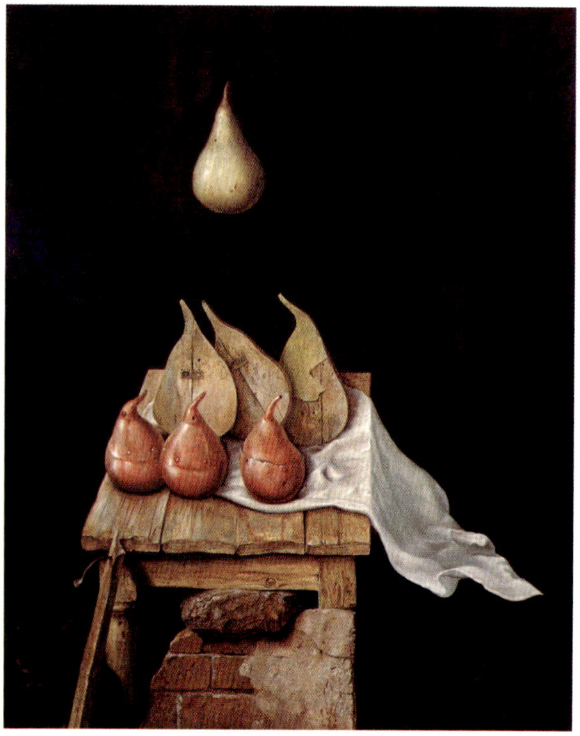

Still Life, 1969
Oil on Canvas, 39 1/4 x 32"

Parable, 1975
Oil on Canvas, 50 1/2 x 38 1/4"

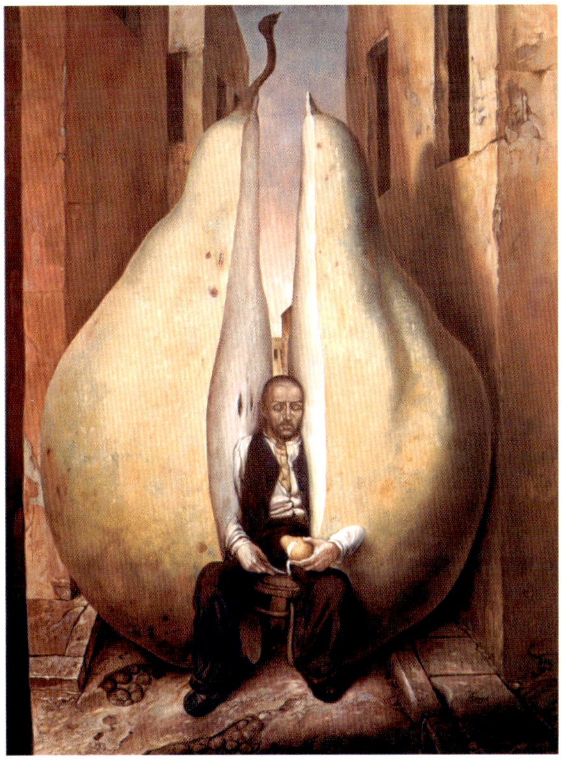

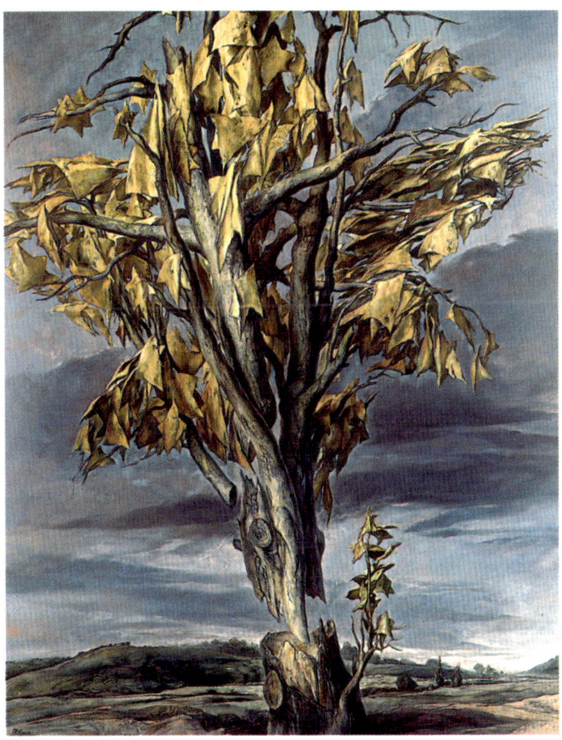

Family Tree, 1995
Oil on Canvas, 78 3/4 x 63"

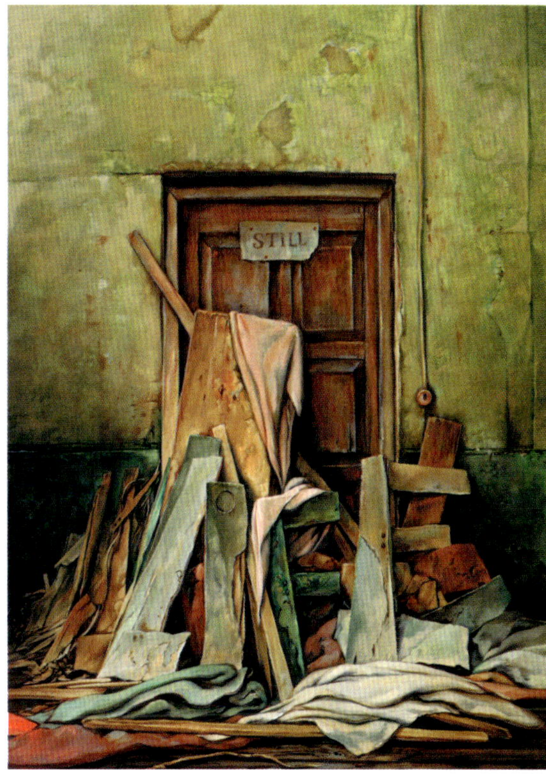

Still There, 2005
Oil on Canvas, 36 x 24"

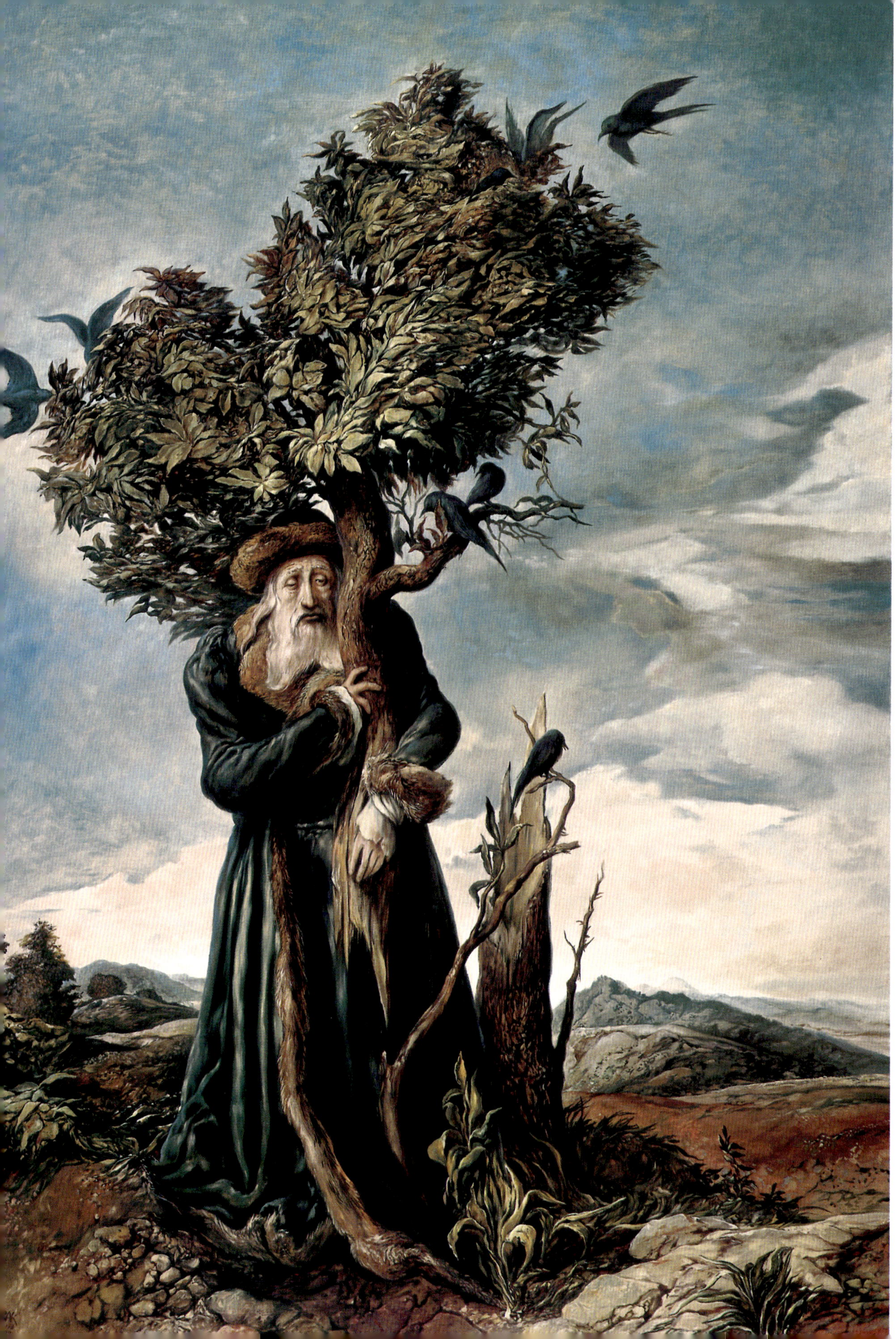

Myth, Midrash, and Mysticism: The Painting of Samuel Bak

MICHAEL FISHBANE

We look upon the world with our natural eye, but we see it through inner-vision. For some, raw experience projects outward upon the world in untamed tempos; for others, the private world of memory collides with the everyday, and wrestles with it in titanic embrace. Forms rise and fall—color and sound and light appear and disappear. Worlds are born with the heartbeat of art. And then they are bound in pages or set in frames for others to come and see and learn. Thus our masters teach us. They teach us to hear with their hearing, or see with their seeing. And if we respond, it is not solely because of the immediate beauty of the seen or the heard, but because something more universal has been revealed out of the depths: a secret sharing, a community of the spirit. How much more mysterious is the bond created when the forms of artistic representation also echo a tradition? The new then vibrates in a larger tension of continuity and change. And one's personal vision is informed by ancient lights.

The Jewish imagination is primarily a textual imagination, and to the degree that images dominate cultural memory they do so through texts. Indeed, ongoing creativity often heightens and dramatizes, even inverts and spiritualizes, older textual forms. In the library of Judaism, this is the relationship between Midrash and Bible. And one can hardly think of the Jewish soul apart from it. Sometimes the Bible is sparse and the Midrash spectacular; sometimes Scripture is elliptical and interpretation explicit; and sometimes the (biblical) Text is circumspect and Tradition charges the center. Think, for example, of Moses smashing the Tablets at Sinai; and the rabbi's accounts of ascending letters; of human laments at divine punishment transformed into God's mourning and tears; or of the fires of doom becoming the furnace into which the priests leap in self-sacrifice—a grim atonement enacted by confession and returning the Temple keys to God in heaven.

To be sure, some of these topics appear in the miniatures and marginalia of Jewish illuminated manuscripts or in Haggadas from medieval or Renaissance times. But in the main the images

The Wanderer II, 1968-1996
Oil on Linen, 50 x 34"

remain in verbal forms—recited in liturgies, proclaimed in homilies, and brooded in meditations, but textual nonetheless. In the modern period, some of these great themes of suffering and sorrow have been treated by the most national poets who speak for all out of the depth of their pain. Who can forget reading Bialik's "The Scroll of Fire,"[1] in which the tears of the angels fall into our hollow hearts; or Sutzkever's collection of *Burnt Pearls,*[2] in which the letters of the Talmud are melted from their printing plates to provide the bullets for life and survival? Who can envision such things, and where is the artist of their visible forms?

Even the great Chagall often conjured with an alien wand. Faced with the pogroms of his people, he repeatedly, over the span of a lifetime, depicted Jewish suffering through a crucified Jew—wearing phylacteries on hand and arm, and covering his shame with a fringed loincloth. Roundabout this icon in cubic vectors are burning villages and endless lines of exiles, like commentaries of evil. What Jew could see himself reflected in this central symbol? Perhaps Chagall; but hardly, I think, any of the villagers whose blood ran at the point of a cross. Nevertheless, innumerable paintings by Jewish inmates of German Hell depict their suffering through this icon. And what must we think of the boy in *Night* whose faith in God dies on a gallows like a child swinging from its noose in a Christ-like form.[3] Who can comprehend such matters? Must the Jewish imagination sell its soul even in suffering?

It is not inevitable. Time and suffering and talent and vision have given us Samuel Bak. And he may teach us to see (with him) again, or perhaps for the first time.

Bak was born in Vilna in 1933. Before the War, over 80,000 Jews lived in this city; after the roundups and murders, about 250 survived. Bak has sworn to be faithful to the dead and the world he shared with them; but his art evolved over time and place, and it took many years before memory of those years returned and found their present shape. In fact, half a lifetime. He was but eight years old when his talent was discovered in the Ghetto, and no less than Sutzkever himself arranged for the first showing. Many of these paintings have survived and retain a remarkable atmospheric tone and texture. After studies in the DP camp of Landsberg, and later in the academies of Jerusalem and Paris, Bak's talent focused on masterly themes and various stage designs. It is only in the late 1960s, when already a resident of Israel, that the particular historical events of the time combined with deep memories of survival and suffering and a new and remarkable artistic production erupted. Figures from the masters now combine with psychic forms to generate a fantastic world of the everyday; vast landscapes are refocused under his gaze into scenes of barren terror; and homey genre scenes have become tableaux of loss and fracture. Nothing is whole, and yet all is recognizable; everything is real (perhaps all too real) but in the sizes and proportions of an inner-truth. It is therefore often not clear whether the viewer looks outward to a world transformed by unspeakable evil; or inward towards their memory, in its broken reconstructions.

It is not necessary to decide. For the inner and outer realities are linked by a series of concrete images—visual metaphors of a symbolic world. Indeed, out of the concrete particularity of the images a metaphysical dimension is disclosed, and the viewer crosses over into living myth. Landscape and home, like trees and candles, all have archetypal qualities, and evoke the ultimate mysteries of space and nature and light; all the while the same images, when fractured and isolated, may conjure more chaotic terrors of human existence. Here is life as such, or so we imagine until, on second thought, we remember that life is always embodied in specific forms. And then we are struck by the particular historical and cultural valence of the images, and the specific shapes of universal forms. Surely it requires a high art to keep these poles in proper balance (or tension). But this has been achieved by Samuel Bak. Like no other contemporary artist, to my mind, he has recovered the archetypal quality of Jewish images and thereby opened a mythic passage to the heart of darkness and destiny. And in other cases, we are initiated into mysteries of creation and the letters of life.

Candles, for example, and their multi-colored flames have often served as universal symbols of light and the desire for transcendence; of hope and the divine eye—even of the human soul and the spark of primordial secrets. But in a Jewish context each possibility is thickened by specific scriptures and commentaries over the ages. And so they enter religious life. The Sabbath candles will thus lose none of their universal power when their lighting connotes the duty to "remember" and "observe" the sanctity of the day; even as the memorial candle for a specific deceased symbolizes more transcendent mysteries of morality. Bak knows this well. But it is the power of his art to fuse these ritually distinct registers, and even to evoke historical dimensions. And so the candles in his paintings concretize a duty to remember the sanctity of the dead in the Holocaust, and immortalize lost life through memory. Arising out of the fissures of a Jewish Star, cut into the earth, or standing within a ghetto shaped like a Yellow Badge, the candles dramatize the mythic magnitude of Jewish suffering. Elsewhere the dripping tallow clings like tears of an enormous sorrow on a bent frame. And who cannot almost see in these smoking, tapered wicks the chimneys of the ovens in which millions were consumed? Candles, like so many other images, thus become multivalent icons in Bak's work—complex symbols of a complex and hard truth.

Symbols do not always stand alone. In addition to their own often interfused and paradoxical logic, they regularly appear in configuration that must be read and reread. Bak's *Nuremberg Elegie* is such a painting—and given its rich thematics, deserves some separate consideration. Indeed, it contains many of the images Bak would develop separately in succeeding years.

Anyone looking at this remarkable piece must recall Dürer's engraving called *Melencolia I*—which celebrates the artist in deep moodiness over his creativity and work. Thus Dürer seats his figure in a brooding, contemplative pose, surrounded by the instruments of Renaissance science at his feet. Incised in the wall at the back are the magical symbols of a decipherer's art; and as the eye moves left, the shape of a rainbow curves off from the edge of the wall. All is monumental; for here sits some new Adam on the ridge of his world, caught for a time in the space of inaction. Some heavenly humour has become incarnate here, to arrest the work to be done. But no larger metaphysical matter need be inferred.

Bak masters the master. For again we see the foregrounded figure in meditative isolation; and at his back is a wall, with the trace of a rainbow at its left edge. But look more closely. The figure betrays a broken sadness, a lament of infinite loneliness. For he sits like some Jonah in a hut of strewn bric-a-brac, propped up by a makeshift Star and a lean-to Cross—a counterpoint to the fractured bow on the side, a ruptured promise held up by stays built by human hands. And now the mysterious script is wiped from the wall which holds in its recessed niches two candles, the grim reliquies of a ruined home. At the base of the wall lie the Tablets of the Law, abandoned, fallen it seems from the niches just above. The candles are thus memorials of this fallen truth, even as their points of light contrast with the closed eyes of the figure. What sadness fills the man, whose pose half recalls Rembrandt's *Jeremiah,* sitting likewise in mourning for Jerusalem! Rembrandt had it from the Midrash that the prophet enacted the divine sorrow beyond understanding. Bak's figure is some other suffering servant: the elegy of Israel incarnate.

The *Nuremberg Elegie* thus gives mythic magnitude to the wreck of wisdom in our day and to the loss of values and hope and home. The human figure sunk in mourning is some Adam—*Everyone,* sitting east of an Eden that is beyond memory. And yet, it is remembered still: as the Tablets of teachings; the candles of home; and the Star of redemption. Bak's paintings remain faithful to both truths.

Like the condensations of dreamwork, Bak's vast oeuvre concretizes around a series of themes that recur as traces of primordial and inescapable trauma. Indeed, the several images of the *Nuremberg Elegie* themselves become the focal points of pain in seemingly endless variations. A condensation of this condensation may sharpen our sense of Bak's mythic and Jewish sensibilities.

Everything begins *All of A Sudden,* with the violent rupture of home—recurrently envisaged as Vilna and its walls, now draped in its prayer shawls like corpses in their shroud. This is the *Shullhoif,* the courtyard of memory. Roundabout, cartons emptied of the warmth of childhood fling their sides upward like flames and cluster in patterns that hint of boxcars and death. Without warning, the contents of Eden have been emptied over a barren world—and the tree of life and knowledge often stands on artificial stays, like the prostheses of the wounded Adams, victims of the *Experiments in Wisdom* east of Eden. Reduced, the tree image appears as a potted plant, the shoot of undaunted hope; while elsewhere it reminds one of the lost home and the camouflage it provided a child in hiding. On still other occasions, the tree is utterly uprooted, carried by a colossal wandering Jew, the eternal *Trans-plant.* Blackbirds endlessly fly from Bak's branches like souls of memory and rebirth. An archetype of Jewish mysticism thus erupts unexpectedly here, from forgotten worlds—a symbol of personal and more-than-personal truth.

The imagery of a lost paradise takes other forms, again with mythic and midrashic dimensions. To do this, Bak often sets his subject within a vast landscape—not the idyllic harmonies of the Dutch masters, but now scenes of vast vacuity. Two figures may sit at a table (is this mother and son?), near broken trees and assorted debris, and ponder an *Explanation* that is already so ironically portrayed; or some lonely Adam peers as an outside *Observer* into a walled-off paradise (a mock "victory garden" for exiles), whose very configuration reminds one of the Tablets of

Torah. But there is no spiritual sustenance here—only a patch of nettles. In another case, the lost fruit of wisdom is an apple rind on a grand table in Nowhere, *Outside Paradise.* But most often, the symbol of sustenance and its subversion is the pear. Like some fleshly form, this fruit is part-human—with wounds of blood; and shielded by the armor of psychic defenses. Imprinted in the earth, the pear becomes a primordial sign of origins; but when surrounded by a pear-shaped wall, the same image becomes a symbol of an irretrievable Eden—and the taste of home.

Indeed, who can still read the words of Scripture? Who will still read them? The ancient letter of *Shema Israel* (Hear, O Israel) of *Amkho* (The People) go up in flames, and with them the teachings on the Tablets. Bak's images are overwhelming. In some cases, the *Othyoth* (or Letters) of the Tablets fly into space—betrayed by bestiality. One recalls here the powerful midrashic lore of the ascending script, which is similarly shamed by earthly idolatry in the time of Moses. As these supernatural embodiments of spirit escape, the stone of the Tablets becomes mere nature and too heavy to bear. For Bak, these Smoke shapes also congeal as gravestones that blow out of Hell's Ovens as some sulphuric Sinai. In other instances, the Tablets stand in monumental isolation on a grim mountain—with the mere word *Lo* (of *lo tirzah;* Do Not Murder) incised upon them (*Tirzah,* Murder, lies below in broken form, as some forgotten conclusion—taken by some as a command in its own right). Ladders and props all hold up these Tablets and their casings, and one wonders if this is a sign of rebuilding. Let us hope. In a similar vein, Bak paints the letters of Genesis 1:1, *Bereshit Bara* (In the Beginning was created). The old letters are reused; the world is recreated from its rubble.

In the Jewish tradition, the letters of Scripture are the primordial forms of the creation itself. The idea is ancient, and appears in mystical and midrashic sources from late antiquity on. The point is powerful, for it expresses an ancient rabbinic belief that Being itself is inscribed with spiritual and moral forms—and that to destroy the letters of the Tablets, with the commandment not to murder, is to destroy more than social order and human value; it is to betray the very principles of existence itself. Bak intuits all this with remarkable keenness. Indeed, he knows that to destroy value is to shatter the very Name of God. Accordingly, in several paintings the letter *yod* is repeated (a symbol of the Name) at the base of broken tablets or in the fires of death. In a most exceptional image, *The Hidden Question* of meaning is posed directly. Our eye is set upon a ruinous heap that entombs a home; and upon the mound is a key whose upturned ridge spells out the double *yod* of the Divine Name. Is this the key of home and heath, abandoned on the rubble of civilization—reminiscent of the keys which the priests misused, according to midrashic tradition, and returned to heaven? Or is this a symbol of the loss of tradition and divinity as a whole? For rabbis, keys also symbolize the mysteries of wisdom, in every mysterious realm. Moses, for example, the consummate seeker of Truth, merited a key called "Eitan," or Strength, according to mystical lore—this being the pass to the fiftieth palace of supernal knowledge. But where might God's Name now be fitted, we wonder, to unlock meaning in our barren time? Might the shape of the ancient Tablets be just the fitting into which our questions might be put?

The series of paintings entitled *Pardes* ponders this possibility. "Pardes" literally means paradise, and thus raises the question of Eden and origins; but it also signifies in rabbinic tradition a heavenly garden of perfection, and thus points to the end of earthly labor and hope. For Judaism, the path from expulsion from Pardes to its re-entry leads through Scripture and Interpretation. For this is the rabbinic way of wisdom. It is therefore significant that the letters of PaRDeS also spell out the acronym for the levels of scriptural interpretation: *Peshat,* being the literal and contextual sense; *Remez,* being the allegorical (philosophical and moral) sense; Derash, being the legal and theological (midrashic) sense; and *Sod,* being the mystical sense. While each sense has its own rules of reading, and exists on its own, the levels move from *Peshat* to *Derash* to *Remez* to *Sod* in an ascending series. One may enter the Pardes of Scripture, then, and through it to every heavenly possibility, through this exegetical rite of passage. The letters of Torah are thus shapes into which human questions may be fitted and through which meaning may be found.

Bak's Pardes images take the shape of the Ancient Tablets of Moses, set on a vast mountainous landscape with a path leading up to it from the distance. The figure of the path suggests the trope of a journey or quest. And this seems confirmed by the fact that the base of the Tablets holds four doors—leading into four distinct areas. Each entry is appropriately marked by the initial Hebrew letters PaRDeS. Within the quadrants are appropriate symbols. The door of *Peshat* is most accessible, and leads to a tree (of knowledge or life). The next two doors (*Remez* and *Derash*) are increasingly closed; and within are labyrinthine patterns through which the seeker must move to more recessed tablets and labyrinths.

By contrast, all access to Sod is barred. This is, of course, consonant with the various prohibitions surrounding it in rabbinic sources, but it may also symbolize the sealing up of the mysteries in our time. Within this ultimate quadrant lies a flaming altar—perhaps the symbol of consuming mystical passions or even the fires of martyrdom (Isaac is a "martyr" on the altar in Jewish tradition; and the smoking flames rising off the altar recall the chimney smoke of other, more devilish immolations). On other occasions the altar is aflame with a book; or it is deformed into a flaming oven. A ladder at the far end of the realm of Sod may connote ascension—or is it escape? But to where? The monumental Tablets are all there on the horizon, being both the visual and spatial center of the painting. The outer landscape is thus no escape. But we wonder: Are the accessible doors for entry, or for flight (like the ladder)? Are the Tablets a new or abandoned Sinai?

The question is insistent, and one must choose. Perhaps just this is the thought of the brooding figure in the *Nuremberg Elegie.* After all, the Tablets lie at his back. Does he, too, like ourselves, absorb this image (of Pardes) with his total being? Is it for him a mythic presence? Or even a passage to more mysterious meditations? Conjured by the colors we are entranced. But a decision awaits us.

1 *Editors' note:* Hayyim Nahman Bialik, "Mgilat haesh" (1905; The Scroll of Fire).

2 *Editors' note: Burnt Pearls: Ghetto Poems of Abraham Sutzkever* (Translated from the Yiddish by Seymour Mayne; introduction by Ruth R. Wisse. Oakville, Ont.: Mosaic Press, 1981).

3 *Editors' note:* Elie Wiesel, *Night.* (Translated by Stella Rodway. Penguin: London, 1981).

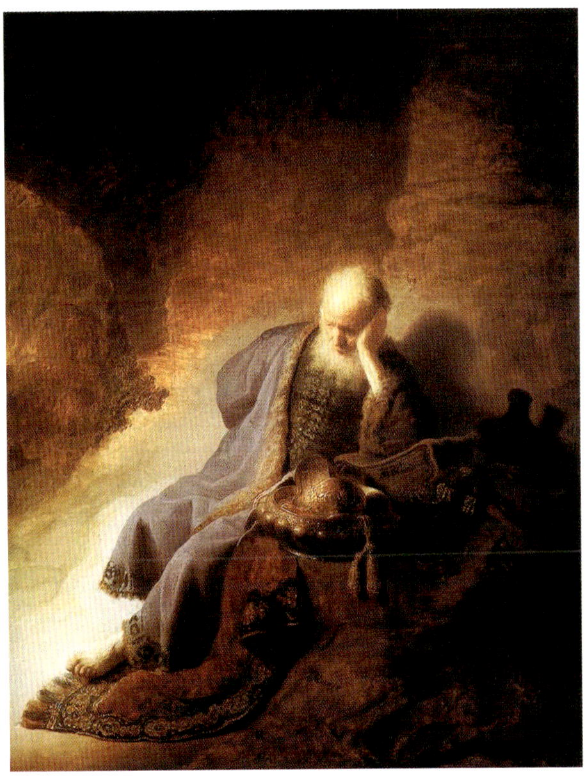

Rembrandt Van Rijn
Jeremiah Lamenting the Destruction of Jerusalem, 1630
Oil on Panel, 23 x 18 1/4"

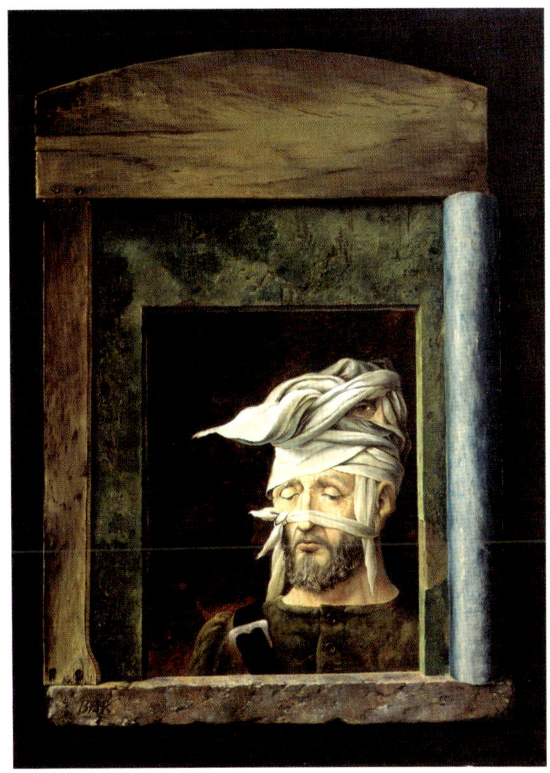

The Observer, 1968
Oil on Canvas, 25 1/2 x 22"

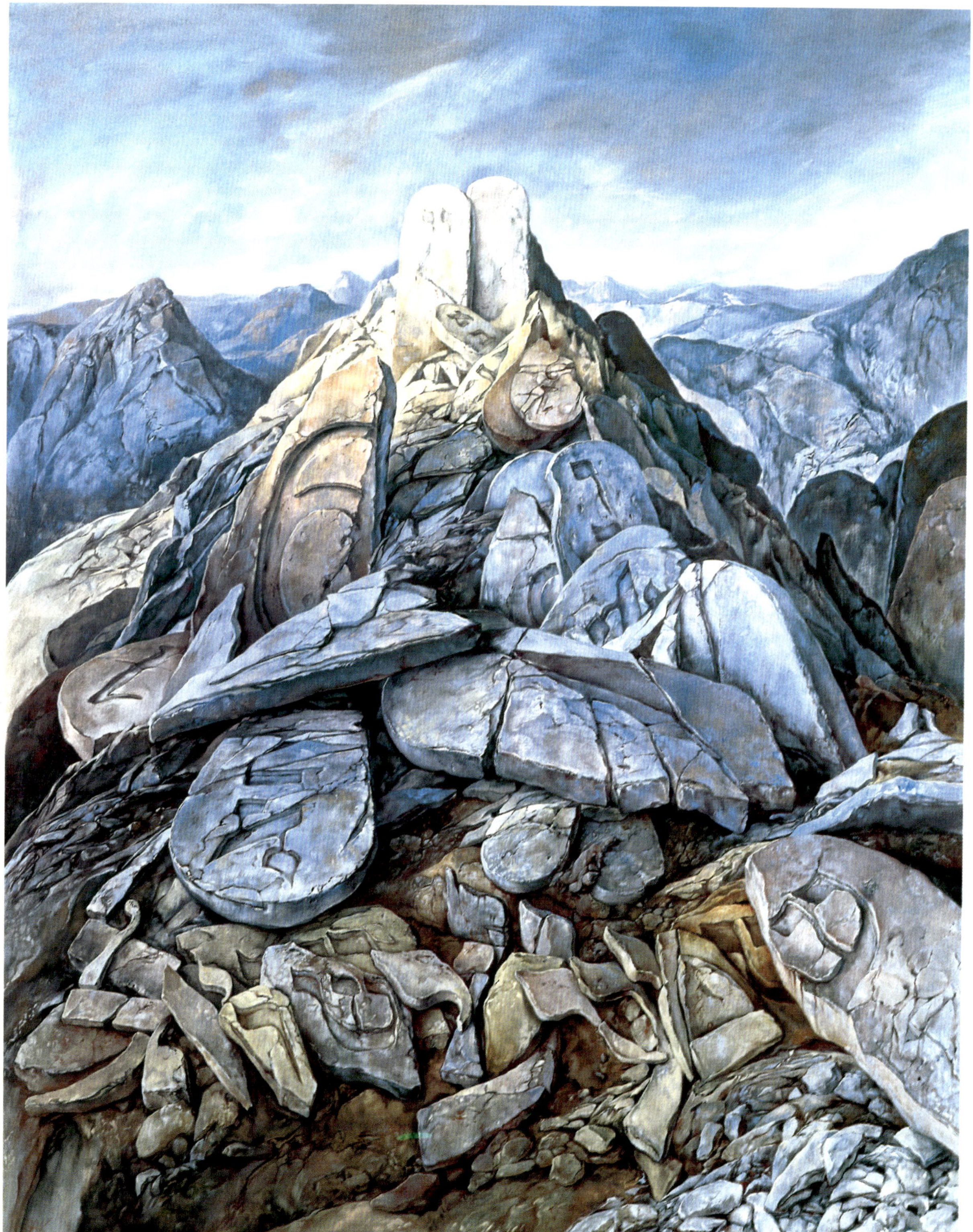

Shema Israel, 1992
Oil on Linen, 32 x 39 1/2"

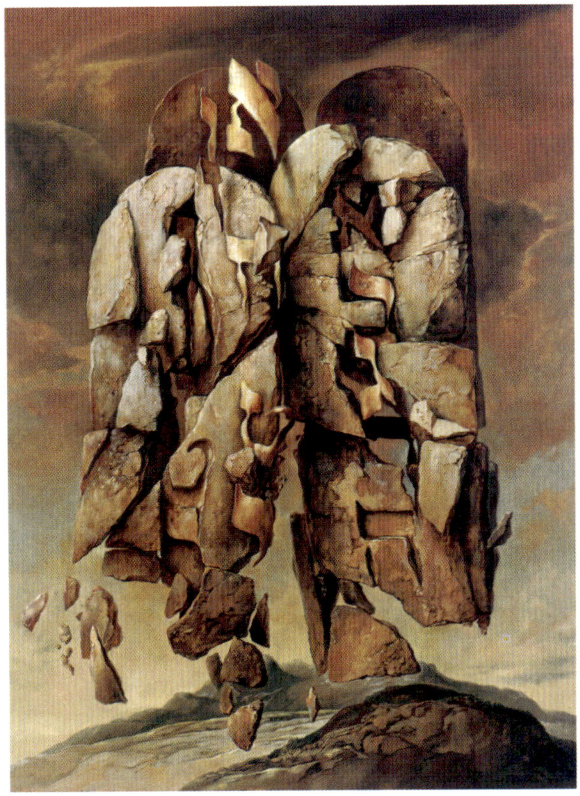

Othyoth, 1992
Oil on Linen, 51 1/4 x 38 1/2"

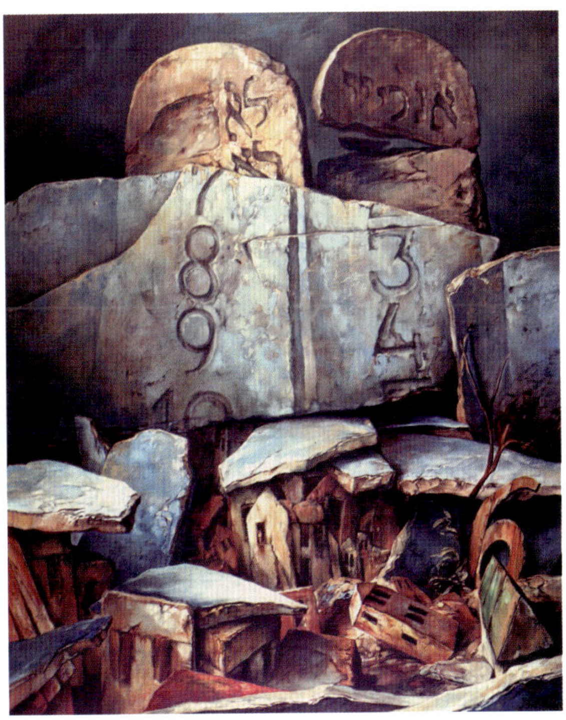

All of a Sudden, 1992
Oil on Linen, 39 1/2 x 32"

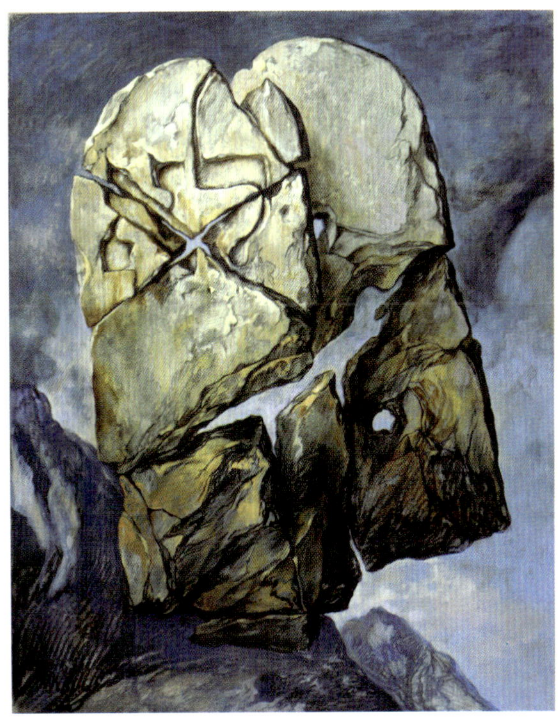

Lo, Against Blue Space, 1976
Oil on Linen, 19 x 23 1/2"

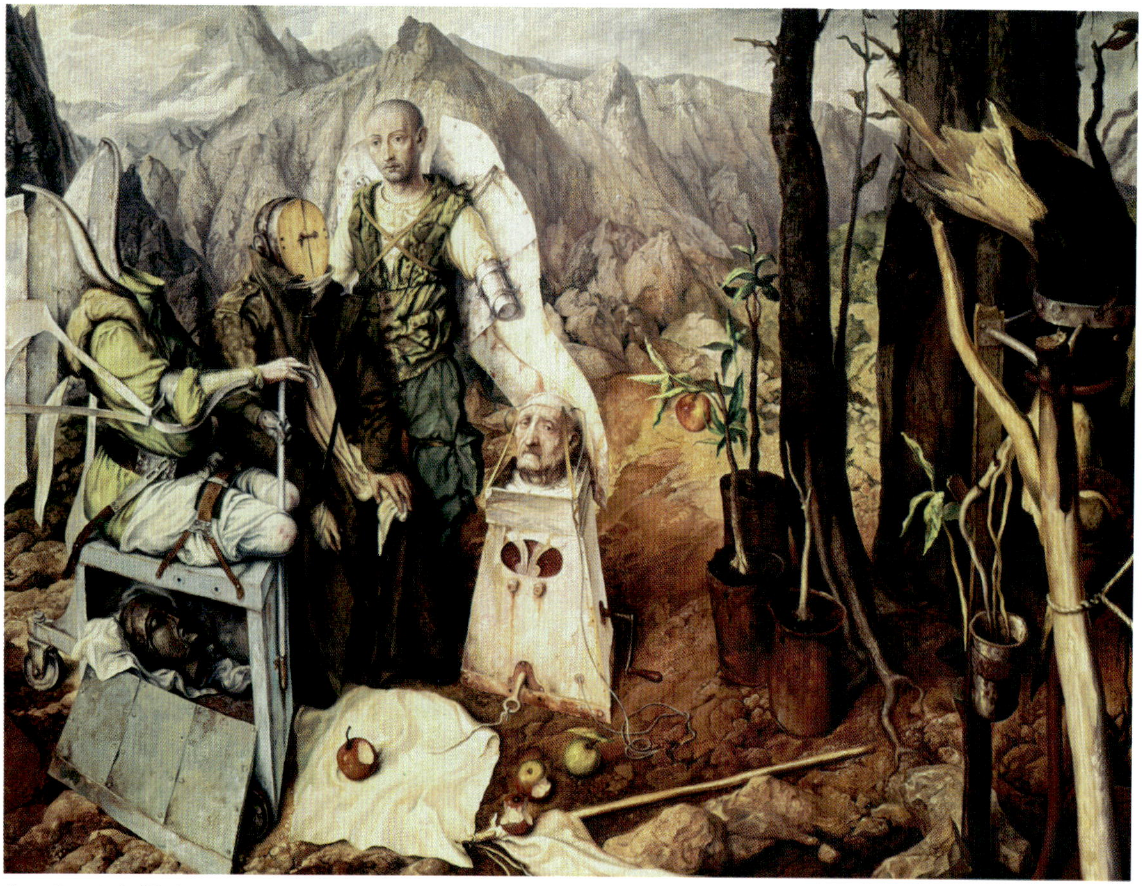

Experiments in Wisdom, 1973
Oil on Canvas, 63 x 78 3/4"

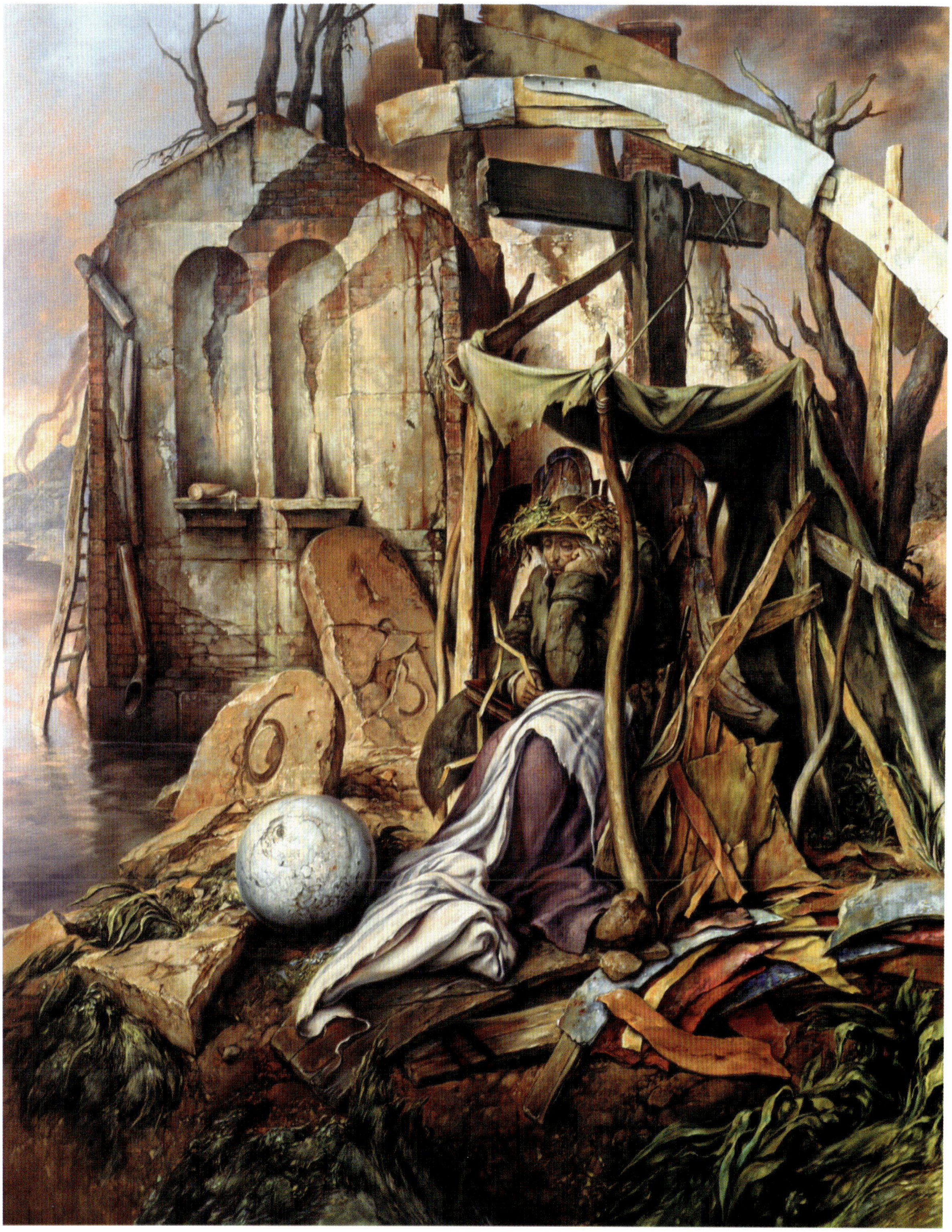

Nuremberg Elegie, 1994-95
Oil on Canvas, 78 3/4 x 63"

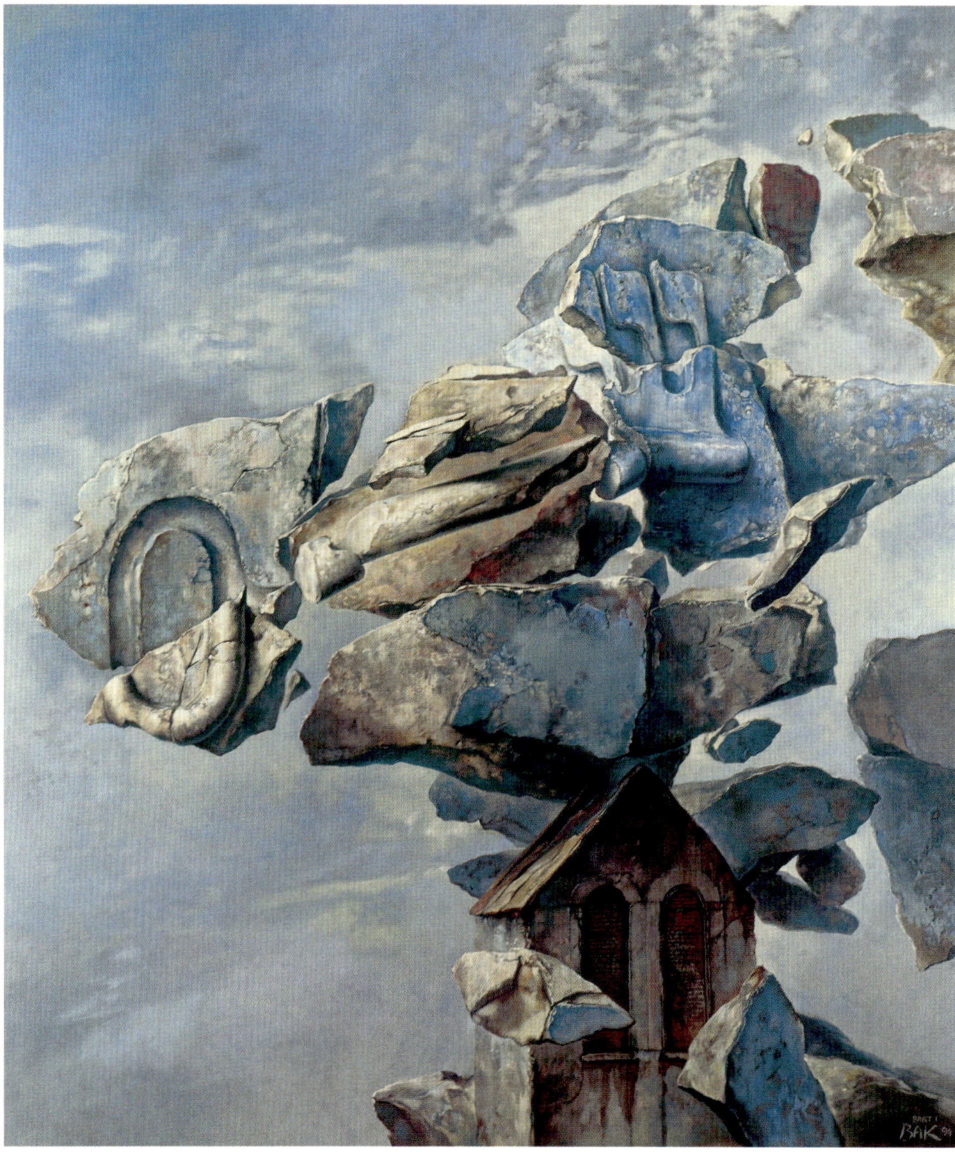

The Hidden Question, Part I, 1994
Oil on Canvas, 63 x 55"

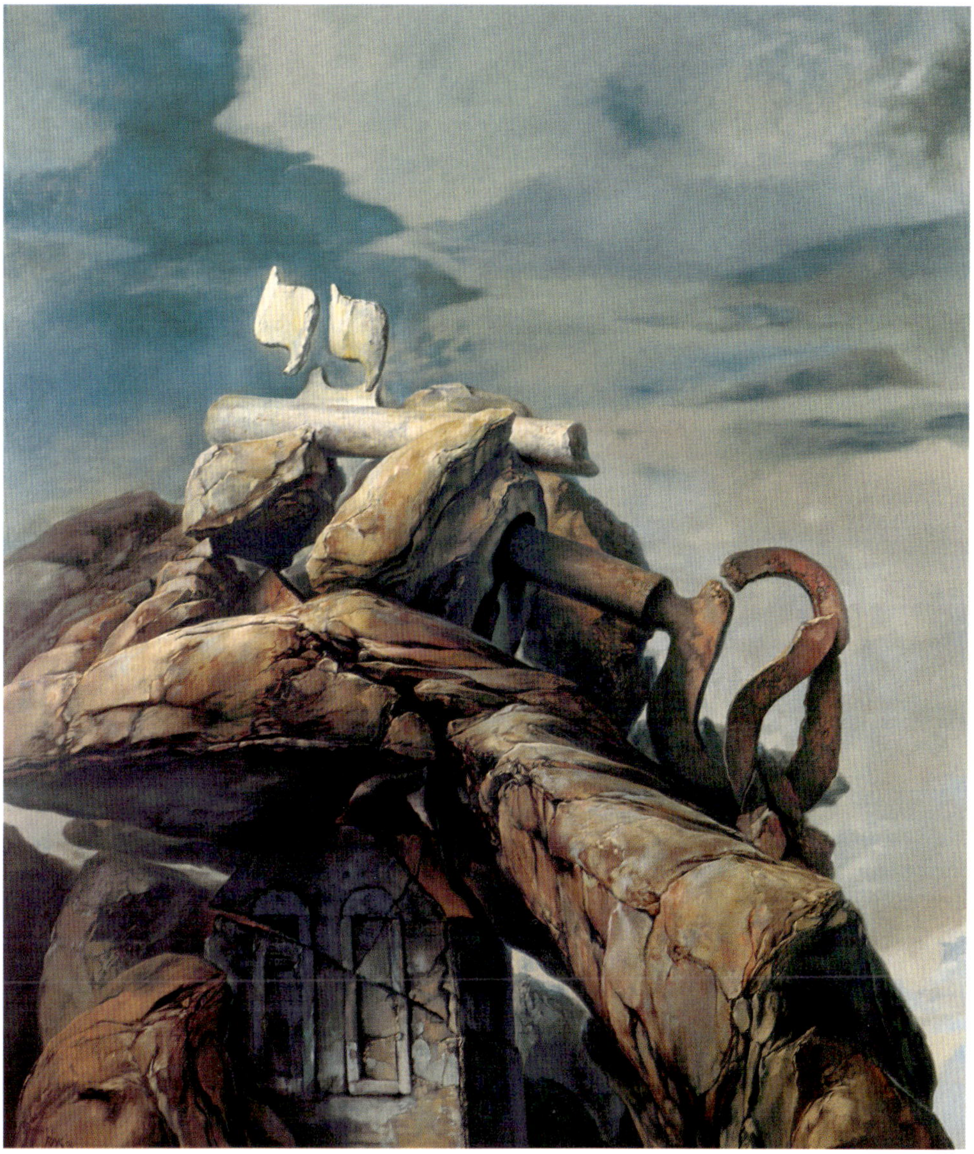

The Hidden Question, Part II, 1994
Oil on Canvas, 63 x 55"

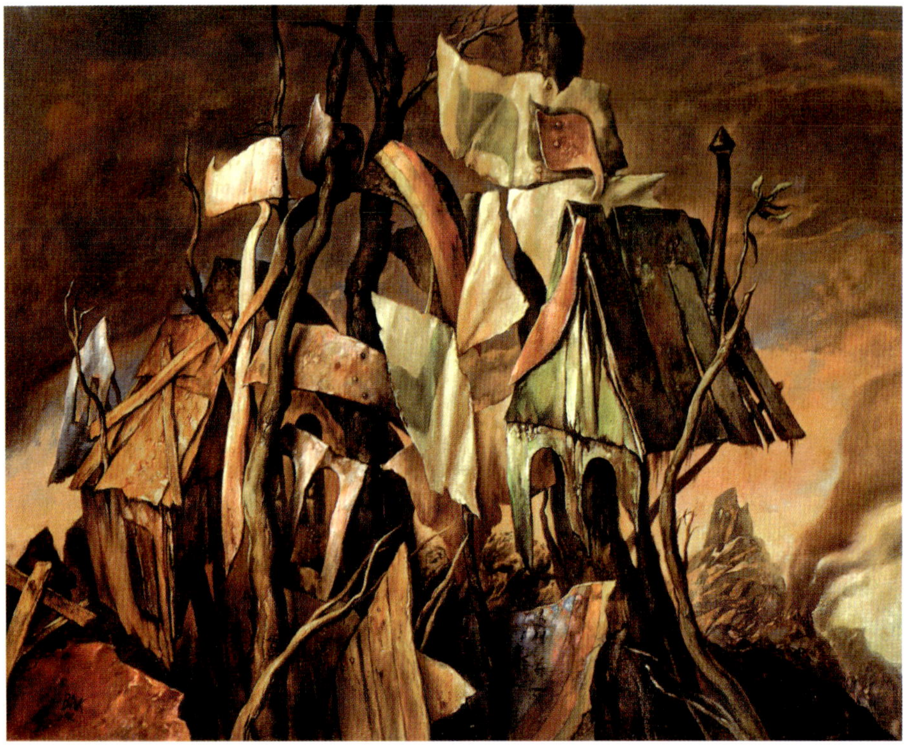

Amkho, 1992
Oil on Linen, 25 1/2 x 32"

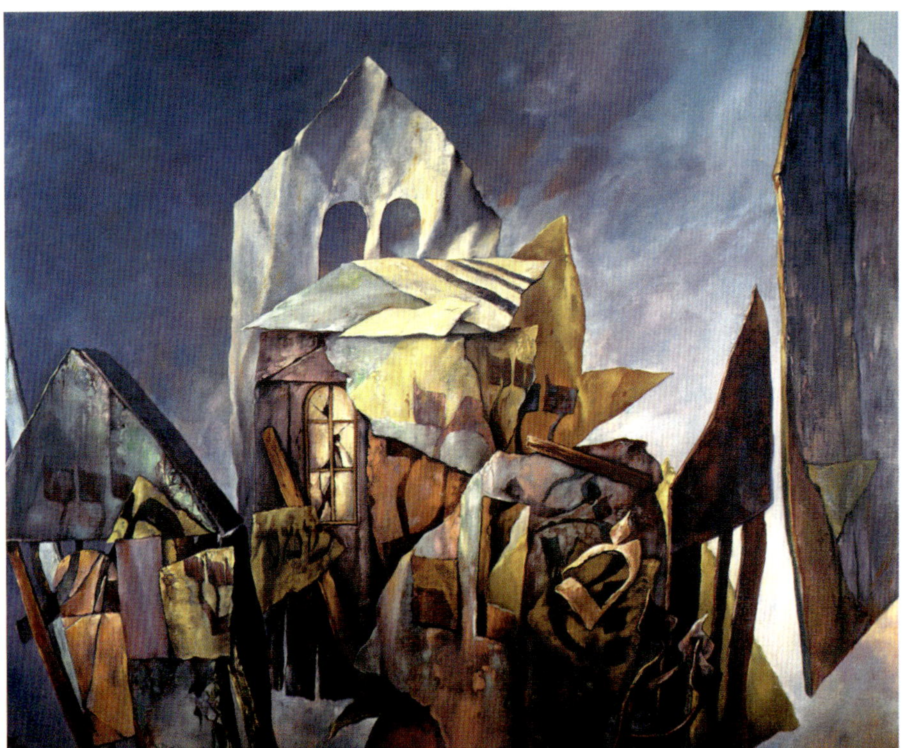

Shemah Israel, 1992
Oil on Canvas, 32 x 39"

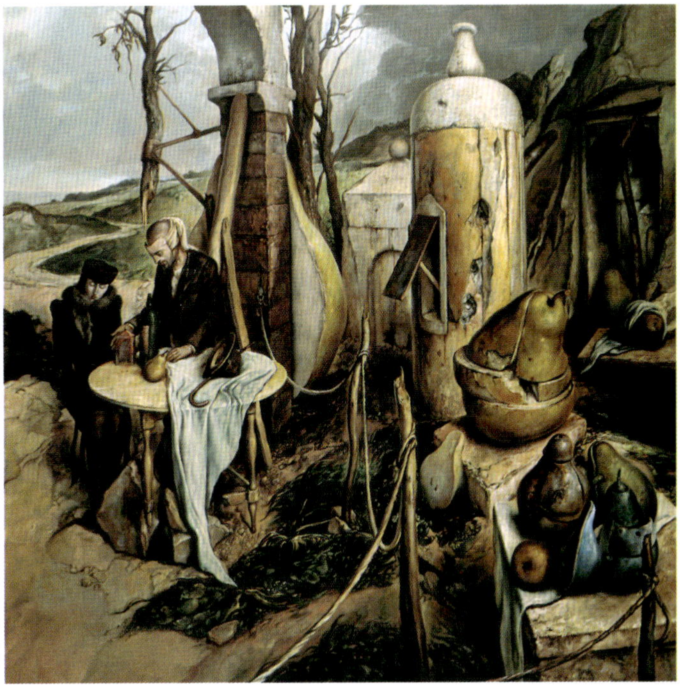

The Explanation, 1977-93
Oil on Canvas, 51 x 51"

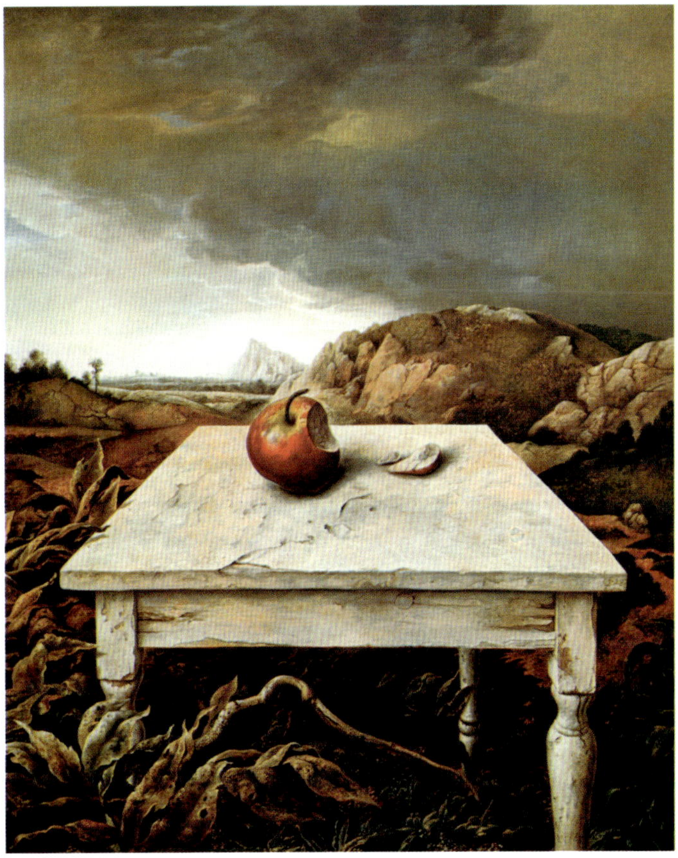

Outskirts of Paradise, 1969
Oil on Canvas, 39 1/2 x 32"

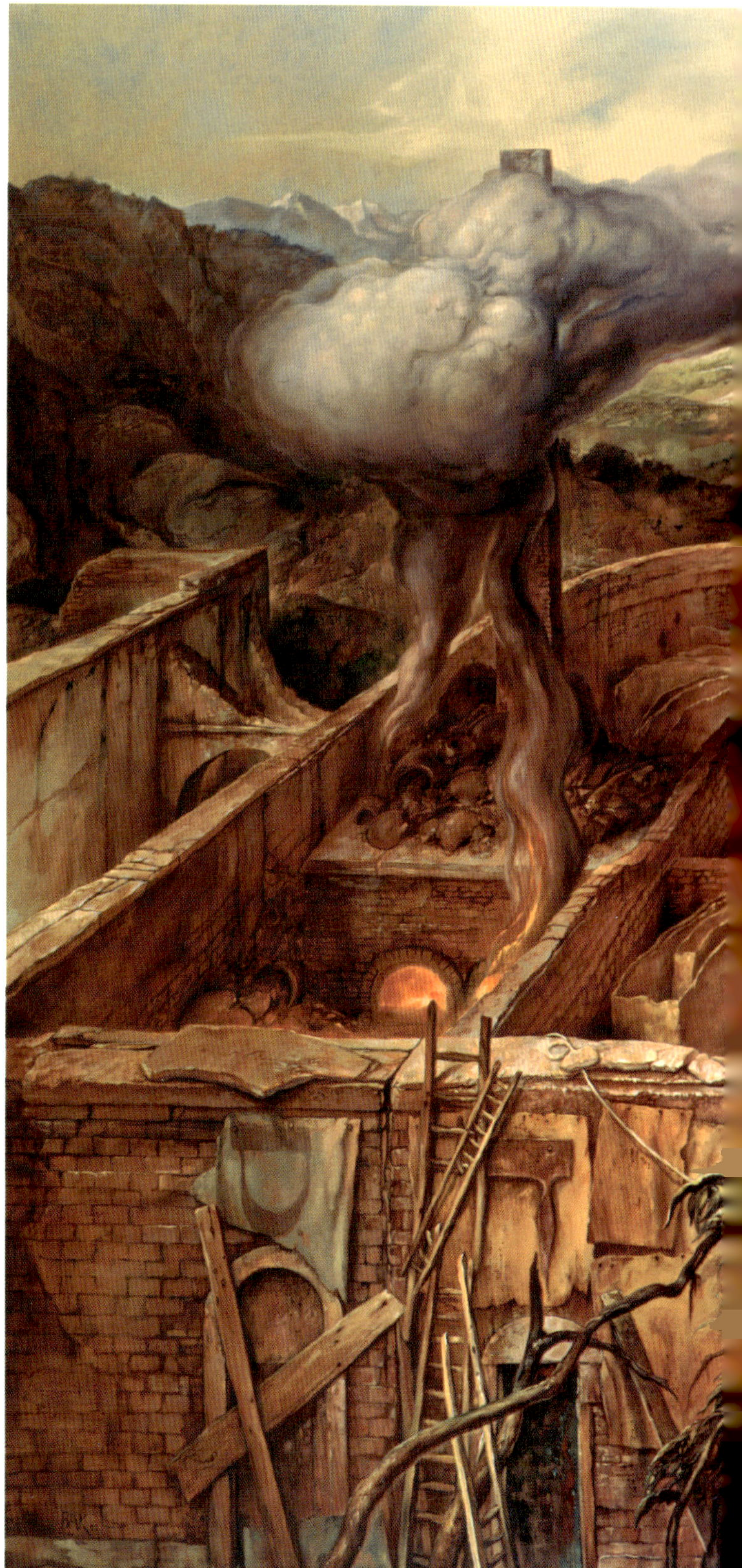

Pardes, 1995
Oil on Canvas, 39 1/4 x 78 3/4"

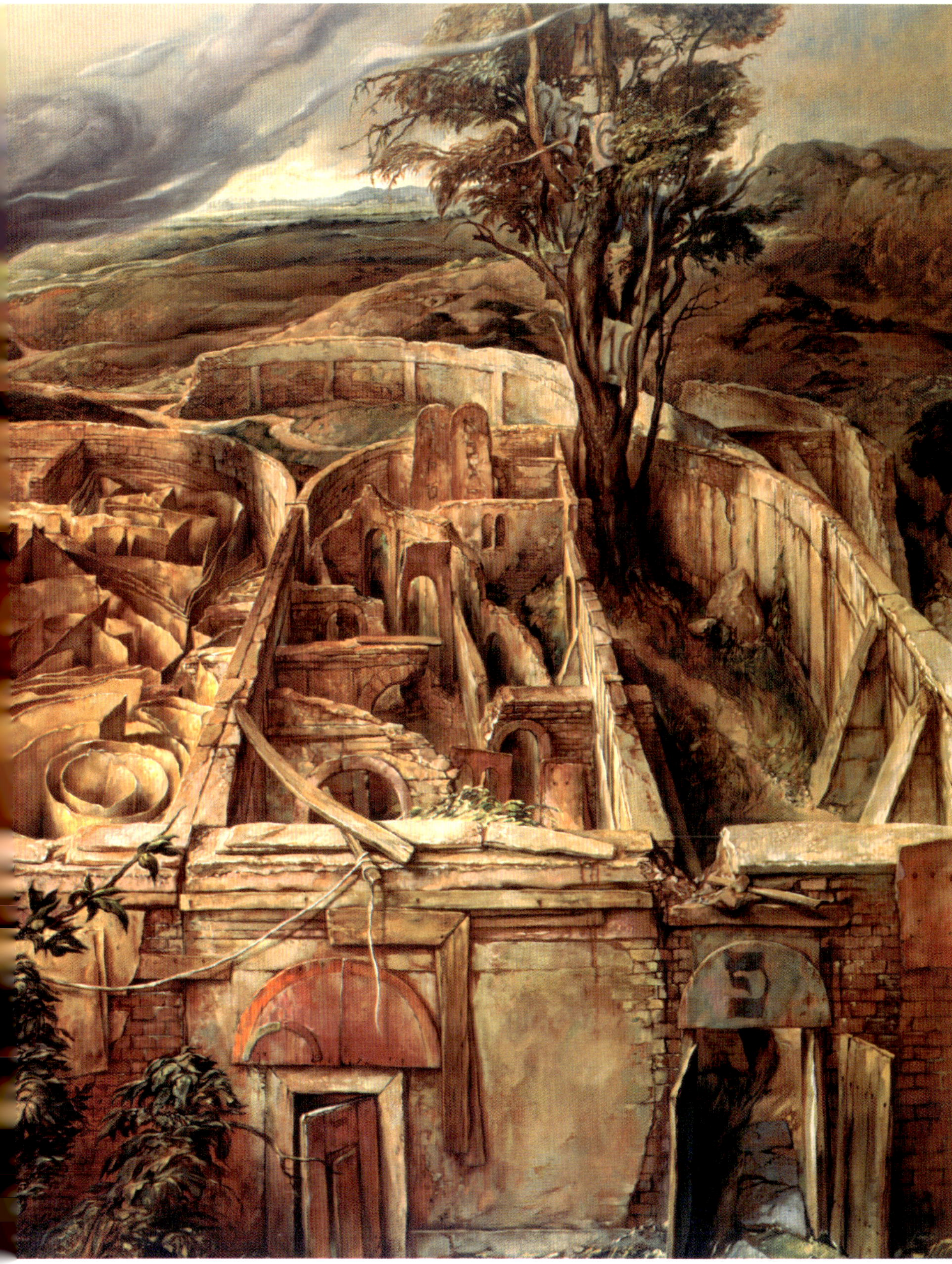

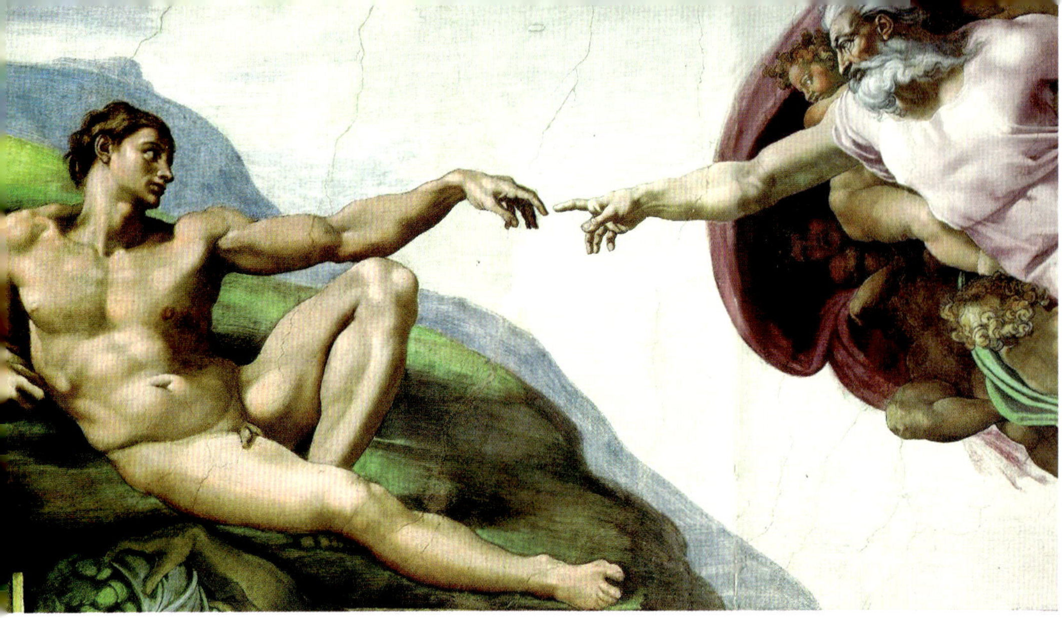

Michelangelo
Creation of Adam, 1508-1512
Fresco

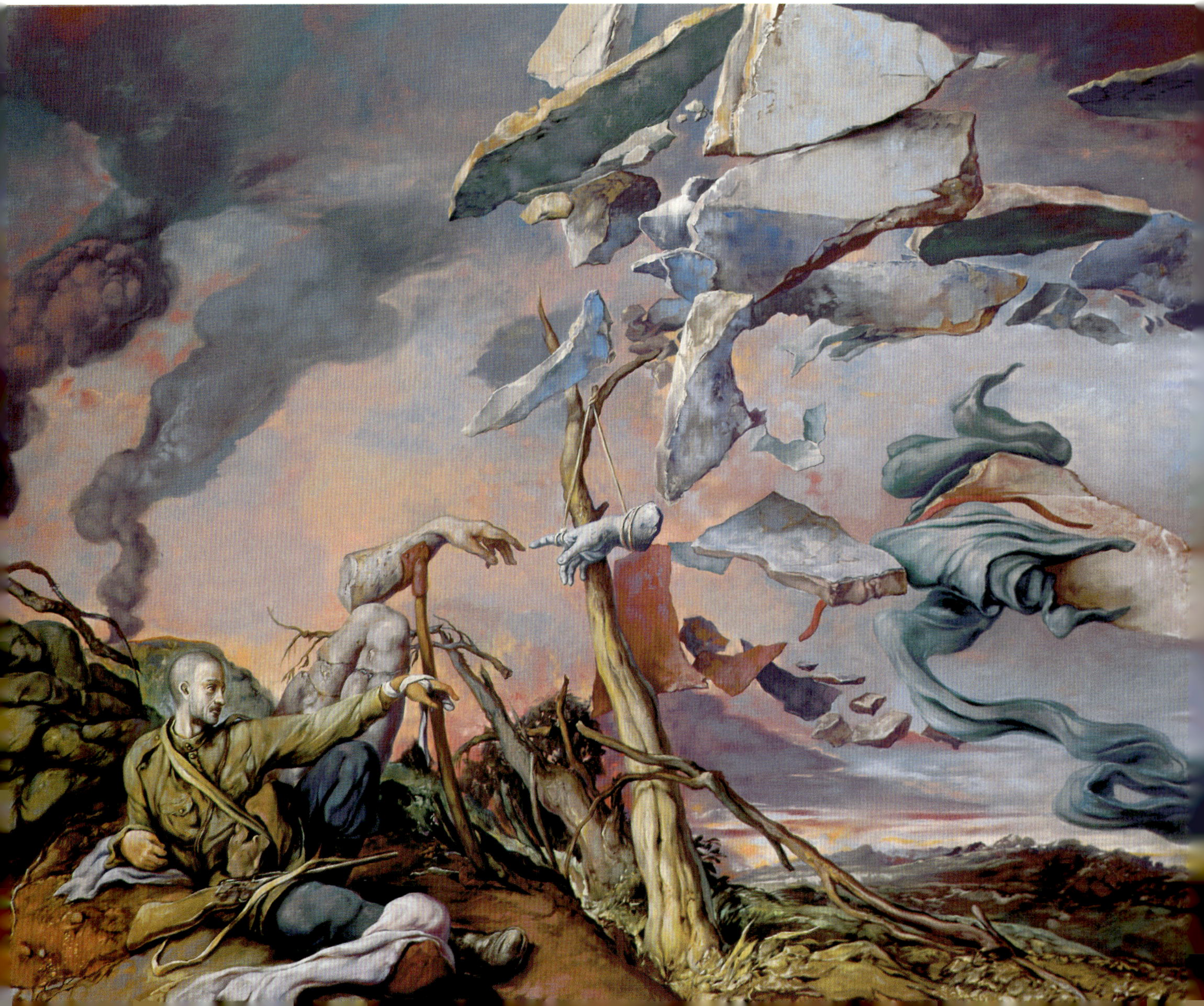

Skeptical Visions and Scriptural Truths: Bak's Genesis Paintings

LAWRENCE L. LANGER

Anyone familiar with Michelangelo's painting of the creation of Adam on the ceiling of the Sistine Chapel who compares it with Samuel Bak's earnest parody of the same episode from the book of Genesis cannot fail to note that something has gone awry in this modern version of the primal biblical scene. In Michelangelo's representation, a powerful anthropomorphic God extends a hand that is about to infuse Adam's reaching finger with the divine spark of life. Although inert, Adam's naked form exudes a radiant beauty, his flesh bathed in a celestial light. In Bak's rendering, called simply *Creation,* the figure of God is barely discernible against a background of natural sky. What was once God's hand, the instrument of divine power, now dangles helplessly from a sling attached to the branch of a blasted tree. It faces the amputated hand and forearm of the original Adam that is supported by a crutch and appears to rest on a huge rock, though closer inspection reveals it to be the ossified remnants of Adam's left leg from Michelangelo's painting. The sky is suffused with a roseate glow, but whether the source is a brilliant sunset above or a blazing inferno below we have no reliable way of deciding.

Like Michelangelo's Adam, the human figure in Bak's painting has an outstretched hand, but it is wounded, its finger bandaged and in no condition to greet its heavenly author. Bak's substitute for Adam is clad in soiled and faded garments; his skull is shaven like the head of a concentration camp inmate, though he seems to be wearing a soldier's uniform. A rifle rests in his lap, its barrel pointing toward the silhouette of God in an unmistakable phallic gesture. The setting is a ruined landscape, not the Garden of Eden. Fragments of stone float through the air, defying nature, as if some nearby monument had exploded, and in the distance two columns of smoke rise skyward, Bak's signature icons, their crematorium origins hidden from view but present to the imagination of anyone familiar with the destruction of European Jewry. Can it be that the title of this work, *Creation,* is meant to be ironic, a devastating critique of the biblical narrative

Creation, 1999
Oil on Canvas, 40 x 50"

of a chosen people who ended up being the people selected, not for covenantal guidance and protection, but for brutal and ruthless death?

Of course, Bak's paintings provide no answers to such bold questions. His stark imagery is part of a retinal audacity designed to stimulate inquiry. The artist's intent is to encourage our educated eyes to witness differently, to see familiar scenes other than they have been trained to do. Bak's violation of fixed visual truth finally forces us to review and revise our memories of earlier artistic and spiritual encounters and the systems of belief to which they were allied. The painting *Creation* suggests that as a result of the violence of recent history the unnatural has displaced much of the supernatural's impact on modern consciousness. The artist Francis Bacon has said that a painter "has to capture not only the look of things but the emotions they arouse." Bak might add to this advice the corollary that sometimes a painter must undo the looks of things in order to discredit the emotions they arouse, so that more credible feelings may infiltrate the vacant space left—using this painting as an example—by the disappearance of divine presence that played such a dominant role in Michelangelo's version. Where has it retreated and why? When will it return? How do we reestablish contact with it? And there are far more audacious questions to ask on this subject, which Bak leaves to the viewer's imagination. His challenge was to find a kind of visual realism—I think it would be a mistake to call this an example of Dali-like surrealism—that would allow him to imprint on the archetypal version of Creation a template of destruction that would substantially modify our response to scriptural and Renaissance visions of human destiny.

In the nineteenth century Friedrich Nietzsche might have viewed this painting as a sign of the loss of contact between the human and the divine, as a hint of God's abdication, for whatever reason, from the human scene, as proof that human renewal could only develop after the withdrawal of divinity from a consciousness struggling to reclaim meaning from an apparently chaotic world. This may be further than Bak is willing to take us; nevertheless, one of the hallmarks of his art is the multiple possibilities of interpretation that canvases like this one offer to the curious and intrepid viewer. John Updike has called Andy Warhol's paintings of Coke bottles and Campbell's soup cans surfaces with nothing behind them, describing them as accurate reflections of much of modern existence. The portrait of God in the painting *Creation* may be named an outline with nothing inside it, though whether this, too, reflects a quality of modern existence is far more ambivalent in Bak than in Warhol's photographic representations of the products of commercial life.

Biblical narrative provides us with considerable evidence for a reciprocal connection between the human and the divine, the most conspicuous of which is the presence of angels. In the book of Genesis, angels are the Lord's messengers, the *mal'akhim,* whose primary Hebrew meaning, as Robert Alter informs us, is "one who carries out a designated task." "It is anyone's guess," Alter continues, "how the Hebrew imagination conceived agents of the Lord three thousand years ago, and it is certainly possible that the original traditions had a blurry notion of differentiation between God's own interventions in human life and those of His emissaries."[1] What is certain, however, is that one role of divine messengers was to remind God's people that He was concerned with their existence. The task of the first angel to appear in Genesis is to urge Hagar to return to Sarah's household and to inform her that she will bear a son to be called Ishmael, which means "God has heard." Its most consoling message of all is that "the Lord has heeded your suffering" (Genesis 16:11). At a parallel moment in the Akedah Ishmael's father is about to sacrifice his other son when the Lord's messenger again intervenes with a promise of divine protection. So the tradition of angels as intermediaries is well established from scriptural precedent, and it is the fate of this precedent that becomes the subject of Bak's portrait of two angels in *Reflecting.*

If human violence has stained the purity of creation, how has that affected the emissaries of divine promise? In *Reflecting* we encounter the dilemma of the angels: they appear as laid-off actors in the drama of God's universe, left to ponder the reasons for the loss of their usual employment. They are poised on a promontory surrounded by waters that once, as a sign of God's displeasure, drowned all living creatures except for Noah and the voyagers on his ark. In the background we see a stranded stone ship—like the angels, its occupation, too, is gone—certainly a reminder, if not a replica, of the vessel from scripture. Rising from its deck, barely discernible, are twin chimneys belching smoke, anachronistic images of a later catastrophe, this one initiated by men rather than God. Is it any wonder that Bak's angels are disconsolate? They seem pensive, gazing into opposite sides of a pier glass that mirrors the double entendre of the painting's title. Despite their wings—which, as Alter points out, are post-biblical additions to the figures of God's heralds—they are earthbound. They meditate narcissistically on their own images, wondering what to do next, like stranded messengers cut off from any possibility of completing their assigned missions—if indeed they have any. Seated beneath the arched remnants of a proverbial rainbow, a breached semicircle deprived of its once luminous promise, they help to portray a world that appears to have lost contact with its heavenly source. Their princely purple robes are sad if vivid signs of their erstwhile task; no bell tolls to summon them back to their assigned purpose. Behind them a ladder, another favorite Bak icon, seems a diminished symbol of the spiritual journey they once pursued between the human and the divine. Is the longing for a semblance of their former selves a mark of angelic nostalgia or a disenchanted critique of our surrender to the illusion that once infused them with vital meaning?

Once more, the questions are more urgent than the answers. Assessing the enigmatic loss of spiritual direction inherent in the modern condition within a framework of biblical meaning leads to some uncomfortable inquiries. Bak might just as easily have given the painting he called *Reflecting* a more explicit title—*Perplexity.* What message can God's intermediaries possibly bring to the people of the Lord after the Holocaust? *In Need of a Tikkun* resumes the angelic theme, while its imagery exposes a major source of the dilemma. One winged figure points to a tear in a fabric that might well be a large crumpled canvas, reminding the artist of his role in restoring integrity to a world shattered by mass murder. Alternatively, when stretched to its full dimensions, it could represent the heavens where once divine power reigned, suggesting that the responsibility for restoring integrity may not lie solely in human hands. As if troubled by its anomalous proximity, the other angelic figure tries to block the smoke pouring from a miniature replica of a crematorium chimney, but its futile gesture only succeeds in focusing our attention on this contradiction to the covenant with which the Lord rewarded Abraham's faith. Of course, in the ongoing saga of divine and human history, this is not the first disruption of the spiritual bond that theoretically joins time to eternity. Both Bak and Michelangelo on the Sistine ceiling find the banishment from Eden a central moment in the biblical story of God's creatures. But there the repair was implicit in the transgression. For Milton, the lapse (or choice) that led to the expulsion of Adam and Eve echoes in the melancholy closing lines of *Paradise Lost:* "They, hand in hand, with wandering steps and slow / Through Eden took their solitary way." But despite their dejected departure we are reassured by the added detail that wherever they choose their place of rest, Providence will be their guide. No such assurance lies concealed in the imagery of *In Need of a Tikkun.* Indeed, except for the tiny model of a vacant house, ominously attached to the crematorium and its chimney, this painting, like so many of its fellows, is marked by the *absence* of human presence, as *Creation* was by the absence of divine substance. Here no hands are joined; instead the hands are given tasks that neither human nor divine energy would cherish: suppressing the smoke of death, or aiming at emptiness.

The paradoxical link between creation and destruction is reinforced by certain spatial relations built into *In Need of a Tikkun,* forcing the viewer to advance from visual to mental perception. The forearm of one angel is parallel to but pointing in the opposite direction from the drifting crematorium smoke, while the forearm of the other angel is parallel to the brick chimney but angled upward as the smoke floats down. Not to be dismissed is the semblance of a finger at the smoke cloud's tip. Does it signify a mute reprimand from the victims who are no longer able to speak for themselves, to say nothing of joining in the necessary act of repair? Or is it perhaps a cautious reminder that creative revival cannot cancel but must coexist with the memory of destructive force? Maybe the tear should remain, as it does in this painting, as a fixed reminder of a loss that can never be retrieved. If angels cannot smother the smoke of mass murder, who can? The images speak vividly to each other, prompting the audience to overhear their disturbing visual dialogue, and to extend the inquiry beyond the frame of the picture.

Yet the first angel's finger is a clear reference to the animating promise of God's digit in Michelangelo's version of human origin, and the biblical narrative that it begins. Was it divine miscalculation or human failure that caused plans to go awry? Or should we readjust our vision to acknowledge that creation and destruction, the innocence of Adam and the murderous violence of Cain, were implicit in Hebrew scripture from the beginning? The pattern of creation and destruction followed by some form of renewal is part of the narrative rhythm of Genesis, from Noah's flood to the reconciliation of Joseph with his estranged family that concludes the volume. But when history introduced the Holocaust into the destiny of the Jewish people, the question of renewal took on dimensions not anticipated by scriptural precedent.

In *Noah's Bird*, an image of God's promise is literally clothed in the garments of Holocaust catastrophe, fusing the two in an indissoluble if paradoxical bond. Remnants of each are scattered across the landscape of the canvas. Since the flood was meant as both punishment *and* renewal, we are forced to ask why signs of the latter do not appear prominently, why reminders of the former dominate the scene. Here Bak blends the twin disasters of water and fire, the one devised by God, the other by man, providing a summary vision of how since biblical times to the present the good intentions of the creative urge have gone astray. One of the strangest consequences of the flood in Genesis is God's own recognition that "the devisings of the human heart are evil from youth" (Genesis 8:21), a line which Robert Alter glosses as follows: "After the flood, God, once more recognizing the evil of which man is capable, concludes that, given what man is all too likely disposed to do, it is scarcely worth destroying the whole world again on his account."[2] Of course, as the Holocaust and subsequent history have shown, supernatural intervention was no longer necessary, since men have proved capable of approaching a natural apocalypse without divine assistance.

But whether the source of the chaotic scenario in *Noah's Bird* be divine anger or human evil, the debris-strewn landscape before us summons us to the ultimate challenge of interpretation. The gentle dove from Genesis, no reassuring plucked olive leaf in its bill this time, stares at the surrounding terrain with a near-demonic intensity. The disquieting sight it beholds dares us to venture toward an even more disturbing insight. Its terrifying gaze, the monstrosity of that mesmerizing eye, betrays far more than the mere ebbing of the waters, though it does not easily reveal the secret of what it sees. It is typical of these paintings that they do not declare their meanings but demand collaboration with the viewer if any significance is to be extracted from their obstinate visual silence. Without such an alliance, they remain mute testimony to an undeciphered if not indecipherable world.

We recall that in Genesis after the flood "God blessed Noah and his sons and He said to them, 'Be fruitful and multiply and fill the earth'" (Genesis 9:1)—a clear allusion to the original creation of humankind in Genesis 1. He followed with a renewal of an earlier promise: "I am about to establish My covenant with your seed after you" (Genesis 9: 8-9). A rainbow is to be the visual sign of this pledge: "And the bow shall be in the cloud, and I will see it, to remember the everlasting covenant between God and all living creatures, all flesh that is on the earth" (Genesis 9: 16-18). Is the bird in Bak's painting, with its alluring eye, searching for evidence of that promise? Scraps of God's rainbow are scattered in the foreground, surrounded by vestiges of the same striped fabric that modify the identity of the bird. As for the clouds that were to be harbingers of the rainbow and thus a reminder of the covenant, they have in *Noah's Bird* a more sinister origin, once a harbinger and now a melancholy reminder of a different kind of destiny for the Jewish people. How is it possible—*is* it possible—to reshape this detritus of history and scripture into a manageable—and even more important—into a life-sustaining form that might renew the human spirit? In the distance a mountain peak hovers over the scene, but whether it signifies Ararat where Noah's ark came to rest or Sinai where the first covenant was certified and inscribed, we are left to wonder. The summit is barren, and there is no hint of divine disclosure. Some traces of the original tablets are sheltered beneath a crude roof, but their surfaces are blank. We would rejoice to find some touch of serenity in the bird's relentless glare, but the more we stare at it, and the more it stares at us, we are forced to ask what token of hope it might bring back were it sent forth to inspect a post-Holocaust terrain. Are we then faced with a return to anarchy, a more despondent version of T.S. Eliot's *Wasteland,* whose fragments we are left with to shore against our ruin?

I think that this gloomy prospect takes us too far beyond the artist's intentions, or more precisely, the intentions of his artistic representations. Bak's most remarkable contribution to the evolution of a post-Holocaust sensibility, and indeed to modern consciousness in general, is the tenacity with which he fashions through visual encounter a point of view for absorbing the implications of our fragmented age, particularly the intellectual and spiritual consequences of the destruction of European Jewry. His use of the catastrophe that undid one version of Creation, evident in his blasted landscapes with their smoke-tainted skies, lay the foundations for a fresh way of seeing, designed to inspire a more complex way of thinking and perhaps a more valid way of knowing, one more consonant with the nature of current reality. We might call it a principle of collateral perception, which must grow slowly into what we might call a collateral mode of thought. It is an empirical rather than a theoretical process, spurring viewers to regard the tensions between the narratives of scripture and history with a double vision that sustains simultaneously in a delicate inner balance the claims upon our attention of creation and decay. They are engaged in perpetual strife, as the search for equilibrium continues to besiege the imagination, though the beguiling appeal of these paintings that urge us to enter into their world of ambivalent duality prevents a victory for either side. At the original instant of creation God forced the darkness over the deep to recede to enable the shaping of our known cosmos, replacing the "wild and waste"[3] of chaos with a human universe from which emerged the covenantal narrative of the Jewish people. These paintings suggest how through the Holocaust those ancient powers of discord have reasserted their primordial rights by trespassing on the orderly world that displaced them. Bak's art captures the resultant stress, leaving to his audience the chore of deciding how it affects and afflicts their consciousness and their lives.

---

1 Robert Alter, *Genesis: Translation and Commentary.* (New York/London: W.W. Norton, 1996), 69.

2 Alter, 37.

3 This is the translation of Everett Fox, *The Five Books of Moses: A New Translation with Introductions, Commentary, and Notes* (New York: Schocken Books, 1995). Robert Alter prefers "welter and waste," while other variations offer "waste and void" and "waste and empty." Most familiar, of course, is the King James Version, "without form and void." Fox and Alter prefer to approximate the rhyme of the original Hebrew *(tohu wabohu)* through alliteration.

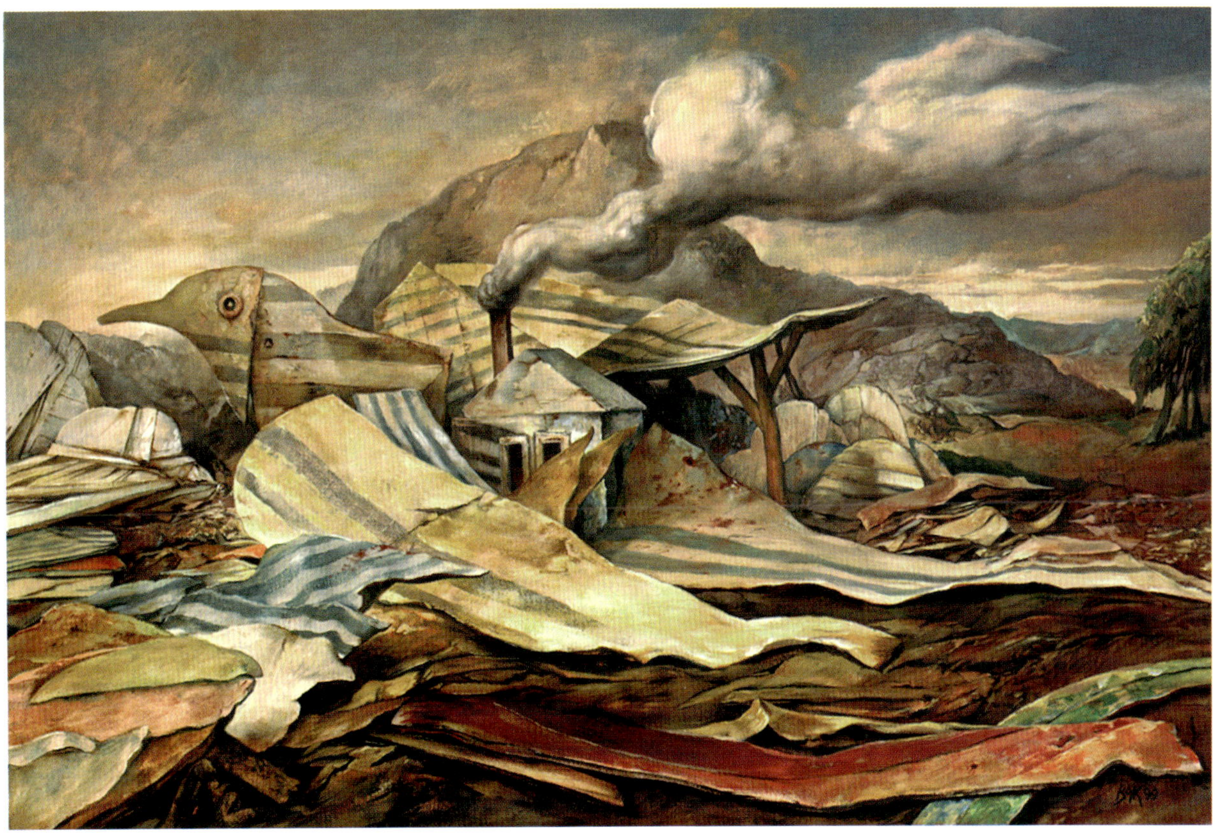

Noah's Bird, 1999
Oil on Canvas, 20 x 30"

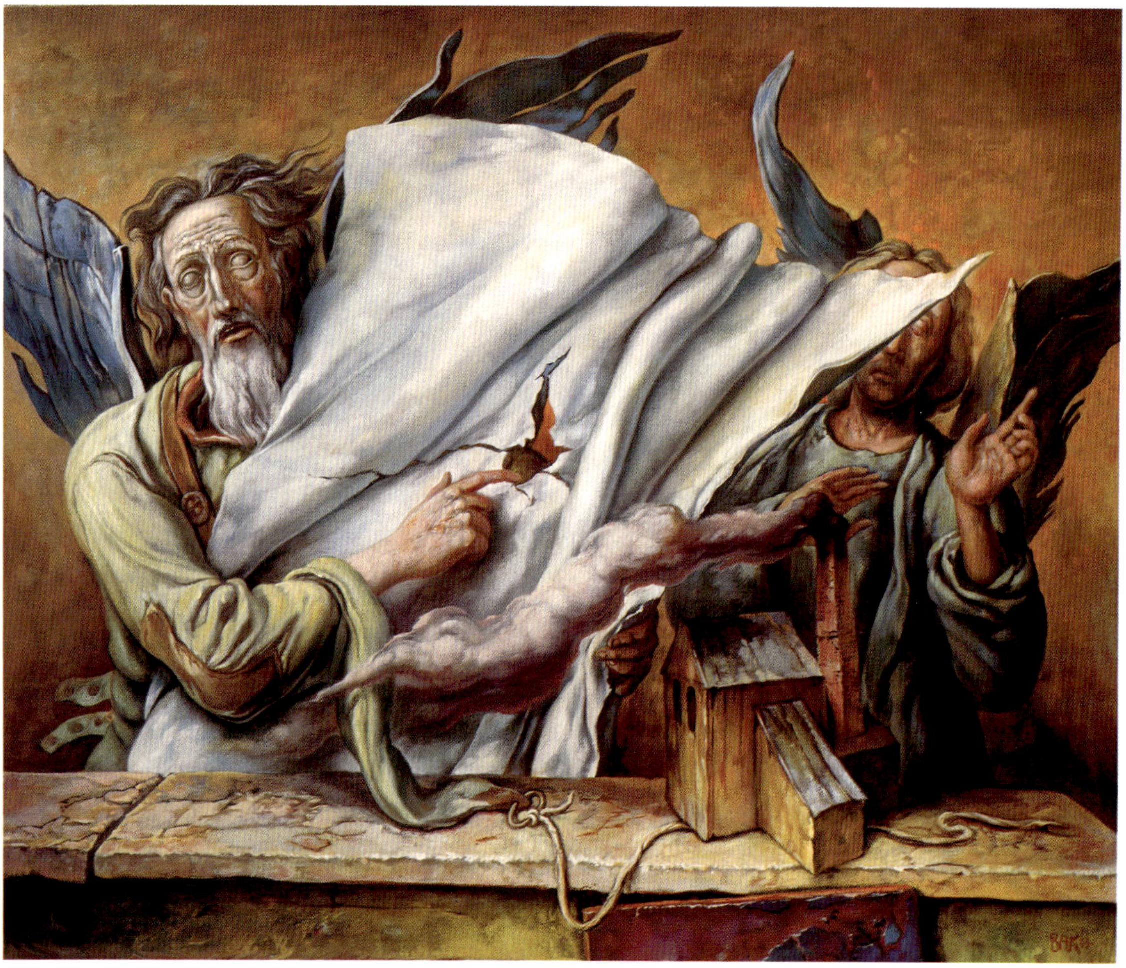

In Need of a Tikkun, 1999
Oil on Canvas, 22 x 26"

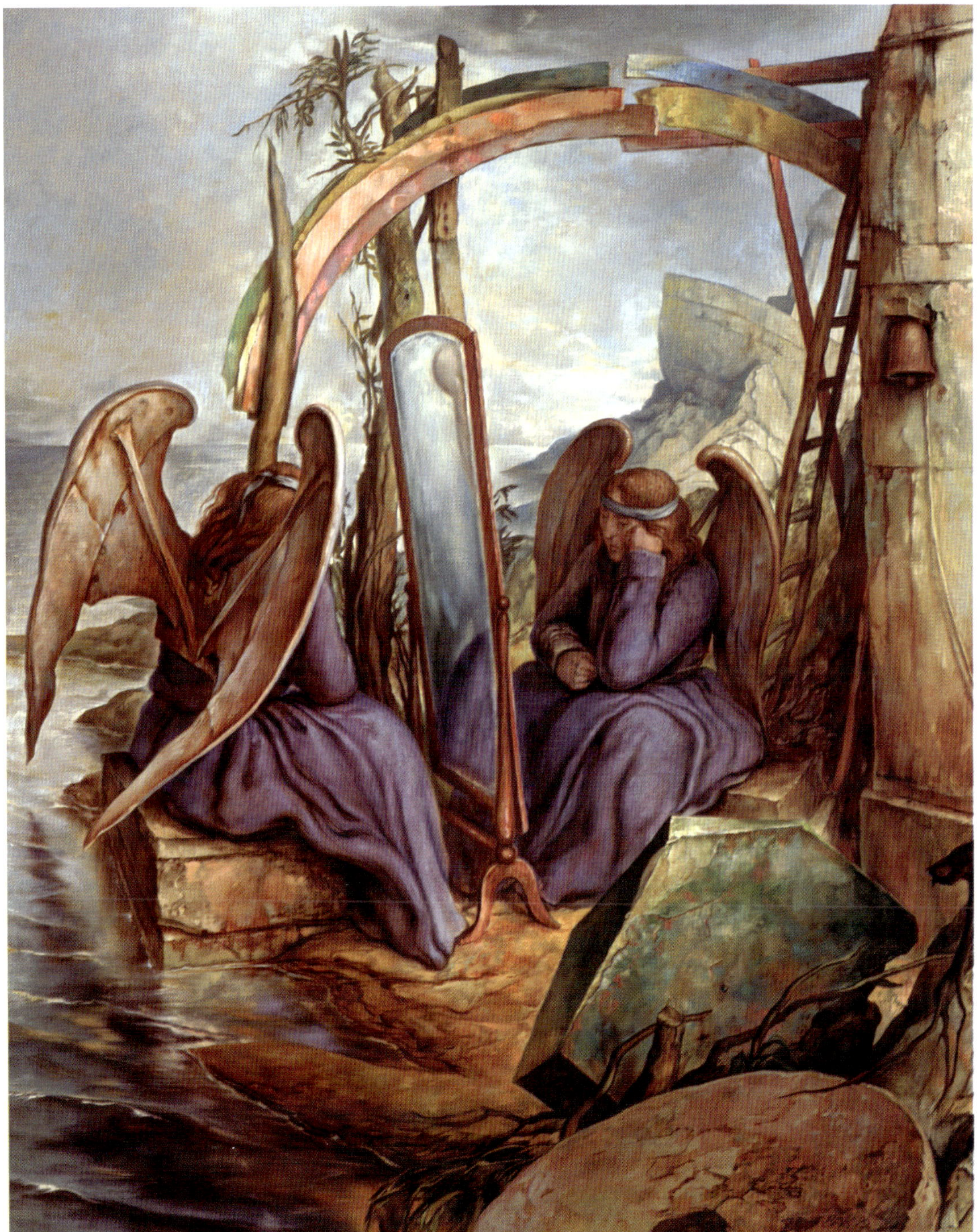

Reflecting, 1999
Oil on Canvas, 40 x 32"

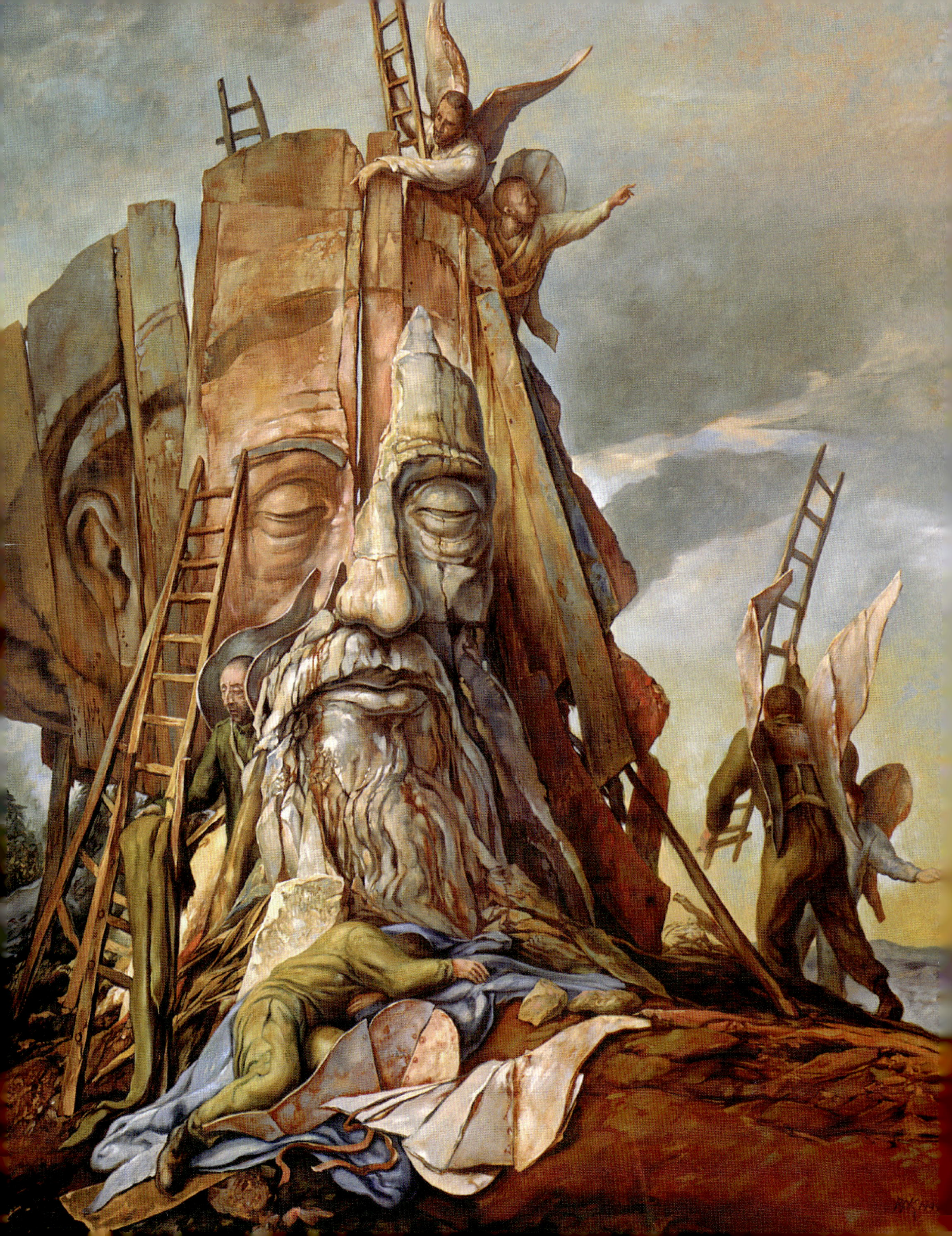

Bak's Dreams: Painting as Midrash

ALICIA OSTRIKER

> The imagination may be compared to
> Adam's dream, - he awoke and found it truth.
> — JOHN KEATS
> Letter to Benjamin Bailey, November 22, 1817[1]

The biblical book of Genesis is filled with dreams, mentioned and implied, major and minor. Adam's dream, unmentioned in the Bible, is described in John Milton's midrashic epic *Paradise Lost.* John Keats makes this dream a figure for the truth of the imagination, in the same letter as his ardent declaration that "What the imagination seizes as Beauty must be truth—whether it existed before or not." In a sequence of visions or dreams in Genesis 15, God announces his covenant with the patriarch Abraham. In Genesis 20, when Abimelech, king of Gerar, takes Abraham's wife Sarah for himself, God in a dream commands Abimelech to restore the woman to her husband, which he does. The nocturnal appearance of God to Isaac in Genesis 26:24, promising to bless him for Abraham's sake, is perhaps a dream. Jacob's dream in Genesis 28:12-15, however, has produced a major image in Western thought. Fleeing his brother Esau, who has threatened to kill him, Jacob goes to sleep somewhere between Beersheba and Haran, with stones for his pillows:

> And he dreamed, and behold a ladder set up on the earth, and the top of it reached to heaven: and behold the angels of God ascending and descending on it. And, behold, the Lord stood above it, and said, I am the Lord God of Abraham thy father, and the God of Isaac: the land whereon thou liest, to thee will I give it, and to thy seed; And thy seed shall be as the dust of the earth, and thou shalt spread abroad to the west, and to the east, and to the north, and to the south; and in thee and in thy seed shall all the families of the earth be blessed.[2]

At the close of this dream of the ladder, God promises to be with Jacob wherever he goes, and upon awakening Jacob says "Surely the Lord was in this place; and I knew it not...this is none

Dreaming Jacob, 1999
Oil on Canvas, 40 x 32"

other than the house of God, and this is the gate of heaven." Years later, in Genesis 31:10-13, Jacob tells his wives that an angel of God has spoken to him in a dream and told him to return to the land of his kindred. When he flees with his family and is pursued by his father-in-law Laban, God in a dream tells Laban to take heed and "speak not to Jacob either good or bad," a dream Laban reports to Jacob as his reason for not seizing Jacob's wives, children, and cattle (Genesis 31:24, 29).

In the long climactic narrative of Genesis, yet another set of dreams gathers around the figure of Joseph, Jacob's favored son. Genesis 37 tells that as a boy, Joseph dreams that his brothers' sheaves of wheat bow down to his sheaves, and that the sun and moon and eleven stars bow down to him. His eleven brothers, envious, plot to kill him, and end up by selling him into slavery in Egypt. In Genesis 40, Jacob becomes an interpreter of the dreams of his fellow prisoners, and in Genesis 41 he is called to interpret Pharaoh's dreams of the fat and lean kine and the full and thin ears of corn. His successful interpretations of forgiveness and death sentences, good years and years of famine, ultimately result in his being made prime minister of Egypt, and in his reunion with his brothers and his mourning father who has believed him dead. In each of these Egyptian episodes, Joseph mysteriously attributes the capacity to interpret dreams to God, and then proceeds to interpret them himself:

> And they said unto him, We have dreamed a dream, and there is no interpreter of it. And Joseph said unto them, Do not interpretations belong to God? Tell me them, I pray you. (Genesis 40.8)
>
> And Pharaoh said unto Joseph, I have dreamed a dream, and there is none that can interpret it: and I have heard say of thee, that thou canst understand a dream to interpret it. And Joseph answered pharaoh, saying, It is not in me: God shall give Pharaoh an answer of peace [RSV: a favorable answer]. (Genesis 41:15-16)
>
> And Joseph said unto Pharaoh...God hath showed Pharaoh what he is about to do....What God is about to do he sheweth unto Pharaoh....the thing is established by God, and God will shortly bring it to pass. (Genesis 41:25, 28, 32)

In case there might be any doubt, the Joseph story seems clearly to imply that dreams—especially dreams having to do with life and death matters and the fate of whole peoples—come from God, and, further, need to be interpreted by one who is on good terms with God. It is as if Joseph's deferring to God *makes* him a correct interpreter.

The case is rather different with Samuel Bak's dream paintings. Among his many revisionist visions of Genesis, Bak has three paintings on the theme of the "dream" referring to Abraham and Isaac, Jacob, and Joseph, which use images of a broken ladder, in mysterious dialogue with Jacob's ladder in Genesis 28:12-17, the ladder of promise. They also use images of barren mountain landscape, wooden or metal-winged angels, and the fragmented or broken face or hand of a

Holy One in dialogue with the familiar image of Michelangelo's God. A fourth painting, *About Dreaming,* depicts a figure looking rather like the iconographic Jesus of Western painting, but this Jesus is a vagabond figure resting with his shoes off, reading, gazed at by a white-bearded God/Abraham. Who is dreaming what in all these paintings remains open to speculation; inevitably a sense of despair is implied by the scenes of barrenness and brokenness, dilapidation, rubble and junk, supported by broken *tfillim,* prison uniforms, smokestacks, etc., suggesting the aftermath of World War II. At the same time, the precision and clarity of Bak's draftsmanship, the subtlety of his palette, and the complexity of his compositions, constantly ask us to see his paintings as artifacts of beauty. And this contradiction is but one of many.

Bak's variations on biblical themes are midrashic in their insistence on locating contemporary meaning in the ancient text. What, then, is midrash? And why is it important to frame Bak's paintings in such a context? From a Hebrew root meaning *seek* or *investigate,* traditional rabbinic midrash exists to fill in the gaps in biblical narrative, to clarify confusions, to deal with the inconsistencies, the contradictions, the absurdities in the tales—to make them meaningful, morally and spiritually, to a community. In other words, it exists to keep the stories alive. For my purposes here I want to emphasize two aspects of midrash: first, that it must always speak to the present time, the lives we live. As Deuteronomy 30:11-14 declares, Torah "is not in heaven…neither is it across the sea....The word is very nigh unto thee, in thy mouth, and in thy heart." The rabbis tell us that there is no "earlier" or "later" in Torah, that chronology is irrelevant to it, that any portion down to single phrases and words may be related to any other portion, their meanings intertwined. Second, what follows from this is that midrashim are never *final* interpretations. An array of midrashim can stem from a single text, they can contradict each other, a biblical text is always a seed that can keep yielding new and various fruit.[3] Within Judaism, we are enjoined to interpret and re-interpret and re-re-interpret until the coming of *Moshiach,* Messiah. Torah is a tree of life, we say, and the way we know a tree is alive is that it grows. "There is always another interpretation," say the sages. "Turn it and turn it, for everything is in it." Torah is deeply archaic, yes, and at the same time completely contemporary. For as Gerald Bruns argues in his classic essay on the origins of scriptural interpretation, "If the text does not apply to us it is an empty text....We take the text in relation to ourselves, understanding ourselves in its light, even as our situation throws its light upon the text, allowing it to disclose itself differently, perhaps in unheard-of ways."[4]

In thinking about the explosion of midrashic writing in America in the postwar period, I have elsewhere argued for three basic interpretive modes that seem to underlie all biblical commentary—a hermeneutic of desire, a hermeneutic of suspicion, and a hermeneutic of indeterminacy.[5] In what I have called the hermeneutic of desire, the interpreter discovers in a text what he or she wishes to discover. We bend the text to our needs; we claim that it affirms what we already believe, whether those beliefs be personal, social, intellectual, or institutional. This is, of course, simply what pious biblical exegetes have been doing since the history of exegesis. Theologians and scholars, priests, ministers and rabbis, makers of sermons and makers of literary commentary, all for the most part see in the Bible what they wish to see. Indeed, it has been said that the New Testament itself interprets the Hebrew Bible through a lens of hermeneutical desire. The hermeneutic of suspicion, on the other hand, looks at biblical texts for evidence of fraud, bad faith, inauthenticity, injustice. Obvious instances may be found in feminist biblical criticism, which looks insistently at issues of gender relations in the Bible and finds it a tissue of patriarchal texts dominated by men and masculinity, in which women and females are at best subordinate, and at worst abused. What I call the hermeneutic of indeterminacy differs from that of desire and that of suspicion, though it may overlap with either or both, and is for me at the core of the most valuable midrashic work in our time. Resting on the assumption that scriptural texts not only can but *must* always yield multiple meanings, that they can *never* be correctly understood once and for all, the hermeneutics of indeterminacy seeks to foreground its own contingency, its own activity. Unlike traditional midrash, the midrash of our post-Holocaust time depends on this last approach—an approach in which it is understood that Torah comes to us through time and place and must be understood in time and in place; that it is created by human beings and must be interpreted by human beings; that no interpretation of a biblical text is or can be final.

The Bible is our collective dream. As we are told that when we dream, every character in our dream is a facet of ourselves, to the contemporary midrashist, every character and every situation in the Bible may reveal us to ourselves, may give us information about ourselves and the societies we inhabit. What might it say to us in the post-Holocaust world? Conversely, what new meanings might our midrashim discover within the text? Midrash is a mirror. It is also a window. In Bak, this doubleness, this complexity, is not unconscious as it tends to be in most commentators, but overt and explicit. When Bak writes that thinking of his ancestors awakes in him "a desire to reach over the chasm of time and touch with my finger the moment of Adam's creation," he speaks as an intuitive, yet self-conscious, midrashist; and all the more so when he adds that "something surely made me land in the arms of that bewildered couple, Adam and Eve—or is it perhaps that the mythological couple has landed in mine?"[6] Bak calls the stories of Genesis "entrancing tales" whose essence was "darkened" after his wartime experiences, and notes that, "At least for me, a post-Holocaust journey to Genesis must pass through the book of Job. Job was one of the six million."[7] All this is deeply Jewish, deeply midrashic thinking. Most Jewish, most midrashic of all is Bak's repeated insistence that his paintings ask more questions than they answer.

Isaac's Dream

The four paintings I want to discuss are all from 1999; I do not know in what order they were painted, but I begin with *Isaac's Dream,* both because the Abraham and Isaac story comes before the others in Genesis, and because this work is so complex visually and raises so many unanswerable questions. The complexity of *Isaac's Dream* is linked to what Mikhail Bakhtin would call its dialogism, or its heteroglossia, terms coined to explain how great writers of fiction make strands of language deriving from different systems, different sub-languages within a culture, play against each other. Bakhtin notes that fiction's "usually parodic stylization of generic, professional, and other strata of language is sometimes interrupted by the direct authorial word."[8] In this painting, which so powerfully revises the story of the Akedah, the binding of Isaac, the "direct authorial word," the Hebrew *malach,* angel, is itself parodic, or at any rate fragmented, painted on cracked wooden panels leaning on trees or suspended on cables from above. From behind another panel, on which two *yods* representing God's name are inscribed, the boy whom we automatically identify as Isaac peers out. Pale, with a high smooth brow, possibly wearing a skullcap. Of his clothing we see only a rolled-up white sleeve. Behind him stands the figure of a white-bearded man dressed in East European garments, whose one visible hand holds a leafy twig. His face is at a three-quarter angle to us, and his eyes are closed. The Word stands in a sacrificial mountain landscape of dead trees, broken ladders, a ripped cloth rainbow, a stone (petrified?) ark from which rise the iconic chimneys, presumably, of Auschwitz, and a stone to which a knife—not a boy—has been bound. All these details are in elliptical dialogue with their prototypes in Genesis. Around the boy's wrist twines a torn strip of *tfillim.* At his feet lies a castoff jacket with a yellow star. The palette is mostly browns, grey-browns, reddish browns, faded blues. Text, visual image, distant past, recent past, reference and distortion co-exist uncomfortably in a destabilized present.

To sleep, perchance to dream, the poet says. *But in that sleep of death what dreams may come / when we have shuffled off this mortal coil / Must give us pause.* Many of Bak's figures offer themselves to us with eyes closed, in sleep, or trance, or dream. Or is it blindness? We see them, they do not see us; they are too inward. They endure our gaze. We are drawn to imagine what they imagine. We imagine grief, hurt, loss; we imagine death. In this most complex of Bak's "dream" paintings, called *Isaac's Dream,* who is the dreamer—the man or the boy? Is it the man, the father, who has not sacrificed his son, but has not protected him either? Behind his closed eyes does he encounter his conscience? Or escape from it? Or is the boy dreaming with open eyes of the future we have experienced—the devastation which is the Western world's immediate past, or perhaps what James Joyce's Stephen Dedalus called all of history: "a nightmare from which I am trying to awake"?

Among the many possibilities here, we might say that if it is the boy Isaac who is dreaming, a fearful or traumatized Isaac who is dreaming the future of his people, then perhaps Abraham behind his closed eyes is recognizing his error in the events of Genesis 22. Perhaps he is regretting the obedience from which history has so disastrously unrolled. We are accustomed to the brilliant defense of Abraham as a "knight of faith" in Kierkegaard's *Fear and Trembling.* Carol Delaney's *Abraham on Trial* questions the morality of an obedience willing to sacrifice children, and the influence of the Akedah as a founding story in the three monotheistic religions of the West.[9] Numerous recent midrashim by contemporary Jewish writers see the Akedah as a test of

Abraham, which he failed. In the Israeli novelist A.B. Yehoshua's *Mr. Mani,* the eponymous Avram Mani indeed sacrifices his son; in an essay on the novel, Yehoshua has described his intention of turning the biblical threatened sacrifice into "an awesome reality...by actualizing the murderous threat I could perhaps discredit its appeal...this is what I refer to when I say I am annulling the sacrifice of Isaac by its fulfillment."[10] In Samuel Bak's own comment on the painting, he declares that "Isaac did not die physically on Mount Moriah, but his father Abraham's willingness to accede to God's demand must have crushed him. Generations of Isaac's descendants have pondered that nightmare."[11] An alternative possibility, if we remember that the biblical Isaac as an old man is blind, and that a rabbinic midrash claims he was blinded by angelic tears falling at the scene of the Akedah, is that the old man in the painting is actually the aged Isaac, helpless to save his descendants. The image of the boy looks significantly like Bak's self-portrait of himself as a child in the painting *A Return to Paradise* (1996). Bak's commentary identifies him as "probably a child of the Ghetto." Perhaps what is most curious about the painter's commentary is that in a single paragraph he tells us first that "The elderly man is not Abraham, but clearly one of his descendants," and in the paragraph's last sentence "Abraham's figure is partly obscured by a broken tree, perhaps the tree of life."[12] Perhaps, perhaps. And perhaps the painting is quietly telling us that past and future are both present, perhaps it is telling us that what we consider fixed identity is actually a blur and a puzzle, perhaps—as the boy looks at us, who look at him—it asks us where we stand and who we are.

Dreaming Jacob

What immediately captures the viewer's attention in *Dreaming Jacob* is the head. The giant sculpted, cracked, crumbling, and layered head. Bak has described how struck he was as a child by the image of the head of Michelangelo's Moses and somewhat later by Michelangelo's Creator God.[13] An interesting analogue, or perhaps gloss, for this painting, is the sculpted "shattered visage" in Shelley's sonnet "Ozymandias," a "colossal wreck" half sunk in the desert, beside a pedestal reading "My name is Ozymandias, king of kings,/Look on my works, ye Mighty, and despair." The sonnet closes,

> Nothing beside remains. Round the decay
> Of that colossal wreck, boundless and bare,
> The lone and level sands stretch far away.

"Ozymandias" is among the first poems Samuel Bak remembers reading when he was learning English,[14] and it is easy to imagine what an impression such a poem about the pride of rulers and the collapse and disappearance of kingdoms might have made. Equally interesting and more intimate is the stone father-figure in Sylvia Plath's post-Holocaust poem "The Colossus." "I shall never get you put together entirely," laments the poet, snidely remarking as well, "Perhaps you consider yourself an oracle, / Mouthpiece of the dead, or of some god or other,"

> I crawl like an ant in mourning
> Over the weedy acres of your brow
> To mend the immense skull-plates and clear
> The bald, white tumuli of your eyes...
> A blue sky out of the Oresteia
> Arches above us. O father, all by yourself
> You are pithy and historical as the Roman forum.[15]

Plath's combination of love and scorn for the colossal lost father is not unlike Bak's. The head of a Moses/God/father-figure, a leader, but one who is trunkless, unable to lead, unable to protect. An artifact of clay or stone, which is what idols are made of, but impossible now to worship. Is the apparently wooden head propped up behind this fragment the scaffolding on which the mask was built? Is it too falling apart, or is it being reconstructed, repaired? The eyes of both mask and head behind it are closed, raising the same questions as the eyes of Abraham in *Isaac's Dream.* The expression is neutral and might be mournful, or merely meditative. Inward, inward, it will not reveal its secrets. Two broken ladders lean against it. Two angels with rickety wings of metal or plywood are bringing another ladder, too short to be useful. Two more angels perch near the head's crown, and one ladder reaches past the top of the painting—possibly a hopeful sign! Might this one lead to heaven?

At the head's foot lies a sleeper, presumably Jacob, much less striking than the head, and next to him a pair of unstrapped wings. Does this suggest that Jacob is himself an angel, albeit an ineffectual one? A weary one? The scene plays most obviously on Genesis 28:10-22, in which Jacob's pillow is a stone, he dreams of a ladder of angels and wakes to say, "Surely God was in this place and I knew it not." But if the head is God's head, it is only a contraption. Or is it the head with its closed eyes that is dreaming this Jacob? I am reminded of the most famous dream story in Chinese philosophy:

> Once upon a time, Chuang Tzu dreamed that he was a butterfly, flying about enjoying itself. It did not know that it was Chuang Tzu. Suddenly he awoke, and veritably was Chuang Tzu again. He did not know whether it was Chuang Tzu dreaming that he was a butterfly, or whether it was the butterfly dreaming that it was Chuang Tzu. Between Chuang Tzu and the butterfly there must be some distinction. This is a case of what is called the transformation of things.[16]

The standard interpretation of the story explains that, although in ordinary appearance there are differences between things, in delusions or in dreams one thing can also be another. The "transformation of things" proves that the differences among things are not absolute. This version of blurred identities fits nicely with both Bak's painting and the Biblical Jacob story in which twins wrestle for precedence in the womb of their mother, and one twin steals the birthright and blessing of the other. In Genesis 32:24-30 "a man" wrestles with Jacob all night and in the morning blesses him with a new name, Israel, meaning that he has prevailed with God and man. Is Jacob himself the man he wrestles? Is the place holy? What is the angel with the arm out gesturing at? The palette of *Jacob's Dream* is governed by warm and rosy terra-cotta tints tending toward pink, and delicate blues. The sky looks like dawn. Is something coming?

Joseph's Dream

Joseph's Dream at first seems rather divorced from its biblical source. Instead of the coat of many colors and the egocentric dreams of triumph over his brothers and over the sun, moon, and stars, this Joseph has a prison uniform pulled open around the navel, and the posture of Michelangelo's Adam with hand extended toward a hollow sculpture of God's disembodied hand. The hand of God, made perhaps of bronze, is suspended by strings knotted around its wrist and index finger. The hand of Joseph/Adam has broken *tfillim* hanging from the wrist, looking as if they are made of the same string. Of the several similar images he has painted, Bak asks, Is God creating Man? Or the reverse? "Could their gestures express any disappointment or accusation?...Surely Man has failed his Creator with his endless history of injustice, cruelty, and war; and God, by allowing it, has invited the accusing finger that mirrors his own."[17] Yet the image need not suggest accusation. It is difficult, in fact, to guess what it does suggest. Not as direct a riff on Michelangelo's creation scene as the similar image of *Creation of War Time II,* its hand-of-God is larger than Joseph/Adam's hand, and its index finger does not point at his, so there is not that sense of electrical charge leaping from one hand to the other. It is more as if a prop has been left over from a theatrical performance of some sort, and that the Joseph/Adam figure does not know this yet but is about to find out, when he fully awakens. Does this imply that when we fully awaken we will understand that Joseph's apparent reliance on God as the giver and interpreter of dreams is itself a dream, a fantasy, a piece of theater?

A few points about this specific Joseph are notable. We would not know his identity if it were not for the painting's title. Yet we may remember that the grandiloquence of the boy in Genesis precipitates his brothers' jealousy: "Behold this dreamer cometh...let us slay him and cast him into some pit...and we shall see what will become of his dreams," they say in Genesis 37:20. Here, Joseph is not in a pit, but he is certainly in exile. Should this also be said of Adam, of all humankind—and is it only *after* exile is inflicted on us that we begin to awaken, as this Adam/Joseph seems to be doing? And what is the triangle doing on his uniform? Inmates of the Nazi camps wore inverted triangles of various colors to identify them as criminals, gypsies, homosexuals, political prisoners, etc. But it is difficult to say what the color of the triangle on Joseph/Adam's chest is. It is certainly not the yellow assigned to Jews. The painting is suffused in warm siennas, terra-cottas, brick, and rose tints, so that the triangle might possibly be considered pink, which was the color assigned to homosexuals. There are traditional midrashim that imply a certain girlishness about Joseph, perhaps to explain why he resisted Potiphar's wife; they say he minced when he walked. On the other hand, the yod imprinted on the triangle looks a bit purple, which was the color used for Jehovah's witnesses. Perhaps color is irrelevant here. The *yod* or *yesod* in kabbala is identified with Joseph—it is the 9th of the *sephirot* and is understood as phallic—it channels divine energy toward creation. Is this Adam/Joseph then a figure for some sort of quasi-sexual, quasi-mystical generativeness? Is this the reason for his conspicuous navel?

About Dreaming

This last image is a surprise and a puzzle. *About Dreaming* depicts a long-haired figure in a blue garment covered by a brown cloak, looking like the iconographic Jesus of Western painting, except for his unconventional pose. The figure is reading, gazed at (or *not* gazed at) by a white-bearded and battered-winged God/Abraham, with the by-now-familiar closed or half-closed eyes, whose torso is hidden by a wooden slat with a ladder painted on it. Behind the old man's head smoke rises. At his side is something that looks like a rifle. Some flimsy broken ladders stand around, but a rather solid one rises beyond the picture frame. The Jesus figure sits on a trunk, his shoes and socks off, a pack and stick at his feet. It seems clear that he is resting his feet, and perhaps his whole self. Is the book a Bible or a prayer book? Maybe, maybe not. Is he reading about himself, his ancestors? Lost in thought, what is he learning? There are three pointing hands painted on scraps nailed to the wood scraps: one points at his head, one at his book, one—on the ground—at the sky. Reminding, rebuking?

Meditating on the image of Jesus as a weary Wandering Jew, I find myself feeling pity—but not at all the pity evoked by images of the crucifixion. Rather the pity for a Jesus whose afterlife has nothing to do with salvation but looks like weariness and confusion—a Jesus who may have been witness to the Crusades, the inquisition, the religious wars of Europe fought in his name, and most recently the genocide against his own people—who might be asking himself where his dream went wrong. Or, if it is the Father who is dreaming this son, is the son the projection of the Father's disappointment—or the Father's error? What does the painting mean to teach us about dreaming? Does it say that dreaming is folly, or that it is necessary for healing? Is the book to be seen as a text of dreams, and should we place our hope in it, or should we distrust it?

Conclusion

Toward the close of Shakespeare's *Tempest,* Prospero—an exile like Samuel Bak, and also a father, and something of a God-figure or Christ-figure—says, "We are such stuff / as dreams are made on, and our little life / Is rounded with a sleep." Should Samuel Bak ever do paintings based on Shakespeare, I believe I know what his Prospero will look like.

Of all these paintings, if we ask what light they shed on the biblical texts that are their sources, the simplest answer might be: the paintings enact a hermeneutic of suspicion. They critique the stories by depicting promises broken, peoplehood nonexistent, the milk and honey dried up, angels absurd, God himself merely an artifact, or even an idol, and a decapitated and fragmented one at that. But this is too simple. Bak is not doing satire or caricature of the Bible. The tone of the paintings is not bitter, though it is surely disturbing. Besides, did not Moses himself shatter his first tablets? And is not Job as biblical as Abraham? "A post-Holocaust journey to Genesis must pass through the Book of Job," Bak writes. I see the paintings as embodying a hermeneutic of indeterminacy that is their strength as art and their strength as moral meaning.

"Since my paintings reflect the contradictions of my own nature," Bak explains "they are themselves complex. Far from offering ideologies, beliefs or answers, they ask questions. Any inquiry into their meanings must be undertaken in this spirit....Once a painting has been exhibited to the public it no longer belongs to me. Anyone who contemplates it with interest may well come up with different and equally valid interpretations."[18] This is exactly what God tells the Israelites about Torah. It is precisely the stance rabbinic midrash takes to the Bible, and the stance current midrashists take: that there is always another interpretation is our core principle. These stories, these dreams, collective, individual, never yielding a correct final single meaning, always entailing a burden, a responsibility of interpretation, always refusing a stance of power and authority, always refusing dogma, refusing ideology. And if it is ideology that has produced Bak's barren, wrecked landscapes, these broken ladders, these failed artifacts, these sad exiled men—then the refusal of ideology and dogma, the absence of authoritative once-and-for-all meaning, is our only hope.

It is good not to know if I am dreaming the butterfly or if the butterfly is dreaming me. It is good not to know if there really is a God or only our collapsing artifacts. It is good to be made to wonder about the mystery behind the eyes of another. It is good not to have an Absolute Truth but an array of possible truths. I think it is good to imagine that Abraham might be sorry he obeyed God, that Isaac's blindness as an old man might be the consequence of seeing too much as a boy, that Jacob himself is the antagonist he dreams, that Joseph is also Adam and also a kabbalistic phallus capable of renewing itself, that Jesus is tired and puzzled. It is striking to me that none of Bak's paintings of a post-Holocaust Genesis evoke the sort of pathos produced by the paintings that use the image of the "Ghetto boy." It is as if the implied texts of Genesis, while deflating the biblical promises to which they refer, somehow also confer a kind of strength and serenity. Suffused with sadness, they differ from almost all representations of the Holocaust in that they accuse neither perpetrators nor victims. I am reminded, at last, of a Blake poem entitled "To the Accuser who is the God of This World:"

> Truly my Satan thou art but a Dunce
> And dost not know the Garment from the Man
> Every Harlot was a Virgin once
> Nor canst thou ever change Kate into Nan
>
> Tho thou art Worshipd by the Names Divine
> Of Jesus and Jehovah: thou art still
> The Son of Morn in weary Nights decline
> The lost Travelers dream under the Hill.[19]

The compassion in Blake's poem is also in Bak's paintings, and ultimately suffuses all his subjects. Like Blake's critiques of conventional religion, Bak's critiques somehow do not destroy the grounds of hope. By requiring a viewer to engage interpretively with his paintings—but making "meaning" indeterminate—Bak gestures toward a future as well as a past. We live in a broken world; we can see the Bible as predicting and producing that world; if we can interpret both Torah and our world without reverting to the blame game, the accusations so familiar to us, the certainty of our own victimization and our own righteousness, if we can look with perplexity rather than righteousness, perhaps repair is possible.

---

1 *The Selected Letters of John Keats,* ed. Lionel Trilling (Garden City, New York: Doubleday Anchor Books, 1956), 99.

2 The Biblical citations throughout this essay are from the King James Version of the Bible, also known as the Authorized Version.

3 See, e.g., Mary Callaway, *Sing, O Barren One: A Study in Comparative Midrash* (Atlanta: Scholars Press, 1986); Geoffrey Hartman and Sanford Budick, eds., *Midrash and Literature* (New Haven: Yale University Press, 1986). James Limburg, *Jonah: A Commentary* (London: SCM Press, 1993) includes Appendices (105-106) which excerpt several texts from early Jewish and Christian commentaries on Jonah. Yvonne Sherwood, *A Biblical Text and Its Afterlives: the Survival of Jonah in Western Culture* (Cambridge: Cambridge University Press, 2000), surveys "mainstream" and minority interpretations of Jonah down to the present day, including Jewish interpretations from Rabbinic sources and contemporary literary sources. Yael Feldman surveys rabbinic and modern versions of the story of Jephthah's Daughter in an unpublished manuscript, "Rightly is thy name Called She'ula": pseudo-Philo' in Israel, or: a Female Aqedah by Amos Oz." Sherwood and Feldman are both engaged in studies of the multiple interpretations of the Akedah.

4 Gerald L. Bruns, "Midrash and Allegory: The Beginning of Scriptural Interpretation," in *The Literary Guide to the Bible,* ed. Robert Alter and Frank Kermode (Cambridge, Mass: Harvard University Press, 1987), 633.

5 See Alicia Ostriker, "A Word Made Flesh: The Bible and Women's Poetry," in *Feminist Revision and the Bible* (Oxford, UK and Cambridge, USA: Blackwell, 1993), 56-91, and "A Triple Hermeneutic: Scripture and Revisionist Women's Poetry," *A Feminist Companion to Reading the Bible: Approaches, Methods and Strategies,* ed. Athalya Brenner and Carol Fontaine (Sheffield: Sheffield Press, 1997), 164-89.

6 *In a Different Light: Genesis in the Art of Samuel Bak* (Pucker Gallery Catalogue, Boston, 2000), 2.

7 Ibid., 3.

8 Mikhail Bakhtin, *The Dialogic Imagination* (Austin: University of Texas Press, 1981), 301.

9 Carol Delaney, *Abraham on Trial: the Social Legacy of Biblical Myth* (Princeton, New Jersey: Princeton University Press, 1998).

10 A.B. Yehoshua, "Mr. Mani and the Akedah" *Judaism,* Winter 2001, 61-65. American midrashim on the Akedah include the title poem of Eleanor Wilner's *Sarah's Choice* (Chicago: University of Chicago Press, 1989), Alicia Ostriker, "The Bosom of Abraham," "Sarah, or Defiance," "Isaac, or Laughter," "The Opinion of the Ram," in *The Nakedness of the Fathers: Biblical Visions and Revisions* (New Brunswick, N.J.: Rutgers University Press, 1994), Merle Feld, "Across the Jordan" in Sarah B. Cohen, ed., *Making a Scene: The Contemporary Drama of Jewish-American Women* (Syracuse, N.Y.: Syracuse University Press, 1997). Andrew Lovett's opera, *The Trial of Abraham,* which premiered in Cambridge, UK, in the spring of 2005, is based on Delaney's book.

11 *In a Different Light,* 16.

12 Ibid.

13 Ibid., 2.

14 Bak explained this to the audience at the session on his work held at the AAR/SBL conference in November 2005 and said he had not thought of the poem for many years, but that my presentation reminded him of it.

15 Sylvia Plath, *The Collected Poems,* ed. Ted Hughes (New York: Harper & Row, 1981), 129-30.

16 This version of the story, with commentary, is from C.W. Chan, "The Butterfly Dream," *The Philosopher: the Journal of the Philosophical Society of England,* LXXXIII No. 2, online http://atschool.eduweb.co.uk/cite/staff/philosopher/butter.htm.

17 *In a Different Light,* 9.

18 Ibid., 16.

19 William Blake, *The Complete Poems,* ed. Alicia Ostriker (New York, Penguin Books, 1977), 863. Like Bak two centuries later, Blake went to the Bible to help him deal, artistically and prophetically, with the trauma of his age. In Blake's case the trauma was the failure of the French Revolution.

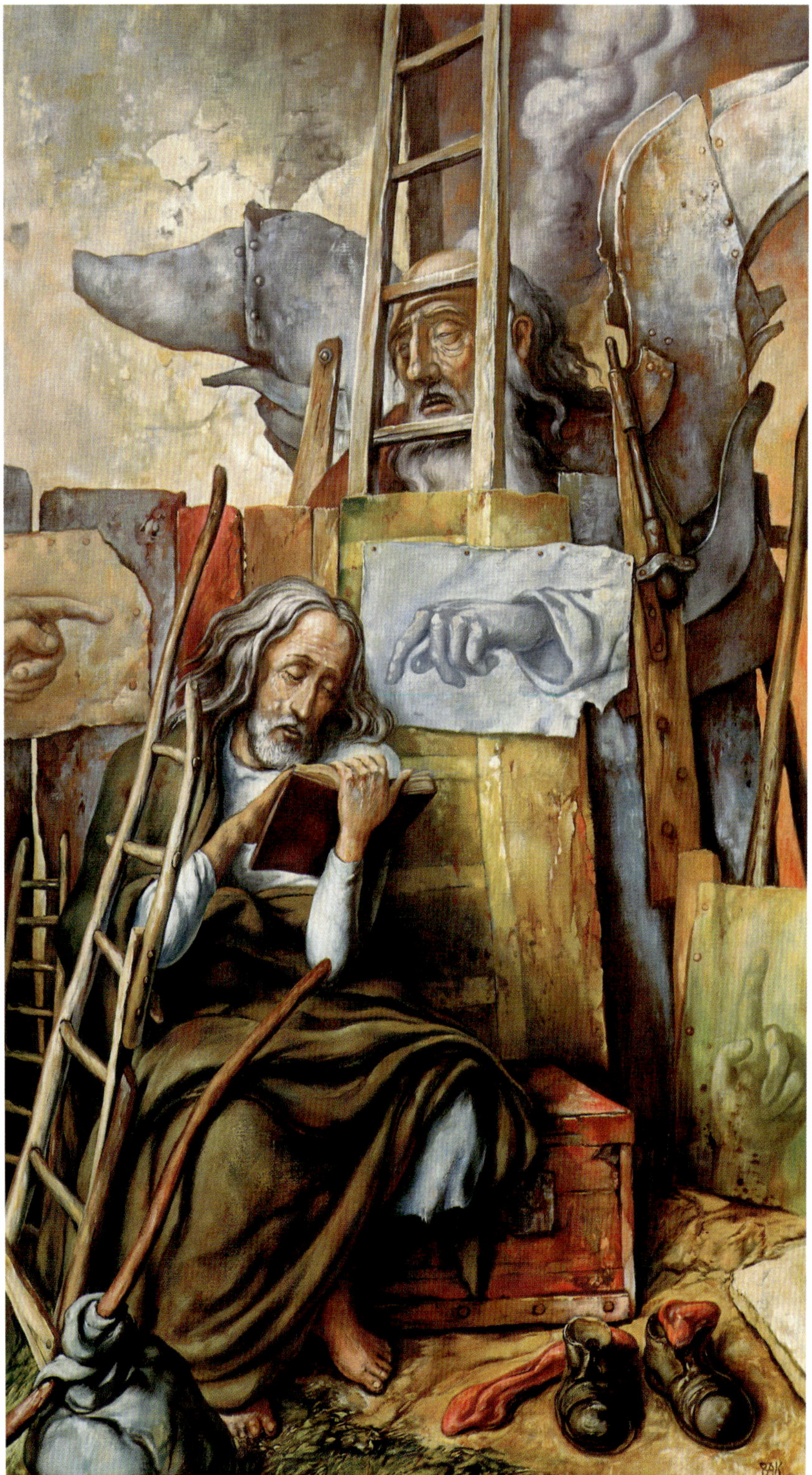

About Dreaming, 1999
Oil on Canvas, 32 x 18"

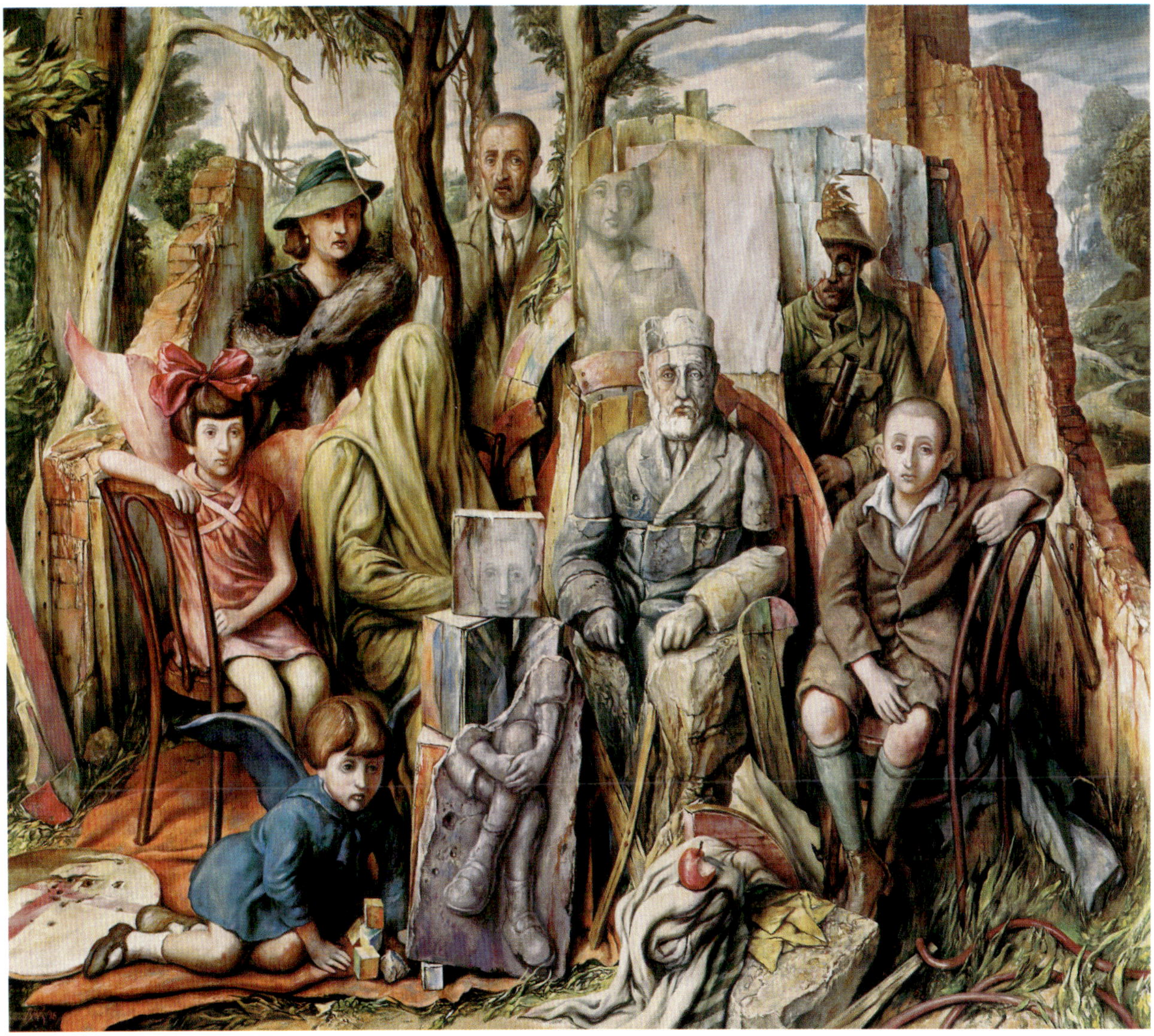

A Return to Paradise, 1996
Oil on Canvas, 44 x 50"

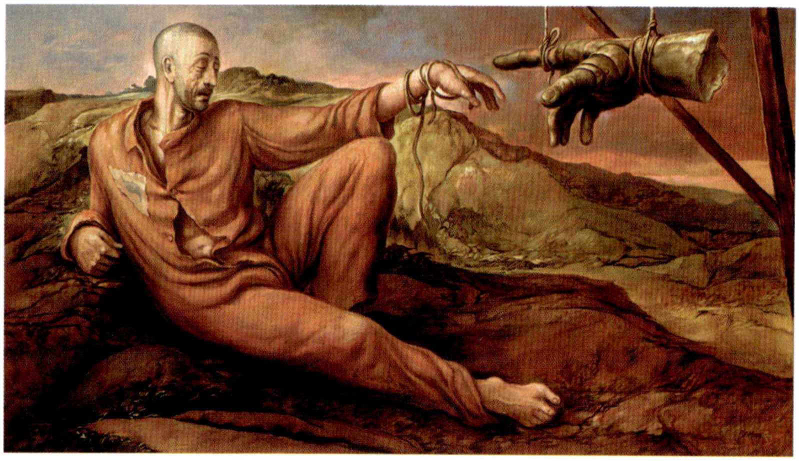

Joseph's Dream, 1999
Oil on Canvas, 18 x 32"

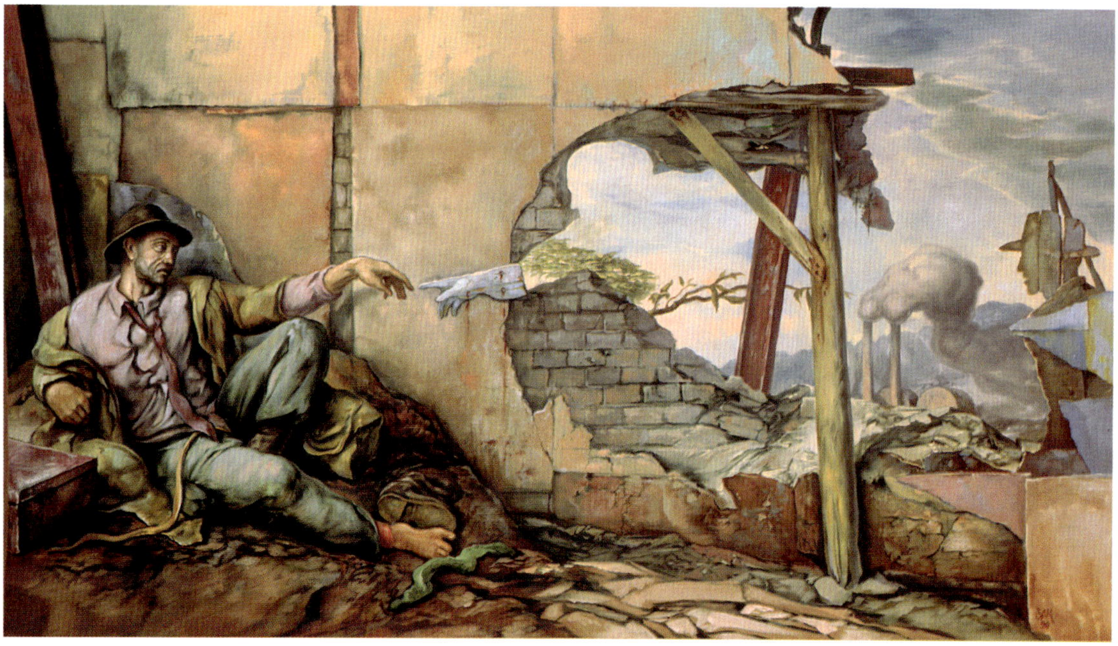

Creation of War Time II, 1999
Oil on Canvas, 18 x 32"

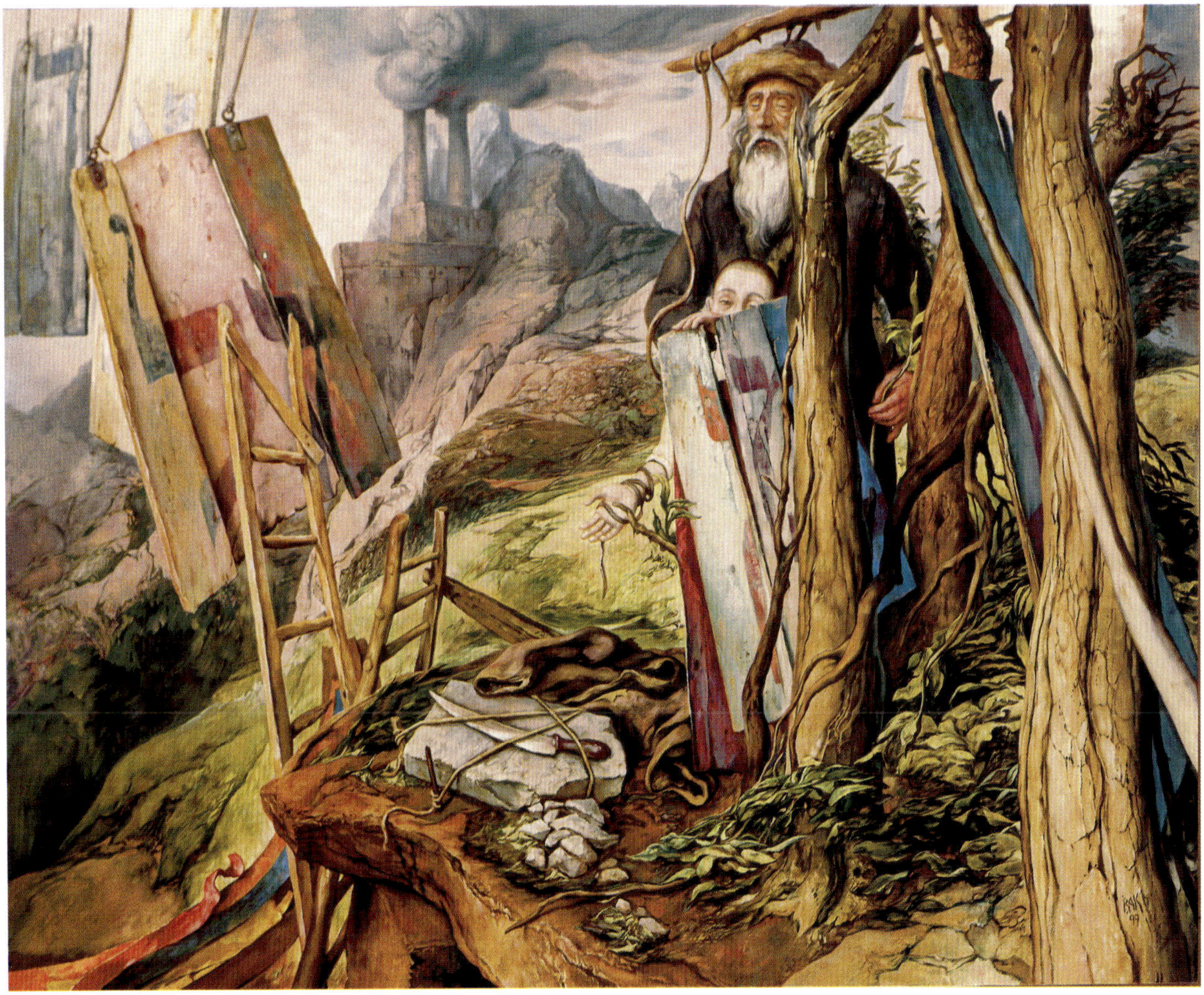

Isaac's Dream, 1999
Oil on Canvas, 40 x 50"

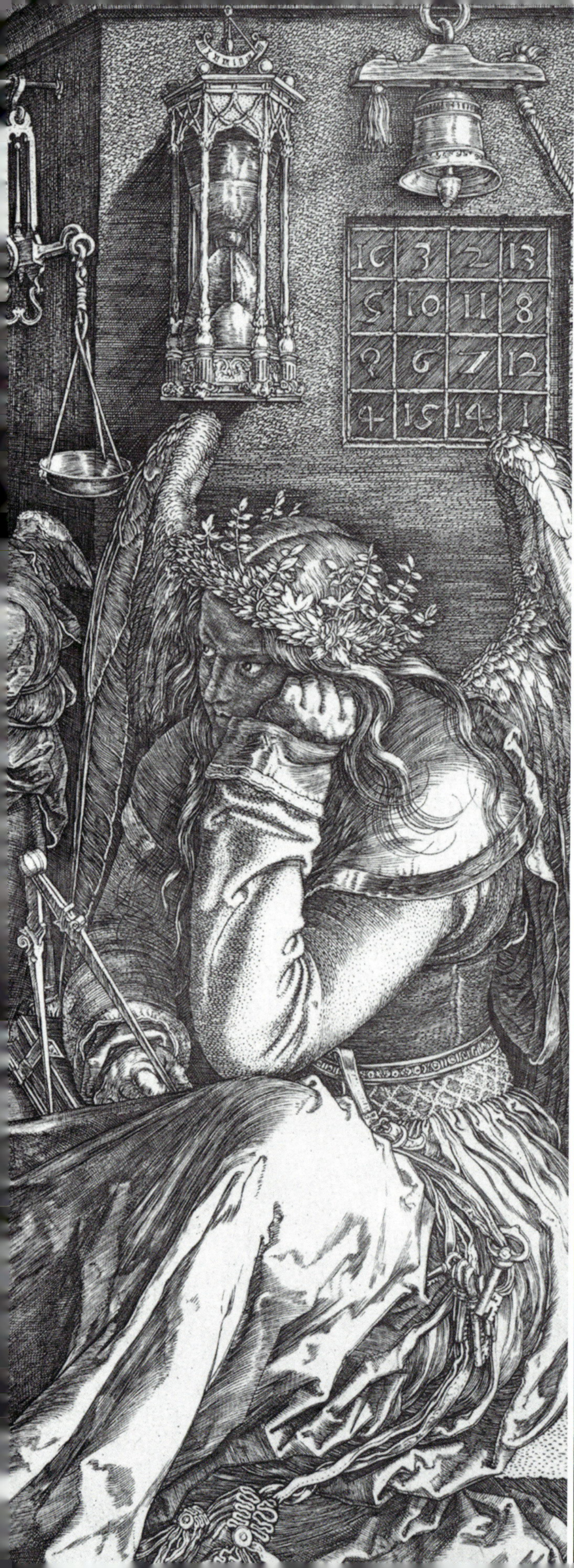
16 3 2 13
5 10 11 8
9 6 7 12
4 15 14 1
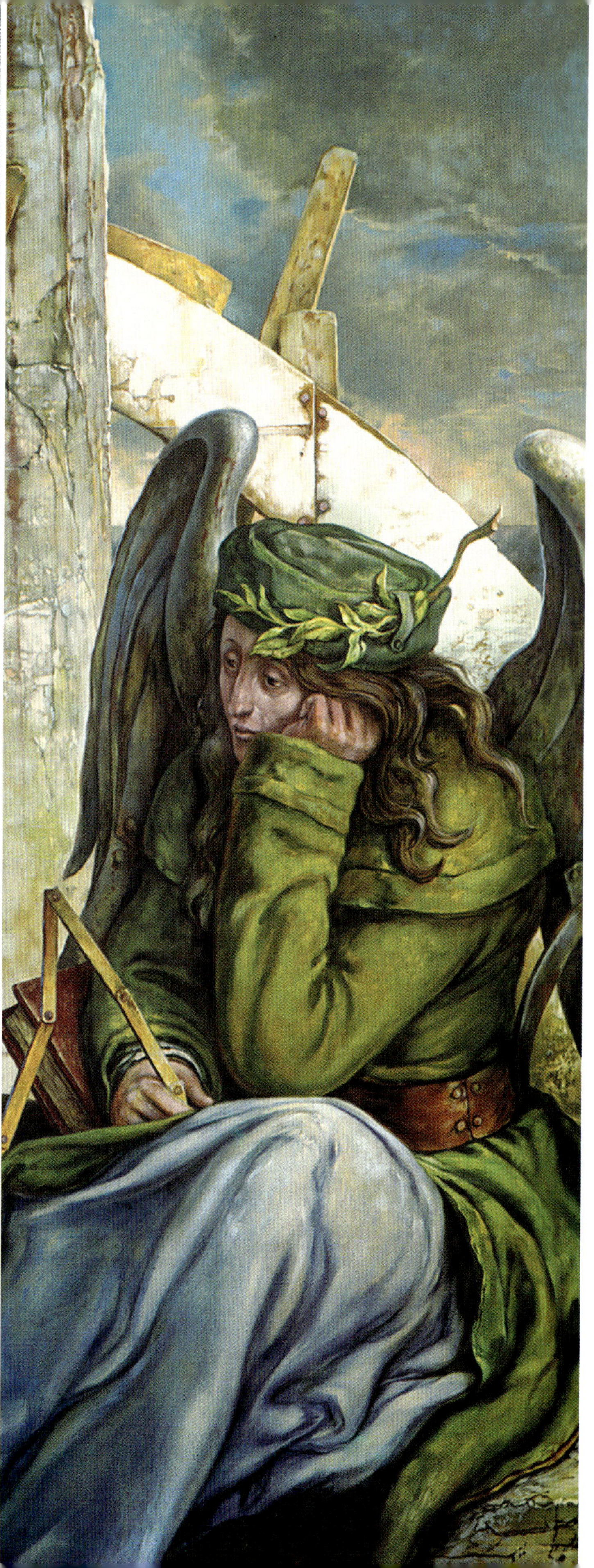

Seeing Words, Reading Images: Allegory and Interpretation in Bak and Benjamin

S. BRENT RODRÍGUEZ PLATE

There are important divergences between words and images; they register in different portions of our minds and must therefore be critically analyzed with divergent tools. Thus, to offer a "reading" of an image, or to apply literary and narrative methodologies to the viewing of film or painting, is simply bad criticism. Yet, there are points of convergence, as with the works of Samuel Bak and Walter Benjamin (1892-1940), where seeing and reading cannot be kept separate and each of them offers new ways of approaching age-old discrepancies between words and images. One often comes to know Bak's paintings by reading them: alphabetic characters, emblems, landscapes, memorials, and scraps of images recast from the annals of art history constitute his literal canvases. In contrary motion, one must be able to envision the writings of Benjamin to realize their critical potentials in twenty-first-century society: photo-texts and fragments, obsessions with graphology and print, architecture and film theory all make up Benjamin's visual writings.

In this essay I explore the cognitive-sensual crossings of seeing words and reading images through a particular archaeology of the ancient literary-visual mode, allegory. I begin with some comments linking a theological account of creation (in the Hebrew Scriptures and the mysticism of Rabbi Isaac Luria) to artistic creation. Then I move to extrapolate on Benjamin's reappropriated version of the trope of allegory, noting how he revises this ancient genre, dragging it through a natural history where it attaches itself to the Lurianic Kabbalah and into twentieth-century avant-garde art movements. Along the way I read Bak's paintings in light of Benjamin's unstable allegorical impulses. At the heart of Bak's and Benjamin's paintings, criticisms, and rehistoricizing movements are dialectical forces of creation and de-creation, of collection and dispersal.

Far left
Albrecht Dürer
Detail of *Melencolia I*, 1514

Right
Detail of *Elegy III*, 1997
Oil on Canvas, 47 1/2 x 51 1/2"

Creation and De-Creation

The creative work of God at the beginning of the Hebrew Scriptures is an activity of setting boundaries. Like any artist, God draws lines. The commonly recalled verb of creation, as found in the first chapter of Genesis, is *to speak:* "And God said...." What is often forgotten is the secondary verb, *separate.* Throughout the first chapter God's creative work is separating: land from sea, earth from sky, and eventually man and woman are separated from out of the original, genderless creature, *ha'adam.* God draws lines, makes decisions, scissions in the originary *tohu wabohu* (the "formlessness and void"). Divinity divides. And so we are given an orderly cosmos, where everything has been separated and concurrently kept in its place. When everything seems to be in place, the separating lines of creation inevitably disappear and the world appears unified.

The tradition of art in the West has worked to represent this orderly world, to portray the hierarchies of the cosmos, seeking symmetry, balance, and eventually the ratiocinated perfection of the single-point perspective where lines of the ordered world are set in place by the solitary vision of the seeing human. Which is to say: art has continually sought what is called Beauty as it seeks to imitate the divinely ordered world. The questions of the artist facing decisions about the form of the artwork are the questions of divine division: Where does one draw lines in a way to maintain the balance of things in their place, of color, shape, and formal arrangement; with hierarchies of angels, demons, and humans, both sinful and saintly; the stars in the heavens and the earth below? Such questions merely beg the further questions: What happens in the face of disaster, if *dis-aster* is literally a "dispersal of the stars"? How to account for things not in their place? What happens when forces of evil and exile disregard proper divisions and leave things scattered?

In my eye's mind, Samuel Bak's fragmented landscapes reveal the world-as-it-is. The true horror of a landscape, especially in art after the Holocaust, would be the sickly sweet image of sunsets, snow-covered mountains, cascading rivers, and proliferations of flowers. Or perhaps, as Lawrence Langer begins to intimate in an essay on Bak's paintings, the terror might also be the hierarchical cosmos as outlined by Michelangelo on the Sistine Chapel.[1] Beautiful landscapes and Renaissance order provide ideal images of a world assembled in perfect perspective, with lines in their proper places. Such images portray a Beautiful world, and may serve as a certain stimulus to hoping, or even working, for the world-as-it-could-be. Yet to reside in such a world is to serve a false messiah. These images are the illusion of a world, the seemingly seamless image of a dreamed-of world—in other words, *surreal.* Among other appropriations, Bak reworks themes found in surrealist painting, particularly those of Salvador Dalí,[2] even as Bak uses surrealism to get to a realism below the perception of reality. His paintings are constantly playing with reality, questioning what it is we call surrealist and what we call realist.

Bak's paintings confront the viewer with a dispersed, disaster-struck cosmos. Taking those originary and seemingly eternal lines of creation, Bak recuts the world, fragmenting it. The lines that demarcate and delimit persons, places, and things from each other are not as they seem. Instead, as Langer notes, "Bak redraws the lines between man and God, Adam and his Creator, human dreams and divine purpose, time and eternity, the whole spiritual drama that inspires the most crucial moments of Hebrew Scripture."[3] Bak re-creates the world of creation by de-creating it, and in so doing reviews the continual act of creation, which is the work of the artist: imitating the dreamed-up, mythic lines of creation is one work of the visual artist; revealing the places those lines were originally drawn is quite another. Bak works in the latter vein.

Bak's 1999 canvas *Creation* displays precisely this. The Adamic figure, borrowed from Michelangelo's famous *Creation of Adam* section of the Sistine Chapel, sits with arm lazily outstretched, resting on weary knee, half-heartedly attempting to reach the heavens. The figure of the divine Creator—which is seen powerfully coming down from the heavens in Michelangelo's painting—is here fragmented, dispersed, Himself de-created. A disembodied divine hand still reaches to the earthly Adam, yet is kept in place only by being tied to a dead tree. The faint outline of God still appears, but is barely sketched among a heavenly realm of bits and pieces that seem to be floating in an in-between world. The fragments of sky swirling along with the creator's form are ossified and give the impression that they are falling, even as they paradoxically appear to be blown about by a wind. In the midst of the falling sky is a piece that looks like the remnants of a book with faint writing and leather binding strap.

Creation deals with, and dwells in, fragments. Separations are made but the lines resemble destruction as much as creation. In this light, Bak's art would have much more in common with an alternative account of creation, that of the Jewish mystical understanding of creation, particularly found in Rabbi Isaac Luria's influential sixteenth-century Kabbalistic writings. This creative account is also significant for Benjamin's aesthetic theories and his work on allegory, as we will soon see. Luria's cosmogonical account is typically paraphrased in three movements. First is *tzimtzum,* the withdrawal of the originary, divine *Ein-Sof,* providing an opening that allows space for the world to come into existence separate from God. Then is *shevira,* the fragmentation and dispersal that results from God's attempt to fill the world with His presence. Divine vessels *(sephirot)* were meant to contain the presence of God, but fail to hold as the vessels shatter and scatter across the universe, with the divine sparks becoming encapsulated within evil-tinged *qlipot* (husks or shells). Finally, *tikkun* (repair, restoration) calls for the work of mending, of freeing the divine fragments from their shells, collecting them, and putting them in their proper place. While there is no space to articulate these movements further, it is this second stage that is crucial for our purposes here.

The divine presence that was meant to fill the cosmic vessels is too much for the created forms, and the vessels break and fragment into many pieces. The divine light is thus dispersed, with some of it returning to its divine source, but some of it falling and scattering in the material world. Shimon Shokek describes the *shevirat ha-kelim* (breaking of the vessels) in terms congruent with Bak's and Benjamin's own allegorical vision:

> The picture of the broken world is a morbid symbol for the total ruin of all; it is a somber myth about the descent and the downfall of a spiritual world that falls into the material

abyss. It is the myth of annihilation and pain; the myth of cosmogonial crisis and of cosmological failure; it symbolized the exile of the Jewish people, the exile of the physical cosmos, and the exile of the Divine Presence, known in Hebrew as *Galut ha-Shekhinah.*[4]

The implication here is that cosmological disaster parallels political disaster; the metaphysical crisis is also a physical one. In the sixteenth century, as Luria conceived of the divine sparks breaking apart, the Jewish people were of course living in exile from the land of Israel, but perhaps more importantly (because more immediate) the Jews had recently been expelled from the Iberian Peninsula where they had flourished for so long. This was the end of the "Golden Age" of Spanish Jewry: when Maimonides wrote his philosophical musings; when Solomon Ibn Gabirol wrote his poetry; when Muslims, Christians, and Jews co-created and co-existed (at least, for the most part) in *convivencia.* Luria's cosmology (like all myths of creation and destruction ultimately) also revealed historical-political realities of the present day.

The exile of God mimics the exile of God's people, with the persistent hope for eventual unity, the healing and putting together of this fragmented world: *tikkun olam* (mending the world). In this final and awaited stage, the mythic cycle comes to completion. But it is only through the work of humans, on Luria's account, that *tikkun* can occur, leading Marc-Alain Ouaknin to consider, "Man and God are associated in Creation."[5] Both humans and God enter into creative history. Ouaknin interprets this final stage in Luria's cosmology as a political and humanistic gesture: "[T]he Messiah is not he who produces redemption, but only the manifestation of his success. One can no longer await the Messiah; one must create him. As a symbol of the completion of the *tikkun,* the Messiah loses his personal value, and we can understand why he is of so little importance in the Lurianic Kabbalah."[6]

Human creation takes its place alongside (or, perhaps, in place of) the divine, though this is not necessarily to give some exalted status to the artist. The romantic notion of a singular artist somehow saving the world must also be abandoned. If "one must create" the Messiah, the creative artist nonetheless works under the guise of the allegorist, as one who de-creates, who seeks to reveal the fragmented nature of reality by ceaselessly writing and painting, melancholically reviewing the archives of past history and bringing bits and pieces into the here and now. Through this de-creative and re-creative activity surrounding the work of art there emerges an interactive connection *between* art and perceiver produced by a melancholic reflection on these fragments. This critical, non-objective gaze produces the revelation, the dialectical image that frees the divine spark. Even if perhaps only briefly. *Tikkun* comes sporadically, in bits and pieces.

Dispersing and Collecting: Allegory

For Walter Benjamin, the role of the critic exploring film, art, or architecture is akin to that of the artist and creator: to investigate and show forth the joints of creation, to take things apart and re-create the world. Criticism is creative. Benjamin was enthralled by Luria's Kabbalistic account of creation, and took its basic structure as a kind of template for contemporary cultural criticism. Throughout Benjamin's aesthetic writings is a dialectic between two terms that can be intimately related to the Kabbalistic cosmology of *shevira* (fragmentation) and *tikkun* (mending). In Benjamin's German these activities become the twin stars of *die Zerstreuung* (dispersal, distraction, dissemination) and *die Sammlung* (collection, assemblage; can also denote a library, and even contemplation; *sich sammeln* is the one who contemplates). A dialectic between these two forces is seen in his accounts of the technologically reproduced work of art, the act of translation, and filmic montage, among other places. The dispersal-collection dialectic is also found in his reworking of the ancient trope of allegory, seen especially in the third and final chapter of his failed *Habilitationschrift, Ursprung des deutschen Trauerspiels* (translated into English as *The Origin of German Tragic Drama;* hereafter *OGTD*). Here Benjamin uncovers an idea of allegory during the Baroque period that is radically distinct from what usually is understood under that label.[7]

To see the fragmenting functions of allegory it must be distinguished from the collective functions of symbolic action. Quoting extensively from a classic nineteenth-century text on symbols, Friedrich Creuzer's *Symbolik und Mythologie der Alten Völker* of 1819, Benjamin retains Creuzer's separation of allegory and symbol: "The [allegorical] signifies merely a general concept, or an idea which is different from itself; the [symbolic] is the very incarnation and embodiment of the idea. In the [symbolic] a process of substitution takes place.... In the [allegorical] the concept itself has descended into our physical world, and we see it itself directly in the image."[8] While Creuzer and others of his time take this difference as a reason to praise the symbol and denigrate the allegory, Benjamin revisits the Romantic hierarchy and rescues the lesser term. Whereas the symbol aims at a single meaning, directly related to one idea and provides a "coming together" of image and idea, Benjamin's version of allegory is open to a multiplicity of meanings due to its descended, earthbound, and constantly visible existence. While both function within a relationship between a material thing and mental/spiritual idea, the material dimension of the symbol is usually disregarded once the meaning is grasped, but allegory cannot be understood apart from its physical nature.

The origins of Baroque allegory are found in the middle ages and Renaissance commentaries on ancient hieroglyphs and various other "emblems" (in German, *Sinnbild,* literally "meaning picture"). Antecedent writers employed allegory as an exegetical tool, seeing hieroglyphs as "an image of divine ideas," as Marsilius Ficinus comments and quoted by Benjamin (169). Terry Eagleton notes that the emphasis on hieroglyphs brings allegory around to the materiality of aesthetics in Benjamin's thought and runs counter to the "phonocentrism" of Saussure and others: "the *Trauerspiel's* preoccupation with script as against voice, its ceremonious arranging of matter-laden hieroglyphs like so many embalmed emblems, returns to us an awareness of the bodily nature of language."[9] By emphasizing the materiality of the Baroque allegorical script, writing becomes visual: "Both externally and stylistically—in the extreme character of the typographical arrangement and in the use of highly charged metaphors—the written word tends towards the visual."[10] Allegorical language is physical, visible, and in this way words and images are not entirely separable. In contrast to Gotthold Ephraim Lessing's aesthetic distinction between poetry and painting (word and image) in his *Laocoon* as two "friendly neighbors," Benjamin's idea of allegory always reveals, as Benjamin quotes Carl Horst, "a crossing of borders of a different mode, an advance of the plastic arts into the territory of the 'rhetorical' arts." In this act of transposition, the visuality of the Baroque allegory was seen as a mode of contamination on the literary. Indeed, Michel Foucault has stated that "the relation of language to painting is an infinite relation,"[12] and such overproduction of meaning is characteristic of the relation of words and images within Benjamin's reading of the Baroque.

The relation of words and images is also central to much Kabbalistic thought. When the *Tragic Drama* study was published, Benjamin gave a copy to his friend, Gershom Scholem, who was almost solely responsible for rescuing the Kabbalistic tradition in the twentieth century. In the copy Benjamin inscribed: "To Gershom Scholem, donated to the *ultima Thule* of his Kabbalistic library," and in comments to others he specified that the book could only be understood by those familiar with Kabbalah.[13] Within the Kabbalistic tradition, the materiality of the alphabet plays a vital role, and Divine energy is seen as manifested not only through the ten *sephirot,* but also in the Hebrew letters. Thus the "Book of Creation" states, "In thirty-two wondrous paths of wisdom God…engraved and created his world."[14] The twenty-two consonants of the Hebrew alphabet, plus the ten *sephirot,* become "building blocks" of the cosmos with which God engraves creation. Each character has its own set of symbolic meanings, yet must also be seen in relation to the other characters, as well as astronomical cycles, human attributes, and other relational systems. "For the kabbalist, the paths to understanding are necessarily infinite, reflecting the boundless and infinite character of Divine energy."[15] Meditations upon the Hebrew letters in their physical form thus have become part of the tradition and spark the relation between language and image by showing how language is an image, a material entity.

Samuel Bak hints toward such a mystical-allegorical view with his 2003 painting, *Interpretation.* Three giant books, however illegible, are strewn across a desolate landscape—one of them stands upright, open, pierced through with a keyhole. A key that just might fit leans against it, with a key chain containing an equally illegible tag. We the viewers wonder if the key fits, if we might be able to unlock the mysteries of the created world by reading these books of the earth. The books become landscapes (*geo-graphies* in the literal sense) there to be impossibly read as they depict a humanless, sunset-less, snow-covered-mountain-less, space. The bound pages represented in oils are nonetheless inspiring for the viewer, sparking vigilance, attentiveness, a contemplation even while such collective awareness cannot ultimately be brought about. While encouraging focused attention, Bak's painting disallows a completed interpretation, a final reading, and ignores the symbolic "coming together"[16] of image and idea. If Benjamin's recounting of allegory sheds light on the imagistic nature of allegorical words, Bak's image of *Interpretation* becomes a challenge to reading. Nothing, finally, can be collected.

Under Benjamin's critical gaze and Bak's decisive brush, the world viewed becomes a text to read, while texts become illegible and can only lead to further meditation. Allegory works in the visible, material realm, and challenges its viewers/readers to constantly take note of our mediated reality, the very boundaries, borders, and structures of creation. To further demonstrate this point, both Bak and Benjamin turn to Albrecht Dürer's 1514 engraving, *Melencolia I.* Dürer's piece becomes a prime emblem for Benjamin as he suggests, "In it the knowledge of the introvert and the investigations of the scholar have merged as intimately as in the men of the baroque. The Renaissance explores the universe; the baroque explores libraries. Its meditations are devoted to books."[17] The Baroque takes the cosmic speculations of the Renaissance, and miniaturizes them into books, turning macrocosm into microcosm. Meanwhile, meditations on such books do not arrive at simple conclusions but lead beyond themselves to the other books in the library, to the overwhelming phenomena of the universe. Reading becomes a contemplative act that, because it takes one in so many directions, can only lead to melancholy.

As is discussed by Fewell and Phillips in this volume, Bak has also taken Dürer's engraving as a key emblem for his post-Holocaust view of the world, as it fits within his "landscape of Jewish experience." If *Interpretation* prompts a mystical wonderment about reading the world, then his 1997 *Elegy III* pushes the possibilities and impossibilities of reading even further. Bak extricates Dürer's winged figure from its original sixteenth-century setting in which an angel sits with eyes down turned, trying to take some measure of cosmic divisions with geometric instruments. Geometric calculation, from Pythagoras forward, has offered the promise of being able to read the ordered, created world, to chart the divisions and ratios between the small and the large. Dürer's angel as allegorical figure, however, and as Benjamin and Bak understand, reveals that any geo-*metry* is always a geo-*graphy,* and writing is endless. Measurements are taken, order appears, but the lines of creation can always be redrawn.

Between History and the Present: Angels and Ruins

Within Bak's de-creative enterprise, Dürer's angel becomes a post-Holocaust "angel of history," as Benjamin might have called him. Benjamin's description of the angel of history was prompted by a 1910 painting by Paul Klee entitled *Angelus Novus,* and while Benjamin writes about this image of an angel in the decade preceding the full force of the Holocaust, his description of this melancholic allegorist is eerily prescient:

> His face is turned toward the past. Where we perceive a chain of events, he sees one single catastrophe which keeps piling wreckage and hurls it in front of his feet. The angel would like to stay, awaken the dead, and make whole what has been smashed. But a storm is blowing in from Paradise; it has got caught in his wings with such a violence that the angel can no longer close them. The storm irresistibly propels him into the future to which his back is turned, while the pile of debris before him grows skyward. This storm is what we call progress.[18]

From among the catastrophic ruins, the strewn wreckage that is progress (dispersal/*die Zerstreuung/Shevira*), may come the possibilities of recollection, bringing the dead to life and restoring the whole of the cosmos (collection/*die Sammlung/Tikkun*). But it is the stormy wind from Paradise itself that keeps the angel from gathering the whole together within its enclosed wings. The angel, for Benjamin, is an allegorist, collecting and collecting but without end. Bak takes Dürer's angel and resituates him in a post-Holocaust world; the historical pile of wreckage is the promise of Enlightenment rationalism, the work of Christian imperial nations, and, finally, the Holocaust itself, most strikingly emblematized by the Holocaust icon of the Warsaw "ghetto boy," also detached from its original photo and recast in *Elegy III.* We are left with fragments, of a de-created world, of images taken from context and recontextualized for the here-and-now. Dürer's angel is seen through Klee's angel, redescribed by Benjamin and reimaged through Bak.

History for the angel does not operate along a timeline, with simple cause and effect, but is gazed upon from the here and now as visual object, a "pile of debris." So within the dialectics of reading and viewing, and of collections and dispersals, Benjamin's allegory also reveals an alternative relation between space and time. Benjamin says of the tragic drama that "what is vital is the transposition *(Umsetzung)* of the originally temporal data into a figurative spatial simultaneity."[19] In the transposition, the chronology of history is flattened into an all-important synchronic dimension. History thus renders itself to the senses, to be seen and perceived in the present. And as it is grounded in space, we reach a decisive trait of Baroque allegory: the "spatialization" of history is also the "secularization" of history. If linear time is bent into a spatial figure (which is, finally, an image), there can be no eschatologically redeemable time, no sense of teleological progress. What this amounts to is a "hopelessness of the earthly condition," "a flight into a nature deprived of grace," and a "rejection of eschatology."[20] Time does not steadily move upwards to some greater and clearer vantage point; rather, natural history is one of decay and death. Benjamin's interest in the Baroque rejection of progress is not merely due to its secularized vein, but he sees such rejection as vital to any deconstruction of myth, whether from twentieth-century capitalism or from the mythical telos of Marxist utopias, or any system (including the Hegelian) that views "History" as a whole entity which can be safely contemplated and understood from an objective distance.

Because the allegory remains physical, imbedded in the created earthly realm, materiality constantly threatens to swallow up meaning. There is no symbolic elevation, no transcendent Beauty to lift one up and out, offering a God's-eye view. Instead, "the *eidos* disappears, the simile ceases to exist, and the cosmos it contained shrivels up."[21] Here in the realm of nature is the land of death and decay. Because of this the allegory finds its greatest emblem (its own allegory) in the ruin:

> The allegorical physiognomy of the nature-history, which is put on stage in the *Trauerspiel,* is present in reality in the form of the *ruin.* In the ruin history has physically merged into

the setting. And in this guise history does not assume the form of the process of an eternal life so much as that of irresistible decay. Allegory thereby declares itself to be beyond beauty. Allegories are, in the realm of thoughts, what ruins are in the realm of things.[22]

Allegory is "beyond beauty," beyond the unity of form and content, appearance and essence. With the ruin as the key emblem of allegory, allegory does not create a total system, but must remain incomplete in the realm of fragments and leftovers. There is no lofty flight of thought, but rather the allegorical struggle is one of stumbling over ruins, of limping, and finally, of breaking the inevitable fall. Working in the ruins shows the lack of control on the part of the artist/critic/individual subject. The allegorist may collect the ruins, but a unified, original structure cannot be (re)built. Instead, the *modus operandi* of the Baroque was one of invention, of accumulating fragments "without any strict idea of a goal,"[23] and hoping for a "miracle" to occur in their arrangement. Haphazardly collecting, the allegorist acts in alchemical faith as she or he arranges the pieces. The finished work of art then reveals its own processes of the creative act, shows the mortar in the walls, the infrastructure on which the superstructure rests. In the Baroque allegory, as in Benjamin's often fragmented writings and Bak's paintings, the artifice of the edifice shows through; there is no recourse to an original nature even as the works of art constantly point backward to other "originals" like Michelangelo, Klee, or Dürer. In so doing, Bak and Benjamin simultaneously point out how these were always pasted together as well.

Still Life with Words

Because of its relentlessly profane character, allegory might fruitfully be understood in relation to the genre of painting called "still life." Even the label "still life" hints toward the allegorical nature of this genre of painting with its "stilling" of life, its spatialization of history, a connection that is all the more apparent in its French translation, *nature morte.* Indeed, Bak seems to have considered still life as allegory, and in several 1999 paintings he creates still life images in a curious juxtaposition with the activity of *tikkun,* such as his *Still Life with Tikkun.* This painting reveals two key crossings that are implicit in my account of Benjamin's allegory. The first is the mix of words and images; the second is the mix of the sacred and profane.

In his book on still life painting, *Looking at the Overlooked,*[24] art historian Norman Bryson considers the genre to be the furthest removed from narrative structures. In other words, there is little or no relation between words and images here. Still life paintings are pure image; they do not tell stories, they do not contain human characters, they are intensely local but also somewhat universal. They are painters' experiments, ways to play with form, color, and light.

Bak takes the traditional Western genre and bends it slightly in *Still Life with Tikkun.* While the foreground of the painting has the traditional vases and fruits, albeit in non-traditional arrangement, there are words added to the background, specifically, the word "tikkun" in Hebrew, which is quasi-legible across several fragmented panels. Still life, a genre seemingly removed from its ongoing location in history, without narrative, in Bak's canvas begins to tell a story. And as we look closer at the "traditional" subject matter, we find a few things amiss. A goblet is overturned, a pear fragmented and surrealistically merged with the outline of a vase, another pear half gone and left in a state of decay. Here is the allegorical chronology of history, physically merged into the spatial setting, beyond beauty. The objects are left to decay, but at the same time the painting captures them in an instance and preserves them. "For an appreciation of the transience of things, and the concern to rescue them for eternity, is one of the strongest impulses in allegory."[25] The ruins of the still life mix with the ruins of the space in which it was set: broken walls, panels in pieces, rubble on the ground. The still life literally makes life still, arrests a moment from time and in so doing points toward a future and a past, bringing it into a kind of narrative structure. We are not told what has happened, why the "repair" of *tikkun* is in a state of disrepair, but the arrangement shifts the typical spatial orientation of still life painting into a narrative and, therefore, temporal dimension even if the story is not fleshed out.

This contrast of spatial and temporal, image and word, leads to the second main juxtaposition in Bak's painting: the relation of the profane and sacred. Bryson considers the profanity of the still life genre since it is located at:

> ...the life of the table, of the household interior, of the basic creaturely acts of eating and drinking, of the artifacts which surround the subject in her or his domestic space, of the everyday world of routine and repetition, at a level of existence where events are not at all the large-scale, momentous events of History, but the small-scale, trivial, forgettable acts of bodily survival and self-maintenance.[26]

Such highly imaged profanity makes Bak's associations between still life painting and the world re-creating activity of *tikkun* all the more curious. Still life relates to "basic creaturely," "forgettable" acts, not to the "momentous events of History," of which *tikkun* would certainly be a part. In Benjamin's Baroque observations on the impermanence of things, the decay of nature, after the violence of the Thirty Years War, allegory surfaces as a mode of rescue, "where transitoriness and eternity confronted each other most closely."[27] So how does the sacrality of *tikkun* relate to the profanity of still life? Especially when the word *tikkun* is itself imaged in a state of disrepair? The life of the table, its routine and repetition, seemingly interrupted? Is there anything sacred left? Is this the allegorical way of the world, the "hopelessness of the earthly condition," "a flight into a nature deprived of grace?"

Conclusion: Allegorical Tikkun

In his writings on Bak, Lawrence Langer begins to answer some of the questions about the artistic potential for *tikkun:* "art supplies the ravages of history with a lasting habitation, offering them up for scrutiny and analysis to future generations. The act of restoration in the studio becomes a bold alternative to the prior parallel practice of spiritual repair."[28] Or as Marc-Alain Ouaknin was quoted above, "One can no longer await the Messiah; one must create him." Indeed this is a logical answer to the open-ended form of Bak's canvases and brings such creative activity in line with the allegorical impulses as described by Benjamin. The inventive, pasted-together fragments of allegory are ultimately recreative. By creating a new work of art, the allegorist, who is also finally the painter and the poet, attempts to open a space for repair. And in the act of creating, s/he has already given a kind of re-created world through formal attention to the de-created world. For while the panels with the word *tikkun* are fragmented, while God's hand in *Creation* is amputated, while the "ghetto boy" is no longer in Warsaw nor Dürer's angel in the sixteenth century, all of the fragments have come together under Bak's paintbrush. What is *in* the painting is ruinous, but the painting itself is still created with precise paint lines and particular colors, set on rectangular canvases all stretched to perfect perpendicularity. The subject matter may be fragmented, but the work of art is collected.

And so, finally, the painter and poet offer a kind of restoration "in the studio," but they do not have the final say. There is the further activity of dispersal and collection which can only take place when the viewer confronts, is faced with, the work of art. Allegory is literally a "speaking (otherwise) in public" (from the Greek *allos,* "other" + *agoreuein,* "to speak publicly"; the "Agora" in Athens was the public square, the city's cultural and religious center). Allegory takes what is obscured (the other) and brings it to light, encodes it in speech and presents it in public. Through this process of "publication," the other is always transformed, transposed—no thing is left whole and intact.

Put bluntly, there is no allegorical art that is not made public. And in its orientation outwards, the allegorical work of art that was brought to completion in the artist's studio is again disseminated to a public that takes from it what they will. The allegorical dialectic between collection and dispersal (which, as I have been suggesting, can be transposed as the Kabbalistic movement between *shevira* and *tikkun*) is a dialectic without foundation, without final collection. Repair, mending, gathering together are achieved, if only briefly and without finality. The allegorical work of art cannot maintain its own readings but ceaselessly deals in fragments waiting for a miracle of collection, some reversed thunder of a disaster that might bestow meaning. The work of the melancholy gaze, the song of lament, the work of interpretation, is the work of re-creation, allowing another re-binding to occur.

---

1 See Lawrence L. Langer, *In a Different Light: The Book of Genesis in the Art of Samuel Bak* (Boston: Pucker Art Publications, 2001), 3-4.

2 There is no space for a full comparative analysis here, but alongside Michelangelo's *Creation of Adam*, Bak's *Creation* painting also appears to borrow from a much different source, Salvador Dalí's *The Metamorphosis of Narcissus* (1943). In Dalí's wartime painting, the figure of Narcissus is repetitiously painted, being refigured at each stage (like Bak's use of Michelangelo's Adam and God), and there is likewise bodily fragmentation, and the ossification of bodies. Other relations of Bak's paintings to Dalí's paintings include use of crutches to support body parts, desolate landscapes, and the use of chess boards, as in the *Metamorphosis of Narcissus.*

3 Langer, 3.

4 Shimon Shokek, *Kabbalah and the Art of Being* (London: Routledge, 2001), 44.

5 Marc-Alain Ouaknin, *The Mysteries of the Kabbalah,* trans. Josephine Bacon (New York: Abbeville, 2000), 200.

6 Ouaknin, 205.

7 Walter Benjamin, *The Origin of German Tragic Drama,* trans. John Osborne (London: Verso, 1977). Much of the following account of Benjamin's allegory can be found in fuller detail in my book, *Walter Benjamin, Religion and Aesthetics: Rethinking Religion Through the Arts* (New York: Routledge, 2004).

8 *OGTD,* 164-65.

9 Terry Eagleton, *Ideology of the Aesthetic* (Cambridge, MA: Blackwell, 1990), 335.

10 *OGTD,* 145-76.

11 *OGTD,* 177.

12 Michel Foucault, *The Order of Things,* trans. Alan Sheridan (New York: Random House, 1970), 9. See also Foucault, *This Is Not a Pipe,* trans. James Harkness (Berkeley: University of California Press, 1982).

13 Quoted in Susan Handelman, *Fragments of Redemption* (Bloomington: Indiana University Press, 1991), 137.

14 Quoted in Gershom Scholem, *Origins of the Kabbalah,* R.J. Zwi Werblowsky, ed., Allan Arkush, trans. (New York: The Jewish Publication Society and Princeton University Press, 1987), 25-6.

15 Johanna Drucker, *The Alphabetic Labyrinth* (New York: Thames and Hudson, 1995), 141. See the section on "The Kabbalah," 129-58. See also, Ouaknin, *Mysteries of the Kabbalah.*

16 Martin Heidegger highlights the "collected" nature of the symbol: "In the work of art something other is brought together with the thing that is made. To bring together is, in Greek, *symballein.* The work is a symbol" ("The Origin of the Work of Art," trans. Albert Hofstader in *Basic Writings,* ed. David Farrell Krell [New York: HarperCollins, 1993], 145-46).

17 *OGTD,* 140.

18 Walter Benjamin, *Selected Writings, Volume 4, 1938-1940,* ed. Howard Eiland and Michael W. Jennings (Cambridge, MA: Belknap Press of Harvard University Press, 2003), 392.

19 *OGTD,* 81.

20 *OGTD,* 81.

21 *OGTD,* 176.

22 *OGTD,* 177-78.

23 *OGTD,* 178.

24 Bryson, *Looking at the Overlooked: Four Essays on Still Life Painting* (London: Reaktion Books, 1990), 24.

25 *OGTD,* 223.

26 *OGTD,* 14.

27 *OGTD,* 224.

28 Langer, 35.

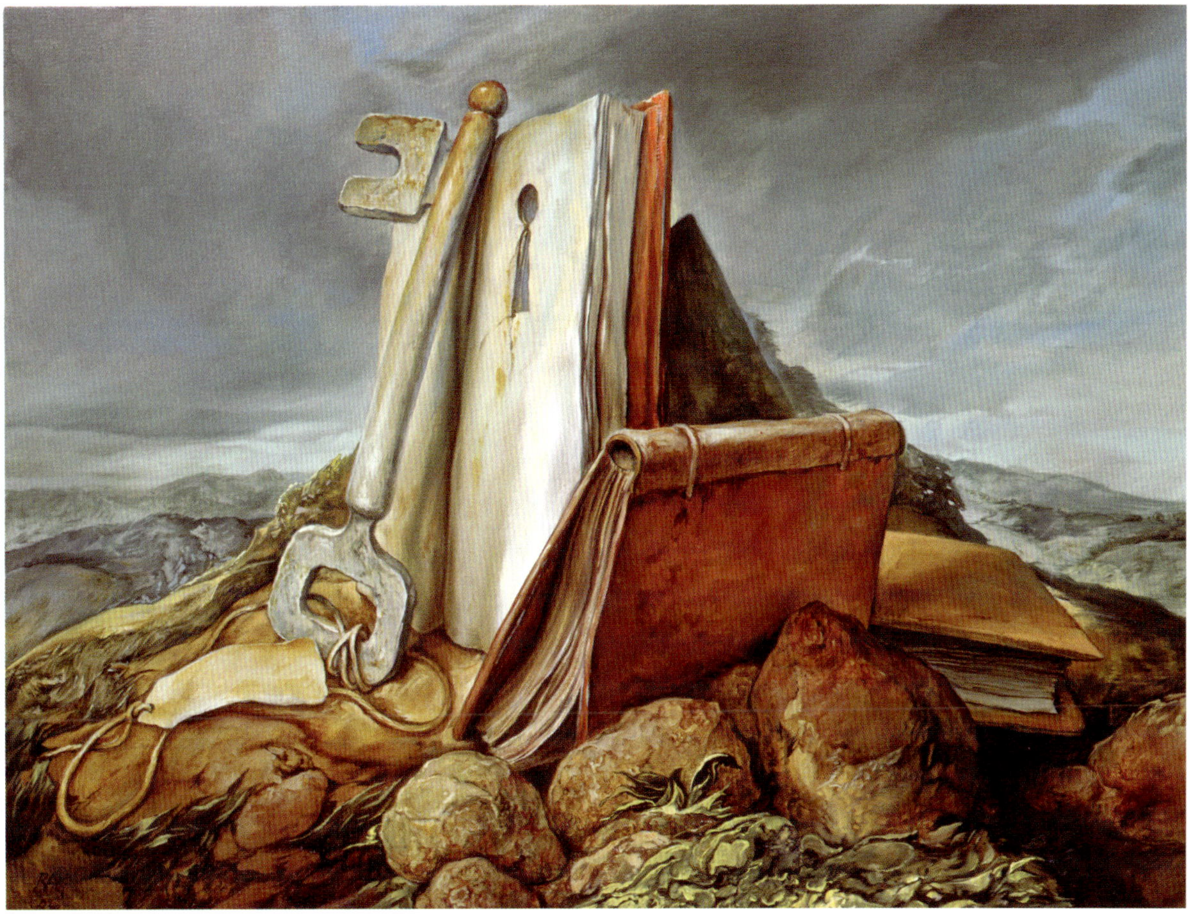

Interpretation, 2003
Oil on Canvas, 18 x 24"

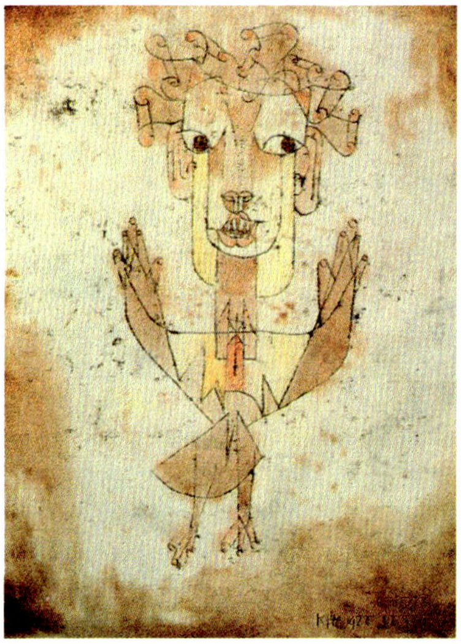

Paul Klee
Angelus Novus, 1910

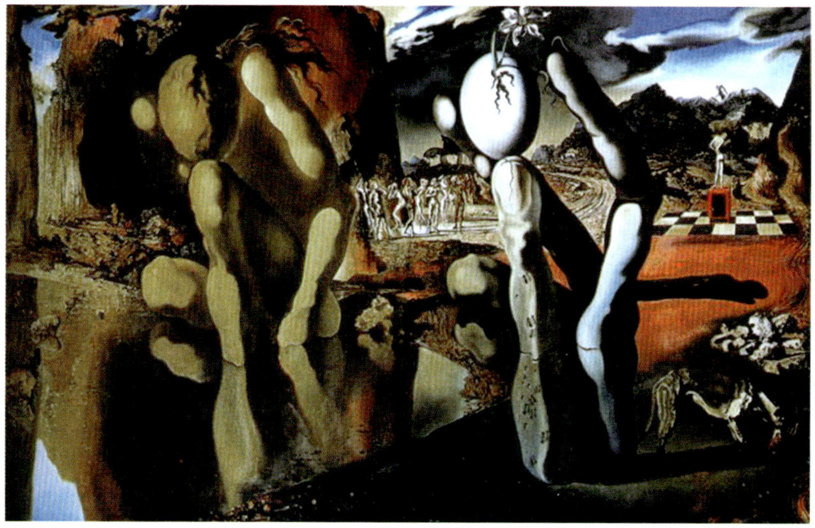

Salvador Dali
Metamorphosis of Narcissus

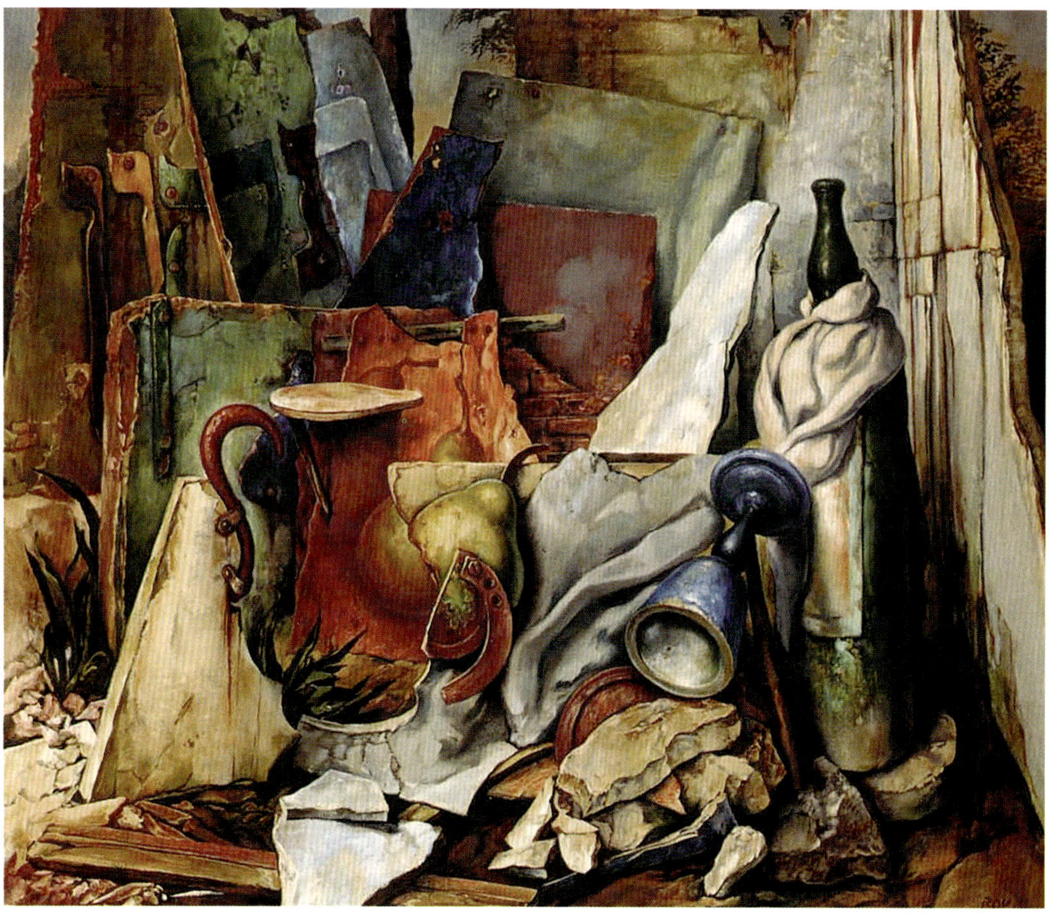

Still Life with Tikkun, 1999
Oil on Canvas, 22 x 26"

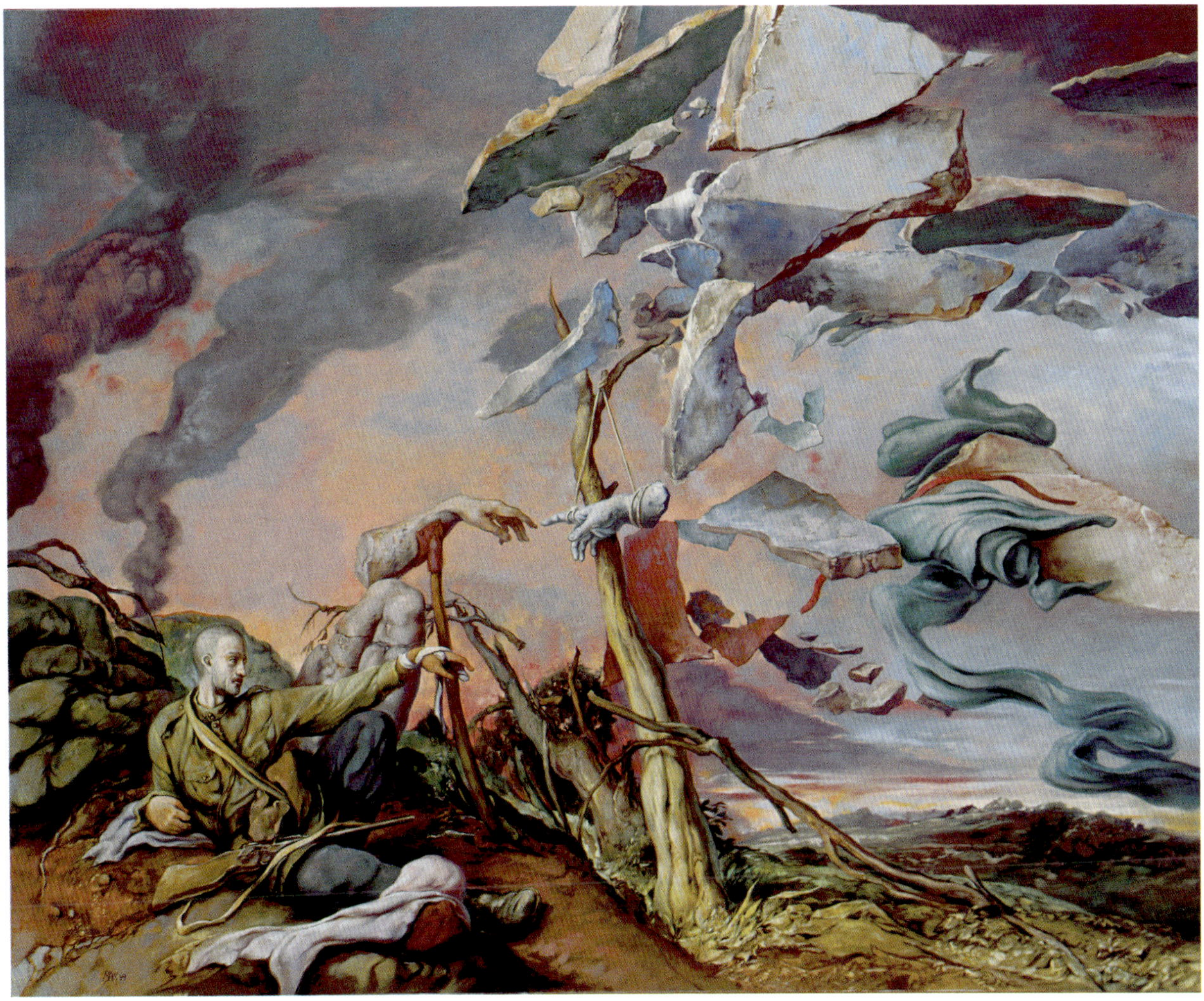

Creation, 1999
Oil on Canvas, 40 x 50"

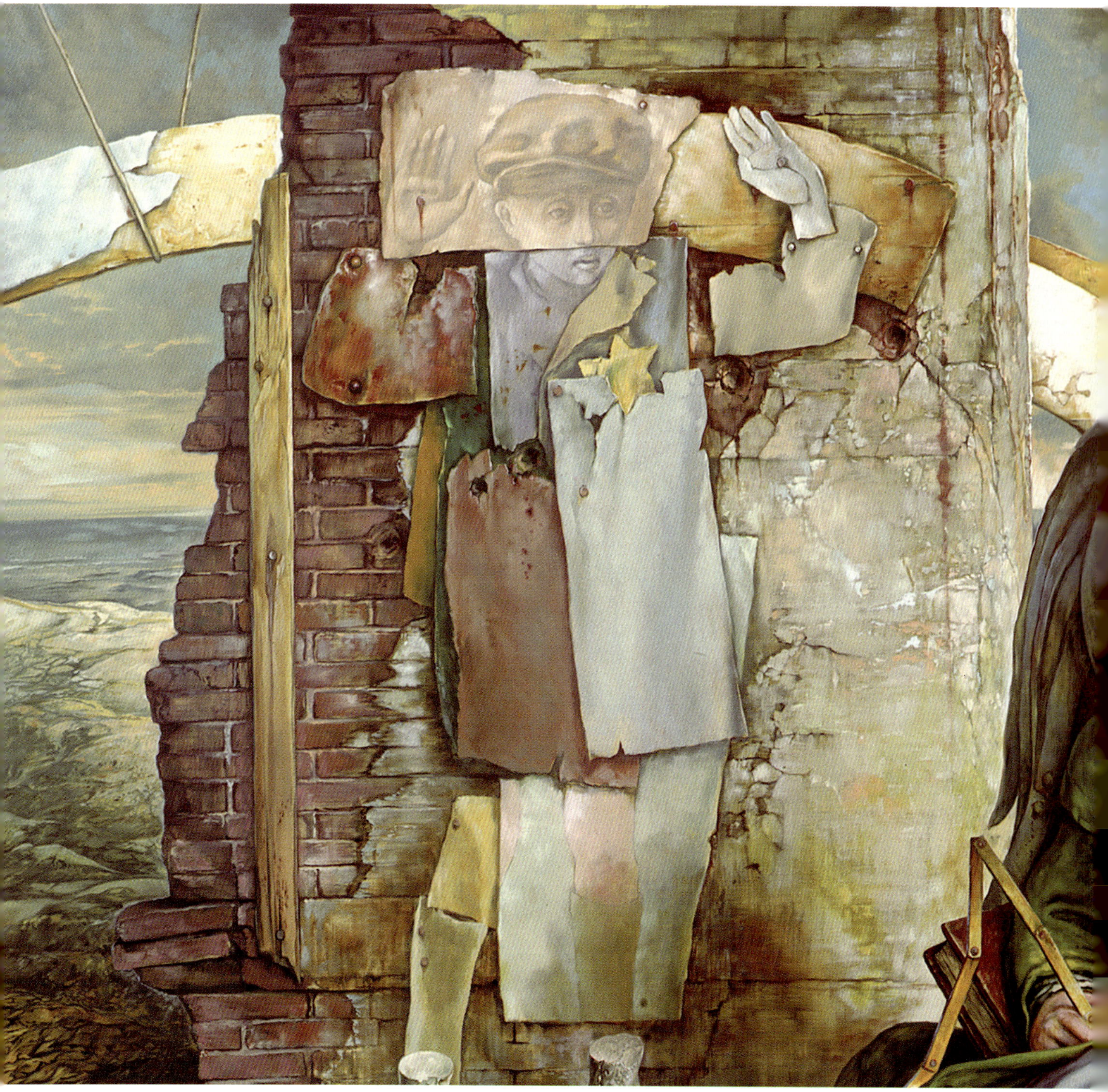

Genesis, Genocide, and the Art of Samuel Bak: "Unseamly" Reading After the Holocaust

DANNA NOLAN FEWELL AND GARY A. PHILLIPS

If, as the late Jewish philosopher Emil Fackenheim has argued, a "seamless" reading of the Bible should no longer be possible after the Holocaust, we now confront the challenge of how to read the Bible differently.[1] By "seamless reading" Fackenheim refers to the ways in which Christian theology and biblical exegesis has proceeded as though the Holocaust had never occurred. The events of World War II, he avers, have hardly caused a ripple in ongoing scholarly and religious discourse as scholars and lay readers alike have "seamlessly" continued to read the Bible as "salvation history" (usually a particularly Christian construction of salvation history), and continued to speak without qualification of Christology, soteriology, and divine providence and sovereignty. By contrast, an "unseamly reading" of the Bible is one that has been deliberately interrupted by the reality of Jewish suffering and Christian complicity in that suffering, rendering suspect any sort of triumphalist reading of biblical promises or accounts of deliverance.

In order to probe what this kind of ruptured, unseamly reading might demand of us, we turn to the work of post-Shoah artist Samuel Bak as a visual model of what our verbal and literary work might entail. Taking as the point of departure Bak's 1997 painting *Elegy III,* we offer here the first of a two-part exploration[2] of how this work of remembrance[3] (both his and ours) disturbs traditional and critical understandings of particular biblical texts and theological constructions, deconstructs time-honored icons, and upsets the meta-narratives of the Enlightenment legacy.[4]

Why Bak? Samuel Bak was a child survivor of the liquidation of the Vilna Ghetto. Vilna, known as the "Jerusalem of Europe," a center of Jewish learning and culture, was home to nearly 100,000 Jews before WWII. All but a couple of hundred of these citizens perished as result of

Detail of *Elegy III,* 1997
Oil on Canvas, 47 1/2 x 51 1/2"

Nazi persecution, including Bak's father and grandparents and his best friend, eight-year-old Samek Epstein, who was publicly executed as a warning to any Jews who tried to escape the Ghetto. Bak, one of a handful of children who survived, was smuggled out of a labor camp by his father, mother, and aunt, and eventually hidden in a monastery. His father died within days of the event. After fleeing with his mother first the Nazis then the Soviets who liberated Vilna, Bak lived as a displaced person, finally emigrated to Israel, and studied painting in Jerusalem and later Paris. He now resides in Weston, Massachusetts. Of Bak, novelist and social critic Amos Oz writes,

> I regard Samuel Bak as one of the great painters of the twentieth century. There are few artists who have so successfully represented the mad cruelty of our era—its horrors, its desolation, its sadness and vacuity. And fewer still are the artists who have created their own unique personal language. In Bak's world, horror, humor, and dreams all solidify into one radioactive mass.[5]

Bak has a distinctive way of bringing together, fracturing, and reconstituting sacred and secular symbols and archetypes to articulate his experience as a child survivor.[6] Bak's surrealism offers a distinctive vocabulary for articulating both ruin and remnant.[7] By visually disrupting biblical stories and themes with fragments of worlds shattered by genocide, he offers an ironic commentary[8] on traditions of creation, catastrophe, covenant, and redemption. He questions these biblical expressions of theodicy: Are they revelatory? Faltering? Moot? His compositions pose a powerful moral challenge to keep our reading of the Bible in direct face-to-face contact with the reality of Auschwitz as well as with ongoing destructive forces in our current world.

Why this particular painting? *Elegy III* is a densely packed painting that stands in a long series of compositions that explore the theme of mourning, biblical images of flood and crucifixion, the brooding angel in Albrecht Dürer's famous engraving *Melencolia I,* and the well-known World War II photograph of the boy from the Warsaw ghetto. *Elegy III* is the first of Bak's midrashic[9] efforts to treat all four elements together. Offering a profoundly ironic questioning of theology, technology, and Enlightenment moral values, *Elegy III* communicates both an excess of meaning and the senselessness of what Emmanuel Levinas calls "useless suffering."[10] In so doing, the viewer is returned to the particular biblical texts Bak employs to reread those narratives anew, to consider who is hidden between their lines, to ask what traumas find expression in the ancient text. Moreover, the child of *Elegy III,* who is at once the historical boy from Warsaw, the memory of Bak's childhood friend from Vilna, and the artist's self-portrait, forces us to recognize that *all* reading of the Bible after Auschwitz must be held accountable to some particular face.

Elegy III

Set against flood waters and storm clouds that are either receding or approaching, stands a colorless rainbow, clearly a human amalgam of scrap metal, wood, and stone. One end of the arch is suspended by a rope; the other is nailed to a wooden stake. In the center of the frame is a brick ruin reminiscent of both crematorium chimney and executioner's wall. Tacked to this battered brick and mortar surface are pieces of metal, wood, and paper that form the image of a young boy.[11] This bricolage child, presented in both two- and three-dimensions, wears a cap, short pants, and a coat pieced together from the faded colors that once constituted the deteriorated rainbow's facade.[12] A yellow Star of David is patched below the left lapel. The boy's face, a misty image—a memory fading or recalled?—peers with vacant eyes from fragments of parchment and metal. His hands, thrown up in a gesture of surrender, are nailed to the wall in a cruciform. The right hand drips blood. Both boy and wall are bullet-riddled. Below his patched body, empty, petrified boots are monumentalized on a stone box, in backwards innocence, soiled with blood. Superimposed upon the image of bronzed baby shoes celebrating birth, innocence, and first steps are other, more sobering allusions. We are reminded here of the thousands of children's shoes discovered in the Nazi death camps, as well as of Primo Levi's sober observation that survival in the camps depended upon shoes.[13] But if we listen as well as look, we might also hear that face-less voice from the burning bush commanding with deep irony, "Take off your shoes. You are standing on holy ground" (Exodus 3:5).[14]

To the child's left sits a bewildered angel in the familiar thinker's pose. Her eyes, like the boy's, stare blankly out into space. She holds a broken carpenter's rule, or one might imagine a fully unfolded Star of David. Under her forearm is wedged a closed book. Her wings are fastened to her belt with metal stays, hinting that she, too, like the rainbow, may be of human construction, and she, too, like the rainbow, is affixed to the earth, grounded in a disaster. A branch, perhaps an olive branch signifying both peace and an end to the deluge (see Genesis 8:11), rims her hat. At her right foot lies a stone globe, once perfectly round and intact, now fractured and chipped, resting in what first appears to be a pile of leaves, residue deposited ashore by receding flood waters. Closer scrutiny, however, reveals a mass of lifeless yellow patches, a yellow tide of stars, detritus of an earlier cataclysm.

Bak's *Elegy III* and Dürer's *Melencolia I*[15]

The angel is Bak's midrash on Dürer's famous engraving *Melencolia I* (1514). Dürer presents a winged female form lost in intense but melancholic contemplation, a state associated then with human creativity and artistic genius. Against a backdrop of a masonry construction surrounded by numerous objects and implements representing mathematics, alchemy, astrology, and scientific inquiry,[16] she sits in the typical philosophical stance of "the thinker."[17] The tools and products of practicing artisans as well as the astrological symbols of comet (or sun) and rainbow evoke the creative work of the artisan and the intellectual.[18]

A locked book (perhaps hinting at the elitism of certain kinds of classical knowledge come to light through the Renaissance) supports the angel's right elbow while her hand fingers an engineer's compass that is open and ready for measure.[19] From her belt hangs a cluster of keys, suggesting the ability to unlock doors and solve problems. Around her head is a wreath of various kinds of plants believed to counteract the bad effects of melancholic humor.[20] Deep in concentration the angel directs an intense gaze upwards toward the rainbow. It is a promising scene that signals a rebirth of human aspiration and hope.[21]

In *Elegy III,* Bak repositions Dürer's angel from the threshold of the German Renaissance on the verge of Enlightenment to a more recent moment, one that questions the very concept of enlightenment and progress that defines the German spirit. If the Enlightenment augured the promise of a rediscovered human self aglow in the classical sciences and the awakening of creativity, Bak's painting invites us to ask: What kind of creativity, what type of self, what era of "rebirth" do we now encounter in the murder of 1.5 million children? It is an age, Bak laments, "that has lost its light and plunged itself back into darkness."[22]

Instead of sitting brooding and introspective encircled by the symbols of human knowledge and the implements of technology, Bak's angel despairs over the scenario surrounding her. Her narrative role is ambiguous: Is she bystander or perpetrator? Has she just discovered this ruin and cannot comprehend what she witnesses? Is her broken carpenter's rule no longer capable of taking the proper measure of the damage and the age? Or is she in fact the architect and builder of these bricolage monuments, remnants of a remembered past that now rupture the present?[23] Is she despondent because this is the best she can do for now, with such few and fragmented materials and only broken tools? Or has she herself precipitated the destruction that now requires this triage?

The book the angel carries is closed. Has she consulted it for answers or blueprints and found it wanting? Has she simply forgotten she has it? Whether the book is a source of secular human knowledge or sacred revelation or both, it remains sealed and impotent. There is nothing there of seeming use. After Auschwitz, the Enlightenment's promise of human invention and creativity has given shape to a different promise, namely that of a problematic human technology whose back has turned upon humanity and the larger creation. Rather than the promised beneficial consequences of knowledge, understanding, and productivity, there is the reality of massacre and devastation.[24] And Dürer's rainbow, of mysterious and ethereal composition and origin, framing a comet, hailing an optimistic future, and posited in the heavens above, is transformed into a mundane construction, pieced together of common materials, both supported and overshadowed by crematorium and crucifix, propped up tenuously, reflecting neither color nor promise.

Bak and Biblical Promises Broken[25]

But Bak's angel in *Elegy III* represents more than Renaissance artistic and technological creativity. It is imbued with other, mostly biblical, understandings of angels: guardian angels, delivering angels, annunciating angels, angels of destruction, divine messengers. If this angel is a guardian angel, one meant to bear up the faithful that they might not dash their foot against a stone,[26] she has failed in her task. If she is a delivering angel, meant to stay the hand of death, she has come too late. If she is here to announce peace and the end of a deluge, there is no one left alive to hear her.

If she has come to destroy the firstborn, she has done her job too well. If she is a messenger, who has sent her? And where will she go from here? With iron-braced wings, how will she ever be able to take flight and leave this desolate si(gh)te behind her?

The rainbow, too, directs us beyond the allusion to Dürer's *Melencolia.* It is also the post-diluvian sign of God's promise never to repeat the flood and destroy creation. One might argue that for Bak, not only has the covenantal promise been shattered by the events of the Holocaust,[27] but the promise has revealed itself to be of human construction, a construction that must be pieced back together—although to what end remains unclear.

Historical critics of the Bible would find the recognition that Genesis is "human construction" hardly surprising. Setting aside the question of the divine origin of the Bible, scholars have long recognized the composite nature of the flood story. One might even venture that the mixture of Yahwist and Priestly sources evidences a kind of literary bricolage, a fabricated narrative that shares something in common with Bak's crude rainbow. The sources combine to form a coherent story line (just as Bak's material fragments form a recognizable rainbow), but not without leaving exposed joints and seams, tensions and contradictions of originally separate traditions. The juxtaposition of different rationales for the flood, different details, and different outcomes, divulges a complicated literary history—which scholars have been only too happy to reconstruct but then smooth out. Consider the commentary of Bruce Vawter who, after having delineated the two literary strands of the flood story, remarks,

> We point out these discrepancies not because they are important but rather in order to suggest that they are not—not, at any rate, to the biblical author or redactor who has given us this composite story. The biblical author, who was well aware of the differences in the traditions he used long before modern critics rediscovered them, was obviously disinterested in such details. He handed on the stories as they had come to him not because he was concerned over water sources or dimensions of time and space, but because he found in this legend from the distant past a suitable means of illustrating a deeply held religious conviction: *the conviction that evil is requited by a just God who is at the same time a God of mercy.*[28]

But is the theological message of the flood story really so simple and reassuring? The competing details of the sources also point to a culture's grave struggle with the character of God and the nature of theodicy—which scholars have, for the most part, read principally in light of older ancient Near Eastern flood stories. In such comparisons, theological understandings of the biblical flood narrative have been largely triumphalist. By contrast to other more capricious ancient Near Eastern deities, the biblical YHWH/Elohim of the deluge is motivated instead by issues of justice and a concern for limiting human evil. The flood, then, is divine judgment against human evil rather than simply a flight of sadistic supernatural fancy in response to human annoyances. For example, in the Atrahasis epic, one of the earliest known flood stories, the gods decide to destroy humankind because they are making too much noise (which, according to some scholars, reflects a problem of overpopulation).[29] The Gilgamesh epic gives no motivation, about which E. A. Spieser concludes: "The biblical Flood...is given strong moral motivation, whereas the cuneiform version—at least the one that is incorporated in the Gilgamesh Epic—fails to suggest a plausible cause; one might ascribe the awesome interlude to mere whims of heaven."[30] Vawter, too, sees the biblical version of divine motive to be of crucial significance:

> In the biblical story the divine motivation for the flood is of its essence. What the Bible has done is *to turn an amoral myth into a highly moral parable of God's retribution and grace responding to the challenge of his creatures' willfulness and evil-doing.* There and there alone lies the biblical message intended by the flood story.[31]

We might also compare Gerhard von Rad's conclusion: "But more important than a neutral, historical, and religious comparison or an elaboration of a relative superiority which is easily established is the recognition that *the biblical story of the Flood has been made a witness to the judgment and grace of living God.*"[32]

Moreover, the rescue of Noah and his family and the promise of eternal divine protection symbolized by the rainbow depict the deity as a merciful God who responds redemptively to human righteousness. Nahum Sarna comments, "In Genesis, the Flood is God's response to the pollution of the earth by the moral corruption of the human race, and there is not the slightest doubt that it is *Noah's integrity that determines his fate.*"[33]

Consequently, critical scholarship of Genesis would resonate with Bak's suggested reasoning that the "divine covenant" is a human construction. However, the exegetical conclusions of both Christian and Jewish scholars alike underscore the more comforting theological messages of cosmic order and divine constancy and mercy. Von Rad's summarizing comment on this text is paradigmatic: "For our narrator, the Flood is the Last Judgment, but one in which God checks sin's spread on the earth; a judgment, to be sure, which at its end reveals more strongly than the stories of the Fall and Cain *a wonderful saving will of God.*"[34] Prime examples of a type of "seamless reading" (à la Fackenheim), such interpretations ignore both the tensions within the text and the tensions caused by historical catastrophes, the very realities that Bak's work and world would have us contemplate.

While the biblical flood story may be making moral claims about God and human suffering that are indeed superior to the Bible's polytheistic literary precursors, and may even be presenting a sophisticated theological paradox of God's judgment and grace, it is, nevertheless, not without ethical difficulties, not the least of which may be the kind of political justifications for genocide that we hear in this century used against Jews.

To begin with, as the story stands now, it attributes to God mixed motives and emotions. In the J source, God unleashes the flood as a response to an indiscriminant, generic, human evil.

Human immorality is to blame for the cataclysm. However, in the P source, God reacts to a polluting violence being practiced by every living creature:

> The land became spoiled before the face of God and the land was filled with violence. And God saw the land, indeed, it was spoiled because every living body had spoiled its way upon the land. And God said to Noah, "The end of every living body is coming before my face because the land is filled with violence from their faces. Indeed, I am despoiling them with the land." (Genesis 6:11-13; authors' translation)

All sentient beings, both human and nonhuman, have polluted the land. God's response to this "spoiling" is a "de-spoiling," a ritual cleansing to purify the earth.

Compare this totalizing rhetoric emphasizing purity and impurity to Nazi affirmations of the purity of the *Volk,* the blood, and the land. In the words of one German pastor, "...[T]he father of lies, the devil, erected the strongest bulwark of his dominion among the Jews....The devil at *all times,* but especially in our times, has used the Jews as his tools and advocates for the erection of his dominion of *darkness, corruption, vulgarity, and uncleanliness of the earth,* that is something that everyone recognizes today...."[35] Or, in Hitler's own words: "What we must fight for is to safeguard the existence and reproduction of our race and people, the sustenance of our children and *the purity* of our blood, the freedom and independence of the fatherland, so that our people may mature for the fulfillment of the mission allotted it by the creator of the Universe."[36] Moreover, the biblical narrative's gesture to turn divine violence into a kind of sacrament ironically echoes the very practice of using the sacrificial term "Holocaust" to label the murder of six million Jews. "Holocaust" by its very label has a way of theologically explaining and justifying Nazi violence.

Moreover, the Genesis story, not unlike modern militaristic rhetoric, stereotypes the victims in order to justify and excuse the magnitude of the act of aggression against them:

> The LORD saw that human evil was great in the land and that all the imaginations of the human heart were only evil all the time. And the LORD regretted that he had made humankind in the land and his heart was aggrieved. The LORD said, "I will erase from the face of the earth the humanity whom I have created—from human to beast to creeping thing to bird of the heavens—for I regret that I have made them." (Genesis 6:5-7; authors' translation)

No distinctions are made. *All* humans, young and old, male and female, are the same. *All* evil is the same. *All* warrant God's judgment.

We might compare again the rhetoric of a Nazi churchman: "We see thus in the Old Testament the desertion of the Jews from God and therein their sin. This sin was revealed before the *entire world* in the crucifixion of Jesus. From then on the curse of God has weighed on this Volk to the present day."[37]

Or, as Hitler explained, "The *personification of the devil* as the symbol of *all evil* assumes the living shape of the Jew."[38]

And if particular faces are erased in the indictment, they are most certainly obscured in the aftermath. Just as in Hitler's Final Solution,[39] the Genesis text, like the Nazis, buries its corpses between the lines, in the unmarked mass grave of a text doing its best to acquit God of mass murder.[40]

The story also offers compromised, even ironic, solutions to ongoing violence. Although it may have vastly diminished the number of possible victims and perpetrators, the flood has ultimately amplified rather than curtailed the violence endemic to the created order. Consequently, God establishes a number of post-diluvial regulations.

First, permission is given to kill animals for meat consumption; however, humans are not allowed to develop "a taste for blood." The blood, with its life-force, is not to be consumed by another. This Priestly concern is starkly juxtaposed to the J source that has God unable to resist the savory odor of smoking flesh (8:21). Second, God institutes the *lex talionis,* a law limiting the penalty of violence to "a life for a life." Not only is this designed to hold humans accountable for their actions, but it limits the extent of retaliation. This, of course, stands in contrast to God's own escalation of violence instigated in Genesis 4:15 where God threatens sevenfold vengeance against anyone who might hurt Cain (cf. Lamech's intensification of vengeance to seventy-fold in 4:23-24) and, most pronouncedly, to God's climactic response here where the retaliation cannot distinguish between the innocent and guilty. Ritually, both stipulations, the prohibition against consuming blood and the *lex talionis,* attempt to limit the spilling of blood that would pollute the ground.

Third, God establishes a covenant with creation, promising not to bring about such massive destruction ever again:

> And God said, "This is the sign of the covenant which I am making between me and you and every living soul with you for ageless generations. My bow I have set in the cloud and it shall be a sign of a covenant between me and the land. And it shall be that when I gather clouds over the land, and the bow is seen in the clouds, I will remember my covenant which is between me and you and every living soul in every living body, and the waters will never again become a flood to destroy every living body. (Genesis 9:12-16; authors' translation)

The designated symbol for this covenant, the bow, a warrior's weapon, is hung in the sky as a gesture of peace. It is intended to be a reminder of this divine promise, not to humankind, but *to God himself.* Hence, the rainbow further exposes God's fallibility: not only is he a forgetful god, but his propensity for violent behavior needs to be held in check.

Hence, despite the text's effort to equalize the crime and punishment with universalisms, it cannot completely succeed. The Yahwist, especially, exposes those who have fallen between the cracks of the predominant logic: not only does the text point to non-human creatures and even the earth itself suffering on account of their human counterparts, but even God himself acknowledges in the flood's aftermath (8:21) that humans are not "only evil all the time" but "from their youth" (a word that we might translate as 'adolescence' or 'young adulthood'). This suggests that the children have fallen outside of God's realm of vision. Moreover, God's own reiterated remorse acknowledges the violent overreaction: "*Never again* will I curse the ground on account of humankind.…*Never again* will I strike every living thing as I have done" (Genesis 8:21). "*Never again* will every living body be cut off by the waters of the flood and *never again* will there be a flood to destroy the land" (Genesis 9:11). "*Never again* will the waters become a flood to destroy every living body" (Genesis 9:15).

The bow, meant to enforce the "never again," is, of course, doubly ironic. Both a weapon and a signal of the storm's end, it stands Janus-faced, pointing back to the past violence of God and forward to a future supposedly without fear of such catastrophe. Whenever God sees it, he will remember his promise; he will be reminded not to destroy all life again. Unfortunately, rainbows by nature appear after a storm has passed, not before it strikes. Moreover, not every storm produces such a phenomenon. Consequently, we may be forgiven a certain gnawing discomfort regarding the effectiveness of this sign. Is this not the very sign that will allow God to be too late, that will allow him either to forget his promise or at least to remember it only after the damage is done?

We witness in this braided story the struggle to make sense of catastrophe that is no respecter of persons.[41] It employs both moral and religious rationales. Its explanations both exonerate and implicate God. Its resolution is colored with hope and resignation and not a little anxiety. Filled with both paradox and contradiction, both ruin and remnant, the story exposes its inadequacy as a coherent statement about the reality of catastrophe and, at the same time, offers in its incoherencies an alternative, honest response. As Jonathan Magonet observes, "The multiple dimensions of the Hebrew Bible become not merely interesting, or disturbing, they provide the key for endless self-critique and renewal. They are not inconvenient complications to our finding the 'truth,' they are the very essence of that 'truth.'"[42] In short, the traces of this text's compositional history signal existential and theological quandaries, human "truths" about incoherence, senselessness, incomprehensible tragedy—all of which are commonly dis/missed in the rush to assert "in truth" a God of justice and grace.

The concern for God's grace has, of course, come predominantly from Christian readers, eager to see in the Flood some prefigurement of Christological salvation (see 1 Peter 3:20). Whether the connection has been made directly in grand theological themes, such as "covenant" or "salvation history," or allusively in the gospels with Jesus as the "master of the sea" pulling Peter to safety, or musically in Christian hymnody[43] equating flood waters with hardship, sin, or lack of faith, or materially in traditional church architecture where sanctuaries are constructed to mimic the inside of a ship, or even in contemporary Christian iconography where a cross rides triumphantly at the top of an ark,[44] there is clearly a covenantal connection asserted between the Flood and the Crucifixion. Hence, the rescued righteous of the Flood have, through the years, taken on a specific Christian identity. But metaphorical comparisons between Noah's family and the Church oblige us to consider what the metaphor leaves out. If Christians are the rescued righteous, who are the non-rescued? All those who are not Christian. While Christians sail on to triumphant redemption, non-Christians are condemned for their evil and meet their deserved end.

However, when, in *Elegy III,* Bak presses the Holocaust onto the same canvas with flood and crucifixion, an "unseamly" reading disrupts this reductive binary thinking. Our focus is shifted away from the rescued righteous to the devastation of the deluge itself. In *Elegy III* there is no ark, no rescue, no "god of grace."[45] Rather, there is the residue of the destruction and the figure of an executed child who disquiets the viewer, rendering void all easy identifications with Noah and his family as the recipients of divine grace, all constructions of God as a one-dimensional savior, all universal pronouncements about sin and retribution, all absolute promises of redemption, in short, all attempts to make sense of undeserved suffering.

In *Elegy III* the storm has hit and left nothing in its wake but the yellow tide and fragments of a shattered childhood,[46] a tattered re-collection of a child crucified on a crematorium chimney and a makeshift rainbow. With its colors siphoned off to form the boy's image, Bak's rainbow at once provides the compositional elements for the boy himself as well as the scaffolding for the crucifixion; and yet, at the same time, it is itself secured by the child's pierced hands. The fractured, battered rainbow with its crucified boy, depicts a shattered covenant, promise, and history for Christians as much as Jews. Both real and unreal, two- and three-dimensional, flesh and stone, paint and blood, Jew and Christian, this boy takes us to where the Bible and the gates of Auschwitz meet in mutual incrimination: *There are no children on the ark.* Neither the Bible nor the Nazis make any distinctions, any exceptions, in their zeal to solve the problem of "evil" and "pollution." And there is nothing in Jewish or Christian theology that can make satisfactory sense of this. No *lex talionis,* or *Torah* of any kind, can bring justice. No atonement can bring salvation. Even the rainbow fails to generate hope. Rather, it stands as a sad and desperate human attempt to remind a God who has come too late—if he has come at all and if, indeed, he will ever come again.

Where does this Christian image with its martyred Jewish boy take us? Or leave us? Of what comfort or promise or meaning is crucifixion, with its accompanying promise of salvation, in light of so many murdered children? Or to frame it in Fackenheim's pointed question: "What are the sufferings of the Cross compared to those of a mother whose child is slaughtered to the sound of laughter or to the strains of a Viennese waltz?"[47] In the words of Primo Levi as he enters the Lager, no sacred face will help us here. Rather, the "serious and gentle face of a child" welcomes us "on the threshold of the house of the dead."[48]

As we cross the threshold into Bak's world, we find ourselves in the same quandary as Bak's angel who sits stultified, mute, and gazing out on a landscape where, as in the world of the Lager, there is no "why."[49] In the presence of murdered children whose images and memories must be pieced together from the fragments of divine promises and the gaps in divine and human oversight, how do we begin to confront the brutality of the world, past and present, biblical and beyond? How do we speak truthfully, honestly, about suffering, evil, the Bible, God? Perhaps we must take our cue from Bak: With coherence now forfeit, and reparation both imperative and impossible, where else can we start but with "unseamly" readings of our cracked, fractured histories, theologies, and sacred texts, tentative constructions that begin the arduous tasks of re-membering past victims and of imagining a world where children no longer pay for divine and human failures.

---

1 *The Jewish Bible After the Holocaust: A Re-reading* (Manchester: Manchester University Press, 1990). If Fackenheim's *God's Presence in History* (New York: New York University Press, 1970) targets a primarily Jewish audience, the audience presupposed in *The Jewish Bible After the Holocaust* is both Jewish and Christian.

2 The second part, "Bak's Impossible Memorials: Giving Face to the Children," follows in this volume.

3 Our understanding of the ethical work of remembrance is informed by Robert Gibbs, *Why Ethics? Signs of Responsibilities* (Princeton: Princeton University Press, 2000), 354-79.

4 In this essay we will deal with the first of these issues; in the second we will address the other two.

5 From the foreword, "Painted in Words, Narrated in Colors and Light," to Samuel Bak's autobiography *Painted in Words—A Memoir* (Bloomington: Indiana University Press/Boston: Pucker Gallery Publications, 2001), vii.

6 Some survivors have been disdainful of art as a medium of expressing experiences related to the Shoah. "Why this determination to show 'everything' in pictures?" asks Holocaust survivor and author Elie Wiesel. "A word, a glance, silence itself communicates more and better....the Holocaust is not a subject like all others. It imposes certain limits." ("Art and the Holocaust: Trivializing Memory," *New York Times*, Sunday, 11 June l989, sec. 2). Bak, however, takes the opposite view:

> My reluctance to deal with these subjects in a direct way must have multiple reasons. Objectively, documents, films and memoirs seem to me more eloquent than a painter's creation. And yet they seldom achieve more than a faint echo of the reality that they try to describe. One might possibly solve this by way of a meaningful transfiguration, but the forms or subjective expressionism, brought to their maximal development by the advent of two World Wars, are at present exhausted. (*Bak: Oils, Watercolors, Drawings, 1972-1974* [New York: Aberbach Fine Art, October-November 1974], 3).

7 See Gibbs's discussion of ruin and remnant (372-79) in conversation with the works of Walter Benjamin and Franz Rosenzweig. "Ruins become the way of remembering what cannot be recalled—in the realm of things" (374). "The remnant waits and promises to remain" (375).

8 Bak explains the ironic use of the Warsaw ghetto boy image in an interview with Richard Raskin, *A Child at Gunpoint: A Case Study on the Life of a Photo* (Aarhus, Denmark: Aarhus University Press, 2004), 153-54:

> The concept of irony is a crucial one, though I find it is not well understood today. Irony carries within it a sad and almost helpless dimension of disenchantment. The great artists of irony were Shakespeare, Kafka, Thomas Mann. Today the word is devalued. It is confused with parody, derision, or sarcasm, whereas irony is actually a system for trying to distance ourselves from something painful in order to see it more richly and fully.

9 Michael Fishbane's and Alicia Ostriker's essays in this volume address in greater detail Bak's midrashic style.

10 See Levinas, "Useless Suffering," *On-Thinking-of-the-Other: Entre Nous,* trans. Michael B. Smith and Barbara Harshav (New York: Columbia University Press, 1998), 91-101. For a short overview of Levinas' thought see Gary Phillips, "Emmanuel Levinas," in *A Handbook for Postmodern Biblical Interpretation,* ed. A. K. M. Adam (St. Louis, MO: Chalice Press, 2000), 154-59.

11 This is Bak's ironic rendering of the famous photo of the boy from the Warsaw ghetto. "The presence of the Warsaw boy's figure in my art is for me an act of remembrance that safeguards our collective memory" (Raskin, 155). See also the chapters "Samek and Samek" in his autobiography, *Painted in Words* (299-306) and "The Ghetto Boy" in *Between Worlds: Paintings and Drawings from 1946-2001,* ed. Irene Tayler (Boston: Pucker Art Publications, 2002), 297-307. For a further description see our second essay "Bak's Impossible Memorials" and the more exhaustive treatment by Raskin.

12 This is even more strikingly apparent when comparing this painting to others of Bak's paintings that include the motif of the flood and rainbow. See, e.g., *Noah's Dream* (1999), *Reflecting* (1999), *Isaac's Dream* (1999) in Lawrence L. Langer, *Genesis in a Different Light: The Book of Genesis in the Art of Samuel Bak* (Boston: Pucker Art Publications, 2001). See also pp. 41 and 57 in this volume.

13 "Death begins with the shoes...." Primo Levi, *Survival in Auschwitz: The Nazi Assault on Humanity,* trans. Stuart Woolf (New York: Simon & Schuster, 1986), 34.

14 Part of Bak's own interpretation of this piece. Private communication, June 9, 2003, Weston, Massachusetts.

15 Albrecht Dürer's *Melencolia I* (1514) ranks as one of the finest examples of Renaissance engraving, a masterpiece whose enigmatic character has challenged the interpretive eye of artists, art historians, and philosophers over the centuries. One of Germany's greatest artists, Dürer is remembered for his unsurpassed technical engraving skill and for his innovation in the arena of self-portraiture. The twentieth-century art historian Erwin Panofsky credits Dürer with being the inaugurator of the Renaissance movement itself owing in large measure to the recovery of classical form informed by mathematical and scientific precision. His prints, Panofsky notes, "set a new standard of graphic perfection for more than a century and served as models for countless other prints, as well as for paintings, sculptures, enamels, tapestries, plaques and faiences" in Germany and beyond. See *The Life and Art of Albrecht Dürer* (Princeton: Princeton University Press, 1943/1955), 4.

16 The hourglass, the magic square, scales, fire, plane, saw, nails, and hammer were tools of the alchemist as well as the artisan and thus reflect an understanding and ability to manipulate the order of the world. The compass along with the geometric shapes of millstone, polyhedron, sphere, and magic square reflect the Pythagorean insistence on the importance of number and form in the Cosmos. The compass, balance, and hour glass also reflect an ordering of all things in number, measure, and weight. The polyhedron, most likely representing the base metal lead, is associated with the Philosopher's Stone (John Read, "Albrecht Dürer's Melencolia," http://www.alchemylab.com/melancholia.htm).

17 The typical reflective pose included sitting with elbow on the knee and face held in one hand.

18 The rainbow was a favorite alchemical symbol for the definite and consistent sequence of colors.

19 The compass was often included in iconography depicting God's activity as creator commonly referred to as the *deus artifex.* Human artistic genius is thus being associated with the creativity of God. See Joseph Leo Koerner, *The Moment of Self-Portraiture in German Renaissance Art* (Chicago: University of Chicago Press, 1993), 26.

20 Walter L. Strauss, ed., *The Intaglio Prints of Albrecht Dürer: Engravings, Etchings, and Dry-Points* (New York: Kennedy Galleries and Abaris Books, 1976), 222. The plants, water ranunculus and water cress, as well as the sleeping dog (lying in front of the angel) were typical symbols of melancholia.

21 For a more detailed and complex reading of *Melencolia I* and Bak's visual commentary upon it, see below part 2 of our study, "Bak's Impossible Memorials."

22 Bak paraphrases his use of Dürer this way:

> Seated among various artifacts and instruments, a brooding angel contemplates a world spread beneath a perfect rainbow. His sad face tells us that he is deeply immersed in his thoughts. Is he pondering the state of mankind in the sixteenth century, poised between the 'the dark ages' and the age of enlightenment? I feel as if the angel had given me a wink: 'Go ahead, explore whatever you wish, transpose me to your time and to your concerns. Show me reflecting on an age that has lost its light and plunged itself back into darkness!' (Bak, "Dürer and I," *Between Worlds,* 272)

Elsewhere Bak speaks of the angel as female. See also his *After Dürer* (1980) in *Between Worlds,* 270, where the same Dürer angel is represented with high-heeled shoes.

23 See Gibbs, 365.

24 On his ironic use of Dürer, Bak confesses further:

> My desire to focus on Dürer and exploit his art came to me from an utterly nonartistic impulse, an old and unadmitted desire for revenge. I wanted to experience the sheer pleasure of looting something that the Germans treasured as being thoroughly German. (*Between Worlds*, 272)

25 An overview of Bak's production shows how potent the biblical text and biblical themes have been. See especially Langer, 2001.

26 Ps 91:11-12 (cf. Mt 4:6), which goes on (vv. 14-16) to say,

> I will protect those who know my name.
> When they call to me, I will answer them;
> I will be with them in trouble,
> I will rescue and honor them.
> With long life I will satisfy them,
> And show them my salvation (NRSV).

27 Though a commentator like Walter Brueggemann (*Genesis.* [Atlanta: John Knox, 1982]) would finesse this critique:

> Certainly, the question may legitimately be raised: Can there be no further destruction? Specific questions of theodicy may be raised about the Holocaust, in which it seems that God again released the flood waters. But all those who regard such events as punishment for sin have failed to understand the change in God. We have seen that in 6:5-7:10 there is a simple structure of indictment-sentence in which God resolves to punish the guilty. But that has now been changed. The one-to-one connection of guilt and punishment is broken. God is postured differently. From the perspective of this narrative, there may be death and destruction. Evil has not been eradicated from creation. But we are now assured that these are not rooted in the anger or rejection of God. The relation of creator to creature is no longer in a scheme of retribution. Because of a revolution in the heart of God, that relation is now based in *unqualified grace.* (84; emphasis ours)

Bak's painting, however, would have us beg for evidence of such "unqualified grace."

28 Bruce Vawter, *On Genesis: A New Reading.* (New York, NY: Doubleday, 1977), 116; emphasis ours.

29 See, e.g., Nahum Sarna, *Genesis* (Philadelphia: Jewish Publication Society, 1989), 49.

30 E. A. Speiser, *Genesis* (Garden City, NY: Doubleday, 1964/1980), 55.

31 Vawter, 116; emphasis ours.

32 Gerhard von Rad, *Genesis* (Philadelphia: Westminster, 1973), 124; emphasis ours.

33 Sarna, 49; emphasis ours.

34 Von Rad, 123; emphasis ours. Cf. Sarna: "Whatever be its literary history, the Flood story of the Torah stands out as an authentic, original expression of the religious genius of Israel. *Conceptually, spiritually, and morally, it stands in striking contrast to all the other versions*" (49; emphasis ours).

35 Pastor Grossman, cited in James A. Zabel, *Nazism and the Pastors. A Study of the Ideas of Three Deutsche Christen Groups;* AAR Dissertation Series #14 (Missoula, MT: Scholars Press, 1976), 165 (emphasis ours). Grossman also adds: "It is sufficient for me to see that the religion of Jesus is not an offshoot [*Abwandlung*] of Judaism...but rather a basically different and essentially foreign type of faith from Judaism. [Jesus] was—no matter how his ancestry appears—in no way `the classical Jewish man,' but much more the `greatest of anti-Jews.'"

36 Adolph Hitler, *Mein Kampf*, ed. Ralph Mannheim (New York: Mariner Books, 1999), 214, cited in Richard Steigmann-Gall, *The Holy Reich* (New York: Cambridge University Press, 2003), 26 (emphasis ours).

37 Pastor H. Beckmann, *Kirchliches Jahrbuch,* 31, cited in Zabel, 159 (emphasis ours).

38 *Mein Kampf,* Vol 1. ch. 11, taken from the website of the Hitler Historical Museum (http://www.hitler.org/writings/Mein_Kampf/mkv1ch11.html; emphasis ours). Biblical texts and images played complex roles in the attitudes and practices of both philo- and antisemites. See David P. Gushee, *The Righteous Gentiles of the Holocaust. A Christian Interpretation* (Philadelphia: Fortress, 1994), 136-40; Douglas Huneke, "Glimpses of Light in a Vast Darkness: A Study in the Moral and Spiritual Development of Nazi Era Rescuers," *Remembering for the Future,* ed. A. Roy Eckardt and Alice Eckardt; vol 1 (New York: Pergamom Press, 1989), 486-92; Doris L. Bergen, "Old Testament, New Hatreds: The Hebrew Bible and Antisemitism in Nazi Germany," *Sacred Text, Secular Times. The Hebrew Bible in the Modern World,* ed. Leonard Jay Greenspoon and Bryan F. Le Beau; Studies in Jewish Civilization 10 (Omaha, Neb: Creighton University Press, 2000), 35-46; see also Doris Bergen, *Twisted Cross. The German Christian Movement in the Third Reich* (Chapel Hill: University of North Carolina Press, 1996).

39 See Julius Streicher, the publisher and editor of the German newspaper *Der Stürmer*, paraphrasing Jn 8:44: "If the danger of the reproduction of that curse of God in the Jewish blood is finally to come to an end, then there is only one way—the extermination of that people whose father is the devil...." From "Trial of the Major War Criminals Before the international Military Tribunal," Nuremberg, 1945, vol 2 cited in www.nobeliefs.com/henchmen.htm.

40 A few artists like Gustave Doré have attempted to exhume the bodies, reminding us that the efficacy of the cleansing waters is severely compromised by the remaining corpses that would have "filled the earth." Yet these are never mentioned in the biblical text itself. The only trace of the dead bodies is the observation in passing that, when released by Noah, the raven, unlike the dove, does not return to the ark. Why not? It doesn't have to—it has plenty of carrion to eat.

41 In our "Suffering Responsibility: Creation, Art, and the Genesis of Ethics" (paper presented in the Theology, Bible and Postmodernism section at annual meeting of the American Academy of Religion, Washington, D.C., November 21, 2006), we suggest a creative link between trauma and the stories of Gen 1-11: the biblical narrative structures suffering, allowing it to be re-presented and thus not forgotten.

42 Jonathan Magonet, *A Rabbi Reads the Bible* (London: SCM, 2004), 26-27. See further our discussion of broken, stammering elegies as communicators of truth in "Bak's Impossible Memorials."

43 Consider the lyrics of the traditional hymn "How Firm a Foundation" (also cited in Brueggemann, 84):

> When through the deep waters I call thee to go,
> The rivers of sorrow shall not overflow;
> For I will be near thee, thy troubles to bless,
> And sanctify to thee thy deepest distress.

44 The logo of Duke Divinity School, and a stained glass window in the Craig Chapel at Drew University.

45 In other of Bak's works employing the flood motif (e.g. *Journey* [1991], *Departures* [1971-1992]), the "ark" is often made of stone, immobile, petrified or fossilized into the landscape, sometimes with smokestacks reminiscent of the crematoria, signifying more of a prison or execution chamber than a vehicle of escape.

46 See Bak's memoir, *Painted in Words,* where he identifies the Boy from the Warsaw ghetto with Samek his close childhood friend and himself. "Samek" is the Yiddish diminutive for Samuel.

47 Fackenheim (1970: 75). A more detailed discussion of the crucifixion motif in *Elegy III* can be found in "Bak's Impossible Memorials."

48 As Primo Levi insists about the Lager, "If one wants to live, one must learn this quickly and well: No Sacred Face will help thee here!" (29, 31).

49 See Primo Levi's story of the concentration camp guard who refuses to let Levi grab an icicle to slake his thirst (29). Levi asks "why?" The guard replies: *Hier ist kein warum* ("There is no `why' here"). Building upon the experience of Levi, James Hatley writes of the importance of demanding *"why"* in the face of those who were "intent on constructing in Auschwitz a mode of history with '*Kein Warum,'* with no why." See his *Suffering Witness: The Quandary of Responsibility after the Irreparable* (State University of New York, 2000), 37-38.

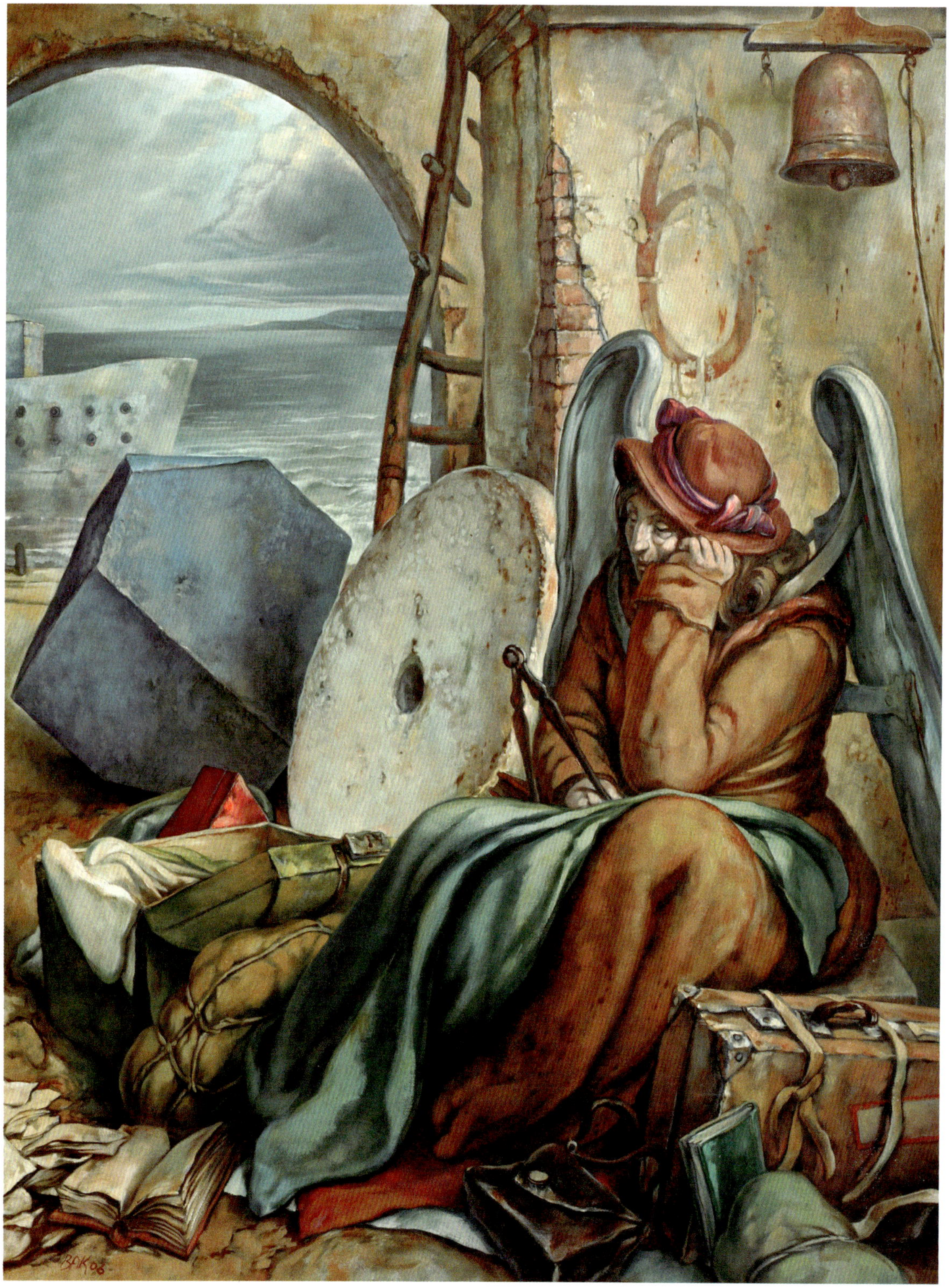

Boarding the St. Louis, 2006
Oil on Canvas, 40 x 30"

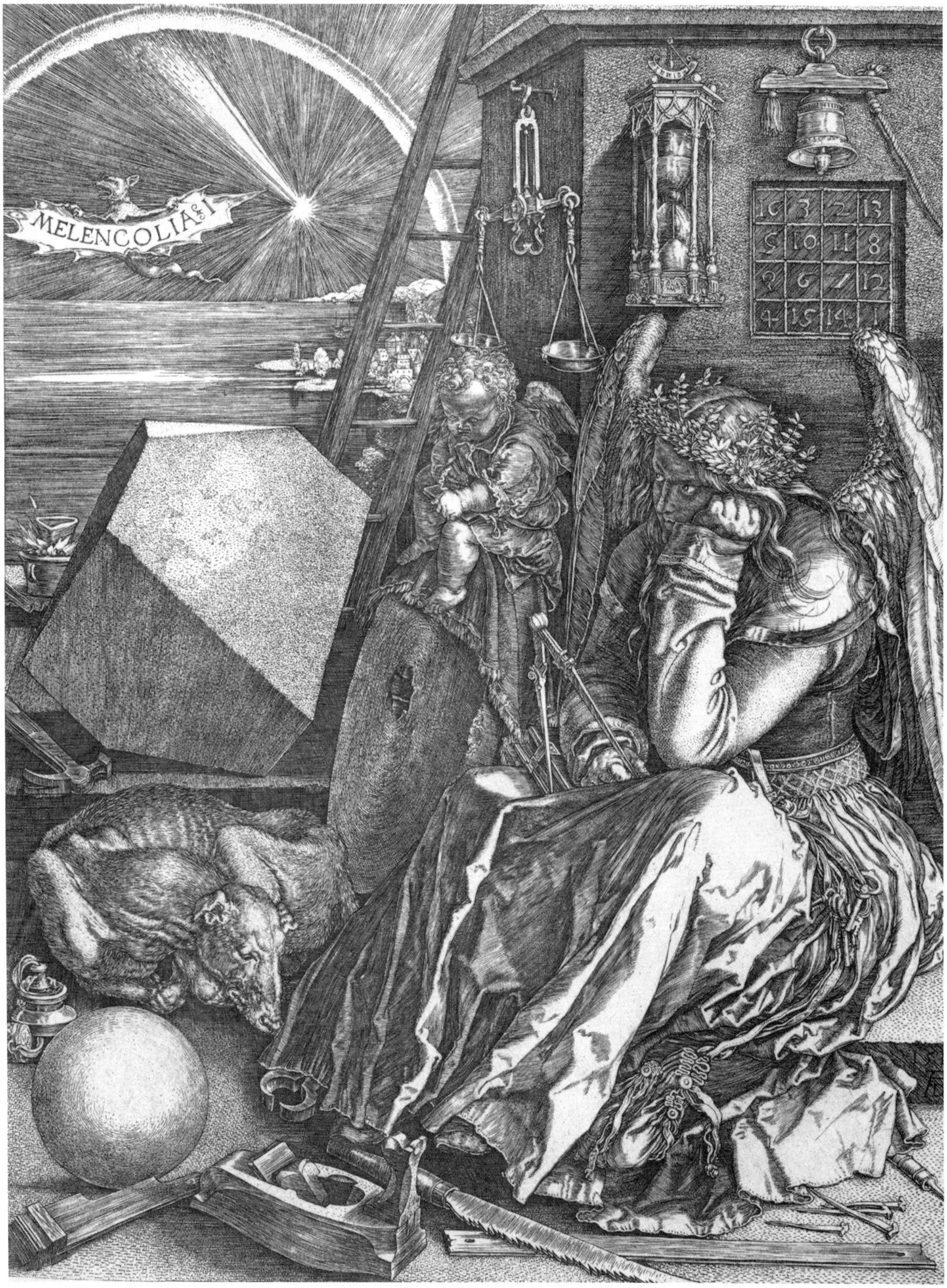

Albrecht Dürer
Melencolia I, 1514

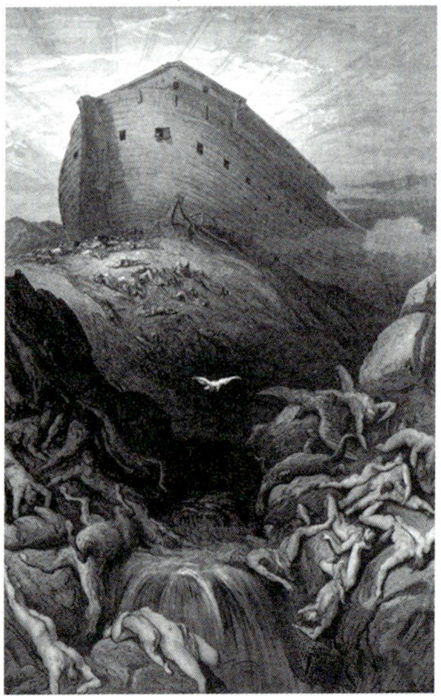

Gustave Doré
Noah's Ark

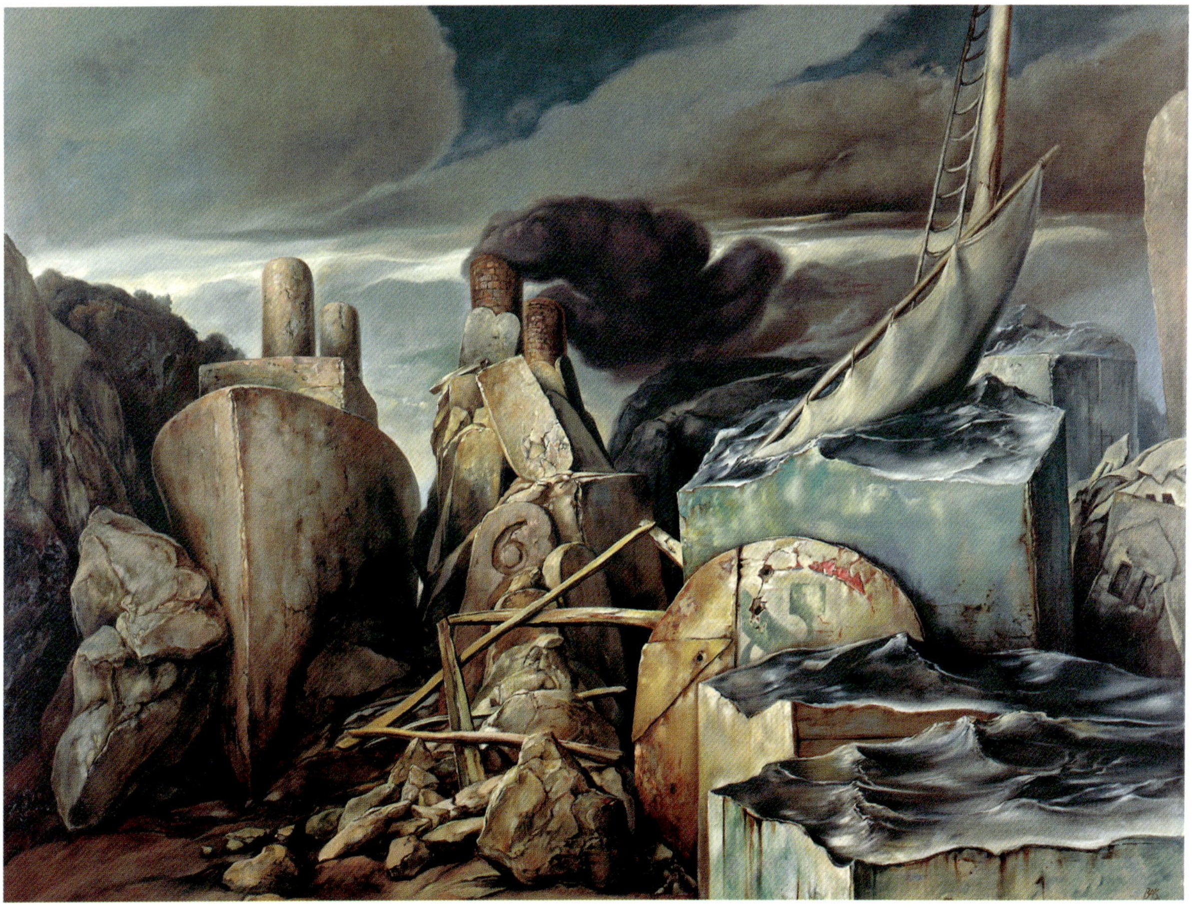

Departures, 1971-92
Oil on Canvas, 35 x 51 1/4"

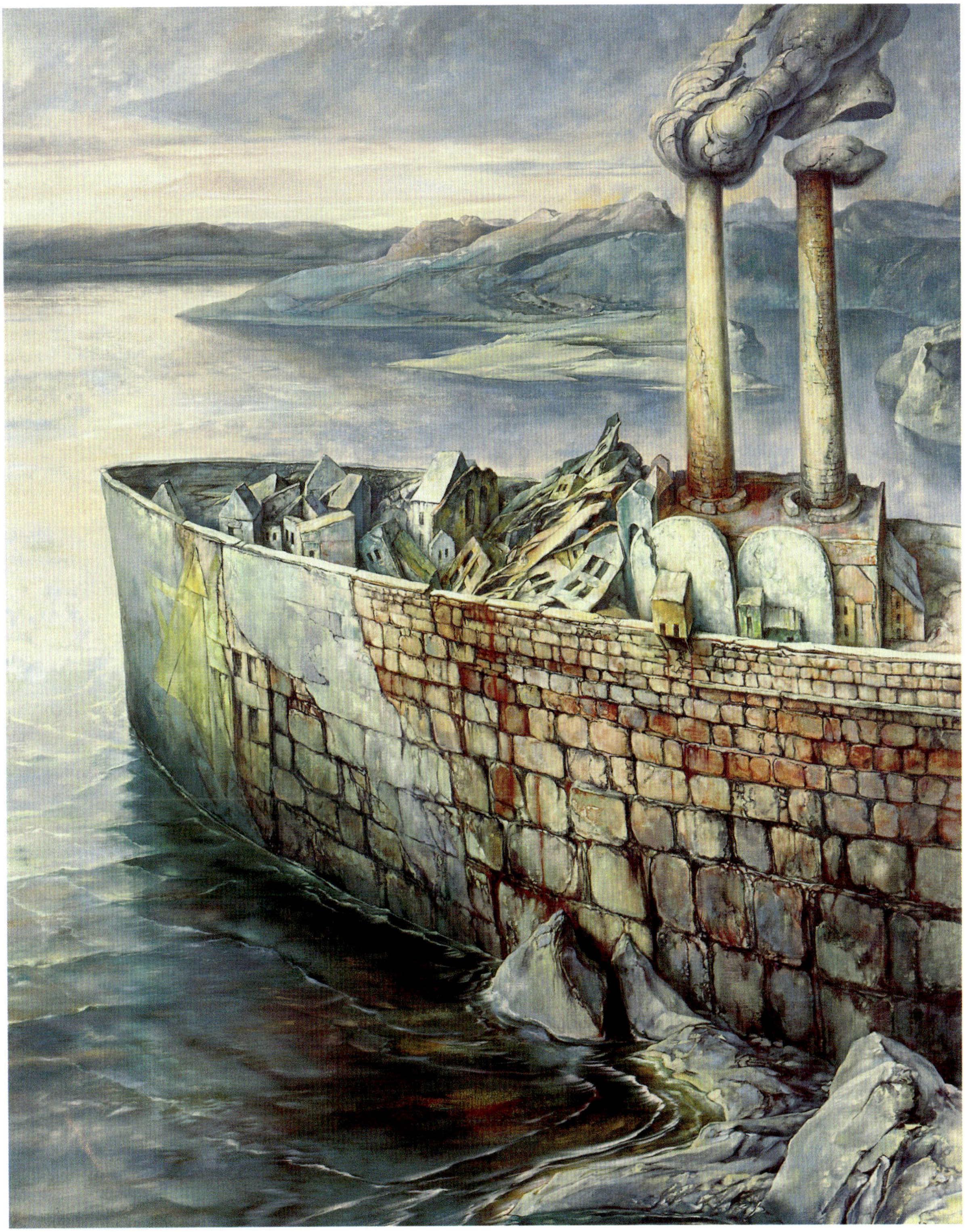

Journey, 1991
Oil on Canvas, 78 3/4 x 63"

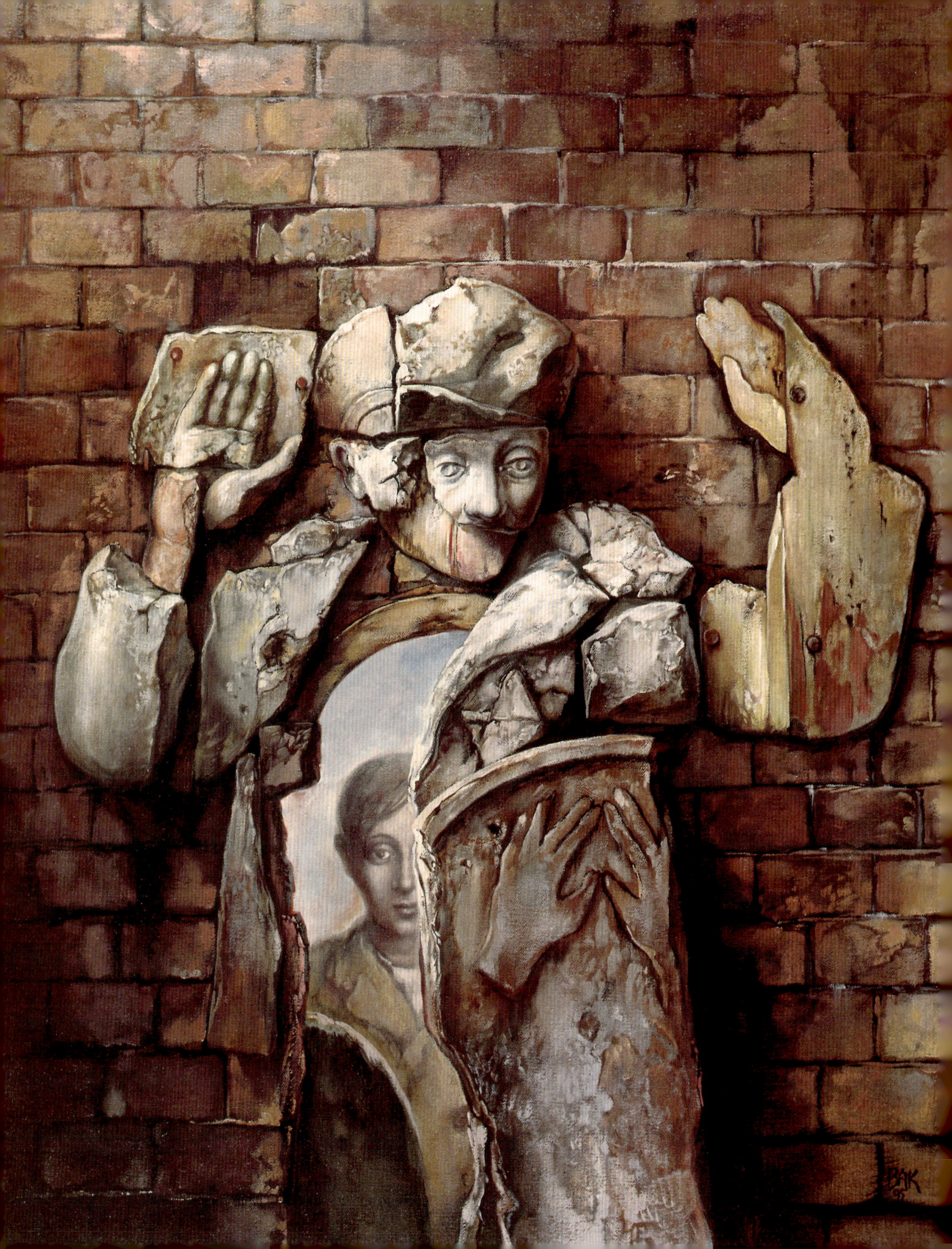

Bak's Impossible Memorials: Giving Face to the Children

DANNA NOLAN FEWELL AND GARY A. PHILLIPS

Reading over the Abyss

How does one go about remembering a million murdered children? And what does this question have to do with reading the Bible? When we read the Bible, with all of its varied explanations for human suffering, with its covenants and promises of divine protection and redemption, with its continuous insistence on justice, with its blueprints for sacred history, should a million murdered children give us pause?

The late Jewish philosopher Emil Fackenheim says "yes" and calls for an end to the "seamless" reading of and theological reflection on the Bible that has proceeded in recent decades as though the Shoah never happened: "An abyss has been opened up between the Book, then and there, and this 'generation' here and now," he insists. "Seeking to build a bridge over the abyss, I shall dwell on it; if the bridge collapses, I shall locate myself amid the heap of whatever fragments of the scaffold remain."[1]

What does it mean to build such a precarious bridge "between the Book, then and there, and this 'generation' here and now"? What does it mean to live and read suspended over an abyss where a million murdered children lie in unmarked graves or, if necessary, to position oneself in the rubble that remains? What would such unstable, interrupted reading of the Bible look like? Sound like? How would it in turn disrupt our theological enterprises, our study of religion, our teaching practices, our scholarly habits and projects as Fackenheim avers? What difference would such interrupted reading and reflection make?

The question is not merely a philosophical challenge to biblical scholarship. Because we know that *some kind* of reading of the Bible, *some kind* of understanding of religion, *some kind* of construction of self and community, *some kind* of teaching and scholarship contributed to, or passively allowed, the murders of the million and of their families. And we also know that violence against children is not simply a thing of the past: our religious, personal, communal, and professional

Study A, 1995
Oil on Canvas, 25 5/8 x 21 1/8"

practices today are implicated within global economies of trade and war that disregard and damage children.[2] The bridge to the past is also a bridge to future. Are we not called to do better? To do otherwise? Are we not confronted with the most profound moral questions as Emmanuel Levinas poses them:

> Is humanity, in its indifference, going to abandon the world to useless suffering, leaving it to the political fatality—or the drifting—of the blind forces which inflict misfortune on the weak and conquered, and which spare the conquerors...? Or, incapable of adhering to an order—or to a disorder—which it continues to think diabolic, must not humanity now, in a faith more difficult than ever, in a faith without theodicy, continue Sacred History; a history which now demands even more...?[3]

How do we, as scholars and teachers of religion, build a bridge over the abyss "in a faith more difficult than ever, in a faith without theodicy"? How do we build and live on and think on a structure that must inevitably lack coherence, that might collapse at any minute and leave us in the rubble among the remains? How does one represent such a world in moral fragments in a way that speaks the truth about suffering and evil? How does one read the Bible and remember the children at the same time?

We take our cue once more from Post-Shoah artist Samuel Bak. In Part I of our study[4] of Bak's work, we addressed the way Bak's use of Dürer subverts traditional Enlightenment values and examined in depth the ways his allusion to the biblical flood story and his exploitation of the crucifixion motif disrupt traditional understandings of these icons as salvific and redemptive. We sought to explore not only how Bak grapples with the challenge of representing the unrepresentable, but also how his work drives us as scholars back to the Bible to discover the ways in which it, too, is straining to articulate irreparable trauma. We ended our piece with theological and ethical questions about children, theodicy, and theological representation that Bak's painting forces upon us: Is theodicy possible in the face of what Emmanuel Levinas calls "useless suffering"? How do we now read biblical covenants and promises of protection and salvation that ignore the wellbeing of children? How do we continue to read the Bible, to do theology, to construct religious meaning in light of the mass murder of children? Is there any covenant, any biblical vision, any theological concept that can restore hope, justice, life, or meaning after such damage to the world? What work of repair or *Tikkun Olam* is at all possible in light of the abyss, and what are we being summoned to do?

In this essay we re-engage these questions, still focusing mainly on *Elegy III,* but in the context of a series of "impossible memorials" that Bak has painted to remember the million murdered children of the Shoah. We pick up the threads of our earlier reading, concentrating here on Bak's use of the boy from the Warsaw ghetto, particularly his superimposition of the image onto the biblical and artistic archetype of the Crucifix, his "plundering" (as he calls it) of Dürer, and the ways in which Bak evokes and subverts Dürer in his gestures of self-portraiture.

The Boy from the Warsaw Ghetto

The famous photograph of the Warsaw boy being held at gunpoint by SS officers was taken during the clearing of the Warsaw ghetto that took place between April 19 and May 16, 1943.[5] It was one of 49 photographs contained in an album assembled by Jürgen Stroop, the German police commander in charge of putting down the Warsaw uprising and cleansing the ghetto of its remaining 60,000 inhabitants. The album, intended as a report and birthday present for Heinrich Himmler, the *Reichsführer* of the SS, was entitled "THE JEWISH QUARTER OF WARSAW IS NO MORE."

Though originally taken to illustrate and to boast of the thoroughness of the SS operation, the photograph has taken on iconic status for the post-Holocaust world due to its content and composition. Against the backdrop of a terrified group of Jews being herded from their hiding place, the boy stands isolated with his hands in a gesture of surrender as though he were an apprehended criminal. He stands unprotected by his family and community in a fearful solitude at the moment when his fate is sealed, his childhood ended.[6]

The pathos evoked by the boy's isolation, his uplifted arms and outwardly turned palms makes the image, in Bak's words, "the most poignant image of Jewish Crucifixion."[7] The boy, like Jesus in crucifixion iconography from the 17th and 18th centuries, appears to be reaching out to God, desiring, pleading for life in the face of imminent death. The gesture, however, is a double one. As Bak observes, "[A]rms that reach for the sky are also a gesture of surrender, of giving up. When you superimpose the image of a crucified Son on the image of the little Warsaw boy with his uplifted arms, you wonder where is God the Father?"[8] Or, we might add, you wonder where is anyone who would play the part of God the Father? This tragic image of a helpless child submitting to the Nazi death machine unprotected by parents, human or divine, has, according to Bak, "become a universal emblem of the million children murdered in the *Shoah*."[9]

The years following the photograph's discovery have seen the image of the Warsaw boy reproduced hundreds of times as a "logo" of Holocaust martyrdom, its symbolic status so firmly entrenched that a public outcry arose in 1982 when *The New York Times* reported that the boy had actually survived and had now been identified. One Holocaust historian claimed in protest against the story that the photograph was "too holy to let people do with it what they want"—even in service of historical investigation.

But whether the child pictured actually perished or not, we know that "such a boy did perish, one among an entire million of Jewish children."[10] Bak identifies him as his eight-year old best friend Samek who was executed by the Nazis and left lying in a pool of his own blood as a warning to any other Jews who might try to hide outside the Vilna ghetto. Moreover, in addition to representing the vulnerability and loss of the million Jewish children, for Bak, the Ghetto boy's image (as condensed symbol) invokes both the particular face of his childhood friend and his own narrow escape from a similar fate. Of the boy Bak writes:

> With his arms lifted in an attitude of resigned and bewildered surrender and his depleted gaze focused on my eyes, he has never stopped questioning me. In the Vilna ghetto, I was his age and I looked—as did thousands of other children destined for the same fate—exactly like him. Same cap, same out-grown coat, same short pants. I always considered this picture a kind of portrait of myself in those times. This may be a presumptuous thought because we do not know if the authentic boy survived, whereas I did.[11]

As the photograph has threatened to lose its symbolic intensity by its very familiarity and predictable uses,[12] Bak has countered with an effort to "reinvigorate" it by disrupting its conventional status. In a series of "monuments that could never exist,"[13] Bak has disassembled and reassembled the Ghetto boy across a series of canvases in an attempt not only to preserve the picture's power to depict a specific historical person, but also to communicate the convergence of multiple identities and references—the executed friend, the martyred million, the child survivor, the crucified son Jesus—that have been evoked for him by the image of a boy who "never stopped questioning." In an act of *re*-membering, *re*-collecting, he repeatedly reconstructs the Ghetto boy as a means of safeguarding the memory of a million murdered children, the aborted life of his friend Samek, his own shattered childhood and, we would surmise, as a means of coming to terms with his own inexplicable survival.

What sorts of monuments has Bak fabricated? Unlike monuments that try to express permanence by ignoring their own material making, unlike monuments that blend into their backgrounds as though they are indigenous to the landscape, unlike monuments that attempt to universalize through abstraction or particularize through recognizable figures,[14] the paradoxical memorials that emerge on Bak's canvases are fragile, temporary constructions, fragmented and incomplete, depending as much on absence as presence, assembled from scraps of debris that should have been discarded, or carved from stone that decomposes as we watch. They advertise their own handmade quality, their dependence upon human labor. They interrupt the landscape, sometimes bursting forth from the earth itself, disrupting, obstructing the view, demanding attention. Neither completely lifelike nor surreal,[15] recognizable nor abstract, these constructions generate distance while at the same time inviting proximity, or in Bak's words, they "protect the scar of an ancient wound while remaining true to [the] knowledge of the wound itself."[16] They interrupt the propensity to collapse all suffering and death into the Same;[17] yet at the same time, they invite us into the empty shoes of the Warsaw boy and of all of his murdered brothers and sisters. "It is no dream world," insists Bak, "but rather reality experienced and expressed through metaphor. If you look at what happens on my canvases, if you focus your eyes onto the decomposed image of the Warsaw boy, you will discover what I feel about the destructured world in which we live, our troubled times, the contradictions and losses that we must face."[18] Bak's memorials, anchored in time, look at once both backward and forward.

Moreover, unlike monuments that do the work of memory for us, allowing us to give in to the desire to forget what is troubling and tragic,[19] we are confronted with the unspeakable, repeated again and again, in an artistic stammering that demands to be heard and eludes being fully comprehended. "When we identify with victims, whether in films, books, or paintings," Bak muses in a later moment of self-reflection, "we become aware that something unforgivable has happened, perhaps it is still happening, maybe one day it will happen again."[20] Past memory is not enough. There are present and future consequences. In James Young's words,

> It is not enough to ask whether or not our memorials remember the Holocaust, or even how they remember it. We should also ask to what ends we have remembered. That is, how do we respond to the current moment in light of our remembered past?...[T]he shape of memory cannot be divorced from the actions taken in its behalf....[M]emory without consequences contains the seeds of its own destruction.[21]

Elegy III and *Melencolia I*: The Work of Mourning, the State of Melancholy, and the Artistic Impetus

There is no little irony that, in addition to utilizing the Warsaw boy photograph in *Elegy III,* Bak also plunders the work of Albrecht Dürer, an artist of monumental importance to the German Renaissance[22] and a cultural icon for Germans even to the present day. Celebrated as the artist who "inaugurates the modern age of representational art," whose very work announces a "pivotal moment in the history of modern subjectivity,"[23] Dürer is noted for his remarkable realism and attention to detail. Like other artists of his day, Dürer understood his skills to be perfectible, but his talent to be a gift from God,[24] the *Deus artifex* who, as creator, was thought of as the "most accomplished painter and sculptor." The belief that the human artist is the *imago dei*[25] allowed Dürer to associate the creative genius of the artist with the creative power of God.[26] The artist is entrusted, indeed anointed, with the power to create, and is called upon to become evermore like God, an endeavor colored by both divine-like achievement but tempered ultimately by inevitable limitations of skill and insight.[27]

This tension between artistic confidence and human limitation is nowhere more clearly imaged than in Dürer's *Melencolia I* (1514) where the divine but melancholy angel represents human intellect and potential that has become paralyzed by introspection on perfection that can never be attained, problems that can never be solved, limits never breached.

Melencolia I has been described by more than one critic as Dürer's spiritual self-portrait.[28] According to Erwin Panofsky, the contemplative but immobile angel and the feverishly productive putto project an image of the violent struggle between the two sides of Dürer's personality. On the one hand, angel and putto associate Dürer's artistic talent with divine abilities, while on the other hand, the angel's inactivity and the putto's blind busyness express his frustration with intellectual and practical limitations.[29] In the words of Joseph Koerner, the overall image "becomes wholly the product and reflection of the unique, creative self of Albrecht Dürer."[30]

But *Melencolia I* is about more than Dürer's preoccupation with his own creative genius and limitations. With its rich and complicated imagery, its endless interpretations and associations, the engraving (in a way perhaps suggestive of the Warsaw ghetto boy photo itself) takes its viewers into a vortex of self-reflection. As Koerner writes,

> ...*Melencolia I* seems designed to generate multiple and contradictory readings, to clue its viewers to an endless exegetical labor until, exhausted in the end, they discover their own portrait in Dürer's sleepless, inactive personification of melancholy. Interpreting the engraving itself becomes a detour to self-reflection....[The] print pictures a relation of the self to itself, inflected...in intellectual, spiritual, and moral labor and enacted...against the temporalizing horizon of death (the ubiquitous hourglass)."[31]

Consequently, *Melencolia I* lures the viewer into identifying with Dürer's psychological predicament. Against the backdrop of impending death, the self, like Dürer's angel, confronts the absolute limits of its capacity to create. Freud's distinction between mourning and melancholia helps illumine this condition. Whereas a mourner can eventually let go, separate from, a lost object of desire, can acknowledge the loss and recognize that the object is indeed separate from the self, the melancholic cannot. Rather, in the state of melancholy, the object of loss or desire becomes so identified with the self that it cannot be distinguished from it. In *Melencolia I,* the angel's inability to let go of its fixation on unachievable perfection produces a narcissistic turn inward and preoccupation with the self, producing a "state of emptiness and vacancy."[32]

In *Elegy III* Bak has transported *Melencolia I's* self-absorbed angel from a scene of endless technological and creative possibilities tempered by inevitable human limitations to a landscape where human technology has achieved its worst, where human creativity in the aftermath of such destruction is challenged as never before. We do not find here "the ubiquitous hourglass" representing the unavoidable death of the individual; rather, we view a "horizon of death" formed from flood waters, masses of yellow stars washed ashore, a scaffold, and an executioner's wall upon which hangs the remnants of a pieced-together boy—all pointing to the senseless murders of a million children.

Juxtaposed to the boy the vacant-eyed angel persists with her introspective mental labor, but the nature of that labor is now uncertain. Is the angel now a displaced person, missing her projected alter-ego (the putto), her "spiritual tragedy" pointedly incongruous with the scene in which she finds herself? Has she seen the child who threatens to intrude upon a narcissistic moment? Has the child breached her consciousness? Become a jarring Other alter-ego? Has her quandary now been altered from a preoccupation with her own "spiritual tragedy" to the contemplation of a historical tragedy that takes her outside of herself? Or is she oblivious to the entire scene, still lost in narcissistic reflection?

By evoking *Melencolia I* Bak has ironically reframed Dürer's Renaissance concerns about the nature of human creativity, aspirations, and limits. By importing Dürer's "spiritual" self-portrait, Bak forces Dürer and the artistic and religious tradition and culture he represents to face up to the reality of the Warsaw boy.[33] Dürer's self-absorption is confronted with its ultimate consequences.[34] The fractured child is the victim of the technology, ingenuity, and obsession with self-perfection that had so preoccupied Dürer, a deeply ironic sign of the technological success of the Nazi death machine. A challenge to Dürer's (indeed any) melancholic reflection upon the limits of human capability, the boy pictures at least one human capacity that seemingly knows no limit, namely the capacity to deal death and destruction. Rather than a "detour to self-reflection," an occasion for melancholia, Bak takes the interpreter elsewhere, beyond the self, to a million other selves who are no more. He paints an *Elegy,* a work of mourning as a counter to *Melencolia.*[35]

Customarily viewed as a literary work, the elegy is an imaginative response to the trauma of death that invites and challenges the reader, hearer, or in this case, viewer, to identify with the loss. More than a mere remembering of the past, elegy engages mourners by re-viewing, re-collecting, and re-presenting absent ones in order "to affirm that their lives do not fall totally into nothingness."[36] According to David Shaw, "...[T]he most important aesthetic decision an elegist can make is to identify not with consolations that are conventionally available to the mourner, but with the uncertainties of a puzzled and questioning reader, looking perhaps for the first time into the eyes of death or grappling with other limitations."[37] "Desires," insists Shaw, "cannot make consoling fictions true."[38]

As he re-views, re-collects, re-presents the absent children, snatching their lives back from the abyss,[39] Bak's elegaic work engages his fellow mourners with irony. His unconventional use of convention—the displacement of Dürer's angel, the crucifixion of a child, the suspended, colorless rainbow—echoes the "uncertainties of a puzzled and questioning reader" and exposes consoling fictions for what they are. In Bak's world, angels, rainbows, and covenants are not the stuff of solace. Rather, they are the site of questions, of brokenness, of incongruity. Bak's "broken, contingent conduct of...elegy" expresses "the broken, contingent nature of...life,"[40] life in the aftermath of Shoah.

Like its modern literary counterpart,[41] Bak's work is marked by silences, images that neither hear nor speak nor see. His many studies of the Warsaw boy comprise a visual stammering, replete with repetitions, revisions, and ellipses ("unassuming cutouts") tenuous constructions made of refuse, riddled with gaps. His memorials are "sites of fracture and breakdown" ("perishable bricolages") made up of traces and fragments, crumbling statuaries rupturing the earth, breached images offering portals to another age. In the insistent re-envisioning of the Warsaw boy, Bak the elegist looks backward and forward at once, plundering the landscape of his childhood in order to construct impossible monuments, imaging loss, forcing a profound encounter with the past in the landscape of the present.

Self-Portraiture and the Image of Christ

Bak's merging of and identification with the Warsaw boy and the crucified Christ in his works also offers ironic commentary on Dürer's other efforts at self-portraiture. For example, Dürer's famous *Self-Portrait* of 1500 has been described as a veritable "Beau Dieu," a pious attempt to depict himself in imitation of Christ,[42] a perfect reflection of the beauty of God. As Koerner writes, "In the sheer *monumentality* of the picture's design, in the fearful symmetry and directness of address that solemnize our encounter with the artist's likeness, Dürer seems to affirm and *sanctify* the epochal change that his self-portraits are believed, in retrospect, to instantiate."[43]

As a visual formulation of the Christ, Dürer's *Self-Portrait* belongs to a long complex history of pictorial representation that evokes the tradition of the *vera icon,* the "true image of Christ." The *vera icon* originates in the eleventh-century legend of St. Veronica,[44] the one who wipes the sweat and blood from the face of Jesus as he stumbles under the burden of his cross en route to Golgotha.[45] Consequently, in the *Sudarium* tradition[46] (the "sweat" of St. Veronica) Christ is presented as a painter too.[47] When he presses his face into cloth, he creates his image instantaneously, effortlessly, and perfectly in an act of "handless making,"[48] thus setting the standard for human artists: to produce works that give the appearance of not being made with human hands.

Within the German *vera icon* tradition Christ was typically presented as a disembodied head silhouetted against a white cloth background. The figure was either wearing a crown of thorns and expressing the agony of the passion or projecting a serene, unwounded, and omnivoyant countenance that distinguished it as sacred and transcendent. The divine gaze settles on the viewer, commanding attention and subjecting the viewer to a higher moral and ontological authority. Just as God summons Moses, announcing "I am that I am," the viewer, too, is called and has no choice but to respond.[49]

In his self-made *vera icon (Self-Portrait)* of 1500, Dürer softens his features to mirror traditional images of Christ. Moreover, the near-omnivoyance of the Dürer-Christ eyes[50] echoes the self-presentation of God: "I am who I am," "I am who painted me."[51] The near photographic quality, with no visible brushwork or evidence of paint, mirrors Christ's legendary "handless making," and celebrates Dürer's own power of self-creation and perfect, mimetic representation. Dürer thus takes on the attributes of God,[52] summoning viewers to attitudes of devotion to a higher creative authority, his own as well as God's.[53]

Bak's self-portraits as they surface in the figure of the Warsaw boy, are, like Dürer's, multidimensional. As Dürer represented himself as both human and divine, both himself and Christ (or alternatively as angel), Bak, too, presents himself as an unexpected and unsettling image of Christ in the crucified Warsaw boy. However, while Dürer's collapsing of his identity with Christ's is colored by pious devotion and self-preoccupation, Bak's identification with the Warsaw-Christ boy is an excessive act of signifying that points to a million faces at once. Its allusion to Christ is focused not on divine perfection, but on human suffering.

Consequently, in contrast to Dürer's 1500 *Self-Portrait,* Bak's self-portraits do not communicate an air of triumph. They do not signify a person or event that initiates a new historical era nor do they purport to represent "universal humanity."[54] Rather, they indicate an era of anti-Enlightenment, an anti-Renaissance, an anti-rebirth, an era of mass murder on a scale heretofore not seen in the heart of Christian Europe. Rather than being a monument *to* that era, they testify to Bak's survival *of* that era, a survival in the face (literally) of others who did not. Instead of triumphantly announcing "I am who I am," "I am who painted me,"[55] Bak's self-portraits signal "I am the one who barely survived," a claim that automatically points to others—the father who saved him in the knapsack, the children whose fathers could not save them.[56]

Whereas Dürer's ominvoyant gaze demands attention and subjects the viewer to a higher authority, Bak presents his viewers with two or more faces, two or more sets of eyes that peer out, diffusing the link between viewer and image. In Bak's divided *Self-Portrait* (1995-96) the seated child looks directly at the viewer, whereas the Warsaw boy looks askance. In *Study A* (1995) an older child Bak peers straight out while the Warsaw boy stares vacantly past the viewer in a manner that recalls Primo Levi's description of the Müsselman's death gaze. In tension with the omnivoyant tradition, Bak's visages invite viewers to imagine an omnivoyant God/artist not as perfection but as brokenness. Viewers are not called to submit to a higher authority, but are summoned to enter a world of ruin, to put on the empty shoes of the boy, to insert their face where the boy's face has disappeared.[57] It is a call to empathetic response.[58]

Whereas Dürer's *Self-Portrait* of 1500 emerges from nothingness in universal transcendence, the illusion of perfect representation, implying a perfect identification of image to reality,[59] Bak's self-portraits are set amidst rubble and broken remains, grounded in disaster.[60] Over against Dürer's effort to produce a universal, a-historical face of Christ, Bak sets the particular, localized face of a boy, disrupting any easy identification with the Christ figure on the part of the viewer. Historical, worldly, chthonic, Bak's images are the stuff of a particular time and place, from below, not above, made not begotten, an echo of a different creedal confession. They do not seek to disguise their concretion or their material making. The piecing together of the Ghetto boy as Christ-figure produces images obviously, painfully, "made with human hands," "hol(e)y" in a different sense, bricolage not perfected, constructed in a landscape where components have to be scavenged, where the human imagination is failing, where a vision of restoration, regeneration, renaissance must be dredged from the ruins.[61]

In 1503, in the midst of an illness loosely identified as one of the "plagues" that had ransacked the population of Nuremburg, Dürer merges his image once again with the figure of Christ in the charcoal drawing, *The Head of the Dead Christ* (1503). Adapting this time the other image of the *vera icon,* that of the face of Christ with the crown of thorns, suffering the agony of the passion, Dürer identifies himself with Christ's passion, an *imitatio Christi* associated with suffering and penance.[62] Christ becomes an emblem of Dürer's own suffering, Christ's death the emblem of Dürer's worst fears, a "potential last testament" as it were.

In his later work *Self-Portrait as Man of Sorrows* of 1522, Dürer again relates his own illness, this time malaria, to the passion. Partially nude and holding the scourge and whip of the passion, Dürer presents himself *conformitas Christi,* appealing to the healing power of Christ's own wounds. Here the self-portrait, fashioned as he ages and suffers illness, exposes his humanity "as precisely *not* equivalent to God"[63] but rather as so sinful that, in Dürer's own words, "no help could have reached us except that the son of God became a man, in order that he, through his innocent suffering, might abundantly pay the Father all our guilt, so that the justice of God might be satisfied."[64] Consequently, we may agree with Koerner's assessment that the significance of Dürer's peculiar self-portraiture is not so much a sudden epochal awakening to or discovering of the Self; rather, we find in Dürer's self-portraits, the triumphant (1500), the suffering (1503), and the penitent (1522), a reinvention (an inflection/intonation?) of the self according to common cultural notions of Christian piety and Dürer's own religious and personal experiences.[65]

Unfortunately, despite the assumptions of the bulk of Dürer scholarship, Dürer's culturally constructed piety and personal religious experiences cannot stand easily as neutral, benign influences upon his art. Christian identity in the late medieval period on was at least partially constructed in distinction from and hostility toward Jews. In the words of Erasmus, "If to be a Christian is to hate the Jews, then we are all thoroughly Christian here."[66] The underlying rationale for this attitude is the accusation, presented in the gospels themselves, especially Matthew and John, that the Jews killed Christ. This propensity to vilify Jews as Christ-Killers is common among the Renaissance artists and writers of Dürer's day.[67] Devotion to Christ meant disdain for those charged with torturing and murdering him. Any emphasis on Christ's suffering and crucifixion, then, served to incite anti-Jewish sentiment, especially during the Passion season when pogroms could well be anticipated. When Christ's suffering was presented as a focal point for penitential reflection, a common practice in Christian piety, it simultaneously became the occasion and justification for hating Jews.

No artist was more enamored of Christ's passion than Dürer himself. Besides producing numerous individual passion scenes, Dürer fashioned four series of works devoted to the passion, some seventy-five pieces in all.[68] In these works and others where Christ is the subject (see, for example, the portrayal of Jews in *Christ Among the Doctors,* 1506), Dürer adopts the common medieval tact of depicting the Jews as opponents and killers of Christ and Christians, rendering their faces, dress, and behaviors[69] with distortion and caricature to indicate their villainous character. And if the viewer misses the anti-Jewish implication, the text accompanying the images often makes it explicit. *Christ Crowned with Thorns* (1508-10), the central woodcut of the *Small Passion* cycle, is explicated thusly: "It is not enough that they [i.e. the Jews] cut Christ to ribbons with their bramble-whips....he is spit upon, bashed, drubbed with cudgels, ripped from his lofty throne and dragged by his hair."[70] Accompanying *Christ as Man of Sorrows* (1510), the title page woodcut for *The Large Passion* (1511), the epigram jointly authored by Benedictus Chelidonius and Dürer reads as follows:

> Ingrate, you constantly tear open my wounds with
> Your sins. Constantly your crime pelts me.

Let it be enough that I endured such great torture
Under the Jewish foe. Now, my friend, grant me peace.[71]

If allusions to the suffering of Christ and, by extension, of Christians, express subliminal anti-Semitic violence, then, when Dürer merges his features with *The Head of the Dead Christ* (1503) while suffering from a "plague" often blamed upon Jews, we might imagine that he, too, is implicating the Jews not only in Christ's suffering, but also in his own. Likewise, his *Self-Portrait as Man of Sorrows* (1522), with its conspicuous implements of torture and its theme of penitence, assumes and promotes the anti-Semitic pathology of the late-Medieval and early Renaissance Passion observances. Even the *Self-Portrait* of 1500 with its conceit of the *Sudarium* intimating Christ's progress toward Golgotha, and its faint cross in the Dürer/Christ figure's eye, implicates the Jews as foil to Christ and to the Christian as *imago dei.* Is it coincidental that in 1499, the year before the portrait was painted, Nuremburg completed a fifteen year plan to banish all its Jews and confiscate their property? Dürer was there when the last Jew left. In eerie anticipation of the future, Nuremburg would remain *Judenrein* for the next 300 years.[72]

Like the Christ venerated in his paintings, Dürer, too, achieved Christomorphic status in death. Not only did his face become the model for subsequent paintings of Christ, as in J. G. Vischer's *Christ and the Adultress* (1637), but his body and works were treated as relics. Elevated to the pantheon of Germany's great artistic giants, Dürer, the "Prince of Painters,"[73] came to symbolize national unity and the aspirations of the German people. But the positive cultural association of Dürer with Renaissance and humanism had its sinister dimensions: militarism, Jew-hating, and Christian supercessionism. The pre-WWI *Dürerbund*[74] campaign against "smut, decadence and bad taste" whose goal was a "healthy culture" anticipated the Nazi drive for "racial purity."[75] During the Third Reich, Dürer was hailed as that most "German of German masters" from Nuremberg, Hitler's "most German of German cities." Dürer's 1493 *Self-Portrait* appeared on the cover of the Nazi publication *Volk und Rasse,* and his 1515 engraving *Knight, Death and Devil,* adorned with swastika, was a best-selling Nazi propaganda poster. The engraving became the very symbol of the Volkish hero when Hubert Lanzinger transformed it into an image of Hitler himself (*Der Bannerträger,* 1938). The archetype of German aesthetic culture was fused with the architect of Germany's Final Solution.[76]

Elegy and Ethics

If Dürer's Christological self-portraits now stand implicated in mass suffering and murder, how might we see Bak's merger of his own self-portrait with a crucified Jewish Christ-child in *Elegy III* who represents one million of those victims? Have the tables of blame now simply been turned? Or is something more complicated taking place? Is Dürer's self-absorbed angel now a subpoenaed witness? And do those of us who have inherited this Western, Christian, Enlightenment legacy also stand in that role? Will the angel ever be able to bring herself to look upon the boy, to be confronted with the ruinous, concrete, consequences of a history of contempt toward Jews? Will she ever move beyond her melancholic preoccupation with herself to mourn for this child? More to the point, will we?

If Dürer could so completely identify with Christ, with so little remainder, what then do we make of Bak's gesture toward excessive representation? Not only do we repeatedly encounter the boy who signifies a million other children, in *Elegy III* we confront the overlay and juxtaposition of photo, rainbow, cross, and angel, a dense concentration of symbols that are continuously reinterpreting each other. On the one hand, each compositional icon is itself a monument to a past event or story that, in turn, points beyond itself: the twentieth-century arrest of a nameless ghetto child who has come to represent the million child martyrs of the Shoah; the ancient Hebrew flood story with its reassuring rainbow projecting a promise of divine forbearance into the ever after *but whose ark saved no children;* the first-century crucifixion of a Jew who has, in Christian tradition, been made to suffer for the sins of the world; the sixteenth-century anti-Semitism and Christian supercessionism of German Renaissance and Humanistic culture that sowed the seeds for Nazism and the Final Solution.[77] Juxtaposed to one another, the icons crowd the canvas and contest the viewer's interpretive ability to formulate easily a stable, coherent, statement from the parts. It is as if, in photographic terms, we were looking at a double- or triple-exposure: a canvas saturated with fragments communicating too much history, too many harrowing thoughts, too many disturbing cultural and religious prejudices, too much autobiographical significance.[78] As viewers we are overwhelmed with the plenitude of meanings, the many questions left unanswered, the enormity of the suffering of so many children, Bak's impossible project of a million more such monuments.

In a Baroque-like gesture, Bak gives us not "a systematic whole, but"—to borrow the words of Robert Gibbs—"a calculated construction of junk[79] in order to dislodge both present and past, in order to set the present under the sign of loss...."[80] This excessive pile of broken and juxtaposed images, this series of impossible memorials, becomes a sign of *veri-diction.* But what truth does Bak confront us with? The truth-telling here is that the gratuitous, absurd sufferings and deaths of a million children were, and will forever remain, pointless. This suffering cannot be fully represented; it cannot be repaired; it can never be made to be meaningful.

To put it in ethical terms, Bak presents in pictures what Emmanuel Levinas has argued in words: Theodicy in whatever guise—"edifying discourse," "preachment," or "narrative"—is "the source of all immorality."[81] There is a perpetual "disproportion between suffering and... theodicy;"[82] consequently, all explanations of suffering do further violence to those who actually suffer.[83]

This puts into question the ways in which Jews and Christians have understood suffering to play a meaningful part in the "drama of Sacred History." In particular Christians who want to read Jesus' death as a meaningful sacrifice of personal significance to them as individuals, have, in effect, imposed their own self-portraits onto the gospel stories and done further violence to the figure of Jesus. In the words of Thomas Hanna, "[W]hen Christians, viewing this event, accept it as a sacrifice—that is, when they accept it as right and necessary—they have denied the one undeniable truth in this event which is that it is horrible and unjust that an innocent man should be killed."[84] Such Christian attitude toward death "transcends and minimizes the abiding reality of human suffering"[85] by attributing to it metaphysical and theological meaning. A totalizing gesture that turns a tortured victim into a universal Christ who suffers to redeem a universal humanity effectively erases the real faces and obscures the real suffering of all concerned—particularly the children who rarely have a place in these grand theological schemes of sin and salvation except as their victims.

Bak's monuments, raked up from the ruins, historicize death with the re-membered faces of real children.[86] The fragmented images and images of fragments interrupt us, question us, impede our view of more peaceful horizons—coherent theodicies, systematic theologies, religious self-understandings, sensible salvation histories.[87] If a million murdered children disrupt our view of the past, should they not also disrupt our present? Do they not also expose our multiple cultural complicities in the suffering of children now? Bak invites us to do the difficult work of remembering real, historical children "in order to be criticized, to reopen the past in a way that can reopen the present—for the sake of the future."[88] For the sake of the children.[89] Looking backward and forward, these "calculated constructions of junk," these impossible memorials, place all of Sacred History under the sign of lost children, and ask us, to what ends will we remember?

---

1 Fackenheim, *The Jewish Bible After the Holocaust: A Re-reading* (Manchester: Manchester University Press, 1990), 17. His book is dedicated "To the children—ours and all the others."

2 See Danna Nolan Fewell, *The Children of Israel: Reading the Bible for the Sake of Our Children* (Nashville: Abingdon Press, 2003) for a sober, statistical accounting of war- and health-related child suffering.

3 Levinas, "Useless Suffering," *Entre Nous: On-Thinking-of-the-Other,* trans. Michael B. Smith and Barbara Harshav (New York: Columbia University Press, 1998), 91-101; 99.

4 "Genesis, Genocide, and the Art of Samuel Bak: 'Unseamly' Reading after the Holocaust," in this volume.

5 See Richard Raskin, *A Child at Gunpoint. A Case Study on the Life of a Photo* (Aarhus, Denmark: Aarhus University Press, 2004). Raskin includes an interview with Bak and a selection of his photo-related compositions.

6 In the Stroop Report the photo carried the caption "Pulled from the bunkers by force."

7 "The Ghetto Boy," *Between Worlds: The Paintings and Drawings of Samuel Bak from 1946 to 2001,* ed. Irene Tayler (Boston: Pucker Art Publications, 2002), 297. The crucifixion, of course, has not been an uncommon symbol of Jewish suffering in either Jewish art or theological reflection. Two of the most well-known artistic images are Marc Chagall's *White Crucifixion* and *The Martyr.* Literary examples are Eli Wiesel's memoir *Night* and Chaim Potok's novel *My Name is Asher Lev.* As the image of suffering *par excellence,* the crucifixion was used in Jewish art prior to WWII as an expression of the Jewish experience of martyrdom that connected itself to Christianity in a gesture of alliance and (a plea for) cultural truce. The magnitude of the Holocaust, however, creates an unprecedented crisis in artistic representation, raising the question of whether any religious archetypes could ever address such atrocity. See David Roskies, *Against the Apocalypse. Response to Catastrophe in Modern Jewish Literature* (Cambridge, MA: Harvard University Press, 1984); Karl Plank, "Broken Continuities: Night and White Crucifixion" (http://www.religion-online.org/showarticle.asp?title=1069).

8 Raskin, 150.

9 Bak, *Between Worlds,* 297.

10 Raskin, 152.

11 Bak, *Between Worlds,* 297.

12 See Bak's discussion of his response to the banalization of the photo in Raskin, 151-52. On the image as commodified object, see Abigail Solomon-Godeau, "Living with contradictions. Critical practices in the age of supply-side aesthetics," *The Critical image. Essays on contemporary Photography,* ed. Carol Squiers (Seattle: Bay Press, 1990), 59-79. See Walter Benjamin's *The Work of Art in the Age of Mechanical Reproduction:* "In photography, exhibition value begins to replace cult value all along the line. But cult value does not give way without resistance...." Source: UCLA School of Theater, Film and Television; Transcriber: Andy Blunden, 1998; proofed and corrected Feb. 2005. (http://www.marxists.org/reference/subject/philosophy/works/ge/benjamin.htm).

13 In addition to *Elegy III,* other Bak canvases that feature the Warsaw ghetto boy include *Study A* (1995), *Study B* (1995), *Study F* (1995), *Study I* (1995), *Study J* (1995), *Self-Portrait* (1995-96), *Exits* (1997), *Group* (1997), *Little Green Trees* (1997), *For Josée* (1997), *Absence* (1997), *In His Own Image* (1997), *In the Footsteps* (1995), *Messenger* (1997), *Into the Trees* (1997), *The Star of Vilna* (1997), *Double Reflection* (1997), *Small Target* (1997), *Sanctuary* (1997), and *Children's Corner* (1997).

14 See James Young's discussion of monuments in *The Texture of Meaning: Holocaust Memorials and Meaning* (New Haven: Yale University Press, 1993), 1-15.

15 See Bak's comments on his style of painting that creates a certain ironic distance: "I believe that the presence of irony enriches my art. It is to be found in my choice of a style of painting, my use of an 'old-masters' technique as a device for creating distance while retaining specificity. If my paintings seem to evoke a certain kind of surrealism, it is not true surrealism" (Raskin, 154).

16 Raskin, 154.

17 Franz Rosenzweig might well identify this reductive effort with philosophy's fascination with the All, or Totality, which he correlates with the ultimate denial of death. See *The Star of Redemption,* trans. Barbara E. Galli (Madison: University of Wisconsin Press, 2005), 10-11.

18 Raskin, 154.

19 See Young's discussion of "counter monuments" and his discussion of post-Holocaust memorials that require different forms of viewer interaction to advance the "memory work." In particular, the "negative form" monument to Aschrott-Brunnen in Kassel and the "Harburg Monument against Fascism" both employ the concept of disappearance to intensify the shift of memory responsibility from the memorial to the viewer (27-49).

20 Raskin, 153.

21 Young, 15.

22 The allusion to the Nazi theft of Jewish artwork surfaces here. See Bak's comments on his relationship to Dürer in "Dürer and I" in *Between Worlds,* 271-72.

23 Joseph Leo Koerner, *The Moment of Self-Portraiture in German Renaissance Art* (Chicago/London: University of Chicago Press, 1993), 27. Erwin Panofsky describes Dürer's 1484 *Self-Portrait* as "the first independent self-portrait ever produced" (*Albrecht Dürer* [Princeton: Princeton University Press, 1943-48], I:42). Koerner is much more circumspect methodologically and hermeneutically about attribution of "epoch-making significance."

24 Koerner, 45.

25 This was the argument of Johannes Butzbach (1478-1526) in his work, the *Book of Famous Painters* (1505), a chronicle of great artists from antiquity to his day. Cited in Koerner, 125.

26 "God," Dürer writes early in his career, "is honored when it appears that He has given such insight to a creature in whom such art resides." Quoted in Panofsky, I:43.

27 Panofsky, I:43.

28 Panofsky, I:171; cf. Koerner, 27. On the question of Panofsky's self-projection into Dürer's work see Keith Moxley, "Impossible Distance: Past and Present in the Study of Dürer and Grunewalds," *The Art Bulletin,* 86.4, Dec, 2004. Moxley finds in Panofsky a complex displacement of his own tensions back upon Dürer. The conflict between tradition and theory in Dürer's art is analogous to the clash of ideologies in Panofsky's own day. Dürer's inability to reconcile theory and mimesis, characterized by Panofsky as a failure, may be regarded as a metaphor of the art historian's own alienation from German culture, and Dürer's defeat at the hands of tradition as a symbol of the root of Enlightenment values in Nazi Germany.

29 According to Panofsky, the contrast "typifies the artist of the Renaissance who respects practical skill, but longs all the more fervently for mathematical theory—who feels inspired by celestial influences and eternal ideas, but suffers all the more deeply from his human frailty and intellectual finiteness" (I:171). In Dürer's day, great artists were thought to create their works in alternating fits of divine frenzy and despondency (Koerner, 26; Moxley, 74). Yet, the angel in *Melencolia I* seems overcome with anxiety: melancholy as genius is disabled by the impossibility of what in theory it aspires to.

30 Koerner, 27.

31 Koerner, 23.

32 W. David Shaw, *Elegy and Paradox. Testing the Conventions* (Baltimore: Johns Hopkins University Press, 1994), 218. On this point he quotes Freud ("Mourning and Melancholia" in *General Psychological Theory,* ed. Philip Rieff [New York: Collier, 1963], 170):

> First there existed an object choice, the libido had attached itself to a certain person; then, owing to a real injury or disappointment concerned with the loved person, this object relationship was undermined. The result is not the normal one of withdrawal of the libido from this object and transference of it to some new one....The object cathexis proved to have too little power of resistance and was abandoned; but the free libido was withdrawn with the ego and not directed at another object. It did not find application there, however, . . . but served simply to establish an identification of the ego with the abandoned object.

Julia Kristeva (*Black Sun: Depression and Melancholia* [New York: Columbia University Press, 1989], 53) links these psychological states to the nature of language. All signs and symbols are structured by a fundamental loss. We are moved to communicate as a result of loss or lack. Only separation from the object allows one to name it, to mourn its loss. Without acknowledgment of loss there is no separation, without separation "melancholy people are foreigners in their own maternal tongue....The dead language they speak ....conceals a thing buried alive." Cited in Shaw, 218.

33 Bak's insistence upon attending to the reality and not spiritualizing (our word) the experience of the dead boy is a challenge to those who would wax philosophical, theological, or theodical about the "ultimate" meaning what stands before us. Such metaphysical and theological moves are ultimately dangerous. "Why did all of this happen?" asks Bak. "If we start to reflect on ultimate meanings, our endless questioning may depart into the infinite and endanger our passion for life and block our creativity" (Raskin, 152).

34 In a similar fashion at the opening of the death camps by Allied forces, local Nazi sympathizers and supporters were forced to help with the removal of bodies and were thus compelled to confront the horror.

35 On the relationship of Dürer's melancholic to the birth of tragic drama, see Walter Benjamin, *The Origin of German Tragic Drama,* trans. John Osborne (London: NLB, 1977): "Mourning is the state of mind in which feeling revives the empty worlds in the form of a mask, and derives an enigmatic satisfaction in contemplating it. Every feeling is bound to an a priori object, and the representation of this object is its phenomenology" (139). The laws governing *Trauerspiel* are to be found in part in the heart of mourning.

Speaking of the Baroque era, Benjamin writes "[Even from the heritage of the Renaissance did this age derive material which could only deepen contemplative paralysis. It is only one step from stoic *[apatheia]* to mourning, but of course a step which only becomes possible in Christianity." Further, "The deadening of the emotions, and the ebbing away of the waves of life which are the sources of these emotions in the body, can increase the distance between the self and the surrounding world to the point of alienation from the body.... In the proximity of Albrecht Dürer's figure, *Melancholia*, the utensils of active life are lying around unused on the floor, as objects of contemplation. This engraving anticipates the baroque in many respects. In it the knowledge of the introvert and the investigations of the scholar have merged as intimately as in the men of the baroque" (140).

36 Shaw, 8.

37 Shaw, 246-47.

38 Shaw, 9.

39 Cf. Hélène Cixous's description of writing in *"Coming to Writing" and Other Essays,* ed. Deborah Jenson; trans. Sarah Cornell *et al* (Cambridge: Harvard University Press, 1991), 2-3.

40 Shaw's comment upon Yeats's "In Memory of Major Robert Gregory" (148).

41 Shaw contends that in an age of extermination camps, atomic bombs, and other atrocities, "a divided or broken consciousness becomes a mark of 'truth-saying'" (178). Modern elegy is a performance of the inexpressible, characterized by breaks and discontinuities. Or in the words of T.S. Eliot, "Between the idea/And the reality/...Falls the Shadow" ("The Hollow Men," V. 5-6, 9). As Shaw writes,

> The slight impediments to speech become more pronounced and audible. They become open sites of fracture and breakdown. Instead of being interpreted as mere restraints, as meanings half said or intimated, these breaking points dramatize the way a tactical stumble or ellipsis may turn the breakdown of language, a potential awkwardness or stammer, into a moment of breakthrough instead. Breakup itself becomes a sign of *veridiction*...(Shaw, 147; our emphasis).

42 In the tradition of *Imitatio Christi,* usually associated with the passion of Christ.

43 Koerner, 39, emphasis ours. Influenced strongly by the theological writings of Nicholas of Cusa (1401-1464) who had suggested that the individual was a self-portrait of God, Dürer's painting is at once the replication of the artist's body, an emblem of the artist's pious imitation of Christ, a reflection of Christ's physical appearance in an idealized portrait of Dürer, and an illustration of human making participating in divine creation. This act and artifact of mimesis celebrates the power of the human ability to make and to form; the (human) self is identified with the (divine) capacity to produce. In the thought of Nicholas of Cusa, such a "play of likeness becomes finally a spectacle God stages to behold himself" (Koerner, 133).

44 St. Veronica is variously associated in the Western Church with the niece of Herod the Great, the woman with the twelve-year flow of blood in Mark 5:25, the woman who gets healed by touching the hem of Jesus's cloak (*The Acts of Pilate* [4th c.]), and with a woman who suffered martyrdom at Antioch. In an eigth-century manuscript Veronica is said to have painted or caused to have painted a portrait of Christ after she had been healed by him (http:/en.wikipedia.org/wild/Saint_Veronica).

45 This event marks the sixth station in the 14 stations of the cross. His image, miraculously and permanently preserved on her handkerchief (in an alternative tradition it is her veil), was considered to be a perfect likeness, a "true icon," of the face of Christ. This *vera icon* lends the saint her name, "Veronica" (the very word itself an amalgam of Greek and Latin), and becomes the most sacred relic in Western Christendom (Koerner, 82-83).

46 The *Sudarium* has its parallel in the Eastern Church with the tradition of the *mandylion,* (Arabic: "veil"; Latin "towel" or "napkin"). In this sixth-century legend King Abgar of Edessa seeks out Jesus the healer to cure him, promising to become his follower. Christ hears this, praises him for having faith without visual evidence, and sends a likeness of himself produced miraculously on a cloth. Abgar is cured. The mandylion had a history of being kept in Edessa and Constantinople. See Koerner, 83.

47 Butzbach, the *Book of Famous Painters.* Cited in Koerner, 125.

48 *Acheiropoeitos* or *non manufactum,* producing an image "not made with human hands." The concept evokes the claim of Jesus in Mark 14:58 that he will tear down the temple made with human hands and rebuild it himself *acheiropoeton,* "not with human hands." Cf. also Acts 7:48; 17:24; 2 Cor 5:1.

49 As Nicolas of Cusa (1401-1464) would write of the omnivoyance of God in *De visione Dei,* "O Lord, Your seeing is loving; and just as Your gaze regards me so attentively that it never turns away from me, so neither does Your love" (cited in Koerner, 127).

50 One eye appears to be omnivoyant while the other gazes past the viewer, a sign perhaps of the tension between the desire for both a perfect image and a historically credible one.

51 See Koerner, 128 on the issue of Dürer's signature. The monogram on the 1500 *Self-Portrait* reads: "Thus I, Albrecht Dürer of Nuremburg, painted myself with indelible colors at the age of 28 years" (Koerner, 183). Dürer's signature appears to float transcendently in the air beside his face.

52 Becoming, as it were, *alter deus,* another god. Hence, the carefully constructed boundary between human and god is threatened, in part, paradoxically, by a theology and devotional piety legitimating his art (Koerner, 99; 138).

Paradoxically, Dürer's preoccupation with "perfect representation" leaves him less than content with the mythical and mystical attributes of the *vera icon.* His concern for mimetic accuracy and historical realism lead him to follow in the footsteps of Dutch artist Johannes Van Eyck who had already begun to model Christ less in terms of the *vera icon* and more in terms of its prototype, the historical Jesus. Van Eyck, wanting to emphasize Christ as a specific, flesh-and-blood person to be encountered in the present, unmediated by any "timeless" image, had in a 1440 painting chosen portrait over icon, thereby transforming the *"Holy Face."* Not only does he present the holy face in perfect proportions just as he might have been concerned to do if painting a sitting model, he edges the image with a realistic frame, signing and dating it as if on January 1, 1438 he had finally completed Christ's portrait. While he, too, was concerned with *acheiropoetos,* using the frame to conceal the manual application of paint and producing the illusion that the image was made without human hands, he nevertheless celebrates the materiality of his subject, presenting Jesus as a living, historically credible person (Koerner, 105). In the 1500 *Self-Portrait* Dürer carries Van Eyck's innovation one step further by not only invoking the vera icon and its Eyckian revision as historical portrait, but also projecting his own person into the painting.

In order to capture Van Eyck's concern for a historically grounded likeness of Jesus, Dürer availed himself of a popular understanding of the historical Jesus's appearance. A letter purported to be by a Publius Lentulus, supposedly a proconsul of Judea who preceded Pontias Pilate, offered a physical description of the historical Christ. Though in actuality a product of fourteenth-century monastic culture, the letter *(Epistula Lentuli)* was believed by many, Dürer included, to be authentic. It was even cited in a papal bull by Innocent IV in 1454. The depiction of Jesus contained in the letter set the standards of Christ's physiology for artists of Dürer's day:

> His hair [is] the color of ripe hazel-nut. It falls straight almost to the level of his ears; from there down it curls thickly and is rather more luxuriant, and this hangs down to his shoulders. In front his hair is parted into two, with the parting in the center in the Nazarene manner. His forehead is wide, smooth and serene, and his face is without wrinkles or any marks. It is graced by a slightly reddish tinge, a faint color. His nose and mouth are faultless. His beard is thick and like a young man's first beard, of the same color as his hair; it is not particularly long and is parted in the middle. His aspect is simple and mature. His eyes are brilliant, mobile, clear, splendid....He is broad in chest and upstanding....He is the most beautiful among the children of men. (Translation in Michael Baxandall, *Painting and Experience in Fifteenth Century Italy: A Primer in the Social History of Pictoral Style* [Oxford, 1972], 57); cited in Koerner, p 103, FN 71).

In the *Self-Portrait* of 1500, Dürer softens his own features and darkens his hair to accommodate this common impression of Christ as "the most beautiful among the children of men."

53 Koerner writes, "The moment of self-portraiture represents here less Burckhardt's notion of an awakening to or a discovery of self than the self's reinvention within the changing paradigms of religious experience" (137).

54 Although it is worth considering with Fackenheim whether the events of 1933-45, in particular the murder of six million Jews, constitute a *novum* or *caesura* in history that amounts to an apotheosis of the Modern Self that Dürer's work announces. See Fackenheim, 1-26.

55 Koerner, 128.

56 See, in particular, *Self-Portrait* (1995-96).

57 See *Study F* (1995).

58 Levinas would speak of an ethical summoning, the biblical "Here I am," that places an impossible burden of responsibility on the hearer to bear up the suffering of the other. Levinas grounds our moral feet in this world, not out of this world.

59 Ironically, we can also see in Dürer's *Self-Portrait* of 1500 the inability to exclude the outside, namely his painting hand and wandering eye. The "hieratic symmetry and otherworld stasis" (Koerner, 139), proportionality and balance, the "autarky" of the image, its epiphanic quality is unsettled by the right hand which has disappeared from sight; it is the one element of Dürer's body that is not still, but rather busy working. Maker and model, representer and represented, are thus not one and the same. This introduces another instability, a disproportionality between reality and representation.

60 See, in particular, *For Josee* (1997), *Study J* (1995), *Study I* (1995), and *Double Reflection* (1997).

61 Dürer's self-portrait of Christ is interrupted, ironized by Bak's deliberate distortion of the mimetic conceit. Bak's re-presentations thus draw attention to the historical character of mimesis as an artistic expression and invite awareness of the danger that is inherent in failing to recognize the constructed nature of representation. By interrupting the image and the reality, it draws attention to the violence of narcissism. Bak's ironic representation of Dürer's identification of his face with the Christ is the act of mourning that moves and keeps one outside oneself, disrupting any straightforward identification with the Christ.

62 Connecting him explicitly with the subject of the drawing is both his massive monogram and an accompanying autobiographical inscription which reads "These two faces I made in awe (?) during my illness." Koerner writes, "The heavy charcoal lines rendering the sharply lit contours of Christ's face have been invested, through inscription and monogram, with pain and sickness consubstantial with the body that draws them. It is as if, infected with Dürer's disease, the charcoal adheres as much to the picture's author, present in his marks, as to the picture's model, present in his image" (220).

63 Koerner, 183.

64 On a scrap of paper that survives from this period Dürer scribbles:

> Seeing that through the disobedience of sin we have fallen into everlasting death, no help could have reached us except that the son of God became a man, in order that he, through his innocent suffering, might abundantly pay the Father all our guilt, so that the justice of God might be satisfied. For he has repented of and made atonement for the sins of the whole world, and has obtained of the Father everlasting life. Therefore Christ Jesus is the son of God, the highest power, who can do all things and he is eternal life. That person lives, into whom Christ comes; and the person then lives in Christ. Therefore all things are in Christ good things. There is nothing good in us except it becomes good in Christ. Therefore, whoever intends (or claims) to justify himself alone, is not justified. We can intend good, if Christ intends that for us. No human repentance is enough [to atone] for mortal sin. (*Dürer, Schriftlicher Nachlaß*, ed. Hans Ruppercht, Vol. 1 (Berlin: Deutscher Verin für Kunstgeschichte, 1956), 234; cited in David Hotchkiss Price, *Albrecht Dürer's Renaissance, Humanism, Reformation, and the Art of Faith* (Ann Arbor, MI: University of Michigan, 2003), 282.

65 Koerner, 137.

66 From a letter to Hochstraten on Aug 11, 1519. *Opus Epistolarum Des. Erasmi,* ed. P.S. Allen et al. Vol. 1 (Oxford University Press, 1906-58), 4:46 (no. 1006); cited in Price, 169.

67 Price, 169.

68 *The Green Passion* (set of 11 drawings), *The Large Passion* (set of 12 woodcuts and poems, 1511), *The Small Passion* (set of 37 woodcuts and poems, 1511), *The Engraved Passion* (set of 15 engravings, 1512). See Price, 174-76.

69 Dürer commonly includes a Jew deriding Christ (so *Christ Crowned with Thorns* from the *Small Passion*) or a kneeling Jew who spits on Christ. See Price, 178.

70 Price, 181.

71 Price, 181. Although not authored by Dürer himself, the poetic language associated with *Christ before Pilate,* also in *The Large Passion,* is even more venomous:

> Circumcised race, hating God, ungrateful, haughty!
> Shaking your godless necks free of the yoke of him
> Who once led you across the sea and fed you from the heavens.
> Are you ashamed to have him as king and God?
> Do you dare to condemn him to death,
> Race full of deceit, bile, and envy? (Price, 188)

72 Even after all the Nuremberg Jews were expelled Dürer continued to work on the *Small Passion.* The anti-Jewish, hate-filled preface is indicative of the whole work. Ironically the story of the abused Christ employs the abuse of Jews as its means and end. See Price, 176.

73 Jane Campbell Hutchison, *Albrecht Dürer: A Biography* (Princeton: Princeton University Press, 1990), 189.

74 Hutchison (199) describes the *Dürerbund's* various programmatic efforts to promote "cultural purity" by eliminating smut, decadence, and bad taste in the form of traveling exhibitions, promoting German cultural heroes, children's books, communion cards, toys, manuals for bird-watching, sex education, and inexpensive reproductions of *"Meisterbilder"* suitable for framing.

75 Though see Bak's observation that, ironically, Dürer, whose father came from Hungary, was most likely of "impure race" (*Between Worlds,* 272).

76 See Hutchison, 187-206.

77 Franklin Littell's observation captures the significance of Christian contempt in its relation to Jewish mass death: there would have been no "Jewish Problem" if there were not first a "Christian problem." See his *The Crucifixion of the Jews. The Failure of Christians to Understand the Jewish Experience* (Mercer, Ga.: Mercer University Press, 1996).

78 Might this explain, in part, why this is Bak's one attempt to juxtapose photo, crucifixion, and Dürer angel?

79 Compare *Little Green Trees* (1997), *Messenger* (1997), and *Into the Trees* (1997).

80 Robert Gibbs, *Why Ethics? Signs of Responsibilities* (Princeton: Princeton University Press, 2000), 374-75.

81 "Useless Suffering," 99. Derrida memorably characterizes the movement of Levinas's thinking as waves hitting the beach, returning again and again with an ever greater insistence and intensity. This compares to Bak's repeated efforts to image the one million dead children through variation upon variation of the Boy from the Warsaw ghetto photo.

82 Levinas, 97.

83 Representations that purport to "give meaning" to another person's suffering are likewise immoral. Mel Gibson's "The Passion of the Christ" is one such. Themes of Jewish demonic associations, blame for Christ's death, and a Christian militarism intersect Dürer-style in the film.

84 See Thomas L. Hanna, *"Albert Camus and the Christian Faith"* in *Camus. Collection of Critical Essays,* ed. Germain Brée (Englewood Cliffs, NJ.: Prentice Hall, 1962), 48-58; 49-50.

85 Hanna, 50.

86 See, e.g., *Small Target* (1997), *In his Footsteps* (1995), and *Children's Corner* (1997).

87 Cf. Arthur A Cohen's *The Tremendum: A Theological Interpretation of the Holocaust* (New York: Crossroads, 1981), a theological meditation on the inadequacy of post-Holocaust theological language, including the accompanying logic of theodicy. Cohen's concept of "subsension" appropriates and inverts Rudolf Otto's language of the *Mysterium tremendum et fascinans* in an effort to give expression to the rupture that is the Holocaust. Alternative language, thought, and image is required to do justice to the magnitude of useless suffering.

88 See Gibbs, 365. Historiography, when done right "juxtaposes the past and present, not merely to learn something new for the present, but to interrogate my present, and to address my responsibility for the other's suffering from which I have directly benefited" (368).

89 For an example of this memory work see Danna Nolan Fewell, *The Children of Israel: Reading the Bible for the Sake of our Children* (Nashville: Abingdon, 2003).

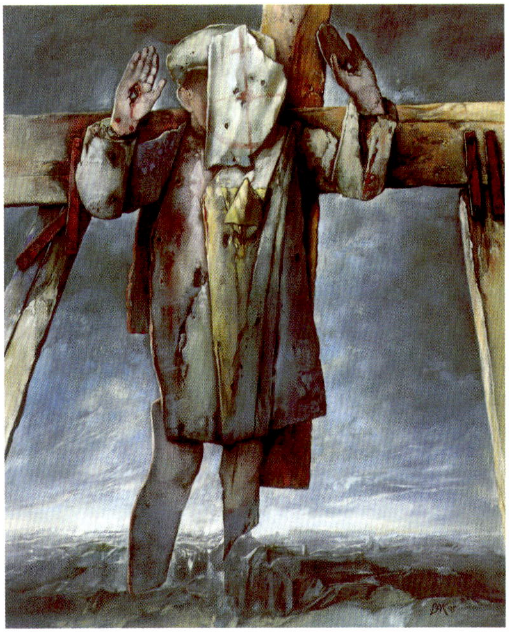

Study B, 1995
Oil on Canvas, 25 5/8 x 21 1/8"

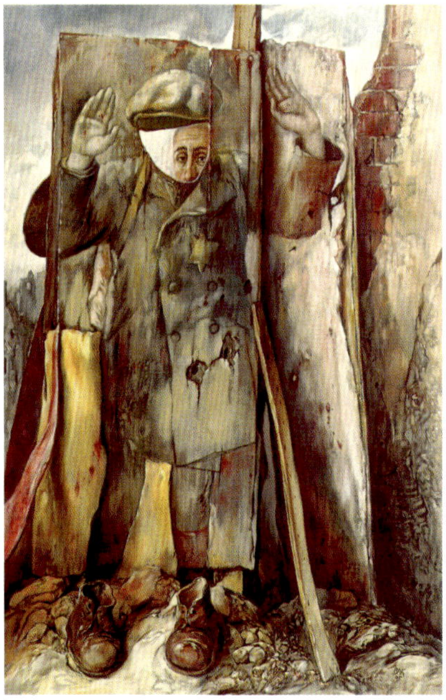

Study F, 1995
Oil on Linen, 23 7/8 x 15 5/8"

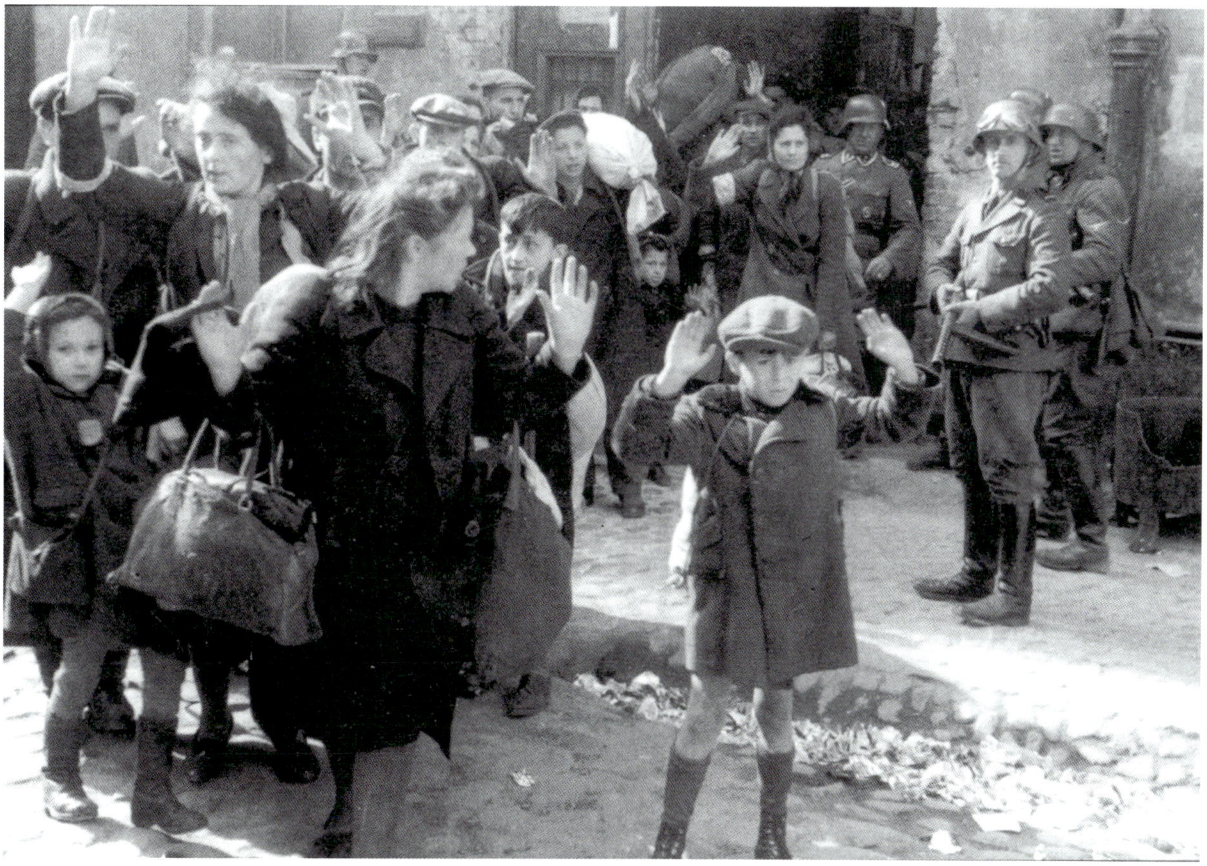

Photograph of the boy from the Warsaw ghetto

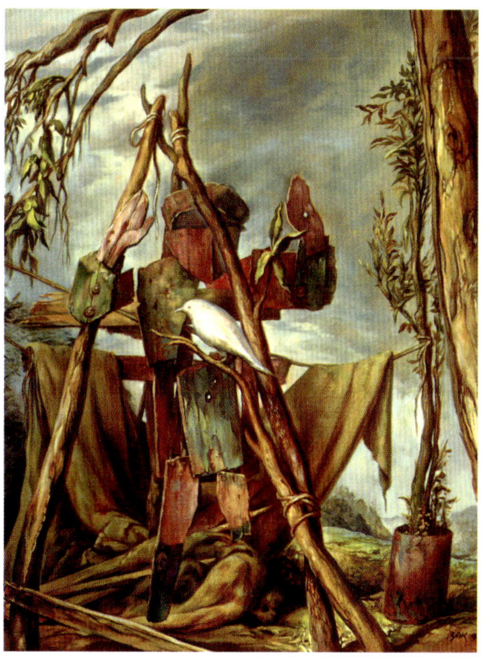

Messenger, 1997
Oil on Linen, 18 1/2 x 15"

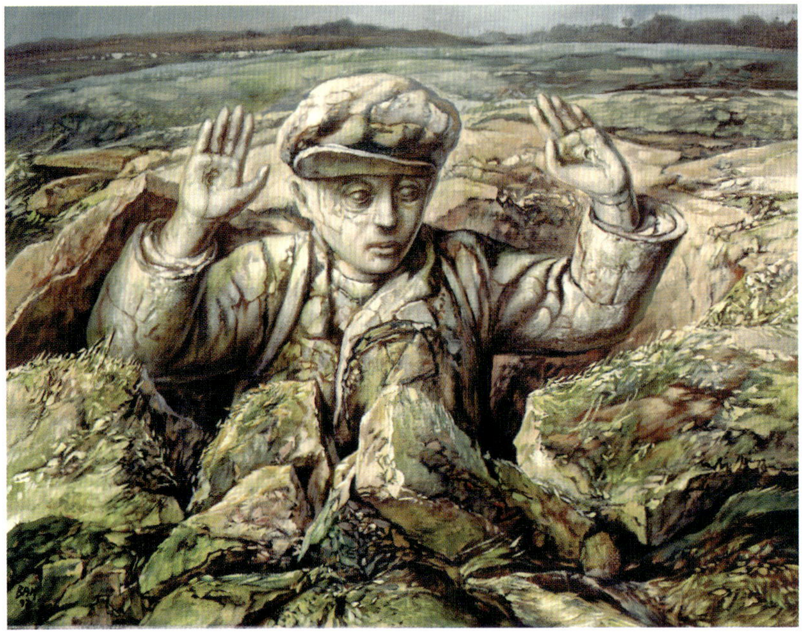

In His Own Image, 1997
Oil on Linen, 11 x 13 3/4"

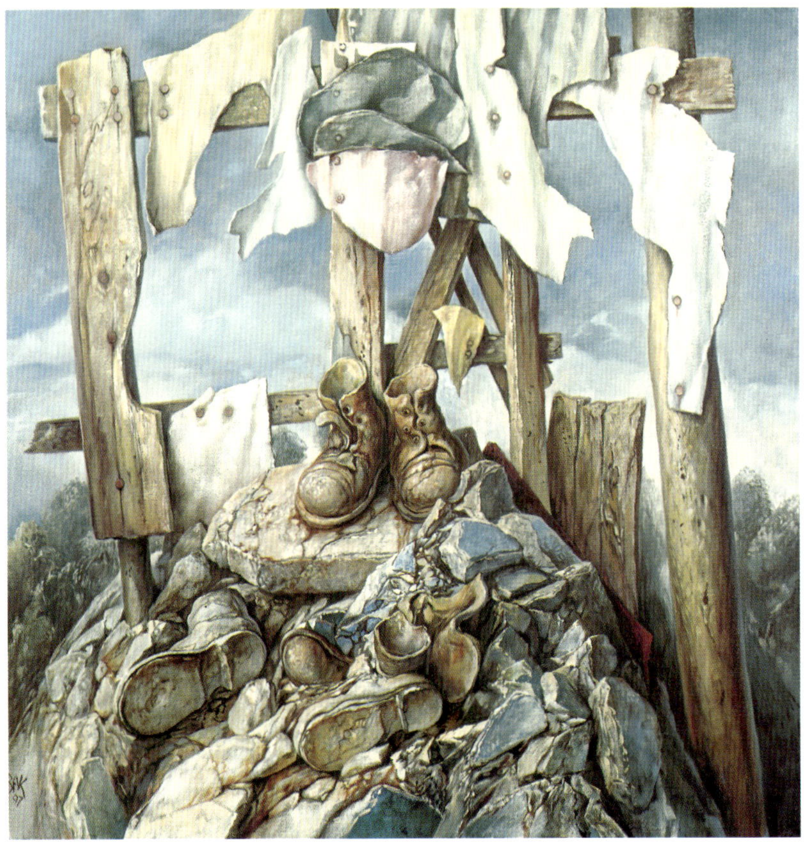

Absence, 1997
Oil on Linen, 20 1/8 x 20"

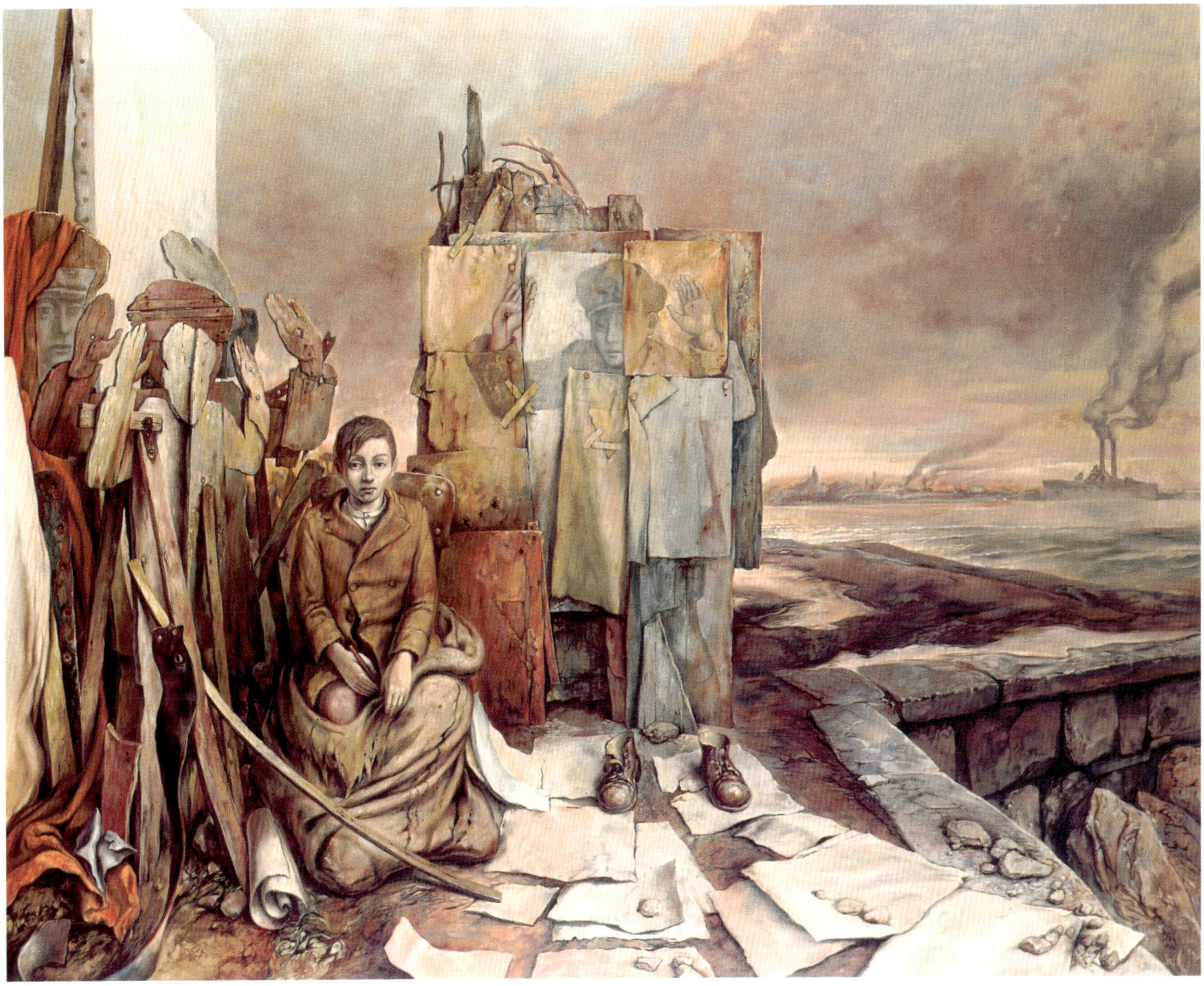

Self-Portrait, 1995
Oil on Canvas, 63 x 78 3/4"

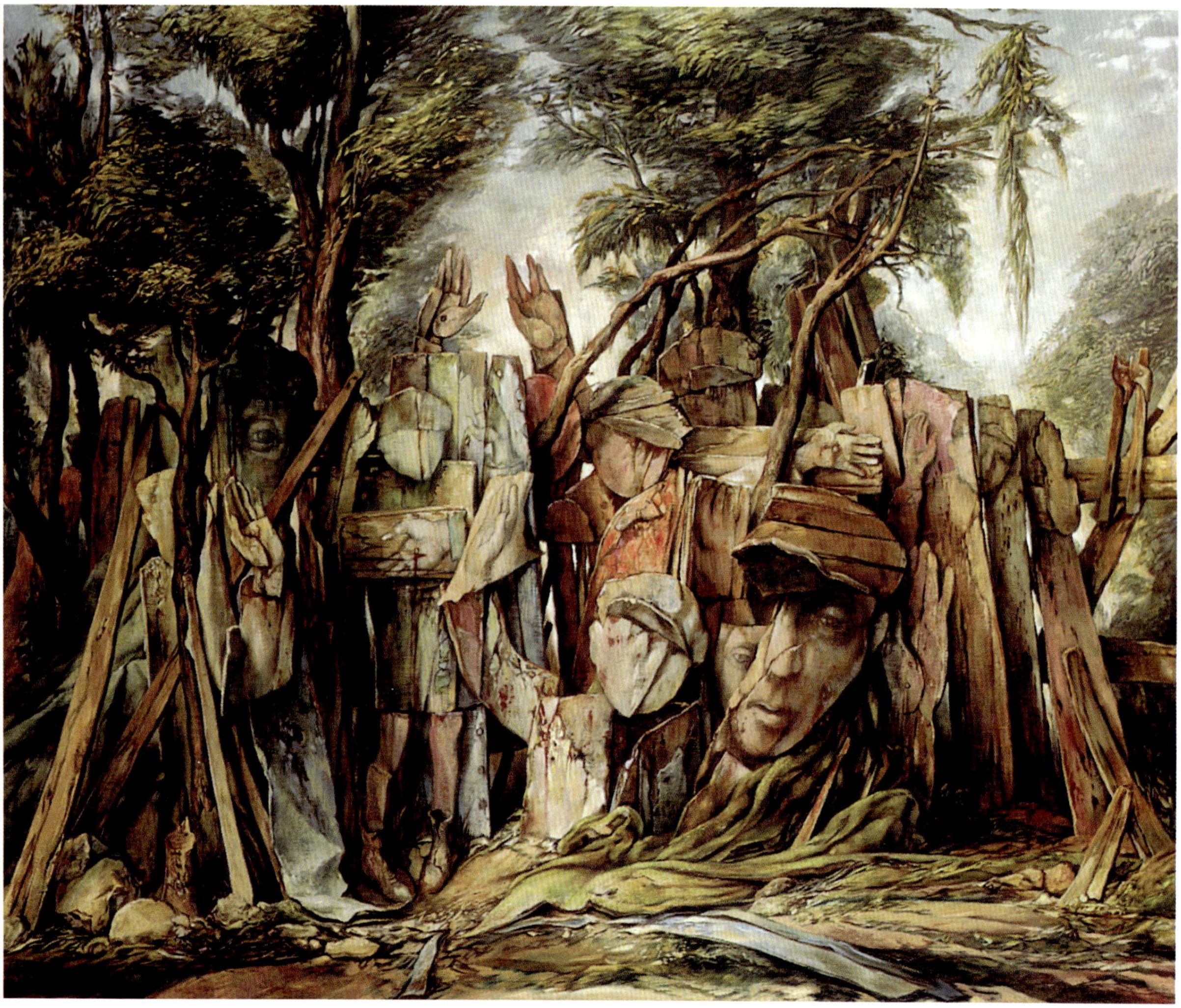

Little Green Trees, 1997
Oil on Linen, 26 x 32 1/2"

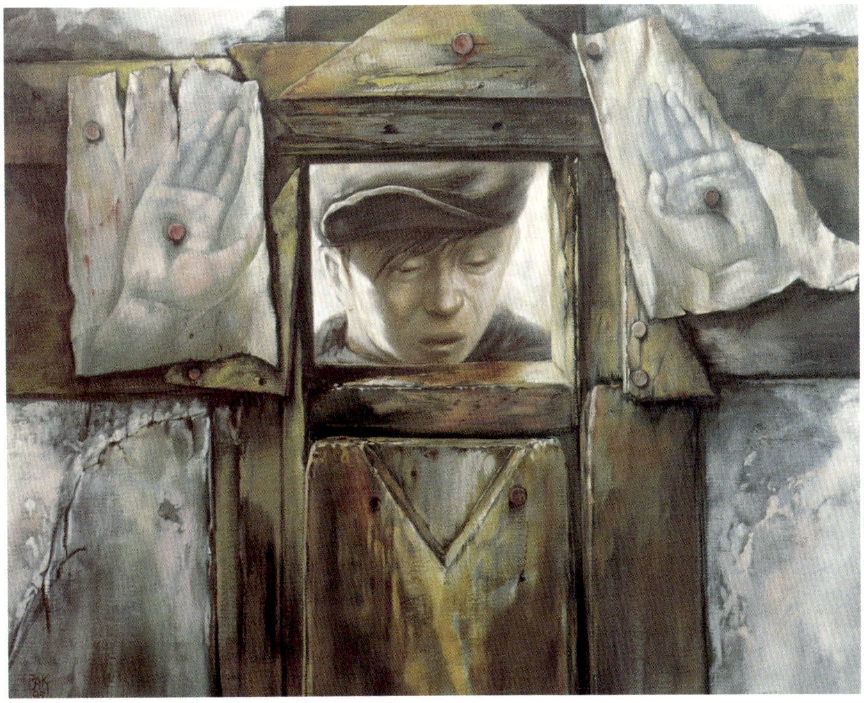

Study I, 1995
Oil on Linen, 18 x 21 3/4"

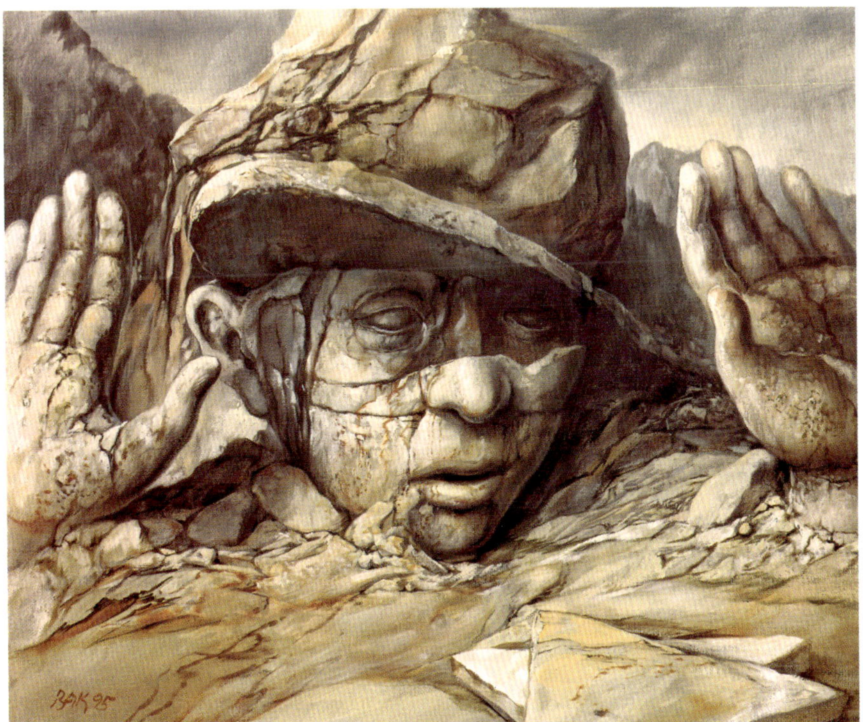

Study J, 1995
Oil on Linen, 13 1/4 x 16"

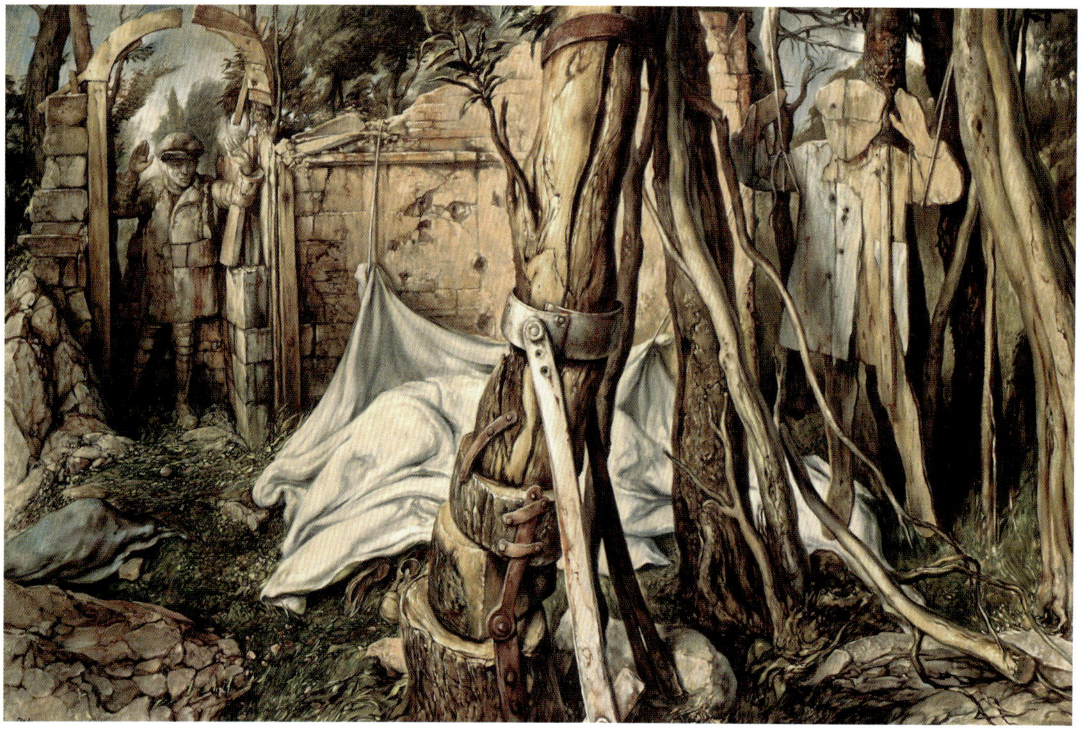

Exits, 1997
Oil on Linen, 26 x 39 1/4"

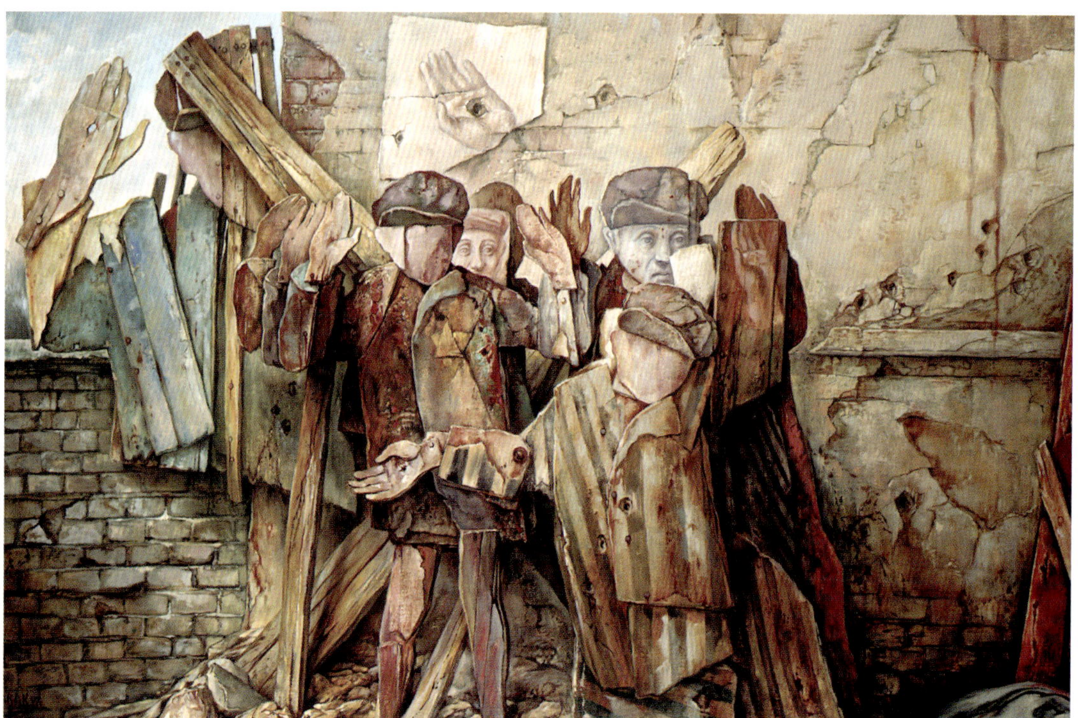

Group, 1997
Oil on Linen, 26 1/4 x 39 1/2"

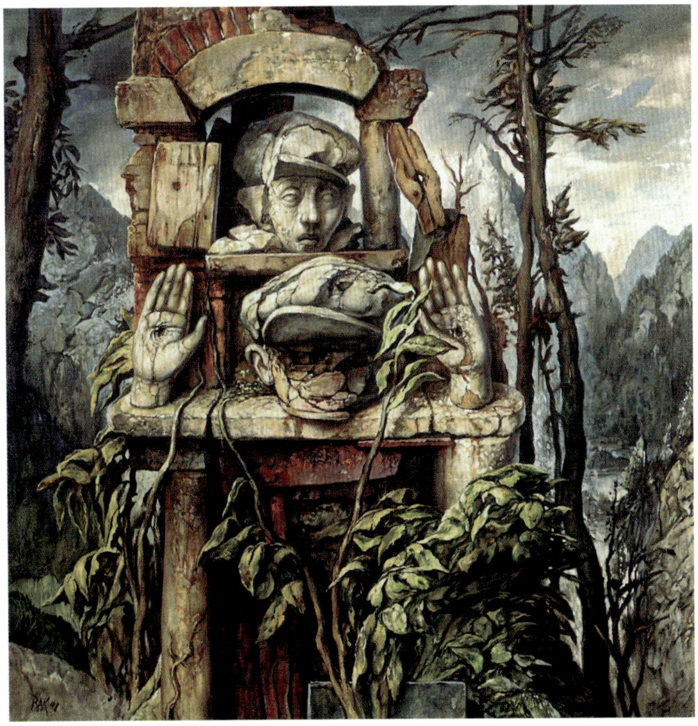

Sanctuary, 1997
Oil on Linen, 20 1/8 x 20"

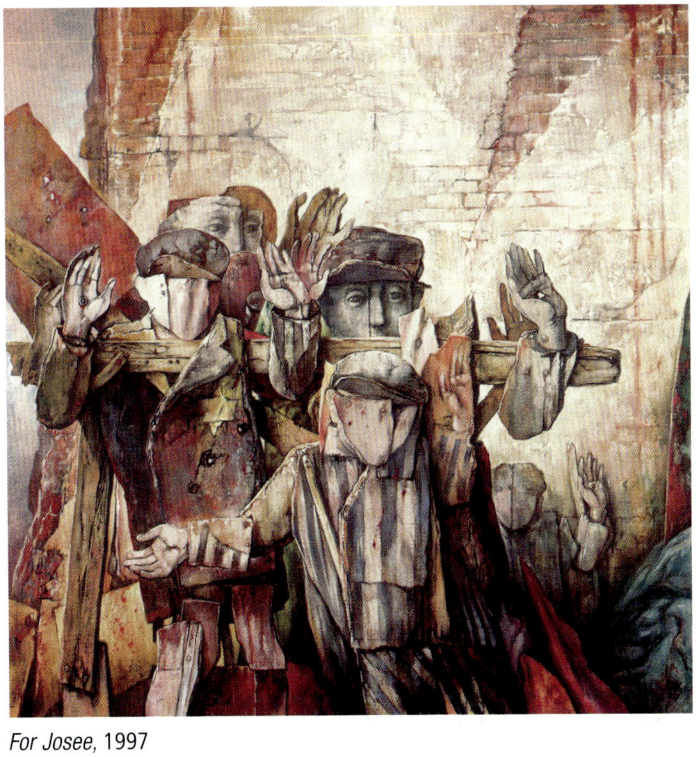

For Josee, 1997
Oil on Linen, 26 1/4 x 26"

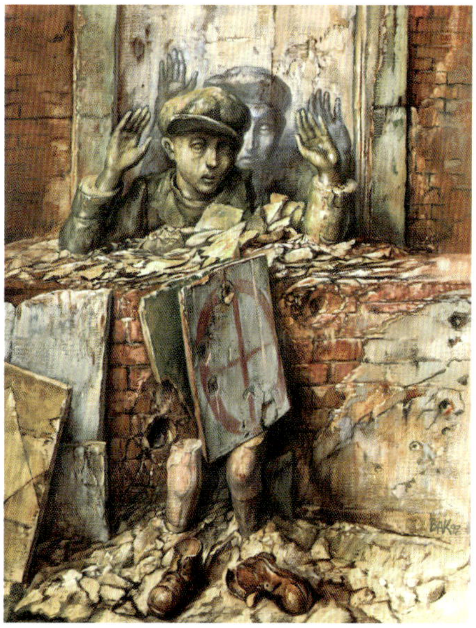

Small Target, 1997
Oil on Linen, 14 x 10 5/8"

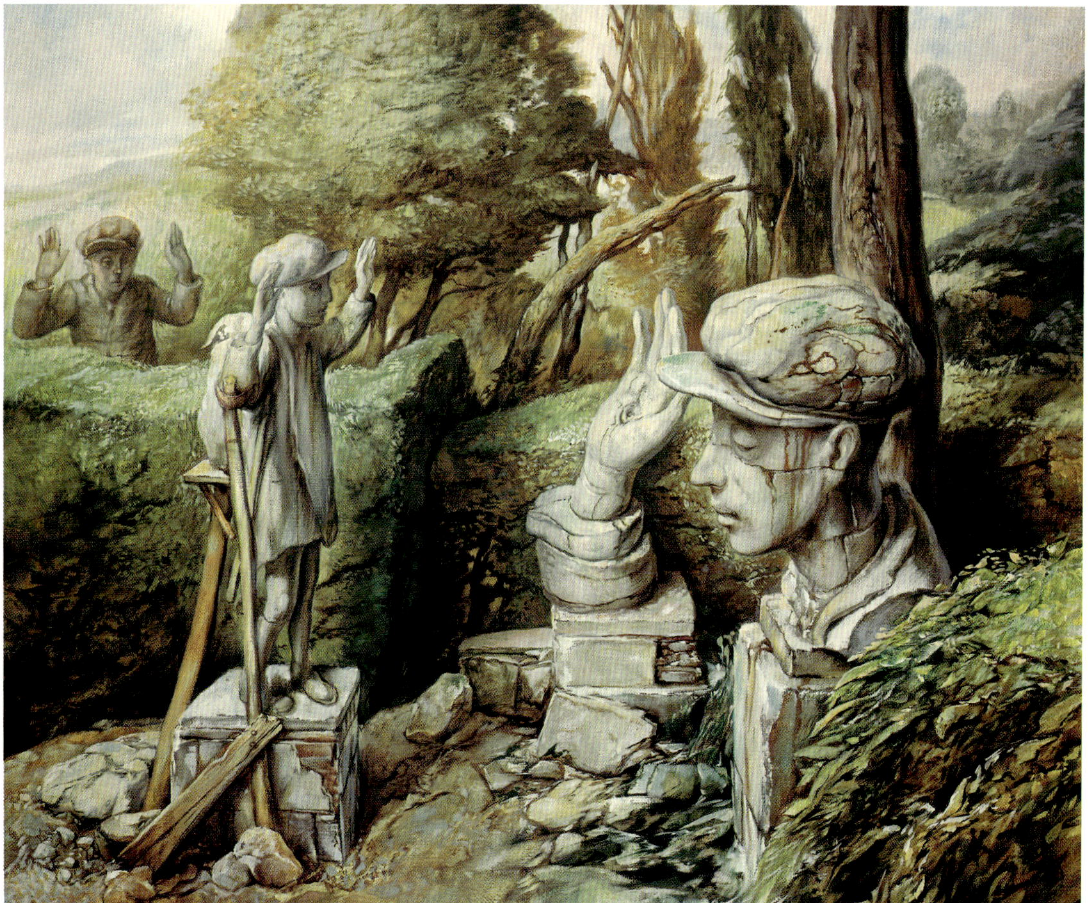

Children's Corner, 1997
Oil on Linen, 15 1/8 x 18"

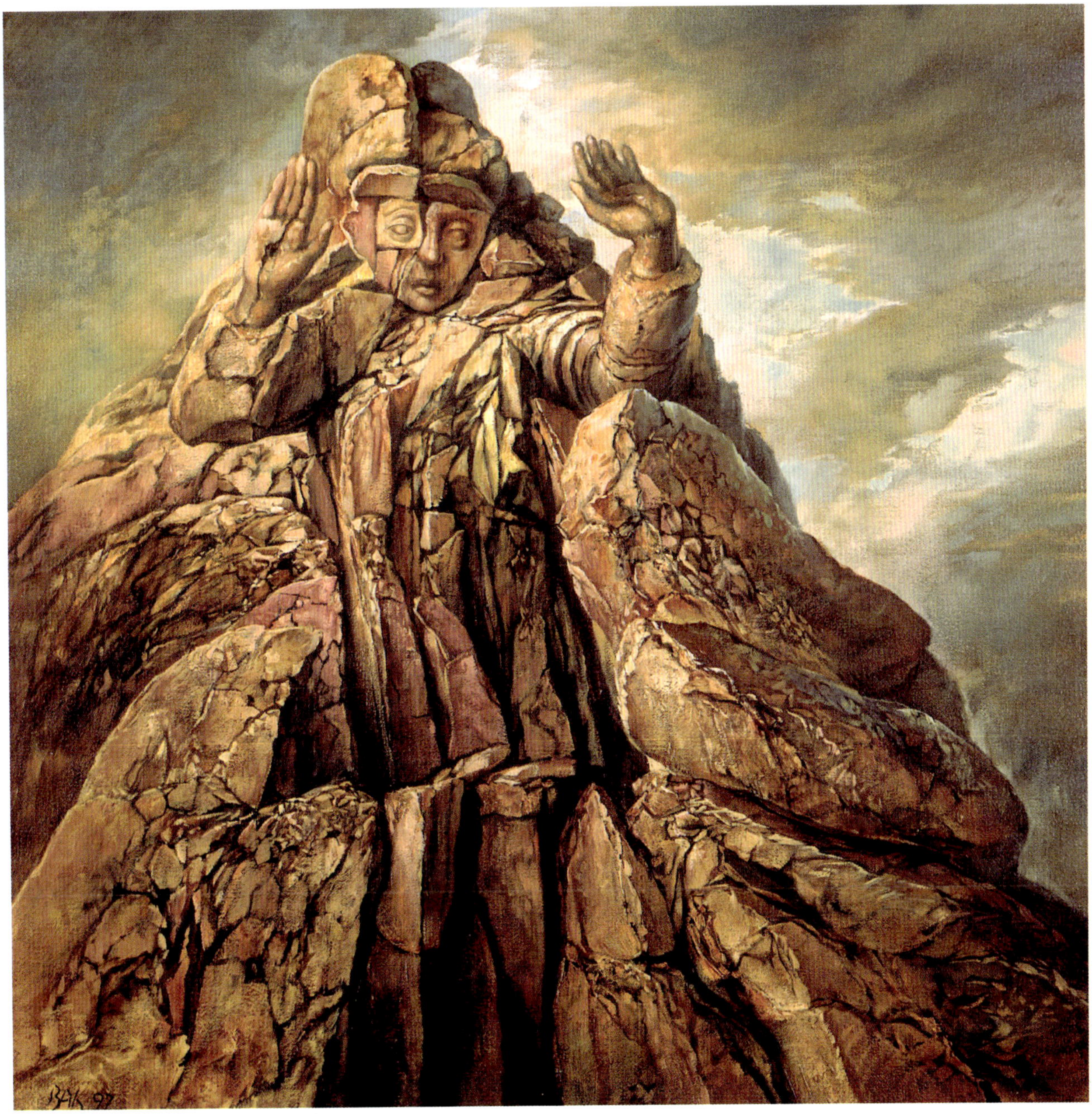

In the Footsteps, 1997
Oil on Linen, 20 1/8 x 20"

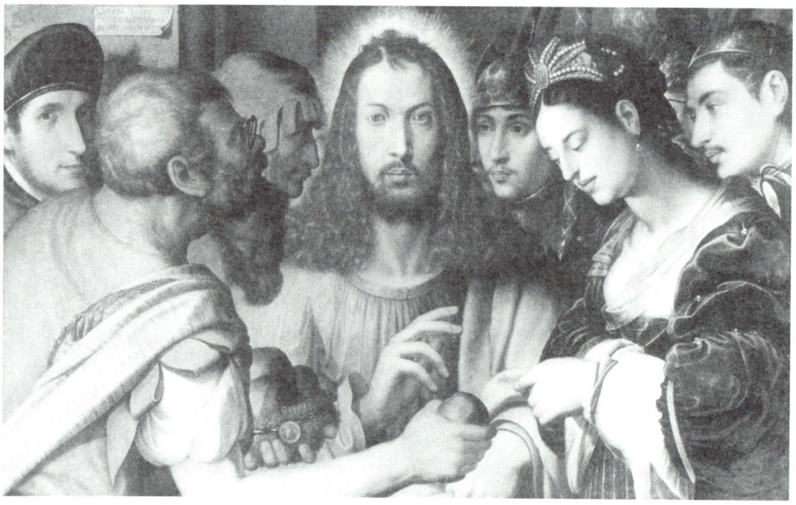

J.G. Vischer
Christ and the Adultress, 1637

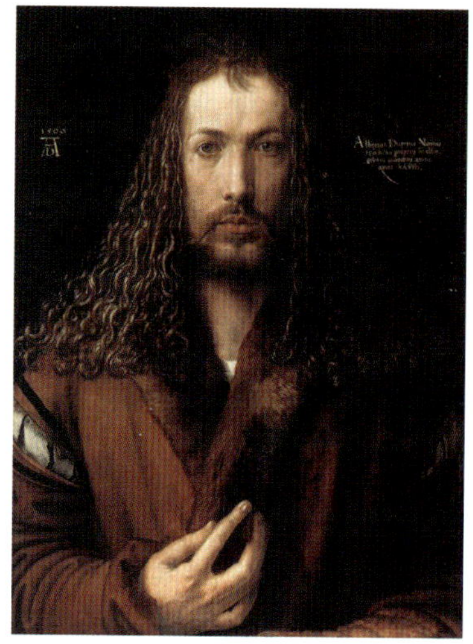

Albrecht Dürer
Self-Portrait, 1500

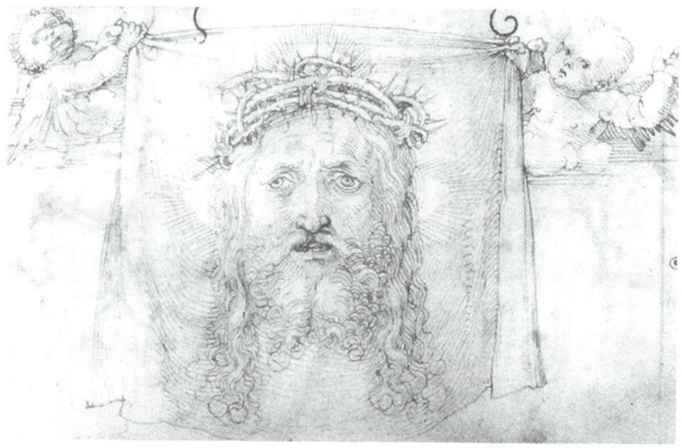

Albrecht Dürer
Sudarium from the *Prayer Book of Maximilian,* 1515

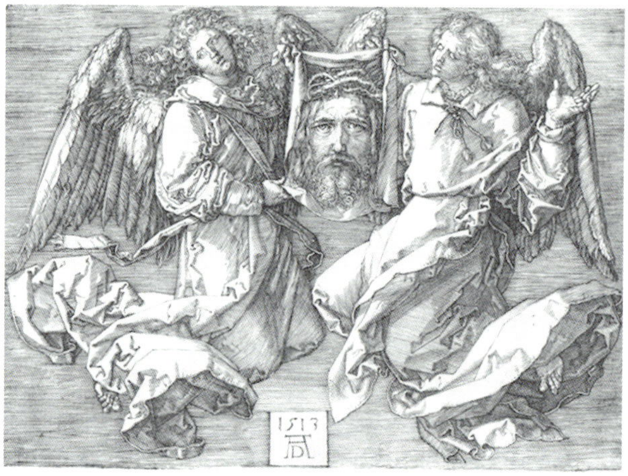

Albrecht Dürer
Sudarium Held by Two Angels, 1513

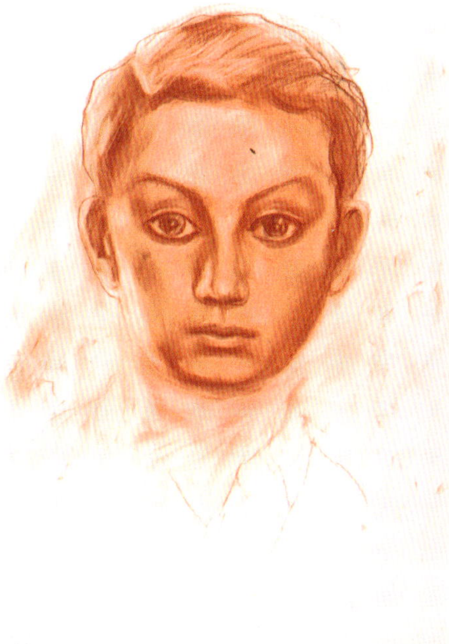

Samuel Bak
Self-Portrait at Thirteen, 1946/47
Red Chalk, 19 3/4 x 15 3/4"

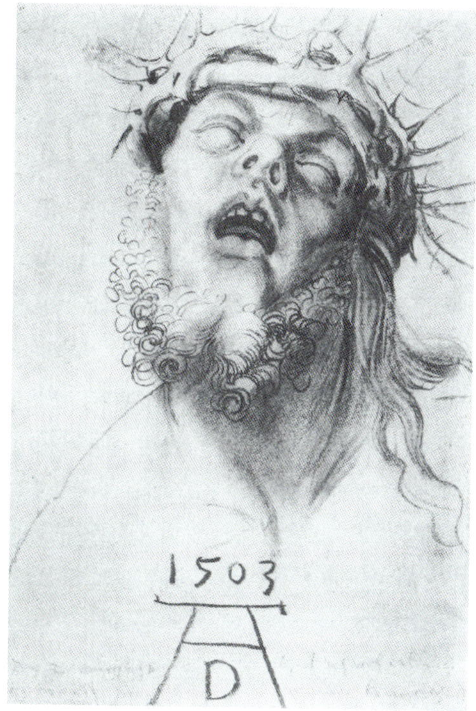

Albrecht Dürer
Head of the Dead Christ, 1503

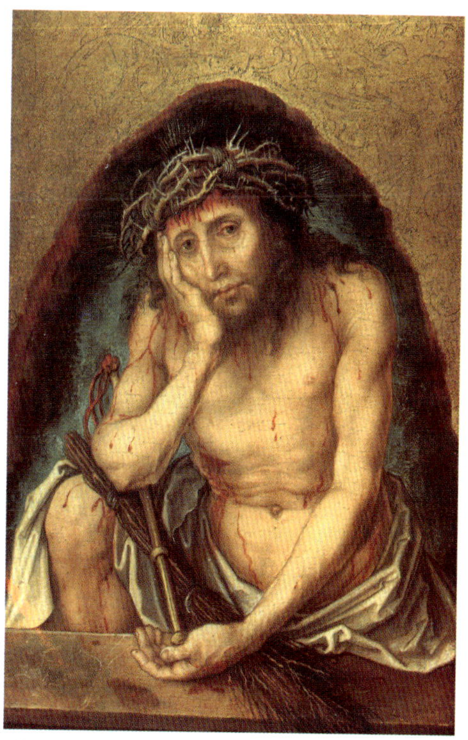

Albrecht Dürer
Christ as Man of Sorrows, ca. 1510

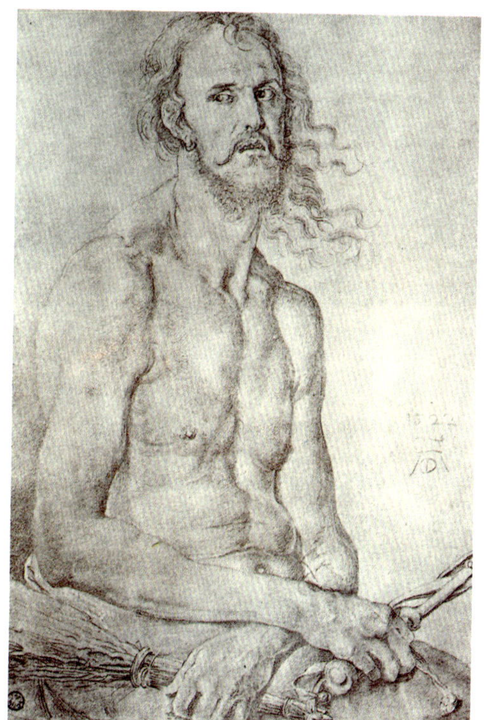

Albrecht Dürer
Self-Portrait as Man of Sorrows, 1522

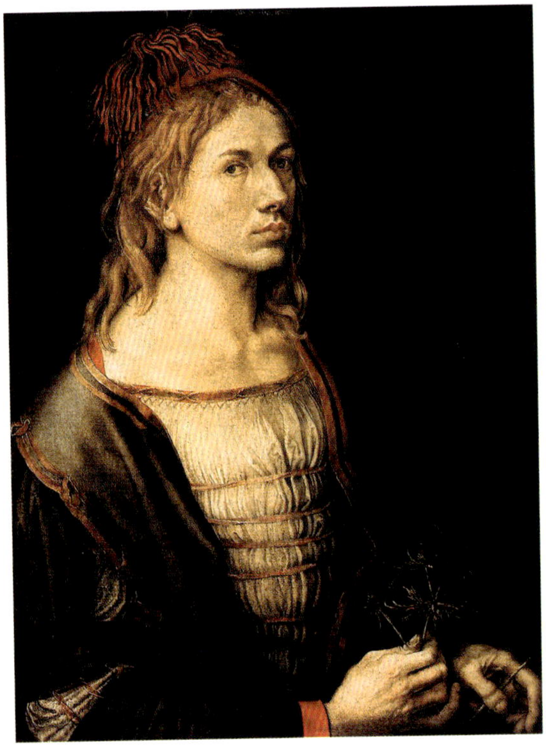

Albrecht Dürer
Self-Portrait at Age 22, ca. 1493

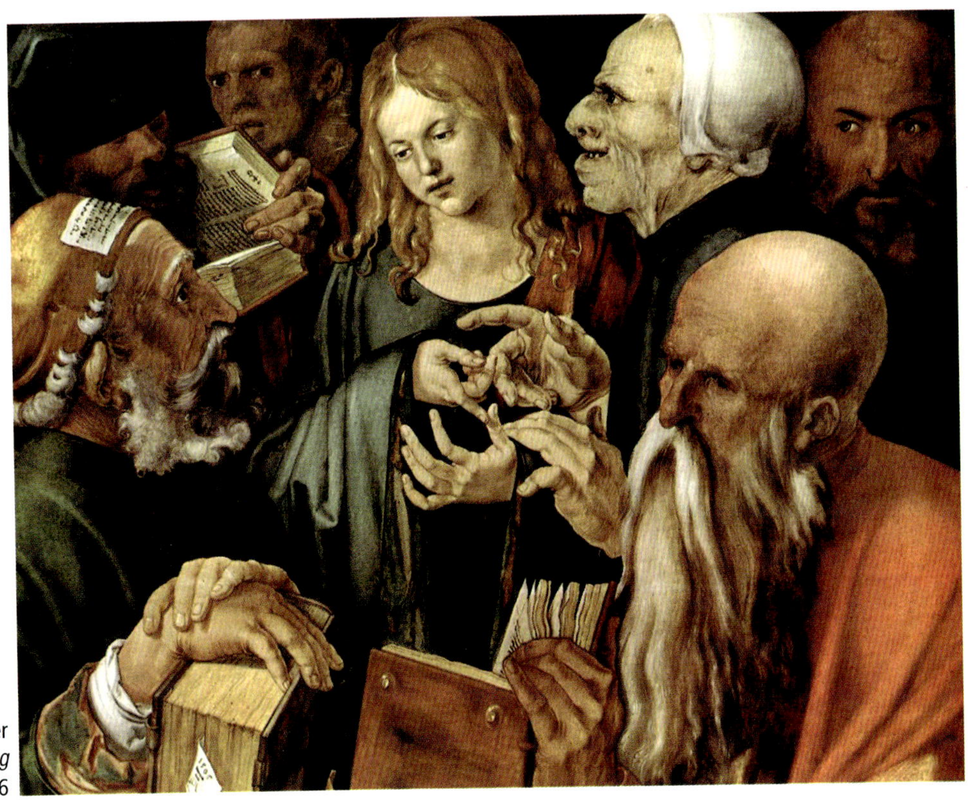

Albrecht Dürer
Christ Among the Doctors, 1506

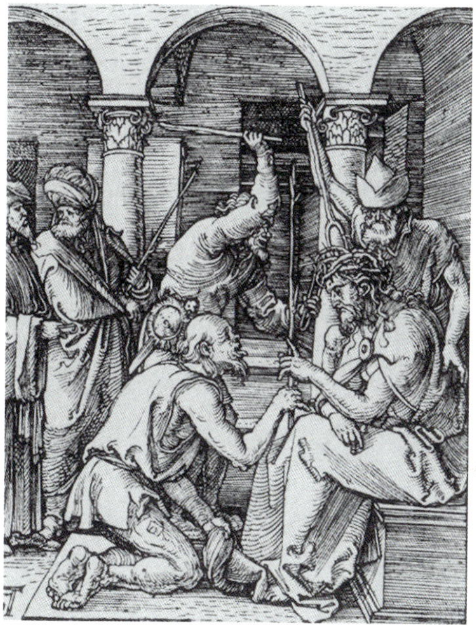

Albrecht Dürer
Christ Crowned with Thorns, ca. 1508-10

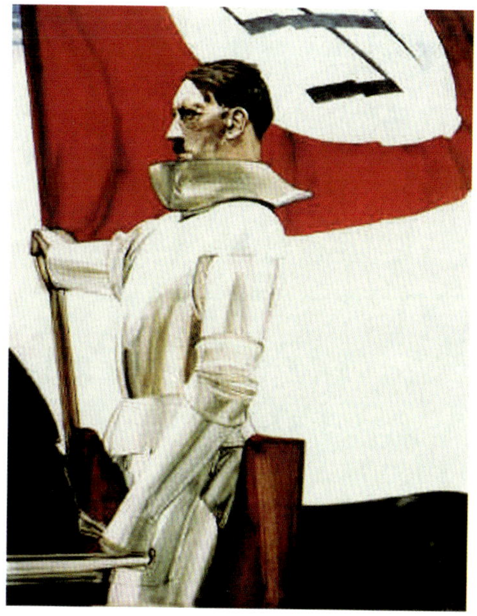

Herbert Lanzinger
Der Bannerträger, 1938

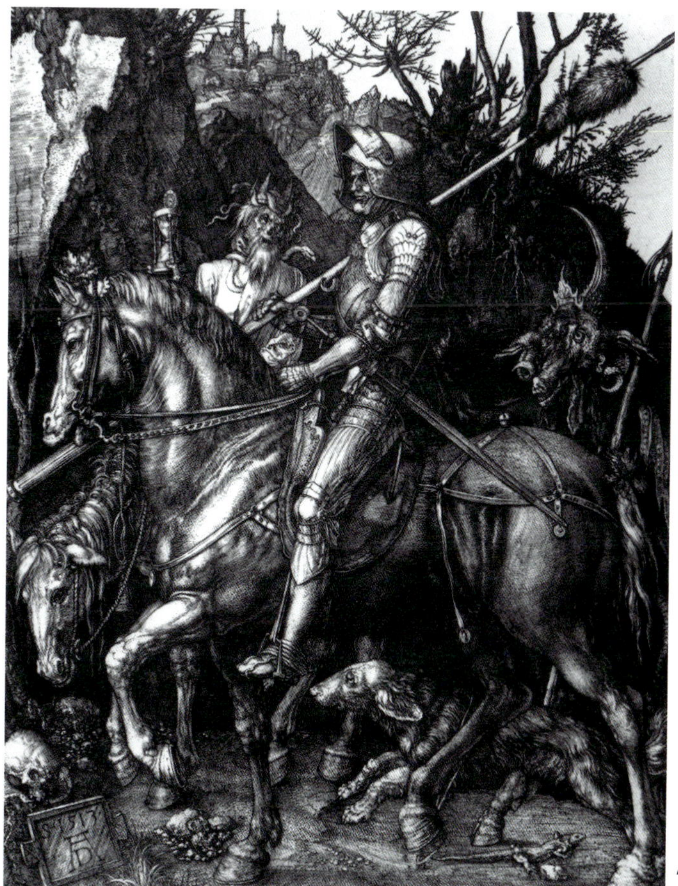

Albrecht Dürer
Knight, Death and Devil

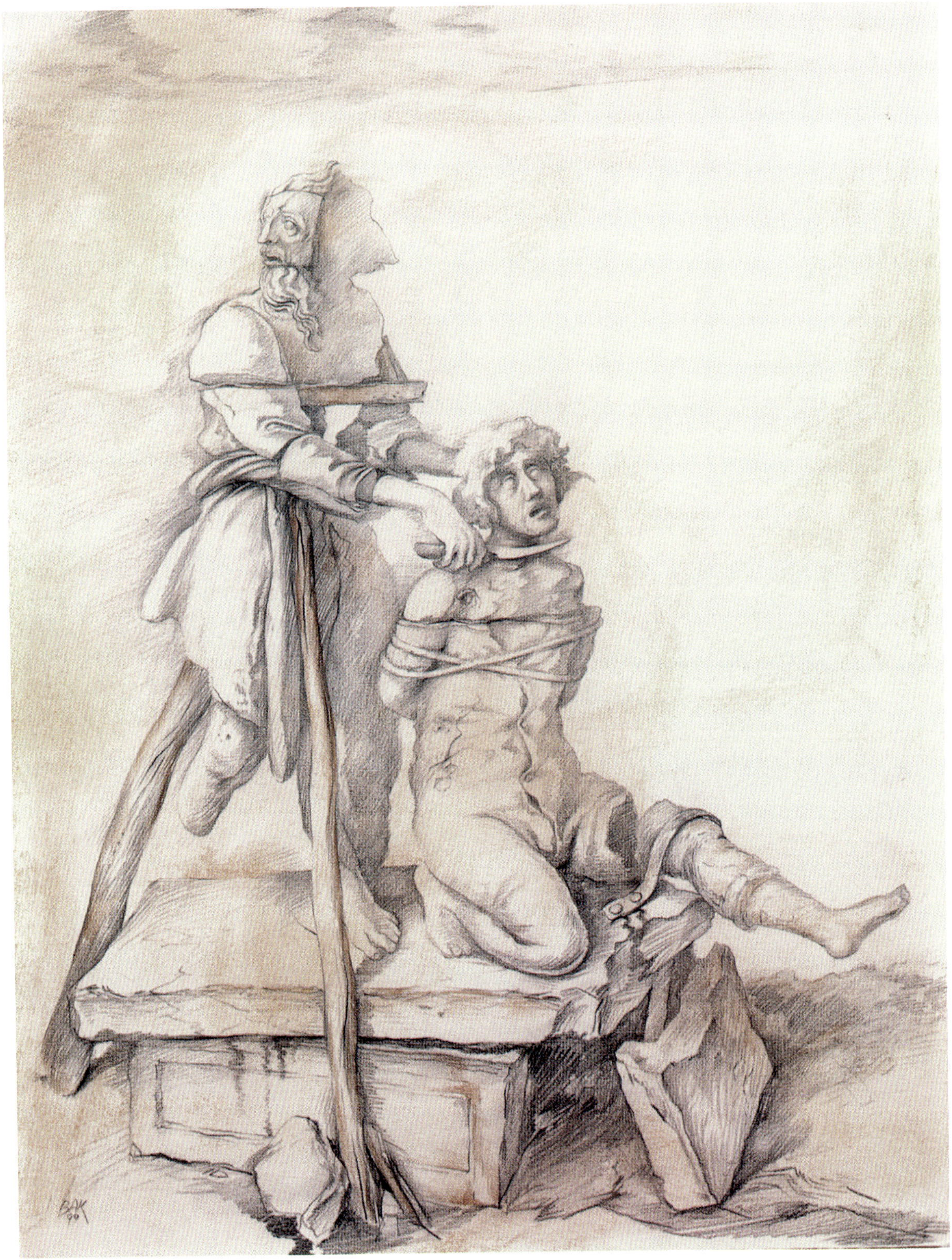

Iconoclash and Akedah: Holocaust and Sacrifice in the Art of Samuel Bak

YVONNE SHERWOOD

> Are not museums the temples in which sacrifices are made to apologize for so much destruction, as if we wanted suddenly to stop destroying and were beginning the indefinite cult of conserving, protecting, repairing?
>
> — BRUNO LATOUR, *Iconoclash.*[1]

> The weapon and the tool seem at moments indistinguishable, for they may each reside in a single physical object...and may be quickly transformed back and forth, now into the one, now into the other. At the same time, however, a gulf of meaning, intention, connotation and tone separates them....The hammer that hammers a man to a cross is a weapon and the hammer used to construct the cross is a tool.
>
> — ELAINE SCARRY, *The Body in Pain.*[2]

Iconoclash[3]

When Reformation vandals broke the limbs of Christ on a small fifteenth-century French pietá what were they doing? When the Chludov Psalter polemically portrayed iconoclasts as spearing Christ's crucified body what was happening? Closer to (my) home, what was a Glaswegian Protestant doing when he took a knife and slashed Salvador Dali's *Christ of St. John on the Cross?* Does the act of crucifying an already crucified icon involve you in a double negative that comes perilously close to a positive? Does it leave you sticking your spear or brush or knife into a place already liminally positioned between destruction and re-creation (resurrection), death and life? Such questions are raised by Michel Serres who wants to know whether, "[t]he holes in the hands and feet of the dead Christ, the gaping wound in his flank, the traces of spears or hammered nails" are different in order from the blows of the iconoclast, and whether they, in turn, are different in kind from the blows of the sculptor who carved the stone.[4] They are amplified by Bruno Latour

After Mantegna, 1999
Pencil and Pastel on Paper, 24 3/4 x 20"

in his reflections on the exhibition and related book *Iconoclash.* "Iconoclash," as opposed to "iconoclasm," is when "one does not know, one hesitates, one is troubled by an action for which there is no way to know, without further inquiry, whether it is destructive or constructive."[5] Iconoclash is, in short, when the eye is unsure of the artist-creator's hand. The hand may be holding a knife (a sacrificial knife or a palette knife?); but it may (also?) be a palm open to catch and preserve/conserve the tradition—even perhaps "a hand that is praying for the hammer to rest, or for an angel to come and arrest the sacrificial arm holding the sacrificial knife ready to cut the sacrificial lamb's throat."[6] And it's no accident, I suspect, that in order to illustrate the paradoxes of iconoclash, Latour selects those two primary scenes of creative wounding: crucifixion and Akedah.[7]

I find Latour's concept of iconoclash and some of the words in this voluminous collection thought-provoking and important. The lavish visual gallery, however, seems rather disappointing, largely because I feel I could have predicted this radical canon in advance. Art is represented, so to speak, by the defiantly non-representational, an-iconic, non-figurative, non-narrative. The gallery is dominated by conceptual art, installations, computer-generated images—very little painting and drawing, with painting only featuring in the form of purer abstract or expressionist art. Though there are some unexpected elements—reflections on the fall of secular monuments of Mao and Stalin, thoughts on the Jewish midrash on Abraham smashing his father's idols—the question of the religious icon spawns (as might be expected) a myriad of crucifixions and extensive work on the Reformation and Counter-Reformation, with other religions featuring in a peripheral role in the Taliban-devastated Bamayan Buddhas and bits of Jewish text. As the art represented tends to be art at the end of, or against, the image, so contemporary religious art seems to be represented by the kind of art that is (most sensationally), teetering at religion's apocalyptic edge. The religious pieces chosen are """'religious'""" in heavily ironized inverted commas, and tend to be more about the "kidnapping, destruction, distance, parody" than about the "quotation" and particularly "struggle" that Latour also claims.[8] The collection highlights such works as the Pope being hit by a meteorite in Maurizio Cattelan's *La Nona Ora* (1999), but you could equally have had Andreas Serrano's *Piss Christ* (1989) or Rudy Giuliani's favourite, Chris Offili's *The Holy Virgin Mary* (a black virgin Mary composed partly from cut-outs of female genitalia and partly from elephant dung).[9]

My point here is not to ally myself with Giuliani or those who assemble annually to mock the kind of work that gets shortlisted for the British Turner Prize. I don't want to defend the holy purity of art or apostrophise nostalgia, though I am weary of the assumption that, in order to matter, art must be at a certain narrowly defined and highly marketable, sensational edge. Rather, my point is that, in the iconoclash collection, the very extremity of the now-familiar edge seems to limit the potential of iconoclash as an idea. Processed through a rather staple collection of avant-garde art, the timely and important concept of iconoclash turns out to mean little more than the clichéd truism that because these seemingly guerrilla acts "generate such a fabulous population of new images" then even these seeming iconoclasts are working creatively, so "iconoclashtically."

(Warning: It's better to read the term than to attempt to pronounce it—as I did in the oral version of this paper—because pronouncing it makes it sound as if you haven't put your teeth in).

It is the contention of this article that we can find tenser, tauter, and more complex examples of iconoclash if we move outside the pure and rather reverent un-traditionalism that circumscribes both art and religion in Latour's collection. Iconoclash becomes far more meaningful at those deeply contested religious sites where a very great deal is still at stake in the struggle between affiliation and disaffiliation: for example, the Akedah after the Shoah. Poised between God's first word "Take your son and offer him as a Holocaust" and his second word "Do not lay a hand on the lad, or do anything to him," Genesis 22 already hovers uncertainly between creative and destructive forces. These tensions have been amplified as—partly because of the uncomfortable relationship of the word "Holocaust" to "sacrifice" and so to "Akedah"[10]—experimental conversations between Bible and Shoah have returned, again and again, to Mount Moriah. Isabel Wollaston, Alvin Rosenfeld, and Gershon Greenberg have already gathered and analysed some—though not all—of the many conversations that take place in the domain of words.[11] Revealingly, writers who write the kinds of words that feel compelled to sort themselves out into theological or philosophical statements tend to produce interpretations that are conservative in both senses of the word: "characterised by caution, moderation, or reluctance to make changes [to the biblical original]," but also dedicated to the "action of keeping from harm, decay, loss or waste."[12] These poignant but disturbing readings include attempts by Hasidic Jews during the Second World War to appeal to the Akedah as an unviolated site of sacred metaphysical truth and redemption; the claims of Ignaz Maybaum and Emmanuel Levinas that the Jewish Akedah is the antithesis of Holocaust and Christian sacrifice (and is essentially about a ram and an angel); even the assertion that "the Holocaust is a modern Akedah" in the sense of "a test of our faith."[13] They also include Eliezer Berkovits's slightly more ambiguous claim that the Akedah functions as a biblical screen for a nightmare scenario in which providence is absent and the promise is retracted, but in which Abraham's trust in the hidden God becomes a figure for the trust of the "authentic Jew in the ghettos and the camps."[14] Only one of the philosophical/theological writers, François Lyotard, goes to the opposite end of the spectrum, arguing that Akedah is an inappropriate, indeed scandalous, template for Shoah. Asking what in fact distinguishes the command that Yahweh gives to Abraham ("that Isaac die") from the command issued to the Nazi guards ("that the Jews die"), Lyotard concludes that, since the distinction is not absolutely solid, the Akedah is as inappropriate a paradigm for the Shoah as the "The Holocaust" is an inappropriate name.[15]

For dissonant, riven, and multi-facted conversations (or arguments) between Akedah and Shoah we need to turn to more poetic forms of writing that court and tolerate ambiguity—pieces such as George Steiner's "A Conversation Piece," Elie Wiesel's *Night* and "Isaac: A Survivor's Story," Saul Bellow's *Mr. Sammler's Planet,* and various Jewish poems such as Amir Gilboa's "Yizhak."[16] Such pieces enact "skewed" and "twisted" relations between the Bible and Shoah that go well beyond the fairly soft dissent implied by Roskie's term "sacred parody," or Wiesel's "irony."[17] They portray sons forced to put their fathers' bodies into the crematoria and sons who let the fathers die, or literally steal bread from their mouths, exploring the death of humanity as much as the death of God (Wiesel). They evoke intense midrashic study sessions on the Akedah, suspended, as it were, in metaphysical, timeless, eternity—only giving away the context in the final paragraph:

> *Up steeps of air.*
> *Which grew steeper and steeper.*
> *Mountainous. Higher than Moriah.*
> *—Dance, Miriam dance, said the spigot in the ceiling.*
> *—There is no ram now and the bush is burning.*
> Dancers, their mouths wide open. So that the hive swarmed in their throats. And hummed to them the slurred slow song of ash.[18]

Or they make scrambled Akedahs in which Isaac is the iconic, lone "survivor," and the son walks with his father through nightmarish European forests, sees "blood on the leaves" and cries "Father, father come quickly so that no-one will be missing from the midday meal."[19] (Amir Gilboa's "Yizhak" has always felt to me like a textual version of Bak's *Study for Akedah,* at the same time seeming to evoke the interrupted domesticity of Bak's un-still "still-lives" [cf.] *Still Life with Tikkun,* and *Study for Akedah.* And they portray men like Mr. Sammler who, having accidentally survived an act of Nazi destruction as arbitrary and massive as shooting through all the names in a telephone book, believes he knows "things about murder which might make [the knight of faith's] choices just a little more difficult."[20] For Sammler, Abraham as Kierkegaard's "Knight of Faith, capable of cutting the throat of his Isaac upon God's altar" is nothing but a symptom of a "modern, middle-class" fascination with those who are strong enough for violence and strong enough to go outside the law.[21]

Using the stage of the Akedah as a descriptive echo-chamber rather than a forum for prescriptive response, these readings create dismembered, chaotic Akedahs that imply that "yearnings for the traditional Abraham of faith will have to wait until Isaac, orphaned and bloodied, has had a chance to say what his wounded eyes have seen."[22] As if taking up the inner-biblical tension between God's first command to kill, and his second to save, and then refracting it through the tensions between ancient text and contemporary biographies (multiplied a millionfold), they create kaleidoscopic scenes of creation(s) and destruction(s), repetition/reperformance and distortion/attack.

If such a conflict were performed visually, we would call that "iconoclash."

Samuel Bak

Samuel Bak is the kind of artist who would not get an entrance ticket to a self-consciously fashionable collection like *Iconoclash,* with its dedication to the pure contemporary and the tradition of the new. The story of his artistic development is perversely a story of rewinding backwards from abstraction to verisimilitude, going back to very old things such as oil and paint on canvas and Renaissance Old Masters. He endlessly paints fathers and grandfathers and evokes lost painterly ancestors such as Pierro della Francesca, Michaelangelo, Rembrandt, Mantegna, Massaccio and Albrecht Dürer, albeit in his own trademark idiosyncratic fusion with surrealism and Magritte. In painterly terms, Bak seems not to be wresting his originality from the fathers, so much as "using strong predecessors to break with the style of the present."[23] His work seems to be all about the struggles of affiliation and disaffiliation involved in coming "after" (both in the style of, and irretrievably from a later, more broken time), and also about breaking up any complacent sense of the contemporary as a time that is at one with itself and that knows itself, unproblematically, as "now." Paradoxically, the combination of the uncompromisingly recognisable figurative, combined with the agonising damage all-too-clearly done to the figures, makes his work less (not more) hangable in the living room or gallery than the sensational or abstract works of a more easily consumable "edge." Not only does it go against the ideas of progress inherent in the very idea of artistic trends and fashion, but the portrayal of self-dispossessed and crumbling victims collides with the agency and self-possession/self-presentation that presides over the art markets. His destroyed, crumbling, ruined selves could not be further from Matisse's "art as comfortable as a chair." But at the same time there is also something anachronistically gorgeous and sumptuous about his art—something on a direct collision course with a certain fashion for the brutal, minimalist, repudiation of beauty in favour of the real-as-stark.

Samuel Bak reminds me of Saul Bellow's Mr. Sammler, another survivor from the Holocaust planet who, having been to the very abyss of human experience, is repelled by the fashion for reality-as-brutality and fails to understand the popularity of cultural tourist trips out to the exotic-violent.[24] Though Bak is attempting nothing so bold or impossible as restoration/reparation/redemption—forcing the gold teeth back into the gums, the smoke back into the chimneys, as Dan Pagis sardonically puts it—his intensely colourful oils have the feel and shine of a recently restored "old master" about them.[25] There seems to be something almost argumentative about this restorative gesture, as if Bak is saying, with his own defiant conservati[oni]sm, that not everything needs to be lost.[26] Like Sammler, Bak seems agnostic about whether one can assemble "inorganic, organic, natural, bestial, human, and superhuman in any dependable arrangement"[27] —an uncertainty expressed in the (icono)clash between human, organic, bestial, and inorganic that takes place on his canvasses. And yet, in a place a very long way away from the cliché of redemptive creativity and the insurgent spirit of the human(e), one gets a sense of the green growth (and indeed a whole palette of colour) rising from the burnt black of the "onetime human, onetime precious, life."[28] This colour and form is not crude enough to articulate itself as meaning, even less as redemption. But yet it seems to find itself, as it were naturally, organically, obsessively "working, trying to start again."[29]

As what Nigel Whiteley nicely terms a "tourist from a word-based discipline,"[30] I should be relieved that the artist on whom I am attempting to write draws, far more than most, on a visual script, a surreal symbolic language. And yet somehow these paintings and drawings prove more difficult to talk or write about than most. Conceptual art is conveniently verbal and theoretical (which is why it is so welcome in art schools);[31] abstract art paradoxically gives us fairly confined parameters of inner-disciplinary language in which to speak, and also a blank canvas of mute inarticulacy and endless interpretative scope in which to stretch out. But these crowded works seem to gabble verbosely, setting up a complex inarticulacy that comes from saying too much. The problem is not just that an image is a long way from being the visual equivalent of a word, making an exegetical allegoresis of the visual impossible. "Images" are not used by artists as definable entities, discrete objects (with clear space around them) that can be aligned sequentially in sentences to produce statements that can be read relatively unambiguously as they can in writing, or at least certain kinds of writing. The idea of an image, by analogy to the word, is misleading. But the problem of translation/articulation multiplies in Bak's densely compiled encyclopaedic canvases, where different "images" are overlaid on one another, and the same image or scene is split and parsed differently—not just between works but within the same work. Like the words of Steiner, Wiesel, or Gilboa, rather than those of Lyotard, Berkovits, or Maybaum, these images coalesce, connote rather than make a statement. The effect is of what Stephen Feinstein calls a reverse "Dayenu," or the gabbling in- and multi-articulacy of Paul Celan or Nellie Sachs.[32]

Eyes and Hands

To give myself some *focus,* then, and something specific *to do,* I'm going to concentrate on the eye and hand. The eye and the hand relate to iconoclash's core questions of blurred and confused vision ("What are we seeing?") and the undecideable hand ("What are the hands inside and outside the work doing?"). But the eye and the hand are particularly appropriate in this case because they play a crucial role in the biblical text. Constructed around a central punning relation between seeing *(ra-ah)* and fearing *(yarai),* Genesis 22 is a central strand in the optic metaphorical nerve that runs throughout the book of Genesis.[33] It commences with a journey that begins early in the morning (in the half-light?); it then travels three days away as if seeking out a secret place or, in artistic terms, a vanishing point. Finally, it leaves everyone else at the bottom of the mountain, as if the scene is for God's, Abraham's (and Isaac's?), and of course the narrator's eyes only. (Presumably the narrator was hiding in the thicket all along). It climaxes in a scene of microscopic and magnifying seeing. On top of the Mount of Seeing/Revelation/Provision, Abraham's eagle eyes zoom in on a ram obscured in a thicket, and then open wide to see a cosmos full of stars.

At the same time what the reader sees is curiously centred on the hand. Verse six seems very concerned to give us a close up of the knife and the fire in Abraham's hand. The story climaxes in a drama of hands. As the narrative slows to slow motion, Abraham very, very slowly stretches forth his *hand* to take the knife to slaughter his son, until—at the eleventh hour and fifty-ninth minute—the angel says "Do not lay a *hand.*" The narrative is strangely preoccupied with tools and materials (knife, fire, wood, donkey, servants) and the act of building the altar for the sacrifice. It is as if it wants us to notice the way the human hand can slide between acts of destruction and acts of construction, as the knife in Abraham's hand slips undecideably between weapon and tool.[34]

This textual obsession with the eye and the hand seems to be faithfully represented in the Christian post-iconographic art tradition. At the centre of Caravaggio's *Sacrifice of Isaac* is a chain of hands: the angel's hand on the hand of Abraham holding the knife; the other hand of Abraham pressing his son's face down on the altar; the other hand of the angel pointing to the obscured ram in the left hand corner, highlighting that which is not visible—at first. Abraham's eyes are locked on the eyes of the angel; Isaac's eyeballs loll unseeing. He surely can't see much of the scene taking place above him from that angle. Isaac has no hands that we can see. They must be tied behind his back. Rembrandt's *Sacrifice of Isaac* is dominated by a vertical chain of hands, just as Caravaggio's is dominated by a horizontal chain of hands. At the top is the angel-hand gesturing emphatically "Halt." At the centre, drawing the eye towards it, is the white flash of angel hand gripping the earthy old hand of Abraham. This hand has the strength to knock the knife loose, sending it in freefall towards the white torso of Isaac, in an imminent fatal accident that Rembrandt seems neither to have anticipated or intended. It is hard to imagine, gravity being what it is, how Isaac can escape. Our eyes are drawn to those piercing, ghostly eyes of Abraham locked upon the eyes of the angel. Isaac's hands are hidden/restrained; his eyes are blinded by Abraham's hand. And it's this hand of Abraham—undecideably protective and aggressive—that takes us closer to the uncertain hands outwith, and within, the Akedahs of Samuel Bak.

Painting the Akedah: *Dress Rehearsal* and *Isaac's Dream*

I want to begin with what is for me the most amazing and haunting of Bak's Akedah works, *Dress Rehearsal*. No less than five assisting angel hands as stage-hands draw attention to the hand that makes the painting. The Akedah is being put on as a self-consciously staged event. In his own idiosyncratic take on bricolage, the artist seems to be actively assembling an ad hoc Akedah from bits and pieces of different times, an old curtain, a crate, and bits of string. Magritte-like, the painting foregrounds the fact that *"Ceci n'est pas une akedah."* It's just a piece of improvisation, a performance, a dress-rehearsal. The Akedah and Shoah are placed uncertainly between life and theatre, as in Charlotte Salomon's *Life? or Theatre?*[35] The performance has clearly been put on in haste. Grabbed suddenly, Isaac is still in his underclothes (not yet dressed, or perhaps undressed in readiness for sacrifice). The very un-Abrahamic Abraham seems to have raided a pantomime costume box from Ali Baba and the Forty Thieves. The hand of the metal-winged angel on the left (let us call him "First Angel," because the theatricality of the scene seems to call for this kind of credit-designation), almost brushes Abraham's hand. But he entirely lacks the divine authority and firm hand of Rembrandt or Caravaggio's angels, and Abraham still clutches his knife, or rather scimitar, firmly. By re-sharpening Abraham's knife's blunted, over-familiar edge, the scimitar seems to over-inflate Abraham as top-billing cinema hero (Lawrence of Arabia/Knight of

Faith). The weak and aging angel is one of that peculiar Bakian breed of heavily qualified "angels," stranded somewhere between the *malkhamoves* ("angel of death") feared by his Grandfather Chayim, and the kind of mad flight machines that could have been dreamt by his inventor-grandfather Khone. They remind me of those angels in Donald Barthelme's "On Angels" who, cast into crisis by the death of God, come down to the level of *homo sapiens*—who is also *homo quariens* (the man of questions)—and are redeployed from glorias to silence, warning, and lament.[36] The hand of the "Second Angel" on Abraham's shoulder could be attempting to stop Abraham, but then again it could be the hand of an angelic stagehand/choreographer simply saying "Abraham, could you just move a little bit to the right or to the left?" Most ambiguous and disturbing are the hands of the "Third Angel." He seems to be fixing the ropes that bind Isaac (so highlighting that chilling textual detail of binding: no escape). But he might also be hooking up the ropes that will winch Isaac to safety at the last moment. If the *deus ex machina* is reduced to a winch and stage mechanics, this is a weak transmogrification of resurrection and salvation—but, heck, some salvation is better than nothing. Is Isaac looking so unperturbed because he knows (or believes) that, like the biblical Isaac, he is going to be saved/winched away? Or is he deluded? He is, after all, blindfolded (as is Abraham) and blindfolding is a very significant thing to do to eyes. What does it mean that someone has blindfolded them, as if to get them to perform the scene of sacrifice with their eyes wide shut? The altar (reassuringly, perhaps, altar-ed to a mere packing box) opens up in a very-solid-seeming (real?) crematorium oven and, behind it, almost obscured, a chimney. The effect is like coming to the end of Steiner's "Conversation Piece," when the curtains part to reveal the spigots on the ceiling. Is this, then, an Akedah scene rigged up in front of the crematorium, as if a surreal biblical riff on the many Nazi ruses and delusions to screen the truth of genocide? Will Isaac escape from Abraham's Akedah-scimitar (which was always just for show and was never really going to kill him) only to enter the Holocaust that is so much more improbable and more real? Is the Akedah, then, being accused as a screen for the Holocaust? Or is it being dwarfed as a faux-Holocaust? Is a survivor painting a modern version of the riposte of the mother of the seven sons martyred during the Maccabean revolts to Abraham, effectively saying that "Yours was a mere dress rehearsal. But all my sons (and daughters and fathers, mothers, and all my relatives) actually died?"[37] Maybe the sense of improvised, low-budget performance suggests that these days, after the Shoah, the Akedah can no longer be played straight, under proscenium arches, to huge audiences, but fits best in those kind of spaces that theatres call their Studios, or Annexes—set apart for those experimental performances that, among other things, revise and distort the classics. Something about the secret venue and the haste implies that this "Classic" is, *before* all distortions, at least as shocking as any radical performance staged by an *avant garde* theatre group. This sacrifice of Isaac does not look like any sacrifice of Isaac that we know, asking, therefore how much we really know or own it. The painting evokes an *unheimlich* sense of disorientating, or rather dis-occidentalising, familiarity-unfamiliarity. Pantomime collides comically, blasphemously, with Scripture; the Turk and Arab, Europe's others, intrude into a scene from European painting, rendered in the rich terracottas and olive greens of the southern Mediterranean. The disjunction seems to suggest that now old cliché of Shoah—the shock of something other, foreign, irrupting in the heart of civilised Europe—while also suggesting something pagan, "infidel" and "other" about "our" scriptures.[38] It calls to mind Søren Kierkegaard's "what if": what if we imagine the sacrifice of Isaac being performed not in some remote, exotic oriental ur-time in the "beautiful regions of the East" but here in Europe.[39] The question becomes more pressing in the second half of the twentieth century than it was for Kierkegaard in Denmark in 1843. The foreignness of the scene takes this performance of Shoah/Akedah beyond the Jewish, the biblical, the religious, to all acts of genocide and terror. This scene from the theatre of the absurd seems to come by way of warning from one who calls himself a "God-fearer" in the sense of one who fears "the atrocities man perpetrates in the name of his militant Divinities"—secular and religious.[40]

It is hard to imagine an Akedah that is more different in tone to "Dress Rehearsal" than *Isaac's Dream* . Weakly "dominating" the painting, if such a tiny thing can be said to dominate, is the central point of Isaac's hand. This hand—which is also the hand of Sam, Samek, and the boy from the Warsaw ghetto[41] —is loosely draped in tefillin. In Latour's terms, it seems to be held, palm out, to catch, preserve/conserve, and to pray *"for an angel to come and arrest the sacrificial arm holding the sacrificial knife ready to cut the sacrificial lamb's throat."*[42] And the prayer or dream does seem to be "answered" in the bound knife to which that extended hand weakly gestures. But this is not a strong gesture, like Caravaggio's angel pointing to the ram. The bound knife is weakly mirrored in the "angel," who turns up as an ad hoc assemblage of boards, like a stage-prop hanging from the sky. As a *mem* and a *lamed* (m and l), and so only half of the Hebrew word for messenger/angel *(mlk)* this is but an amputated angel, a half-angel, an obscure angel-as-cryptogram. The bound knife does not allow itself to be interpreted as a straight illustration of the second word of God: "Do not lay a hand on the lad." Rather it is the kind of "Do not lay a hand" that seems to redound on a God and an ur-text that breaks God and humanity's primordial sixth commandment, "Do not Murder"—resonating with all those broken sixes and broken tablets that tumble across Bak's canvasses. Might the most destructive thing that you can do to an Akedah be to bind the knife or cancel out the text with its own "Do not lay a hand?" Perhaps this is also the kind of "Do not lay a hand" that exhorts the viewer to intervene and stop this ur-scene, this almost-Holocaust happening—an exhortation that becomes more insistent in a world where angels are absent or uncertain, and where the only thing that can bind the knife is the human hand.

This is an Akedah as seen through survivor-Isaac's eyes, for Bak identifies with the haunting image of the "bound child."[43] Inverting the artistic tradition of depicting Isaac as unseeing and hand-less, Isaac's half-open eyes are the only open (living) eyes, and it is his small hand that reaches out towards us. It is far from accidental that the painting has the feeling of the chintzy, brightly coloured illustrations of a book of fairytales or a children's Bible. That absurd-impossible garish splash of verdant lime green, sprouting from the stone, seems to me to express the absurd and guilty excess of *sur*-vivre, over-living, in a world where "ten improbable miracles were the minimal rate for survival," and a child's "salvation"[44] (in heavy inverted commas) was at least as improbable as a fairytale, a rainbow, an angel, or a ram. This Akedah is so *difficult* (both to make and to see), because it stages what Bak calls the dwelling together of a child's love and terror "in ritualised interconnection," and what Lawrence Langer appropriately calls the "collateral encounter" between "apparently opposing worlds" of "intimacy with infinite power and mercy," and "mourning, estrangement and unending loss."[45]

Isaac's Dream suggests not only *iconoclash* but what might be termed *chronoclash*: different possibilities, different tenses, colliding at the same time. There is the biblical ancient past, as past historic, the Holocaust as recent past (past simple, also past indigestible), and the subjunctives, the dreams, the futures: what might have been, what could have been, the quest for another story. This Akedah is so difficult (to do/make and to see) because it stages a collision of tenses: the child's natural habitat of future and subjunctive somehow struggling against the implacable, steady thud of past simple—which is also past incomprehensible, and past imperfect, still extending into now. Times collide in a single image: the boat is at once Noah's long-lost biblical ark, a monument of Jewish refugee ships such as the SS Struma or the St. Louis, and crematoria that are still producing smoke, but also past, stone memorials to the horror. The painting sustains both a sense of something that has happened—which cannot be deflected by our hand, or Isaac's or Bak's—but also dreams, interrogations, and reverberations towards the present and the future. For Bak as for Wiesel, "The question is no longer whether Isaac was saved but whether the miracle could happen again. And how often. And for what reasons. And at what cost."[46] The event that the Bible stages three days from home, in secret, is brought into the glare of "full daylight" and bright blinding colour, to ask vividly and insistently what this paradigm of "imposed sacrifice could mean in our time."[47]

In *Isaac's Dream, bereshit,* in some qualified sense, begins again: Genesis regenerates. The sprig in Abraham's hand may be a fragile promise like the sprig in the dove's mouth after the flood (compare the tattered ribbon rainbow-promise on loan both from Noah and from Dürer's *Melencolia I.* Or it may, as I prefer to think, be a fragile little seedling tree of Torah, seeds of a new composite Torah-Shoah that speaks in strange tongues.[48] It reminds me of biblical images of the remnant as almost-destroyed tree-stump (see for example Isaiah 6.13) and also the powerful Jewish image of Torah as living tree. Perhaps these two ideas have been grafted together in this diminished, fragile seedling post-Shoah.

In some respects the hand making the painting seems to be a palm held out to save, catch, and conserve/preserve Torah as a repository of rich, raw fundamental Jewish life. Like the genealogical chains of fathers, grandfathers, and great-grandfathers in *The Wanderer II,* or *From Generation to Generation III,* the cut, frayed, but present tefillin urgently raises the problem of memory, continuity, and connection already present in Kafka's letter to his father, but magnified a millionfold by Shoah.[49] As Elie Wiesel asks, to whom would the father "transmit this faith, this knowledge" if "Isaac were to die?"[50]—or if all the Abrahams were to die. The scene is one of complex affiliation and disaffiliation mirrored, at the level of form, in the conflict between absolute verisimilitude and absolute defamiliarization. In aesthetic terms the traditional Jewish text is "made strange," but in this context the concept has particular connotations of being orphaned from tradition and losing, rather than leaving, home.[51]

Bak's book of Genesis orbits compulsively around four primal scenes: creation and expulsion, the flood, the Akedah, and Jacob's ladder and his encounter with the angel. All four scenes involve a battle between forces of creation and destruction and are threaded together in Genesis to form an ongoing drama of composition-decomposition-recomposition. Bak reworks the iconic scenes by adjusting each scene's internal equilibrium between construction and deconstruction; changing the biblical sequence (so that flood can intrude on Akedah for example); and eroding the cyclic certainty of composition-decomposition-recomposition through the insistent pressure of Shoah. In the primal myths of Akedah and Flood, knife and fire are negated by ram and angel and universal genocide is redeemed by an ark, a dove, and a rainbow—or at least we must believe that it could be so. In *Isaac's Dream,* the destruction in these primal myths has become as traumatic as we always feared it could/must be. Incredulous salvation weakly asserts its hopeful (naive?) self against the scene of universal destruction in the bound knife, the tattered ribbon rainbow, the sprig in the dove's mouth, or the seedling Torah tree.

Monuments and Ruins in Pencil, Pastel and Crayon: *Rembrandt's Angel, Study for Akedah,* and *After Mantegna*

This sense of internal fragility and unstable equilibrium becomes, if anything, more intense and overt in the altogether slighter lines of Bak's drawings. Viewers who have learned to view art through the European art tradition habitually equate drawing with impermanence, preparation, study. When we see a Michelangelo drawing of David we are likely to say "That's a study of David," or "That's a drawing of David," whereas if we see a sculpture or a painting of David we are more likely to say "That's David." Bak uses drawing to evoke a sense of the once-real, once-living, decomposing back into studies: the art world's equivalent of "dress rehearsals" and "dreams." It is no coincidence that one of these drawings is titled *After Mantegna,* for Mantegna (1431-1506) is synonymous with an illusionism that conjures solid stone from paper. Bak reverses the process, causing three dimensions to fall back into two dimensions, or to hover uncertainly between two and three dimensions. Stone and flesh turn back into fragile pastel, crayon, and pencil line as Bak, who declares himself agnostic about the viability of Holocaust memorials, creates "tombstones of sorts, humble 'reliquaries,' unassuming cutouts, and perishable bricolages," erasable "monuments that could never exist."[52]

In *Rembrandt's Angel* the angel, whom we see only from the back (as if in weak imitation of Moses's encounter with the hidden God in Exodus 3), crashes through a wall and instead of holding his arm to cry "Halt," holds up his hand to cover his eyes. "A slight delay in the angel's arrival has changed the whole story."[53] Caught between dimensions he is receding back into mere drawing, and we see for the first time his exaggerated smallness. Did Rembrandt ever think that this youthful little angel was ever going to be enough to halt the demand to kill? *Study for Akedah* sketches Abraham and Isaac as deportees and refugees, travelling through Alpine mountains and the blasted trees of European forests like Ponar/Paneriai, a long way from Jerusalem-Moriah.[54] The deep blue chill (a world away from the dayglo daylight of *Isaac's Dream*) could not be colder, and the spots of flame yellow add to the hazy sense of being suspended somewhere between solidity and smoke. Father and son have the look of the reel (r.e.e.l.) about them. Their footsteps recall the eerie 1940's footage that keeps the victims boarding the trains that have already taken them to their dying. Isaac's eyes are unseeing, barely open, almost blind; the father has his handkerchief over his face, as if hiding his eyes, like Rembrandt's angel, or saying his last *shema.* "It is I who am slain, my son./My blood is already on the leaves./And my father's voice was stifled/And his face pale."[55] The father holds the son's arms, or, more accurately, his arm continues into his son's arm, as father and son meld together as an assemblage of prostheses and limbs. The emphasis of this Akedah is not on hands or eyes—but legs—in those stone legs that so eerily stand free. Apart from his arm, which reaches out, as if trying to be real, three-dimensional, the father is entirely made of combustible wooden board and the spot of flame-light comes to rest most intensely on him. The figures are held between solidity and smoke, the organic and inorganic: monument, pencil, memory, and dream.

The frail Isaac monument of *After Mantegna* is in need of something much stronger than binding—such as iron rivets—to hold him together and to hold him to the altar. His eyes are pupilless: put out, extinguished. "Abraham's" face is nothing more than a mask over a grey pencil shadow, washed with the thinnest lemon yellow. He recedes, like Rembrandt's angel, back into the paper and pencil from whence he so barely came. With just one full leg to support him, propped up by joists, and severely amputated *and* faded, this "Abraham" is an Abraham ruin. He is a long way, however, from the ruins that are such a conventional component of modern aesthetics. From Shelley's "Ozymandias" and the Romantic love affair with the sublimity and grandeur of ruins, to T.S. Eliot's "fragments shored against our ruins," de Chirico's "The Philosopher's Walk" (1914), and Walter Benjamin's reflections on the ruin, modernity has been mesmerised by what Lowenthal calls the "sad, sinister, violated look of ruins," which has always accompanied its alleged drive towards perfection/progress.[56] Works such as Mark C. Taylor's *Disfiguring* and Bruno Latour's *Iconclash* all testify to the postmodern (Sammler would say "dark" or late Romantic) fascination with the seductive end/edge/apocalypse of mortal ruin. Artworks such as Hans Bellmer's dolls bring that sense of ruin to the person, deliberately dis-assembling the composure of portrait or sculpture. But for Bak, who learned to draw from the broken plaster figures that his teacher retrieved from the rubble of the ruined Vilna Academy, ruins are less metaphorised and encrusted with nostalgia. His artistic training seemed to parody the Renaissance convention of practising anatomy drawing from broken Greek and Roman statues.

For him the broken figures imaginatively merged with the everyday sculpting material of his orthodontist-father's dental-plaster and became iconic of "what happens to a human body in a bombardment."[57] His disfigured figures testify to the destruction of the human person, in acts of violence that make Romantic visions of mortality in moss-covered crumbling stone look so tranquil, natural-organic, and desirable by contrast. Saul Bellow's Mr. Sammler, reflecting on the word "dilapidate," literally to "take apart the stones," muses that it cannot be applied to a person.[58] But Bak, as if following Sammler's train of thought, performs the violent "dilapidation" of a person. He foregrounds the atrocity of a person being treated as no more than inorganic material and then performs, in his *ad hoc* bricolage-people, the devastating impossibility of a person-*tikkun*.

Akedah and Crucifixion: Altar and Cross

There is another dimension of iconoclash in *After Mantegna* that begs consideration. For Bak is decomposing a well-known Christian icon. *After Mantegna* is based on "The Circumcision of Christ," one of three panels in a triptych in the Uffizi Gallery in Florence. There the sacrifice of Isaac features as one of two "Old Testament" scenes in two partially represented porticos in a very Italianate Jerusalem temple. (You can just see it if you crane your neck and look up to the left). Propped up by a vertical joist, bisected by a cross-bar, Bak's Abraham, who barely exists, seems to be an *Abraham on a cross*. In Mantegna's original, the sacrifice is already partially obscured, cut, and turned into a shadow of the son/sun below it. You can just make out a tiny Abraham and Isaac, with an altar behind them, and a ram behind Abraham, towards which Abraham turns his head. In the Christian logic of the painting, the two Old Testament porticos—the sacrifice of Isaac, and a horned Moses with the tablets of the law—are invoked to signal the end of the Law/the Old. A compliantly self-defeating Old Testament reassembles itself and makes itself New from within.

Bak, who grew up in a climate of euphemism where circumcision was referred to as "baptism" and Jews were referred to as the "families of Moses' faith," is unlikely to have missed this supersessionist hermeneutics.[59] By presenting a broken Akedah in the foreground, with the "cross" now in shadow, Bak iconoclashtically (that is, destructively-productively) breaks the logic of the Christian icon by reversing the relation of major to minor, foreground and background. He also breaks the "universal" cultural pact which makes the cross the icon of icons, the paradigmatic instance of the image in Western culture, and turns the Jewish (non)image into the non-incarnate, the icon that does not exist.

Insofar as the "No Jewish art" thesis is (at least partly) historically true, contemporary Jewish art offers a rather particular instance of iconoclash that seems to cry out for consideration. For the paradoxical relation between making and breaking goes through a rather fundamental twist in a context where to make is (potentially) to break the second commandment. Protestant iconoclasm is not the only cultural place where construction becomes transgression and destruction is piety/faith. Insofar as the truism about "no Jewish art" is false,[60] it raises the question of why Jewish art is perceived as parochial, while Christian art remains the cipher of the universal, and why *crucifixion, not Akedah, has been perceived as the most natural religious symbol to use for artistic interrogation of Shoah.* Though several powerful Jewish Akedahs were made in the second half of the twentieth century, Jewish Jesuses and crucifixions are far more prominent, and the domination of this image raises the same kinds of questions as the infamous cross at Auschwitz. Just as for Chaim Potok's Asher Lev working on his Brooklyn Crucifixion because (allegedly) there is "no aesthetic mould in his own religious tradition into which he could pour a painting of ultimate anguish and torment,"[61] the Akedah remains curiously invisible in the shadow of the cross. Even specialists on Holocaust art such as Matthew Baigell and Ziva Amishai-Maisels radically under-estimate the number of post-Shoah Akedah images, and then rationalise the absence by arguing, for example, that "The story of Abraham and Isaac was really not appropriate as Holocaust subject matter since for Jews it symbolizes the end of human sacrifice," or that the Akedah does not work as a "basic alternate symbol" because art on the sacrifice focuses on "the dramatic moment of reprieve."[62] Could not the very same points be made of crucifixion? Does not crucifixion, even more than the Akedah, represent the end of sacrifice and even the end of all death? Does not the death of Jesus tend even more dramatically towards the coda of resurrection? And does not Jewish tradition have its own traditions of Isaacs who *actually die?*[63] The fact that such questions are not considered fatal for crucifixion's potential as a post-Shoah icon imply that, at least unconsciously, the crucifixion is being regarded as more malleable and universal, and that the Akedah is being seen (like Christian images of the Jewish "Law" and the "Old") as more specific, local, and inflexibly fixed. And if they persist even in surveys of post-Shoah art, lingering perceptions of "the Christian" (as universal) and "the Jew" (as parochial) must lie very deep indeed.

Post-Shoah crucifixions allow the damage to infiltrate Christian-Europe's central icon, rather as Celan allows the disaster to disrupt the German language and Bak allows it to break open Dürer—sacred icon of German art. But as post-Shoah icon, the crucifixion brings in the added complication that the one who suffers is not just human and is thus always really safe, despite the dying. Moreover, at least according to the theology of atonement, Jesus *chooses* to sacrifice himself in an act necessary for redemption and *infused with meaning for the salvation of the world.* These connotations of crucifixion are contemplated by Bak in theological-aesthetic reflections in his memoirs. Unconsciously crossing paths with recent critiques of the atonement by Christian theologians, he tells how, in various childhood encounters with Christianity, he found solace and adventure in "the sense of *fulfilment* that the Christian faith ascribed to suffering," the "ecstatic bliss" of those who suffer, and the image of the *"strong"* God who saves.[64] Unconsciously intersecting with the kind of work that defamiliarizes the religious through political and social translation and explores the relationship between religion and violence, he puts crucifixion and Akedah in the same aesthetic constellation as Repin's *Czar Ivan the Terrible,* where the Czar holds the dead body of his murdered son in his arms.[65] For Bak, Ivan shades into the implacable, all-powerful Christian deity, who ignores the "Why have you forsaken me?" (Matthew 27:46; Mark 15:34) and seems "willing to see his son suffer," and an "irresponsible" Abraham appeasing a "cruel god." He then juxtaposes these too high and holy fathers with his own weaker, safe, and, as it turns out, saving father Jonas, who saved his only beloved son but died.[66]

In *After Mantegna,* as in all his Akedahs, Bak takes the Akedah (and behind it the crucifixion) out of the binding of the quasi-economic sacrificial logic that makes suffering "worth it," and that makes the meaning/the productive outcome mask the cost to flesh. In Bak's broken Akedah scenes, sacrifice comes out of its economic binding and tips into its perilously close cognate "disaster": *Churban,* Shoah. In the traditional religious reading, God's first command "to offer a Holocaust" is cancelled out by the second counter-command "Do not lay a hand," and the pain achieves an outcome and a meaning because Abraham's willingness to offer his son leads to a burst of blessing, the promise of a nation as numerous as stars. In Bak's distorted re-performances, the primordial act of redemptive suffering (in Akedah, and even more in crucifixion), is turned back into a mere assault on flesh and sacrifice decomposes back into disaster, literally a "dispersal of the stars."[67]

After Mantegna crops the original image so that the ram cannot be seen, thus turning sacrifice into disaster. But this change has knock-on effects, for with no ram to look at, the Abraham-mask seems to be looking guiltily over his shoulder, as if scanning for witnesses. Thus, the image now suggests the guilt of the father. Bak seems to be desecrating the sanctity of the child-sacrificing holy fathers but for (iconoclashtically) preserving, protecting, and so creative ends. The altar is smashed, reduced to barely a plinth, and Abraham and Isaac are both placed on it—so making the father, undecideably, both agent and victim. This lowering strips the image of its height and aura of sanctification, even as it removes Mantegna's original from its temple context. Some might feel that it therefore automatically demotes the sacred image, ruins the sacred truth. But by turning it into a scene played out at our (all-too-human) eye level, it converts the Akedah from a scene which is divinely prescriptive, commanding holocaust, into a scene that is merely descriptive—a sounding-board for incomprehensible and excessive suffering, as the Akedah has also always been in Jewish tradition, particularly since the Crusades.[68] The work, as delicately constructed and lovingly created Akedah ruin, leaves me wondering, as all these works do, what has damaged these Akedah scenes: the internal tension of the Akedah itself, the Shoah, or Bak, or all at once? If the damage has been inflicted by Bak's hand, is he then witnessing to the disaster of the Shoah by taking that disaster into Torah? Or is he, after Shoah, actively damaging a now in some sense unbearable biblical text? Or both at once? Is he testing Abraham's test back, asking it questions it can't endure? And how can we deem this questioning, destructive, iconoclasm merely, when it seems to seek out a certain, very qualified, saving, and uses the artist's damaging-caring hand to extend the text's own "Do not lay a hand" against the atrocities of Shoah—and the biblical text.

1 Bruno Latour, "What is Iconoclash, Or is there a World Beyond the Image Wars?," in *Iconoclash: Beyond the Image Wars in Science, Religion and Art,* ed. Bruno Latour and Peter Weibel (Cambridge, Ma. and London: MIT Press, 2002), 14-39.

2 Elaine Scarry, *The Body in Pain: The Making and Unmaking of the World* (Oxford: Oxford University Press, 1985), 173.

3 This article was completed during a period of leave sponsored by the Arts and Humanities Research Council.

4 Michel Serres, *Statues: Le second livre des foundations* (Paris: Editions F. Bourin, 1987), 195.

5 Latour, "What is Iconoclash?," 14.

6 Latour, "What is Iconoclash?," 15.

7 The "Akedah"/"binding" is the traditional Jewish term for Genesis 22. Christian tradition knows the text as "the sacrifice of Isaac."

8 Latour, "What is Iconoclash?," 36.

9 For discussion of the very American controversy that made Ofili's "The Holy Virgin Mary" iconic of the blasphemy and scandal of contemporary art, see S. Brent Plate, *Religion, Art and Visual Culture: A Cross-Cultural Reader* (New York: Palgrave, 2002), 1-2.

10 For the relationship between "Holocaust," "sacrifice," and "Akedah" see Zev Garber and Bruce Zuckerman, "Why do we call the Holocaust "the Holocaust"? An Enquiry into the Psychology of Labels," in *Remembering for the Future: Working Papers and Addenda,* ed. Yehuda Bauer (Oxford: Pergamon Press, 1989), 1879-92.

11 See Isabel Wollaston, "Traditions of Remembrance: Post-Holocaust Interpretations of Genesis 22," in *Words Remembered, Texts Renewed. Essays in Honour of John F. A. Sawyer,* ed. John Davies, Graham Harvey, and Wilfred G.E. Watson. JSOTSups 195 (Sheffield: Sheffield Academic Press, 1995), 41-51; Alvin H. Rosenfeld, "Reflections on Isaac," *Holocaust and Genocide Studies* 1.2 (1986): 242-48; Gershon Greenberg, "The Death of History and the Life of Akeda: Voices from War," in *The Death of God Movement and the Holocaust: Radical Theology Encounters the Shoah,* eds. Stephen R. Haynes and John K. Roth. Contributions to the Study of the Religion 55 (Westport, CT: Greenwood Press, 1999), 99-109.

12 Citations are from the definition of "conservative" in the *Shorter Oxford English Dictionary.*

13 For Orthodox Hasidic responses, see Gershon Greenberg, "The Death of History and the Life of Akeda;" Ignaz Maybaum, "The Binding of Isaac;" and "Moriah, Massada, Golgotha," in *Ignaz Maybaum: A Reader,* ed. Nicholas de Lange. *European Judaism.* Vol. 3 (New York and Oxford: Berghahn Books, 2001), 78-80, 81-83; Emmanuel Levinas, "Kierkegaard: Existence and Ethics" and "A Propos of 'Kierkegaard Vivant"' [1966] in Levinas, *Proper Names,* trans. Michael B. Smith (Stanford: Stanford University Press, 1996), 66-74 and 75-79; Stephen T. Katz, *Post-Holocaust Dialogues: Critical Studies in Modern Jewish Thought* (New York and London: New York University Press, 1983), 144.

14 Eliezer Berkovitz, *With God in Hell: Judaism in the Ghettos and the Deathcamps* (New York: Sanhedrin Press, 1979), 124-25.

15 Jean-François Lyotard, *The Differend: Phrases in Dispute,* trans. George Van Den Abbeele (Minneapolis: University of Minnesota Press, 1988), 117. Compare Bak's reflections on "Holocaust" in Bak, *Painted in Words: A Memoir* (Bloomington, Indianapolis and Boston: Indiana University Press and Pucker Art Publications, 2001), 481-82.

16 George Steiner, "A Conversation Piece," *Granta* 15 (Spring 1985; reprinted 1986), 166-78; Elie Wiesel, "The Sacrifice of Isaac: A Survivor's Story" in *Messengers of God: Biblical Portraits and Legends* (New York: Simon and Schuster, 1976), 69-97; Elie Wiesel, *Night,* trans. Stella Rodway (London: Penguin, 1981; first published in French 1958); Saul Bellow, *Mr. Sammler's Planet* (New York and London: Penguin, 1995; first published 1969); Amir Gilboa, "Yizhak" (1953) in *Modern Hebrew Poetry,* ed. Ruth Finer Mintz (Berkeley: University of California Press, 1968). Night as distorted Akedah is discussed in A. Neher, *The Exile of the World* (Philadelphia: Jewish Publication Society, 1981), 216-18; Rosenfeld, "Reflections on Isaac" briefly discusses Gilboa's "Yizhak" and (in depth) *Night.*

17 See Rosenfeld, Reflections on Isaac," 242. It is interesting how attempts to describe acts of damaging/distorting the tradition use terms like "irony" (Wiesel) or "sacred parody" (Wollaston following Roskies), which seem to euphemistically contain the level of savageness and distortion. See Wollaston, "Traditions of Remembrance" following David Roskies, *Against the Apocalypse: Responses to the Catastrophe in Modern Jewish Culture* (Cambridge, Ma.: Harvard University Press, 1984).

18 Steiner, "A Conversation Piece," 178.

19 Amir Gilboa, "Yitzhak" ("Isaac"), 1953. The full poem, translated by Glenda Abramson can be found in Abramson, "The Reinterpretation of the Akedah in Modern Hebrew Poetry," *Journal of Jewish Studies* XLI (1990): 101-114.

20 Bellow, *Mr. Sammler's Planet,* 63.

21 Bellow, *Mr. Sammler's Planet,* 145.

22 Rosenfeld, "Reflections on Isaac," 248.

23 Irene Tayler, "Shards of Time: Samuel Bak and the Art of Memory," in *Between Worlds: The Paintings and Drawings of Samuel Bak from 1946 to 2001,* ed. Irene Tayler (Boston: Pucker Art Publications, 2002), 11.

24 Bellow, *Mr. Sammler's Planet,* 42-43.

25 Dan Pagis, "Draft of a Reparations Agreement," *The Selected Poetry of Dan Pagis,* ed. and trans. Stephen Mitchell (Oxford: Carcanet Press, 1972), 26.

26 For Bak's own reflections on the restorative dimension of his work, see *Samuel Bak: Painter of Questions, a film by Christa Singer* (Boston: Pucker Gallery, 2003).

27 Bellow, *Mr. Sammler's Planet,* 277.

28 Bellow, *Mr. Sammler's Planet,* 224.

29 Bellow, *Mr. Sammler's Planet,* 224. In his autobiography, Bak describes his first exhibition in the ghetto in 1942 as a desperate attempt to attest to the Romantic truth of the "indestructible power of human creativity." He comments, with a combination of empathy and critical detachment, that "[p]athetic circumstances breed pathetic clichés." See Bak, *Painted in Words,* 28.

30 Nigel Whiteley, "Readers of the Lost Art: Visuality and Particularity in Art Criticism" in *Interpreting Visual Culture: Essays in the Hermeneutics of the Visual,* ed. Ian Heywood and Barry Sandy well (London and New York: Routledge, 1999), 117.

31 Crammed as it is with letters and verbal gags, Bak's work cannot easily be set up as the opposite of conceptual art, however. For discussion of Bak's complex relationship to surrealism, postmodernism, and conceptual art, see Saul Touster, "In and Out of Surrealism: Placing Samuel Bak," in Tayler *Between Worlds,* 39-56.

32 Stephen Feinstien, "'This is not a Pear:' Reflections on Samuel Bak's Pear Paintings," in *Samuel Bak: New Perceptions of Old Appearances* (Boston: Pucker Gallery, 2004), 4. As Celan famously fractures the German language, so Bak breaks the visual language of Dürer, former citizen of Nuremburg. On the "sheer pleasure of looting something that the Germans treasured as being thoroughly German" see Bak in *Between Worlds,* 272.

33 Images of sight and blindness run through the Genesis narratives. Think for example of the opening of the eyes of the first couple; Hagar's encounter with the 'God who sees' (Genesis 16), Isaac's dim eyes failing to see the difference between Esau and Jacob (Genesis 27), and Tamar's deception of Judah (Genesis 38).

34 Scarry, *The Body in Pain,* 173. See the headquote to this essay.

35 *Life? or Theatre?* Is the title that the artist Charlotte Salmon (1917-1943) gave to a series of over 780 small gouaches chosen from a total of 1,325 painted while in exile in the south of France between 1940 and 1942. In 1943, aged just twenty-six, she was deported from France and murdered in Auschwitz. I visited the exhibition when it was on tour at the Royal Academy of Arts, London (October 1998-January 1999). Segments are exhibited permanently at the Jewish Historical Museum in Amsterdam.

36 See Donald Bartheleme, "On Angels," in *Sixty Stories* (New York and London: Penguin, 1982), 135-37. Bartheleme's story, beginning with the announcement "The death of God left the angels in a strange position," seems to me to come very close to the wry and poignant redeployment of angels by Bak.

37 The lament of the mother Hannah can be found in *Yalkut Deut* 26, and *Lamentations Rabbah;* cf. Shalom Spiegel, *The Last Trial: On the Legends and Lore of the Command to Abraham to Offer Isaac as a Sacrifice* (Woodstock, Vermont: Jewish Lights, 1993; first published in English 1967; in Hebrew 1950), 15. The mother says: "Go and tell Father Abraham: Let not your heart swell with pride! You built one altar, but I have built seven altars and on them have offered up my seven sons. What is more: Yours was a trial; mine was an accomplished fact!"

38 Lawrence Langer also notes the "infidel implications of some of the costumes" and observes how "a holy ritual of sacrifice" has metamorphosed into a pagan rite of slaughter. Lawrence Langer, *In a Different Light: The Book of Genesis in the Art of Samuel Bak* (Boston: Pucker Art Publications, 2001), 23-24.

39 Kierkegaard, *Fear and Trembling,* in *Fear and Trembling and Repetition,* ed. and trans. Howard V. Hong and Edna H. Hong (Kierkegaard's Writings VI; Princeton: Princeton University Press, 1983), 9. Kierkegaard famously asks what if the sacrifice had occurred on a barren heath, in Jutland, not so very far from Copenhagen.

40 See Bak, *Between Worlds,* 173: "But as a God-fearing atheist what I fear are the atrocities man perpetrates in the name of his militant Divinities. I am sure that if God existed, He would never have permitted the horrors I had to witness, and this is a strong point in His favour." See also his comments on devoted cult of Stalin in "Stalin Loves Us," *Painted in Words,* 309-26.

41 Compare the discussion by Danna Fewell and Gary Phillips in this volume.

42 Latour, "What is Iconoclash?," 15; my italics.

43 Compare Bak's comments on being haunted by the figure of Isaac, the "bound child" in *Painted in Words,* 172 and *Between Worlds,* 309.

44 Bak, *Painted in Words,* 342.

45 Bak, *Painted in Words,* 297-98 (On the particular struggle of this painting, see *Between Worlds,* 309-310); Lawrence Langer, "The Holocaust in Bak's Art" in Tayler, *Between Worlds,* 24.

46 Wiesel, "Isaac: A Survivor's Story," 73.

47 Bak, *Between Worlds,* 309.

48 Bak ventures that the broken tree alongside Abraham is the "tree of life" which, in Jewish liturgy and tradition, is connected to the tree of Torah. See *Between Worlds,* 310. I'm extending this possibility to the sprig in Abraham's hand.

49 Franz Kafka's comments on being part of a "transitional generation of Jews" in "Letter to His Father," in *The Sons: The Metamorphosis, The Judgement, The Stoker, and Letter to His Father,* trans. Edwin and Willa Muir (New York: Schocken Books, 1989), 115-17, esp. 146-48.

50 Wiesel, "Isaac: A Survivor's Story," 72.

51 The theory that art makes notice the familiar by defamiliarizing or "making strange" is taken from Victor Schlovsky, "Art as Technique" and *"Sterne's Tristram Shandy: Stylistic Commentary,"* in *Russian Formalist Criticism: Four Essays,* ed. Lee T. Lemon and Marion J. Reis (Lincoln, Neb: University of Nebraska Press, 1965), 3-57.

52 Bak in Tayler, *Between Worlds,* 297.

53 Bak, *Painted in Words,* 172.

54 All of Samuel Bak's grandparents—Khone, Chayim, Shifra and Rachel—were murdered in Ponar/Paneriai on the outskirts of Vilna.

55 Amir Gilboa, "Yizhak."

56 For a fascinating discussion of our complex love affair with ruins see David Lowenthal, *The Past is a Foreign Country* (Cambridge: Cambridge University Press, 1985). The citation is from p. 173. The fragments shored against our ruins are stolen, of course, from T.S. Eliot's *The Wasteland.* Walter Benjamin's reflections on ruins are discussed by S. Brent Rodriguez Plate, "Seeing Words, Reading Images: Allegory and Interpretation in Bak and Benjamin" in this volume.

57 Bak, *Painted in Words,* 221, 370.

58 Bellow, *Mr Sammler's Planet,* 36.

59 See Bak, *Painted in Words,* 287-91. See particularly his astute comments on the experience of being made, self-consciously, into a Jew through violent name-calling by the "other" (291)—a story familiar from other European Jews, including Alain Finkelkraut and Jacques Derrida.

60 On the myth of no Jewish art, see for example Elisha Revel-Neher, "'With Wisdom and Knowledge of Workmanship': Jewish Art without a Question Mark" and Margaret Olin, "Graven Images on Video? The Second Commandment and Jewish Identity," in Matthew Baigell and Milly Heyd, eds., *Complex Identities: Jewish Consciousness and Modern Art* (New Brunswick, NJ; London: Rutgers University Press, 2001),12-33 and 34-50, esp. 42-44. The denial of early Jewish art, to the point where Gombrich catalogues the third century C.E. murals at the synagogue at Dura Europos under "Early Christian Art," is particularly revealing (see Olin, 43). These murals include an Akedah.

61 Chaim Potok, *My Name is Asher Lev* (New York and London: Penguin Books, 1972), 288.

62 Matthew Baigell, *Jewish-American Artists and the Holocaust* (New Brunswick, NS: Rutgers University Press, 1997), 79. Ziva Amishai-Maisels, "The Jewish Jesus," *Journal of Jewish Art* 9 (1982): 90. Amishai-Maisels concedes that the Akedah has far outstripped the crucifixion as a literary image, but argues that the Akedah is ruled out as a visual image because "there is no visual tradition of the sacrifice being carried out'" (90).

63 For discussion of the Isaac who actually dies and the midrashic confusion between the ram called Isaac and the son called Isaac, see Sherwood "Textual Carcasses and Isaac's Scar, or What Jewish Interpretation Makes of the Violence that Almost Takes Place on Mount Moriah," in *Sanctified Aggression: Legacies of Biblical and Post-Biblical Vocabularies of Violence,* ed. Jonneke Bekkenkamp and Yvonne Sherwood (London and New York: Continuum/T & T Clark International, 2003), 22-43. See also Spiegel, *The Last Trial.*

64 For just a sample of the many contemporary Christian critiques of the doctrine of atonement, see for example Rita Nakashima Brock. For Bak's reflections on Christian theology as a stage, where suffering becomes fulfilment, see *Painted in Words,* 375; my italics. Rebecca Ann Parker, *Proverbs of Ashes: Violence, Redemptive Suffering, and the Search for What Saves Us* (Boston: Beacon Press, 2001); Anthony Bartlett, *Cross Purposes: The Violent Grammar of the Christian Atonement* (Harrisburg, Pa.; Trinity Press International, 2001); Timothy Gorringe, *God's Just Vengeance: Crime, Violence and the Rhetoric of Salvation,* Cambridge Studies in Ideology and Religion, 9 (Cambridge: Cambridge University Press, 1996).

65 See Bak, *Painted in Words,* 170-72.

66 Bak, *Painted in Words,* 170-72, 375. Bak, who was nicknamed by his grandmother Shifra as 'Jesusl', little baby Jesus, and was doted on by his parents as if he were the Christ child, was saved (for the last time of many) by his father Jonas who smuggled him out of the labor camp in a sack. His father perished in the camp a few days before its liberation by the Red Army.

67 See Plate, "Seeing Words, Reading Images," 60 in this volume. On stars and disasters and sacrifice as an economic, salvific principle, masking the damage done to flesh, see John D. Caputo, *Against Ethics: Contributions to a Poetics of Obligation with Constant Reference to Deconstruction* (Bloomington and Indianapolis: Indiana University Press, 1993).

68 See Spiegel, "The Last Trial" and Sherwood, "Textual Carcasses and Isaac's Scar."

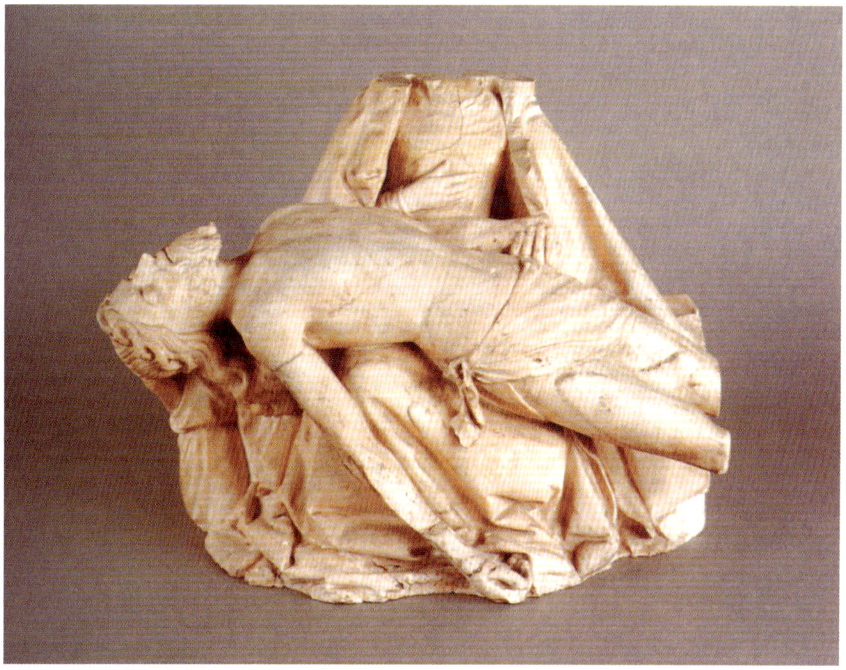

Pietá, fifteenth-century

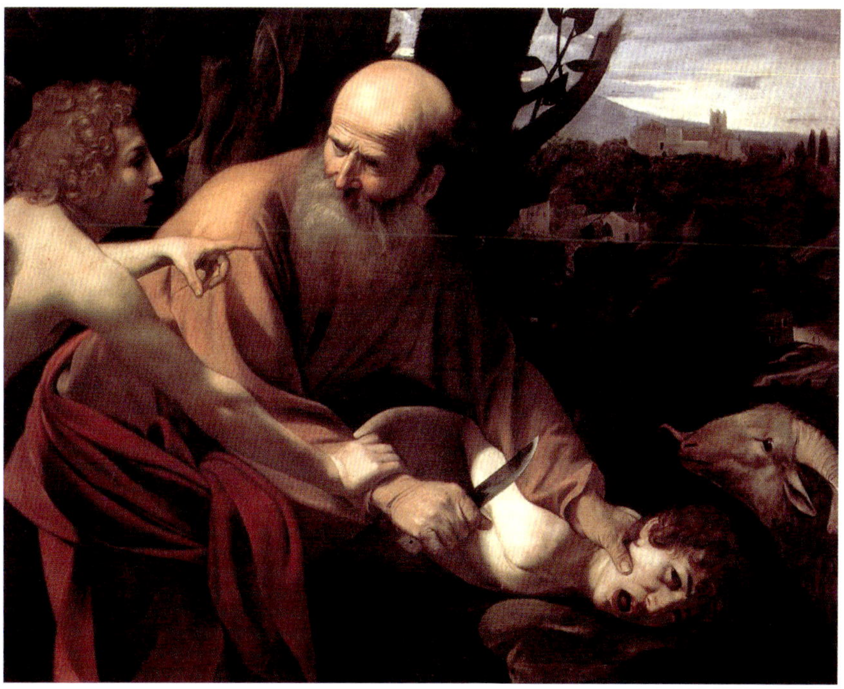

Michelangelo Merisi Caravaggio
Sacrifice of Isaac, ca. 1603

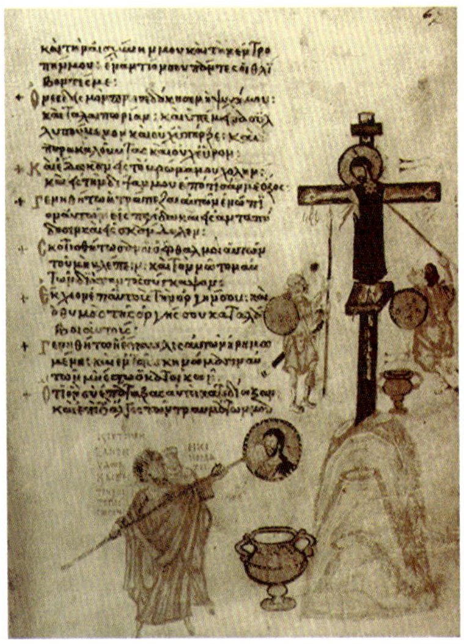

Chludov Psalter, c 850-75 fol 67r

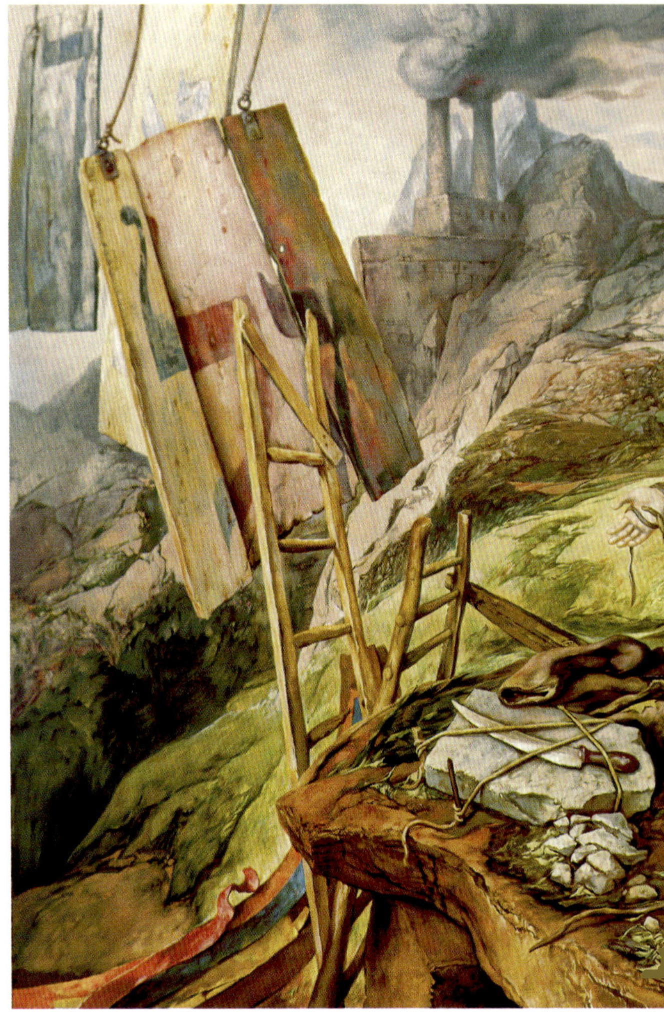

Isaac's Dream, 1999
Oil on Canvas, 40 x 50"

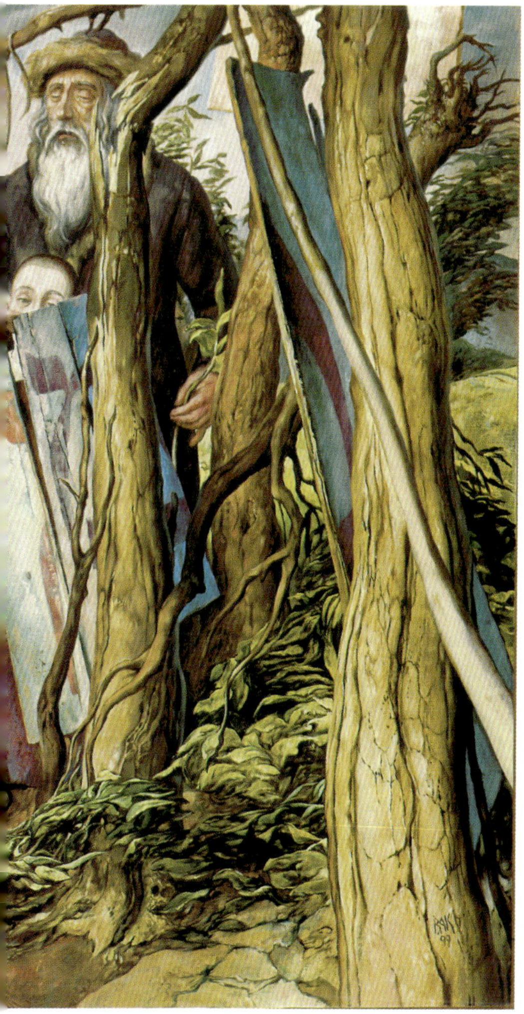

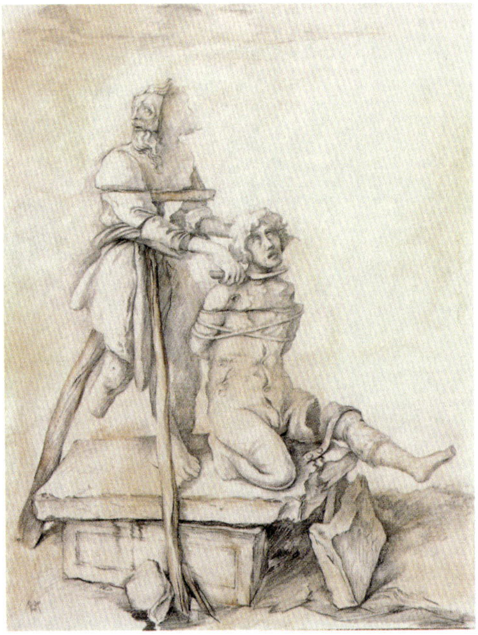

After Mantegna, 1999
Pencil and Pastel on Paper, 24 3/4 x 20"

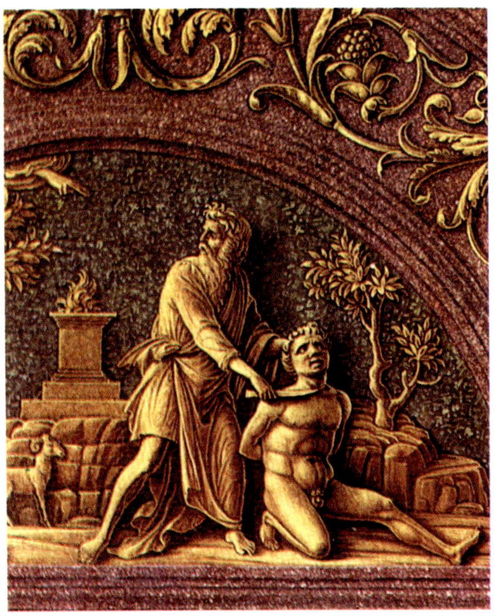

Andrea Mantegna
The Circumcision of Christ, ca. 1470

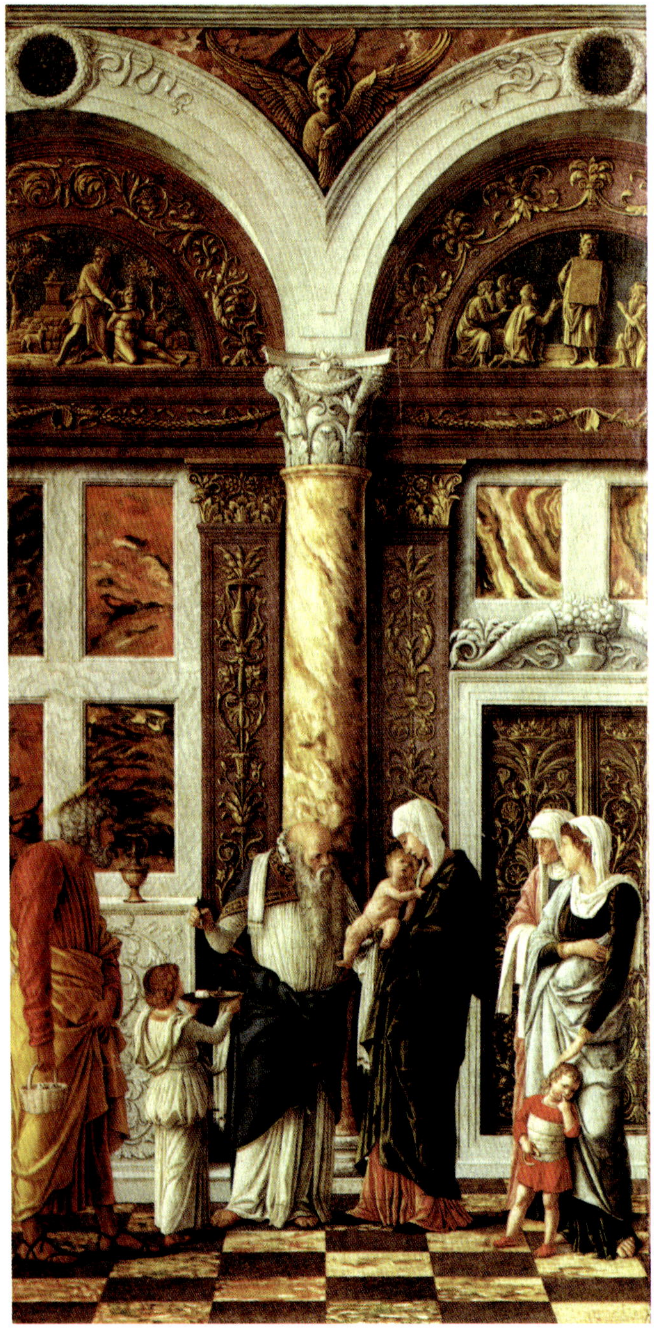

Andrea Mantegna
The Circumcision of Christ, ca. 1470

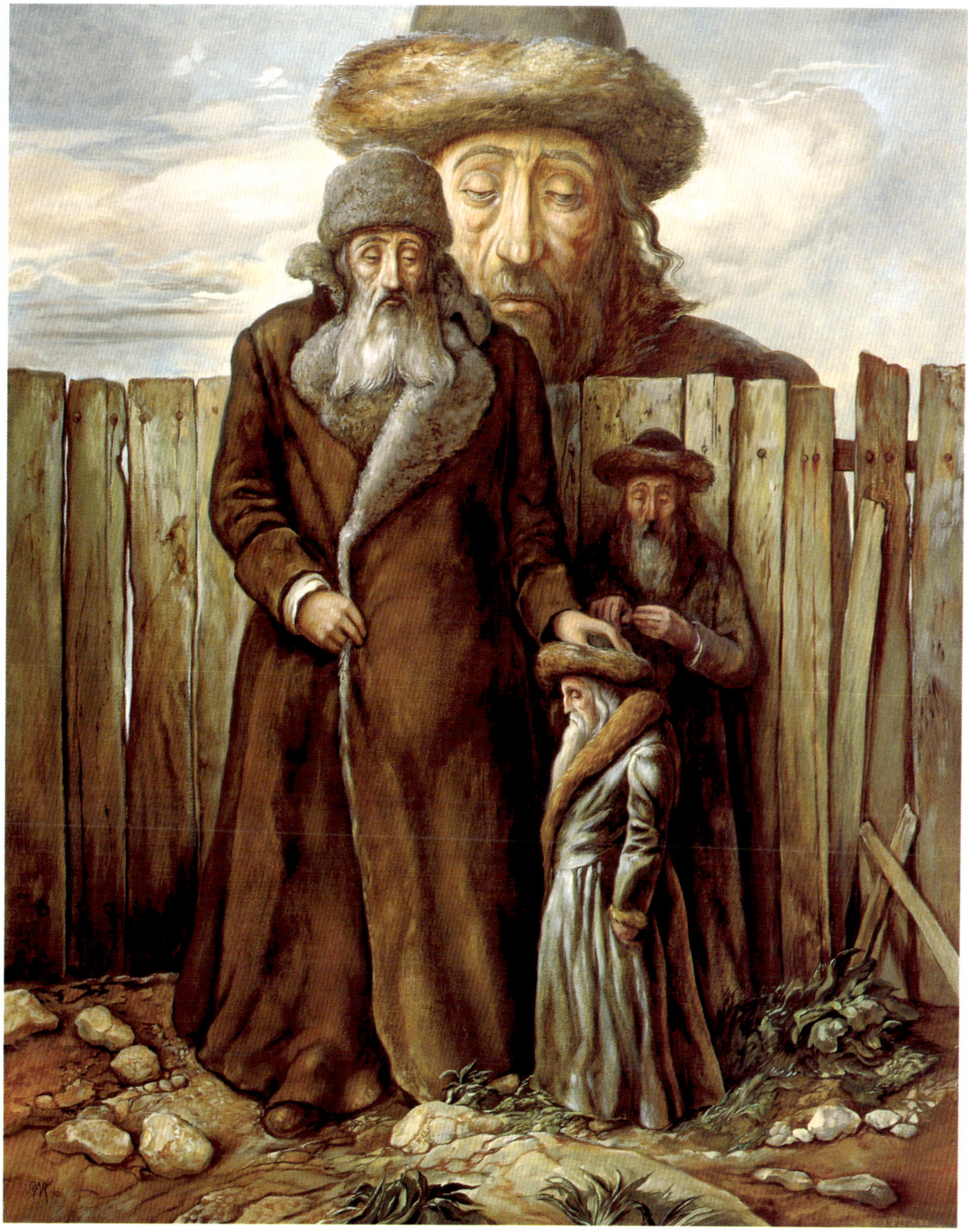

From Generation to Generation III, 1996
Oil on Canvas, 32 1/4 x 26"

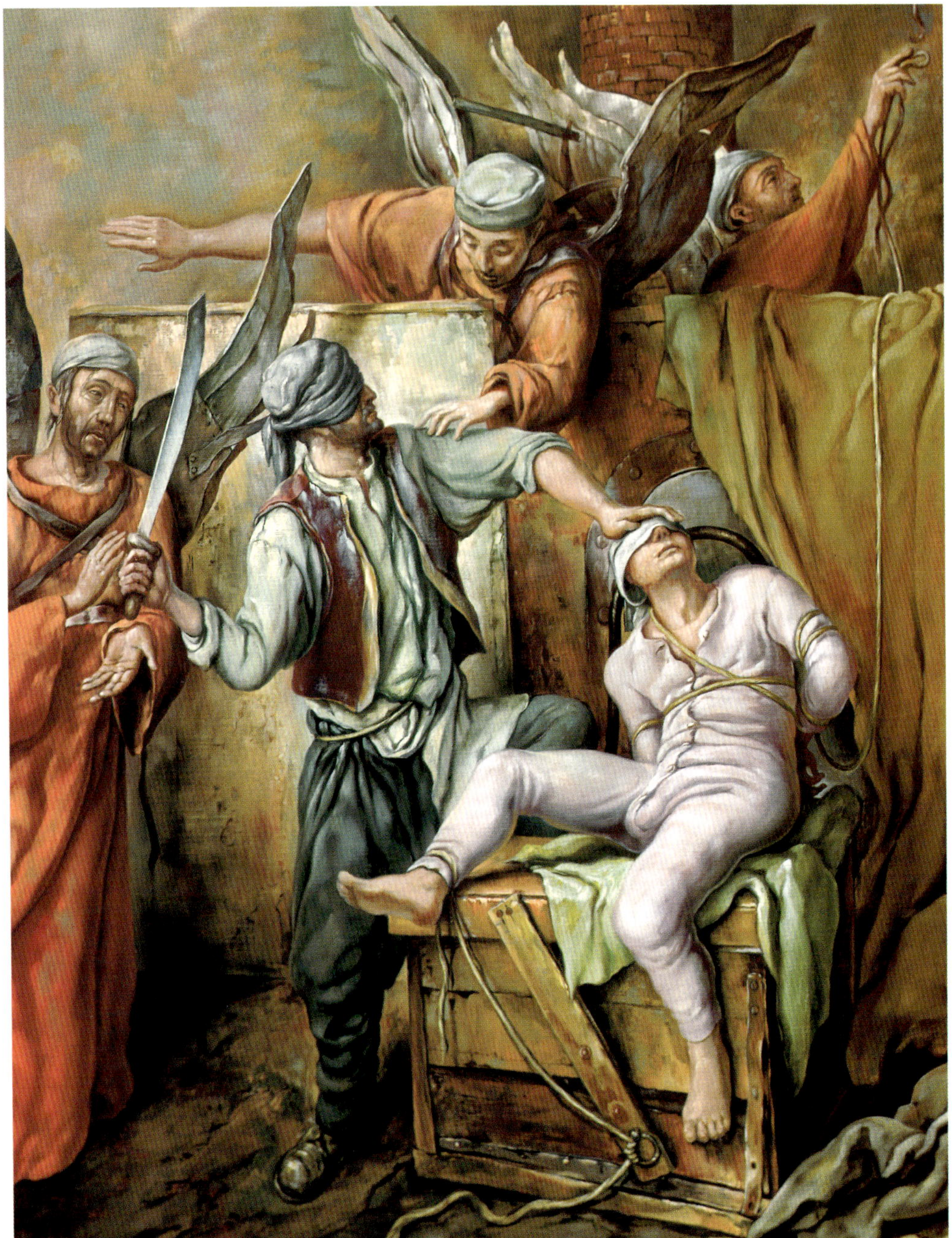

Dress Rehearsal, 1999
Oil on Canvas, 40 x 32"

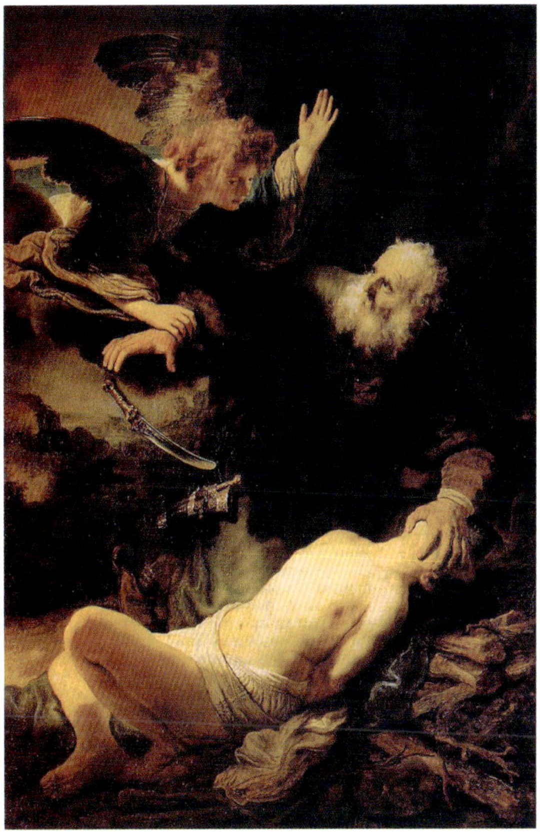

Rembrandt Van Rijn
The Angel Prevents the Sacrifice of Isaac, 1635

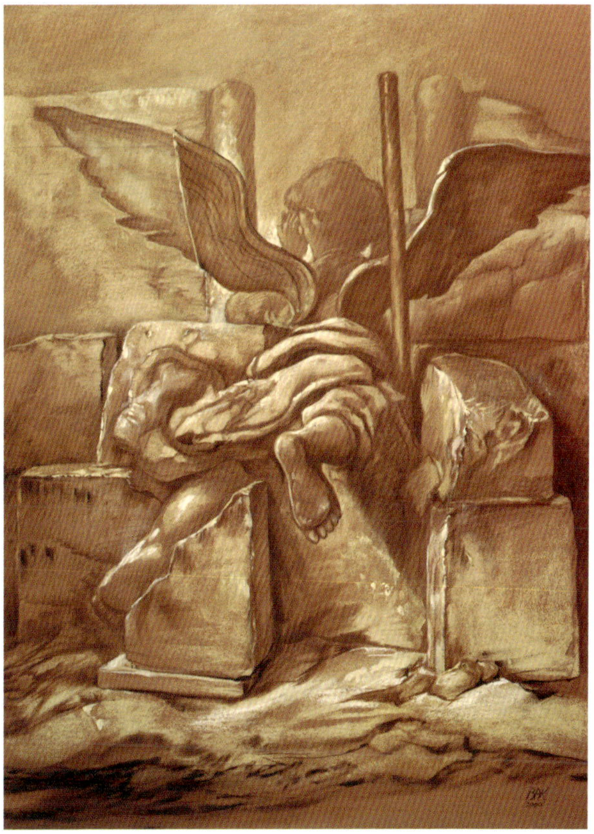

Rembrandt's Angel, 2000
Crayon and Oil on Brown Paper, 25 3/4 x 19 3/4"

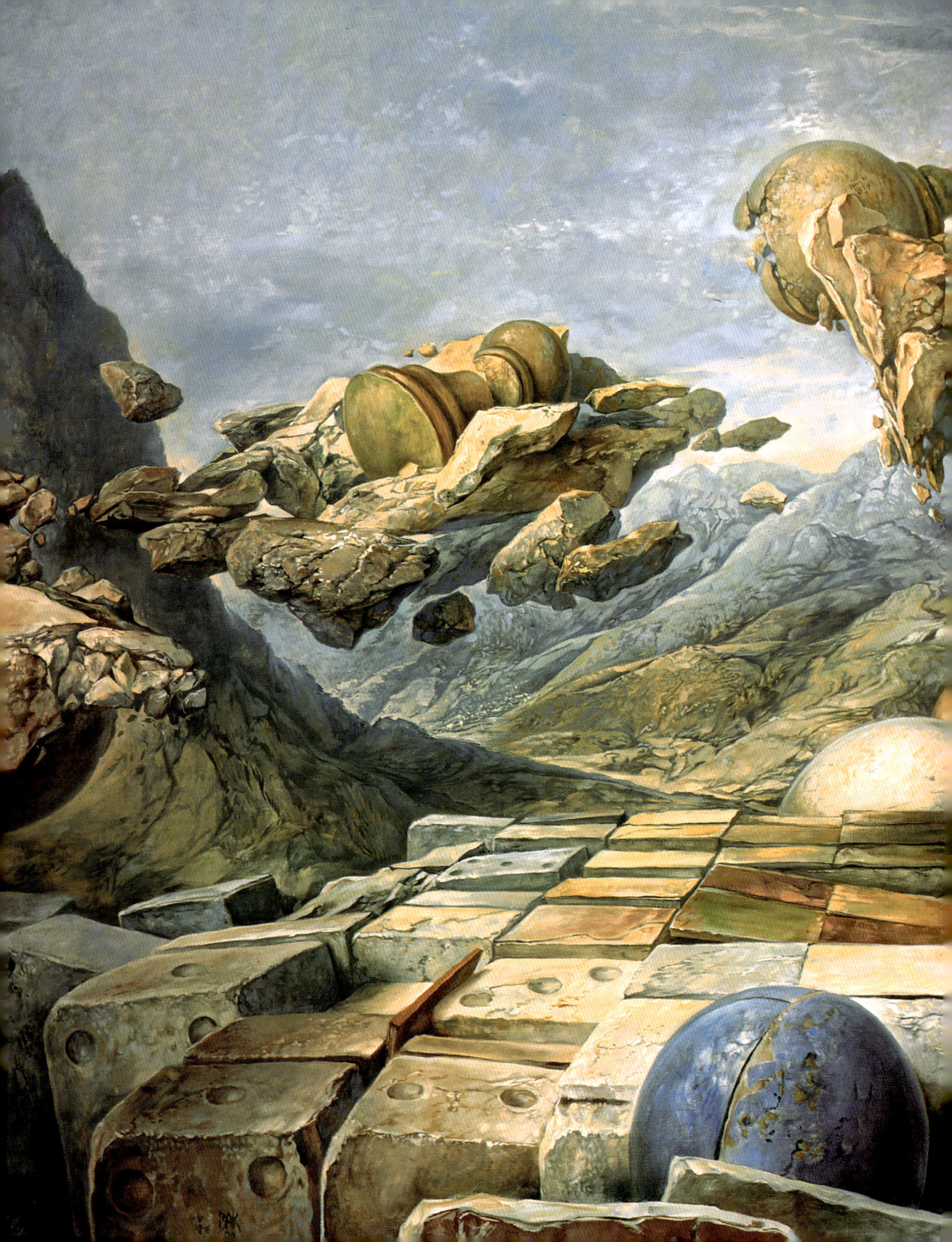

Images of Disaster: Survival and the Impossible in the Artwork of Samuel Bak and the Book of Job

DAN MATHEWSON

> Whenever we attempt to tell our own story [about the Holocaust, about disaster], we transmit [Job's]. The opposite is true also: those of his legends we presumed invented, we live through; those of his words we thought illusory, proved to be true; we owe them our experience of evil and death.
>
> —ELIE WIESEL, *Messengers of God*[1]

> [T]he story of Job is not a legend, for Satan appears in real life: he is Nebuchadnezzar, he is Hitler.
>
> —ANDRÉ NEHER, *The Exile of the World*[2]

Much of the artwork of Samuel Bak is replete with the rich imagery of biblical texts. Mainly drawing from Genesis, Bak finds in these images the malleable clay with which to form landscapes that display the experience of disaster and the difficult issue of Jewish identity in the present. Absent from Bak's canvases (at least as far as I've discovered) is that biblical figure who has become the model of suffering and protest, that character whose story numerous thinkers have reexamined with renewed interest in light of the Holocaust: Job.[3] Though Bak never paints explicitly Joban scenes, he does discuss Job in his commentary on his artwork, specifically on his winged creatures, sometimes called angels, which appear in his artwork with fair regularity. Commenting on these angels, Bak notes that

> The piteously man-made angels that populate my paintings do not pretend to represent... unearthly beings. My spent and aged angels with their heavy wings are emanations of the

Detail of *Passing Thoughts,* 1998
Oil on Canvas, 26 x 48"

> inevitably constricted human imagination....I wonder whether these angel messengers can help us, or whether we don't encumber their ill-fitting wings by giving them impossible tasks. In my perpetual question, I ask them to carry undecipherable messages from a God-fearing atheist to some superior presence, some silent voice from which, like Job, I seek adequate answers but receive none.[4]

Here is a statement of Bak's sense of his own artistic task. He, like Job, delivers undecipherable messages to a deity who responds with silence. And the figure of such a convoluted exchange is this "piteous" angel, the very un-angel-like creature that is distinctly human-looking, clad in a cumbersome flying suit that is itself the composite arrangement of discarded junk. This is hardly the supernatural mediator between the heavenly and the earthly, that guardian angel that Bak as a child learned about while hiding from the Nazis in a Benedictine convent, who miraculously brings humanity in contact with the deity by its very mediation. Bak's (and Job's) angel is a distant echo of such grandeur.

Above all, Bak describes this angel's task as an "impossible" one. He is to deliver the undecipherable message of a God-fearing atheist to a silent deity. This angel, therefore, is the figure of confusion, disillusionment, incomprehension—the figure of a Joban-Bakian task that Bak calls "impossible." Though Job never appears on Bak's canvasses, this angel signifies Bak's connection with Job. By bringing this "impossible" to life, Bak does as Wiesel says: he transmits Job's story (and vice versa).

But what, exactly, is this impossible that Bak's angel signifies? This word "impossible" with all of its synonyms—incomprehensible, unthinkable—and alternate forms—impossibility, incomprehensibility—is a term that the reader of the vast amount of secondary literature on the Holocaust encounters with fair regularity. This "impossible," however, is not a capital "I" impossible, the way the Real is written with a capital "R" in Lacanian psychoanalysis or the way the Other is written with a capital "O" in Simone de Beauvoir's feminist analysis. The "impossible" does not describe a concept or a theory or an idea. Rather this "impossible" is an authorial shorthand for "there's no way to understand this." It is a literary raising of the hands in a gesture of bewilderment. It is a way, in the midst of offering analysis and explanation, of saying "there is no way to analyze and no way to explain."

So, for example, Lawrence Langer, in describing what he calls the "inhuman"[5] actions of the Germans and other perpetrators and the apparent passivity of their Jewish victims, speaks of "impossible" actions: an SS soldier taking a Jewish infant from its mother, grasping the infant by the ankles and ripping it in two; or a Jewish woman "frantically running around the house, begging" for her life from her German tormenters, while her husband, apparently unconcerned, ate his soup.[6] Such actions defy understanding. "What kind of world is this and what kind of people are these who are able to inflict such unbelievable and impossible suffering on living beings?" pens an unknown diarist in the Lodz ghetto.[7] Such actions seemingly exist outside any ethical frame of reference by which humans ought to live. As such, they are impossible to explain, to theorize.

Shoshana Felman and Dori Laub also discuss this "impossible." For them it is the "impossible" of survivors speaking the trauma of the Holocaust. In their account, "the traumatic event, although real, took place outside the parameters of 'normal' reality, such as causality, sequence, place, and time."[8] The effort to speak about this trauma is therefore to speak of an impossibility, something without reference in the world of the known and familiar. Cathy Caruth likewise discusses the "impossible history"[9] that trauma victims carry: an event that stubbornly exists outside all schemes of meaning that would attempt to tame it, to render it comprehensible, to bring it inside the realm of the familiar.

In this line of Holocaust study, to ask "what is the impossible," as if to conceptualize the disaster of the Holocaust, to assign it a recognizable place in the symbolic categories of mentation, culture, and analysis, is to miss the point. The impossible is the negation of all such frames of reference, a gaping black hole of signification.

But how to paint or "speak" this impossible? How to give voice to that which defies articulation without trivializing it or rendering it false? For Bak, as for Job, the answer is through the world of images—or at least through the imaginative bending and alteration of familiar and accepted images and metaphors. Bak speaks Job's story by referencing the known world, but casting it in scenes that only can exist in the world of the imaginary. He rearranges the realm of the known in impossible combinations. Whether the fragmented bodies of human subjects, the absent spaces in the shapes of living forms, or living wholes composed of the discarded remains of war's aftermath, Bak populates his canvases with figures that are at once recognizable, but also deformed and refashioned.

The particular paintings that I wish to examine more closely are the ones devoted to the memory of his step-father in which Bak invokes the familiar world of chess. Chess is a game with its own symbolic field: a self-contained world, governed by a set of rigid rules that define the movement of the pieces about the fixed, carefully delineated squares of the board. Within the symbolic world of chess, there exists a myriad of formations and strategies, seemingly inexhaustible choices within the realm of the possible.

I would argue that chess in Bak's paintings operates as a metaphor for life. Just as humans inhabit symbolic worlds that provide stability and rational structures to the chaotic and overwhelming masses of information and sense perceptions of daily life, so also chess suggests a whole symbolic world—one that organizes reality into conceptual zones. The symbolic world of chess represents life's rational symbolic world with its rules of conduct, ethical standards, social norms, and so on. The world of chess is the symbolic world of human existence.

If the world of chess provides a set of stock images for Bak, in Job the biblical character draws on a traditional set of Israelite stock images, one that he shares with his friends. These images find their home in the rational, symbolically coherent, moral and theological worldview sometimes called "Divine Justice," an idealized world where God is thought to reward virtue and punish vice. Like Bak, Job will select key images from this particular symbolic world, and then will deform them.[10]

In his exquisite opening speech in chapter three, one such image is that of "the way" *(drk)*—an iconic image of the moral-theological world of Divine Justice. "The way" is the concrete image of the path on which one walks, but more importantly "the way" functions as a "ground metaphor"[11] or "nuclear symbol"[12] that "organizes other perceptions and images and conveys a way of perceiving the world" (especially evidenced in Proverbs 1-9).[13] The full image is of two paths, two ways: one could walk along one path that is straight, clear, true, and open; or one could walk on another path that is evil, dark, lawless, and dangerous. To walk on the good path means to act in accordance with Wisdom, which operates as a roadmap for this journey. The way of the good path is the religious way of God, who aids the traveler on this journey (Proverbs 3:23-26).[14] Moreover, the symbolic conception of "the way" implies active agency: one is always *walking* rather than *being* on one path or another. Thus the righteous "walk" along and "keep to" the right path (1:5; 2:20; 3:23; 9:6; 11:5; 28:18), while the wicked "walk" along the evil path, and "forsake" the right one (1:15; 2:13; 4:14).[15] One's actions and decisions determine which path one walks.[16]

For Bak as for Job, however, symbolic landscapes—whether chess or "way"—are invoked only to be disrupted. In one of Bak's chess pieces, entitled *Unexpected,* we see game pieces caught in a deluge that threatens to wash them away and carry them out to the sea. This is not the "unexpected" of a carefully laid trap in the game of chess, a stratagem whereby a player captures an important piece of the opponent's army—the type of move well within the rules and symbolic field of the game of chess. Bak's "unexpected," rather, is the sweeping away of this very symbolic field—a deluge that renders the mobility, strategy, and meaning of chess irrelevant. The symbolic world of chess is punctured, fissured, rent apart by an alien reality. The terra firma of the chessboard, that rigid surface that provided stability and firmness, has now become its opposite: churning liquid, a ferocious force that topples. The squares of the chessboard, once representing individuated autonomous zones in a logically connected symbolic world, now begin to blur together in an undecipherable watery mass. And the chessboard itself, once comprising chess's entire symbolic field, now begins to blend in with the threatening, untamable sea. The rigid rules that once governed the movements of the chess pieces are now irrelevant. Impossibly, the knights, bishops, and queen all occupy the same liquid square. Impossibly, a pawn drowns on the very square that once provided its grounding. Impossibly, the pieces have nowhere to go and have nowhere to stand. They huddle together in fear, even as waves begin to pull them out to sea.

This is the picture of a world whose rules no longer apply. It is the collapse of a world of meaning that leaves its inhabitants seemingly lost and without recourse. It is a depiction of the collapse of meaning and the experience of the impossible. And as Wiesel claims, this is also a depiction of Job's story. For Job, too, describes disaster by invoking the world of the known, namely the traditional world expressed by the "way" image. In the climactic verses of his opening speech (3:20-23), Job wonders aloud why God gives life to a certain class of humans, of which he is the prime exemplar. He identifies these miserable humans as "the sufferers" (*l'ml*; 3:20a), "the bitter of spirit" (*lmry npsh;* 3:20b), and "the man whose way is hidden" (*lgbr 'shr drkw nstrh;* 3:23a). This invocation of the "way" image is brief but particularly troubling, for Job speaks of the "way" in the passive voice: his "way is hidden" from him.[17] This claim of hidden-ness, however, is not an option in the symbolic world of Divine Justice's "two paths." In the expected formulation—in the world of the possible—not to be walking along the path of righteousness would entail walking along its alternative, the path of wickedness. Yet, in Job's reformulation, he has neither continued along the one path, nor has he abandoned it in favor of the other. Instead, Job speaks the impossible image of one who is utterly bewildered, not knowing anymore where a path of any sort might be. Job speaks of the unavailability of a functional symbolic structure that might underpin a rational moral world.

Moreover, Job reveals in his next line (3:23b) that this bewildering non-path, non-place in which he finds himself is the result not of his own shortcomings, but of the very obstructive presence of God about him. "God has hedged him about" *(ysk 'lwh b'dw),* an image of hostility and aggression. Just as the sea in Bak's chess painting overwhelms the symbolic order of the world of chess from without, so also in Job's reformulation the two-paths image collapses "from the outside," as it were, by an uncontainable and irresistible force: here, God's hostile activity. In the traditional image of "the way"—the world of the known—God was thought to be the companion and guardian of those who walked on the righteous path. Here, however, Job suggests that God's presence is far from guardianship. It is, rather, an oppressive barrier that effectively obscures the path of righteousness and causes Job's paralysis—God has "hedged him about."[18]

The linking of a ruptured symbolic world with the sense of paralysis—the inability to perceive a way forward in a world that no longer makes sense—is a feature, too, in Bak's chess series. In another piece in the series, *Passing Thoughts,* Bak again alludes to the impossible as the disruption of life with the image of the permanently scarred chessboard. Once stable squares now crumble and waver. Some squares appear to fall off of the chessboard, while others are replaced with dice, symbols of chance. Life is no longer the security of the logic and cunning of chess, but is reduced to dumb luck. The pawns, too, no longer operate within a once meaningful world of the chessboard. Seemingly terrified of a world that no longer functions properly, they have "escaped" their crumbling world and appear possibly to cower before the uncontainable forces of disruption. The blue pawn in the foreground, in particular, appears trapped, pinned in by the force of a ruptured world, incapable of the very movements that once defined its existence. Like Job's paralysis in view of a collapsed symbol system, this pawn is also trapped in a symbolic world that no longer affords movement but hinders it. Moreover, this image of paralysis is also an image of death, for the pawn's stasis in Bak's depiction is like a symbolic entombment, the descent below into the earth. The stasis of the ruptured world is like the stasis of death.

According to the psychohistorian Robert Jay Lifton, a depiction of symbolic death is common in the attempt to articulate the impossible of disaster. Lifton argues that in light of disaster among survivors there exists an increased awareness of death's place in life. This awareness is expressed by a range of death imagery, of which Lifton emphasizes three groupings: images of bodily disintegration; images of separation (the lack of connection to a human community); and images of stasis or paralysis (the sense of the absence of a meaningful way forward). According to Lifton, survivors of disaster—those who experience the impossible, and live through it—tend to have an increased awareness of death's place in, and claim upon, life. Lifton argues that there is frequently among survivors "an outpouring of death imagery, publicly and privately, as well as feelings of separation, disintegration, and stasis (what I call 'death equivalents') and a questioning of larger human connectedness or symbolic immortality."[19] Where once the meaning of life and death formed a coherent place in a rational symbolic world, now with the shattering of this world, life and death lose their symbolic moorings, lose their once assumed fixed and reasonable meanings, and now exist in a symbolic flux. The artist, claims Lifton, frequently is the one to depict this flux, to probe the relationship of life and death, to explore death's hold on life, and to question their meaning in relation to each other and to the world.[20]

Certainly Job links his sense of stasis or paralysis to death in his opening speech. His paralysis on earth—his lack of a symbol system to provide a meaningful way forward—drives his plea for death, which is the main theme of his opening speech. Life, Job claims, is the experience of the stasis of death—disruption and disaster (the *rgz* of 3:26). Conversely and paradoxically, Job's anticipated and longed for actual death comes to represent to him the experience of true life. In contrast to traditional depictions of Sheol as a place of gloom and darkness, separated from the land of the living, where one would eke out a minimal existence with the life-energies severely truncated (Lifton's death equivalents of separation and stasis), Job in his opening speech fantasizes about Sheol as a place of abundant life. Sheol is a place not of separation but connection to the most venerable of all company—kings, counselors, and princes (3:14-15). Sheol is not a place of stasis and the diminishment of life but a place of life-giving rest and tranquility, a place of renewal that Job describes using key terms of the Psalmist's description of the good life *(shkb, shqt, yshn).*[21] Moreover, in death Job identifies the reversal of death's equivalents on earth. The prisoner who is bound (an image of stasis, paralysis) finds release (liberation, movement), and the slave who is confined (stasis) in death is free (3:18). For Job, Sheol—death—takes on the characteristics of life (peacefulness, rest, tranquility, release, freedom, movement, community), while life—his life—takes on the characteristics of death—stasis, paralysis, lack of movement. And this reversal, this experience of death in life, Job claims in the last words of this speech is the result of *rgz,* disaster, rupture, trouble (3:23).

Job gives voice to the disruption not just of a world, but of the values of life and death in this world. Life and death intermingle and join. So also in Bak's paintings. In *Passing Thoughts* the paralysis of the blue pawn is depicted as a sort of death: though the pawn is upright, seemingly alive, the pawn is entombed below the "earth" as if dead. As in Job's speech, this image of paralysis-as-death raises certain questions: How to move forward when the world has crumbled? How to live when one no longer knows how to move? How to *be* in a death-tainted existence?

The pawns in the upper portions of the painting also depict this intermingling of the experience of death and life in light of the impossibility of rupture and disaster. These pawns appear in death-like poses: lying on their sides, lifeless in the terrain. And yet, unlike their earthbound, alive-yet-entombed counterparts, these dead pawns have seemingly escaped the terror and bewilderment of the shattered earthly world. In death they have broken away from the vicissitude of the earth and appear to be carried upward, heavenward, possibly to a better existence in the world beyond or above. Unlike their earthbound counterparts, these pawns do not cower in fear, but appear tranquil in a sleep-like pose. These pawns seem to reflect Job's vision of the life-giving repose of Sheol: though dead, they appear to have attained that sacred rest that rejuvenates, a repose that brings life and bears one up and away from the disruption of life.

But Bak's image of life-in-death is more complicated. For the pawns that seem to be escaping towards the heavens are being borne upward by rugged clouds of dense rock—quasi-clouds absolutely incapable of floating and rising to the heavens. These stony clouds seem to suggest that perhaps death does not transpose one to the repose of the world beyond, as Job suggests, but that in death one simply sinks more deeply into the rugged earth, and the reality of rupture and impossibility that earth represents.

Further complicating this intermixture of life and death is the fact that, on closer examination, these dead pawns themselves do not seem completely to reflect Job's emphasis on tranquility and wholeness in death. One pawn (is it a pawn?) has a crumbling "head" and badly eroded "torso," while another's "head" is severed from its body. Although escaping the deathly reality of life on earth, these upward-downward borne pawns do not fully enjoy Job's rejuvenation of blissful sleep of death. The brutalities of earthly life accompany them in death. Interestingly, this is a conclusion that Job will also reach later in his speeches. Death, as much as life, is hopeless, Job claims in 14:7-22 and 17:11-16.

For both Bak and Job, this sense of death-tainted life is a corollary of the type of impossible rupture that they depict. It is the paradox of survival. In Lyotard's words, someone "that is dead or ought to be, is still alive."[22] Life is no longer simply life, but becomes death-in-life, a combination of seeming opposites. To live after the disaster is to live impossibly—to experience life as death-in-life or life lived-*through*-death, an experience and conception demanded by the impossibility of the ruptured world. But rupture and death are not the only images in Bak's paintings or in the book of Job. Hope, impossibly, also inhabits their landscapes. Yet this is not a simple, uncomplicated hope; rather, this is a hope that exists only *through* the impossible, and it is not guaranteed, not inevitable, and more gestured toward, rather than precisely revealed.

Bak hints at this slim shadow of hope in most of his artwork. In *Unexpected* hope accompanies the images of the two pawns on the right side of the piece. Have they, perhaps, escaped the terror of the deluge? Have they found new and firm soil in which to exist, in which to experiment with new modes of being in a new symbolic world? Are they beginning to map out existence in an impossible world that did not exist before the deluge, one that only came into existence through the deluge?

Similarly, in *Passing Thoughts* the orange pawn in the middle of the canvas seems to hint at the faint possibility of hope. This pawn is not like the blue one, living and yet entombed; but neither is it like the pawns borne upward: dead, yet reposed and relaxed. This pawn seems to have escaped the ruptured reality of the chessboard and gazes out over a new landscape, a new mode of existence with its own world of possibilities. However, the hope that Bak gestures toward is one that is forever marked by the rupture of disaster and the death-taint of survival. So, for example, this pawn, though perhaps gazing out over a new reality still must go forward with the marks of death inscribed on its shape: a cracked "head" irreparably scarred by the rupture of life. And the hopeful way forward certainly is not assured. How to be a pawn outside of the chessboard in a world of mountains and valleys? This is no longer the world of the possible, the chessboard, but of the impossible.

Finally, I would like to return to Bak's angels to discuss this impossibility of hope. In the piece *Sounds of Silence,* one in a series of paintings infused with a musical theme, Bak's winged figures, the figures of the impossible discussed earlier, reappear. This piece depicts a musical quartet calmly playing their instruments in apparent harmony. Yet the scene of the concert is "off": Rather than in a concert hall, these angels play their music amid the rubble and remains of war. They play surrounded by the remnants of a disintegrated world: a crumbling brick wall, rusted cylinders, crumbling foundations, junk strewn about with the menacing smokestack looming in the background, that icon of death and destruction. The angels themselves also signify death and destruction: their very bodies are amalgamations of discarded junk, the remnants of destruction. One figure's wooden arm is secured to his body by a bolt and propelled by a mechanical devise that, in turn, enables the bow to pass over the strings of the violin. A portion of the torso of another figure appears to be a large wooden box that barely holds its shape. Another figure exists as a badly fading diptych. And the upper torso of the final figure is truly composite: the left portion a fragment of death camp garb, the middle portion the faded remains possibly of a tuxedo, and the right portion a shadow or an outline of a body that once existed.

In the center of the angels seems to be an amalgamation of the collapsed remains of a Jewish ghetto and the scattered remnants of a violated and scattered Torah scroll, both of which blend into each other and into the sheet music that the figures play. Their "music," therefore, is the collapse of a religious system and the destruction of a community. This is the music of silence and negation, of the large "X" that towers above the figures.

The title of the piece, *Sounds of Silence,* however, suggests a paradox: this sound of *silence* is also the *sound* of silence. Despite the bleakness of this scene of destruction and death, still what is on display is sound: the sound of violins and cello played, impossibly, by these hodge-podge angel-musicians. This bleak scene paradoxically also seems to be a scene of hope: the hope of beauty, music, community, and fellowship. But this certainly is not an easy hope, a blind guarantee of some prior notion of virtue that is untouched by disaster. This is not "a simple tribute to the triumph of art over attempted annihilation."[23] Rather, this is a hope that is tenuous and is thoroughly marked by the impossibility of the ruptured world and the impossibility of the death-tainted life, what Langer calls "the charged tension between hope and despair."[24] If music continues to be played, if angel-musicians collaborate in the sonic production of beauty, it is only because they are marked by death; it is only because their lives, indeed their very fragmented bodies, retain the traces of disruption and death. The sound of silence is the sound that disaster-as-silence, disaster-as-negation produces. Beauty, goodness, and hope exist only as beauty-as-disaster, goodness-as-disaster, and hope-as-disaster. And thus, these virtues are impossible virtues: ones that cannot be imagined beforehand; ones that did not exist in the world of the possible before the disaster; ones that are tenuous and, like the angel-musicians themselves, are the cobbled-together assembly of the discarded remains of a disrupted world. Impossibly, this assemblage makes music.

"Modern Job" is the name that Maurice Friedman gives to those whose vision of a way forward after the disaster, whose vision of hope for the future is one that is marked permanently by that disaster. According to Friedman "[Modern Job] helps us to take unto ourselves the problematic of modern man and shape from it an image of meaningful human existence, an image that neither leaves out the problematic, nor simply reflects it, but wrestles with it until it has found a new way forward."[25] I would argue that Samuel Bak is the Modern Job that Friedman describes. Bak's complex, disaster-infused vision of hope truly is the type of hope that the book of Job presents. For Job's hope is also not a simplistic one: easy answers, the triumph of faith over doubt, or even divine recompense. The deity certainly does grant Job's demand for answers, yet God's response is rather bizarre, celebrating the virtues of wild and dangerous animals, and mythical creatures, rather than addressing head-on Job's burning issues. Even the ending to Job where God berates Job's friends, restores his fortunes, and grants him progeny to replace the ones who were killed—even this fairy-tale ending, the seeming triumph of faithfulness over doubt—is full of problems and questions. The God of the ending who praises Job for speaking rightly (42:7) scarcely resembles the God of the divine speeches who berated Job for speaking without knowledge (38:2). The God of the ending who condemns the words of Job's friends (42:7) ends up doing exactly as the friends predicted: restoring fortunes to the faithful. This is to say that, despite the divine voice of authority in the divine speeches, despite the apparent "happily ever after" final scene in Job, despite what on the surface appears to be the answer to Job's "why" questions to the problem of suffering and disaster, the way forward that the book of Job gestures toward is not so simple and not so easily discerned.

The book of Job is eminently complex with competing voices articulating different and often rival perspectives on the experience of disaster: Job's articulation of the impossible; his friends' vision of theological and moral wholeness and consistency; the deity's exploration of images of the sublime; and the theologically simple and rational world of the prose tale—not to mention the Elihu speeches, the Wisdom poem, and other voices inserted here and there. The hope that Job presents, like *Sounds of Silence,* is a hope that arises out of the assemblage of various parts—out of the cobbled-together remains of discarded literary "junk." It is the hope of continued discussion, of continued examination, of continued struggle amid the rupture of disaster. New voices need to pick up the discussion that even the fairy-tale ending of Job could not shut down. But both Bak and Job can merely gesture to the precarious way forward. The shape of this conversation cannot be known, cannot be determined, and must inevitably include the sounds of silence.

---

1 Elie Wiesel, *Messengers of God: Biblical Portraits and Legends,* trans. Marion Wiesel (New York: Summit Books, 1976), 211-12.

2 André Neher, *The Exile of the Word: From the Silence of the Bible to the Silence of Auschwitz,* trans. David Maisel (Philadelphia: Jewish Publication Society of America, 1981), 195.

3 Emil L. Fackenheim, *The Jewish Bible after the Holocaust: A Re-reading* (Bloomington: Indiana University Press, 1990), 71-99; Maurice Friedman, *Problematic Rebel: Melville, Dostoievsky, Kafka, Camus.* Rev. ed (Chicago: University of Chicago Press, 1970), 10-22; Maurice Friedman, *To Deny our Nothingness: Contemporary Images of Man* (Chicago: University of Chicago Press, 1978; repr., Chicago: Midway, 1984), 309-54; Steven Kepnes, "Job and Post-Holocaust Theodicy," in *Strange Fire: Reading the Bible after the Holocaust,* ed. Tod Linafelt (New York: New York University Press, 2000), 252-66; Neher, 27-33; 192-98; Richard L. Rubenstein, "Job and Auschwitz," in *Strange Fire: Reading the Bible after the Holocaust,* ed. Tod Linafelt (New York: New York University Press, 2000), 233-51; Wiesel, *Messengers of God,* 211.

4 Bak, "Winged Figures," in *Between Worlds: The Paintings and Drawings of Samuel Bak from 1946 to 2001,* ed. Irene Tayler (Boston: Pucker Art Publications, 2002), 155.

5 Lawrence L. Langer, *Preempting the Holocaust* (New Haven: Yale University Press, 1998), 2.

6 Langer, 190.

7 Quoted in Langer, 192.

8 Shoshana Felman and Dori Laub, *Testimony: Crises of Witnessing in Literature, Psychoanalysis, and History* (New York and London: Routledge, 1992), 69.

9 Cathy Caruth, "Introduction," in *Trauma: Explorations in Memory,* ed. Cathy Caruth (Baltimore: The Johns Hopkins University Press, 1995), 5.

10 For a fuller discussion of some of the following exegetical issues in Job, see my recent work, *Death and Survival in the Book of Job: Desymbolization and Traumatic Experience;* Library of Hebrew Bible/Old Testament Studies 450 (New York: T&T Clark, 2006).

11 See Michael V. Fox, Proverbs 1-9*: A New Translation with Introduction and Commentary* (New York: Doubleday, 2000), 128-31.

12 See Norman C. Habel, "Symbolism of Wisdom in Proverbs 1-9," *Interpretation* 26 (1972), 131-57.

13 Habel, 129.

14 Habel, 145.

15 Other path imagery in Proverbs also implies active agency. See Prov 1:31; 3:31; 4:26; 5:8; 7:8, 25; 9:15; 10:9; 21:16.

16 See further, Fox, 137-43. See also Prov 21:8 where *drk* is specifically paralleled to *p'l* ("conduct").

17 Many English translations mistakenly render this verse in the active voice, as if the *nip'al* verb *nstrh* were active.

18 Interestingly, Isa 40:27 employs a similar expression as Job 3:23: "Why do you say, O Jacob, and speak, O Israel, 'My way *[drk]* is hidden *[nstrh]* from YHWH; my justice disregarded by my God'?" Like Job 3:23, this expression is used of a situation of disaster (in Isaiah, the experience of exile), though *drk* does not have the same import for moral discourse in Deutero-Isaiah as it does in Wisdom literature. Further, in the Isaiah passage God is not the cause of the way being hidden. In fact, Israel's way is hidden *from* God.

19 Robert Jay Lifton, *The Protean Self: Human Resilience in an Age of Fragmentation* (New York: Basic Books, 1993), 14.

20 Robert Jay Lifton, *The Life of the Self: Toward a New Psychology* (New York: Simon and Schuster, 1976), 114-15.

21 His fantasy of death is based on the belief that Sheol is a place of utter rest and tranquility, which Job describes using three synonyms, *shkb, shqt, yshn.* Of the three, the first is by far the most common word in the Hebrew Bible, whose range of meaning includes sleeping, lying down, having sexual relations, and death. The "death" sense of the word fits with the context of Job's description of Sheol, suggesting that the trio of "sleep" words connote death or the sleep of death. *shkb* frequently has this sense in the Hebrew Bible, normally in the phrase "to sleep with one's ancestors" (Gen 47:30, Deut 31:16; 2 Sam 7:12; 1 Kgs 1:21; 2:10; 11:21, 43; 14:20, 31; 15:8, 24; 16:6, 28; 22:40, 50; 2 Kgs 8:24; 10:35; 13:9, 13; 14:16, 22, 29; 15:7, 22, 38; 16:20; 20:21; 21:18; 24:6; 2 Chron 9:31; 12:16; 13:23; 16:13; 21:1; 26:2, 23; 27:9; 28:27; 32:33). It also suggests the sleep of death in other cases (Judg 5:27; Ps 41:8; 88:5; Isa 14:18; 43:17; 50:11; Lam 2:21; Ezek 32:19, 21, 27, 28, 29, 30, 32).

The other two "sleep" words nuance this "death sleep" by indicating more precisely the nature of the sleep that Job envisions. For its part, *shqt* has several connotations. Most frequently, especially in the prose narratives, the word describes the peacefulness and tranquility of a people or a land, in contrast to the turmoil of war and upheaval (Josh 11:23; 14:15; Judg 3:11, 30; 5:31; 8:28; 18:27; 2 Kgs 11:20; 1 Chron 4:40; 22:9; 2 Chron 14:1, 4, 5; 20:30; 23:21; Isa 14:7; 30:15; Jer 30:10; 46:27; 47:6, 7; 48:11; Ezek 16:49). It also stands more generally for a sense of tranquility and calm as opposed to anxiety, tension, and hyper-activity (Ruth 3:18; Prov 15:18; Isa 7:4; 57:20). In the Psalms and Prophets the word often represents the calm and peacefulness that Yhwh provides, or is urged to provide, for his servants (Ps 76:8; 94:13; 32:17; Jer 30:10; 46:27); or it represents Yhwh's own calm and peacefulness that he is urged to break in order that he deal with his enemies (Ps 83:1; Isa 14:7; 62:1; 47:6, 7; 48:11; 49:23). Similarly, *yshn,* in prose narrative, almost always suggests a deep sleep that comes over individuals who then undergo some sort of ordeal or hardship while asleep (Gen 2:21; Judg 16:19; 1 Sam 26:7, 12; 1 Kgs 3:20. See also Gen 41:5; 1 Kgs 18:27 and 19:5), while in the Prophets and the Writings, the word frequently suggests the tranquility of sleep that Yhwh provides his servants (Ps 3:5; 4:9; Ezek 34:25) or the slumber that Yhwh is urged to rouse himself out of in order to dispatch his, and his servant's, enemies (Ps 44:24; 78:65; Jer 51:39, 57. The word has a related sense in Ps 13:4; 121:4; Isa 5:27). The word can also have the simple sense of "deep sleep" in the Writings also (see Prov 4:16; Qoh 5:12; Cant 5:2).

Both of these "sleep" words stand for the peacefulness, rest, and tranquility that enables the pious to live abundant lives as they are guarded and protected by God. The short psalm of lament, Psalm 3, expresses this nicely. In it the Psalmist laments the foes who attack him (vv. 1-2), but then confesses that Yhwh is his protector and that Yhwh listens to his cry (vv. 3-4). Furthermore, the Psalmist announces that in the face of a myriad of opposing forces (v. 7) he is able to lie down (*shkb*) and sleep (*yshn*) because "Yhwh sustains me" (v. 6). The image is one of Yhwh providing life, sustenance, and rejuvenating rest to his servant even in the face of seemingly insurmountable opposition. Rest and tranquility stand for abundant life.

22 Jean-François Lyotard, "The Survivor," in *Toward the Postmodern,* ed. Robert Harvey and Mark S. Roberts (Atlantic Highlands, NJ: Humanities Press, 1993), 144.

23 Samuel Bak and Lawrence L. Langer, *Landscapes of Jewish Experience;* The Tauber Institute for the Study of European Jewry 25 (Boston; Pucker Gallery and Brandeis University Press, 1997), 114.

24 Langer, *Landscapes,* 116.

25 Friedman, *To Deny our Nothingness,* 347. Friedman identifies Elie Wiesel as "the most moving embodiment of the Modern Job" (348).

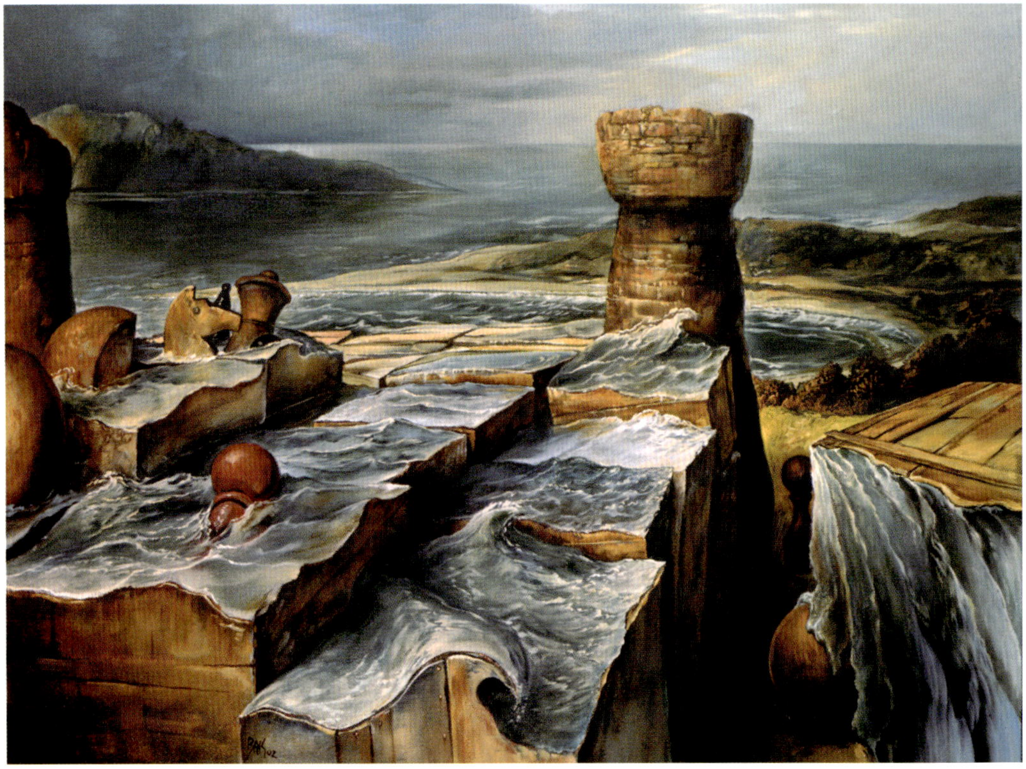

Unexpected, 2002
Oil on Canvas, 18 x 24"

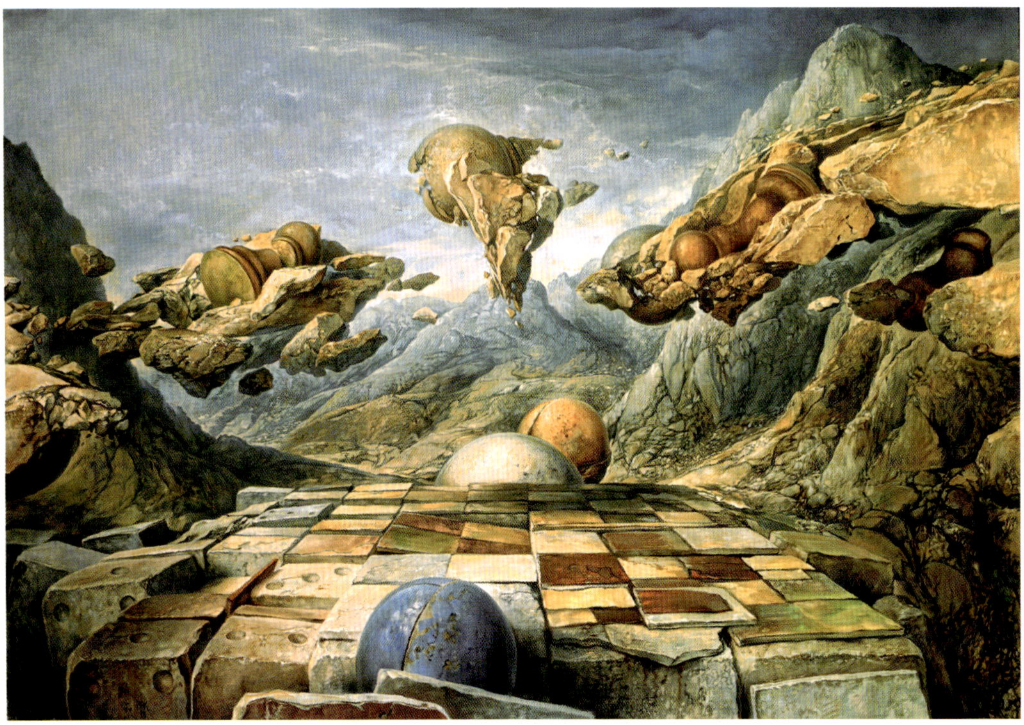

Passing Thoughts, 1998
Oil on Canvas, 26 x 48"

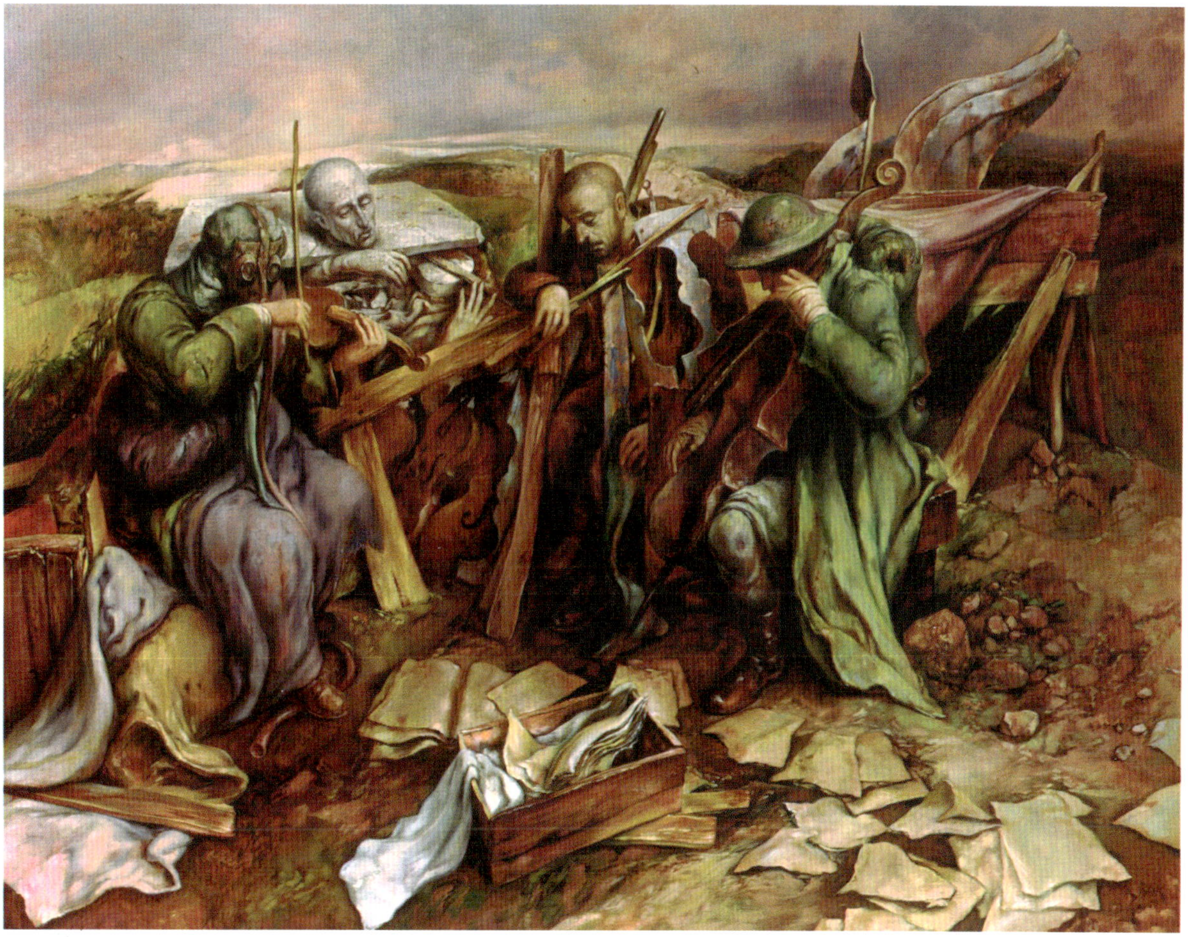

Sounds of Silence, 1995
Oil on Linen, 32 x 40"

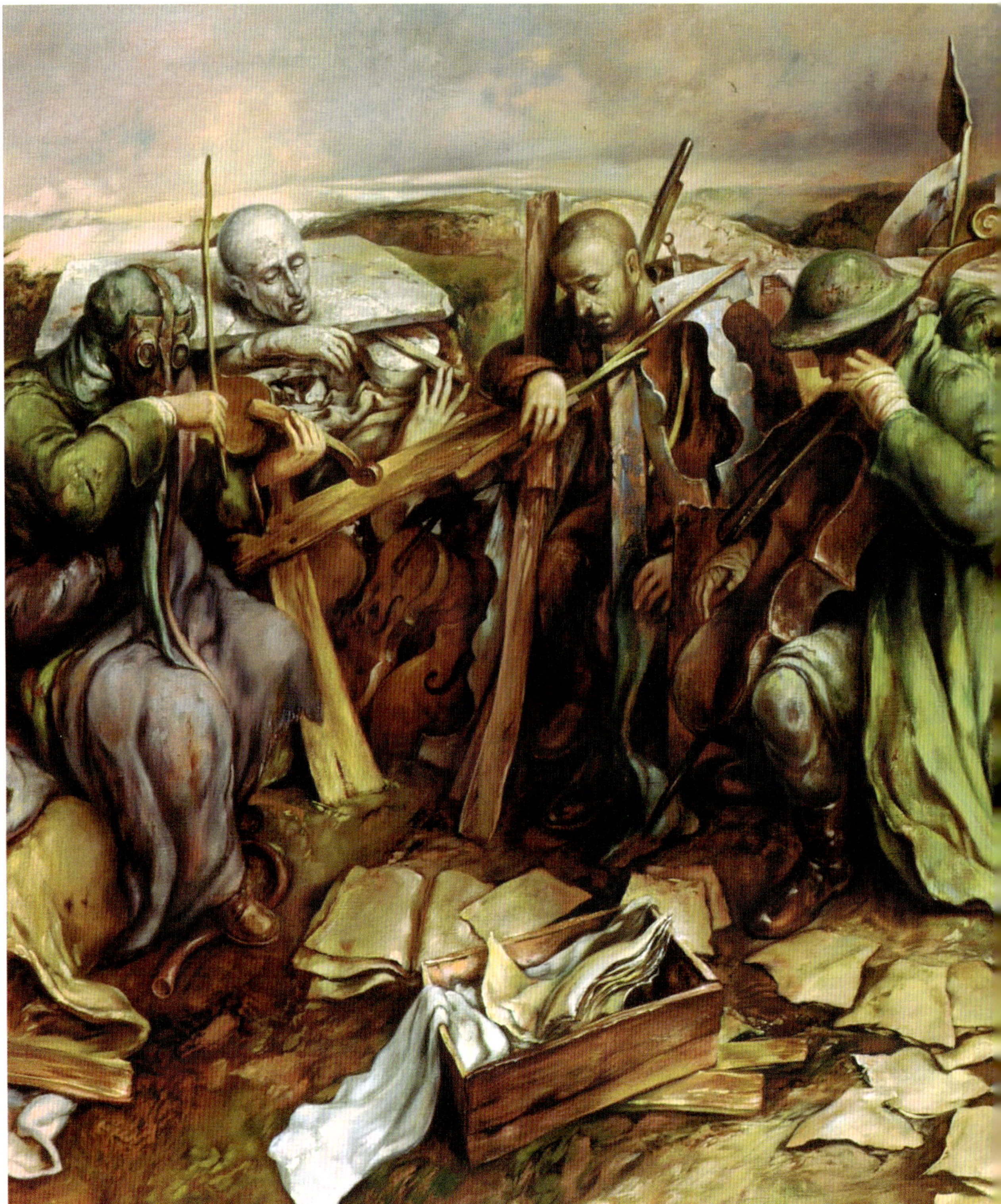

The End of Time: Bak's Art, Messiaen's Music, and Levinas's Ethics

CHARLES RIX

How can we give thanks when we remember Treblinka?
Only silence speaks loudly enough for millions who were marched into the abyss.
We have been where we did not find You, O Hidden one!
Yet even there, even there, our people sang:
I believe in redemption.
And they sang: 'Never say you walk the final road!'
And even then this deathless people was renewing itself, its life.
Whose faith is equal to this people's?
Whose will to live?
The storm ends.
In the sky, a rainbow signals hope and new life.
Again, and yet again, there is a song to sing.[1]

We might imagine attending a soiree of chamber music performed by Samuel Bak's quartet. Several works are on the program: *Elegy for a Town, Solo, Last Movement For the End of Time*, and *Sounds of Silence*. Perhaps we entered the concert hall this evening expecting a stream of familiar *Arabesques, Allemandes, Bourees,* and *Ballades.* Yet for whatever we may have anticipated, the music has now stopped, *subito.* The players have come to a *fermata* in the score, an elongated hold in the music. We expect the music to begin again, yet we remain suspended in silence. It seems this caesura has been held a bit too long. We are growing anxious. With racing hearts, we wonder what is happening.

Two questions confront us: What is this silence about? How should we respond? A low-grade

Detail of *Sounds of Silence*, 1995
Oil on Linen, 32 x 40"

buzz moves around the concert hall as our fellow music-lovers muse over what to make of such a performance. The gentleman to our left reminds us of the courage and maturity it requires to hold a rest for its full rhythmic value so as to achieve the complete interpretive effect of the silence, which as Mozart taught, is the greatest effect in music.[2] The spry musician in front of us reminisces about his lessons with Josef Lhevinne, one of the last century's great pianists and teachers, who insisted his students understand that hurrying over the silences, like the failure to stop and observe one's surroundings, destroys the message of the music.[3] Conservatory students in our audience sermonize among themselves: "We must understand that silence not only rhythmically shapes melodic lines, but also provides a space to reflect on what has just been heard as well as to anticipate what is coming." Others speculate on the aleatoric nature of the composition, and what sense we are to make from a "chance" silence we have encountered. Still, musical theorists in our midst quickly connect this lengthy pause to the achievements of the avant-garde composer Karlheinz Stockhausen, who understood that only when one plays a note and then allows it to die away before producing another sound, is the true individual "voice" of the instrument revealed. Only in the period of decreasing vibration and ensuing silence is there enough space for the listener to be aware fully of shifting colors and meanings of sound.[4]

However, none of these musings relieve our growing tension as the silence expands throughout the concert space. The players have moved from simply being poised, to appearing frozen, stone-like, and propped up. With the score now scattered about their feet, have they lost their place? Or is the uncomfortable truth simply that no one in the hall understands this music? As the silence becomes deafening, we realize that our traditional notions of rhythm have failed. We've lost the beat. The pulse of the music has flat lined. Any calming, mellifluous melodies or plush, Slavic harmonies we have enjoyed up to this point in the quartet's performance have long since dissipated into the rafters. Irreconcilable silence is upon us. We have encountered a rhythm that is completely *Other.*

In this rhythmic disruption, our attention unavoidably shifts to the *otherness* of the faces of players themselves. The cellist, clad in a tattered Czech soldier's coat and knapsack, draws a stringless instrument forlornly into his chest, as the score crumbles among the rocks—just as his hometown was reduced to rubble by Nazi atrocities.[5] In his observance of the rest in the score, we might imagine that he is feeling, as Chopin would say, the weakness in a musical phrase, which naturally occurs at the point of silence.[6] However, we notice that the cellist has no bow. His hand with musculature strong enough to execute the most fiendishly difficult Etudes, yet supple enough to bend with elegant nuances in production of the spiciest *spiccati,* and loveliest *leggieri,* now only lies in his lap laced in linen, having been irreparably injured by the hate and violence of those who have no regard for justice or beauty. The most intimate physical connection with his instrument, the cellist's hand, now weak and stiff, draws our attention to the attendant angel wings behind him, also stiff and ineffectual, suggesting an unimaginable heavenly impotence in response to the useless suffering of the innocent.[7]

The hunched violinist wearing a gas mask conjures up malignant musical mockeries that accompany deportees arriving on the platforms at Auschwitz as they were sent to the gas chambers, hung on the gallows, or burned in crematoria. Just as rests provide music with the opportunity to "breathe," and just as a performer must be conscious of his or her breathing so as to bring vitality and elasticity to the music, so this musician's mask suggests the possibility that music and art now struggle to breathe in order to make meaning amid suffocating atrocities.

In the musical counterpoint of this silence, Bak's violist from Vilna, in the words of the Psalmist, has hung up his lyre. Perhaps he is thinking:

In the ghettos
And in the death camps,
We sat and wept
As we thought of Vilna
There, in the stench of the streets and pathways
We put down our instruments
For the Nazis, our captors, asked us there for songs
Our tormentors, for amusement,
"Play for us one of the melodies of Vilna"
How can we play the melodies of our heart in such a place as this?
If I forget you, O Vilna
Let my right hand wither,
Let my left forever remain in my lap
If I cease to think of you,
If I do not keep Vilna in my memory
Even in my happiest hour.

Remember, O YHWH, *against the Nazis*
The day of Vilna's fall;
How they cried, "Strip her, strip her to her very foundations!"

You predators!
A blessing on him who repays you in kind
What you have inflicted on us
A blessing on him who seizes your babies
And dashes them against the rocks![8]

Our Vilnian violinist still wonders how he can play any melody from his heart on the alien soil of this now irreparable landscape. We notice he has taken up a rifle, and like the Psalmist asks

YHWH to remember the day of the fall of his village, how its very foundation was stripped away as its children were dashed against rocks. Hanging in sorrow between two planks of wood forming an "X," at once a crucifixion, and a reminder of Sinai's Ten Words, our violinist, crest-fallen and lachrymose, confronts us with the surrender of "Thou Shall Not Kill" to the gun.

In such resignation, must we admit that music, as we have known it up to this point, is no longer capable of portraying the emotions of useless suffering? Does the shorn, stone violinist, carved in granite, in a state transcending temporal time, suggest that the horrors of what we have seen with our eyes simply forbid the luxury of making music in the manner we once did? Do Bak's musicians frozen in a world of disrepair, suggesting a performance but not actually playing, raise the question of whether or not art has been trumped by the atrocities of the Shoah, or whether hearing the music we once knew, or any music at all, is simply too much of an indulgence given what we have seen?[9] Has the time for music-making ended?

Elegy for a Town, another in Bak's quartet series, portrays the musicians either wearing masks, blindfolds, or cast in stone. As we contemplate the faces of these musicians, their silence begins to generate melodies composed in our own aural imaginations that, as Lawrence Langer suggests in *Preempting the Holocaust,* are in keeping with the "legacy of atrocity that inspired it."[10] The masked and blindfolded musicians suggest that players of violins, violas, cellos, and other instruments either are not able or are not allowed to realize their own painful experience through the music. Is there any music that can be heard sensibly in the wake of Treblinka? Has the limit of musical language been transcended by the atrocities of the Shoah? The stone wall reminds us of the chimneys of the crematoria, and informs us that any former pleasures we might have taken in lyrical rhapsodic phrases swelling with romantic sweep have been overcome by non-legato sequences of atonal screeches puncturing holes in an Auschwitz nocturnal sky clouded in human cinder-rain. Any catching, toe-tapping, or easily singable melodies have been shattered by dissonant cacophonies of train whistles, fugues of Nazi voices shouting orders (*"Schnell!")* percussive cadences of boots hitting wooden platforms, and endless finales of prison guards crashing together metal gas chamber doors like overenthusiastic cymbalists. Any relief from such intensity will not come, for as Jeremiah recounts, Rachel refuses to be comforted as she weeps for her children who are gone—forever. There are endless repeats of sharp shrill cries of children being thrown alive into the crematoria, and the flat, falling sighs of fainting mothers.

We want this music to stop! We want to run from the concert hall to the cozy familiarities of *chez-nous.* Yet Bak's lone cellist in *Solo* asks us to remain seated. He will not yield up his artistry as a burnt offering in the furnaces of our indifference. In his silence we are obliged to note his courage, carved with flint onto a tablet of stone. His silence boldly proclaims his alterity. Playing alone, in solitude, he proclaims with a resounding *sforzando* the particularity of each individual that cannot be reduced, subsumed, or totalized under any rubric. Making the cello one with himself, the soloist reminds us that music and art, like the human spirit, cannot be completely muted by atrocities. His new song can be played, even on string-less instruments, if we will but listen.

No, we cannot get up and leave the hall, for we have not happened upon a concert but upon a sanctuary inhabited by those who courageously observe the longest of rests—the musical Sabbath, the silence which demands our attention. In *Sounds of Silence*, *Elegy for a Town*, *Last Movement*, *Solo*, and *For the End of Time*, these musicians literally have all the time in the world, until our private worlds are disrupted, and as Isaiah might say, until the cause of those who have suffered senselessly finally reaches us.[12]

In *For the End of Time* Bak's quartet is playing in an unfamiliar harmonic structure—not one bound up in aesthetics that panders to delectable delights or lingers in sensuality. Bak's musicians refuse to provide us with yet another spectacle proposing to manipulate our emotions with *sognandos* and *smorzandos* that are surely pleasing to the ear, but which, through satisfying the self, ultimately hardens the heart against perceiving the needs of others.[13] No. Bak's quartet aims at a music that is released to what Emmanuel Levinas would call the "difficult freedoms" of moral responsibilities and obligations to our neighbor and to all of the extant diversity in creation.[14] It is music that coheres not with childish whims, fancies, and numinous speculations of the divine. Rather, Bak's musicians play the music of a perfectly adult ethic: the acceptance of responsibility towards one's neighbor.[15] If the landscape against which Bak's musicians are poised is to recover its lushness, if Bak's musicians are to rise from the dust of the earth rather than be swallowed up by the appetite of Sheol, a new world must be created not from the refuse of the old world, but with the exigency of a new fabric created from threads of each individual's ethically responsible actions towards others. Just as the Sabbath calls for each individual to stop and consider the face of the other,[16] so Bak's silence, his musical Sabbath, calls for us to stop and look into the face of the *Other*. In Levinasian terms, we are called to be available to the face of the Other who is unfamiliar and strange to us and to say "Here I am."[17]

As a further exploration of the ethical behavior to the *Other* called forth by the silence of Bak's musicians, I will briefly examine the function of silence in the Hebrew Bible as well as the musical language of Olivier Messiaen, whose celebrated *Quartet for the End of Time* provides an historical reference point for Bak's quartet series. Subsequently, I will offer some reflection on how the works of Bak and Messiaen, when experienced together and heard in light of Levinas' insight, might inform our response to this silence emanating from a seemingly irreparable world—a world whose former time has ended.

With respect to the function of silence in the Hebrew Bible, we might reflect on the wisdom tradition of Job where silence is a time for learning (Job 6:24), or according to 4 Esdras a time for mourning and fasting (10:22), and a time to recognize that the blood of the innocent will cry out (15:8). Sirach 20:6 reminds: "Some people keep silent because they have nothing to say, while others keep silent because they know when to speak." However, it is Aaron's silence in Leviticus 10:3 which is most instructive as fire comes out from the presence of YHWH to consume his sons as "holocausts" upon their offering of strange fire.[18] Aaron's silence both subverts and resists Moses' theological doctoring of a tragic event: "This is what YHWH meant when he said, 'Through my near-ones I shall be holy, and before all the people I shall gain glory.'" Moses' all-too-reductive theological explanation in the face of Aaron's unspeakable personal tragedy is, in itself, all-too-familiar as we reflect on the way in which many in our religious communities have quickly attributed the events of 9/11, the Asian Tsunami of 2004, and the devastation of New Orleans by Hurricane Katrina to the consuming fire of the judgment of God upon so-called "evil-doers." Rather than speak too quickly, one might be better advised to follow Aaron's posture and that of Bak's soloist: to remain respectfully silent and to open one's mind first to view and then to reflect upon the faces of the devastated—the families, clans, tribes, and villages that have been divided by untimely death and tragedy. Such a silence constitutes the only appropriate eulogy for pain that is too deep for sound.[19] In view of Moses' totalizing theological explanation for Aaron's unspeakable grief over the loss of his two sons, we might begin to wonder whether or not the production of any art risks the violence of totalizing the suffering and grieving of another, rendering it trivial by subsuming the grief of another too neatly, or even too enigmatically, into an aesthetic display. How can the suffering of another ever actually be "played" or "contained" in bar lines, and rhythms—or words and endless commentary, for that matter? And, in light of the Decalogue,[20] where the Sabbath functions as a stop to the busyness of life for the purpose of regarding the plight of others, Bak's musicians, frozen in the musical rest, suggest a musical Sabbath so that we might observe the faces of those who have suffered senselessly, being serenaded to the gas chambers even by the tawdry little ditties eked out by Nazi platform bands.

It is precisely on this point of cessation that we further sense the function of silence through the music of Olivier Messiaen via the concept of the *Other* as advanced by Levinas. Messiaen wrote the *Quartet for the End of Time* as a depiction of the cessation of the *idea of time* as chopped up and parceled out by our temporal understanding. He intended a musical portrait of the state of timelessness or infinity. It is through the concept of infinity that Levinas characterizes the alterity of the *Other; Otherness* is infinite in the sense that it cannot be contained, reduced, or subsumed. Further, in *Time and the Other* Levinas sets forth the notion that time—not as chopped up and parceled out, but time as it actually is—constitutes the very relationship of the subject with the *Other.*[21] Hence, as we will see, Levinas's concept of the infinite nature of the alterity of the *Other* provides a framework for bringing the work of Bak and Messiaen together.

While imprisoned in Stalag VIIIA Messiaen wrote the *Quartet for the End of Time*—perhaps the most celebrated musical product of a concentration camp experience.[22] Four prisoners, pianist Olivier Messiaen, cellist Etienne Pasquier, violinist Jean Le Boulair, and clarinetist Henri Akoka, premiered the work on January 15, 1941 (a Wednesday evening at six o'clock) on dilapidated concentration camp instruments for an audience of about three hundred and fifty inmates comprised of farmers, factory workers, intellectuals, professional servicemen, doctors, and priests, many of whom were unfamiliar with any form of chamber music.[23] Similar to the musicians portrayed in Bak's Quartet series, Messiaen's quartet members were also dressed in shabbily patched bottle-green Czech soldier uniforms and wooden clogs that made the feet hurt, but which kept them warm. Ironically, Messiaen recalls that the most difficult thing to achieve before the performance could begin was silence. Yet, for all the success and recollection that Messiaen's musicians enjoy to this day in the tradition of chamber music, there were other compositions written by other camp inmates who did not find prison guards sympathetic to their musical inclinations and were exterminated. One of these was Samuel Bak's maternal uncle, the poet, painter, and composer of liturgical music, Arno Nadel (1878 Vilna-1943 KZ Auschwitz) who greatly inspired Bak's artistic journey.[24] Perhaps we are also to be reminded of Czech composers such as Pavel Haas and Victor Ullman.[25] And there are yet other faces we see in Bak's Quartet series: the blind-folded, the masked, the musician with hands but no arms, faces of stone or wood with little or no expression—those musicians, artists, teachers, and composers whose music we will not have the privilege of hearing or celebrating. Bak calls upon us to listen to an *Elegy,* a *Marche Funebre,* and a musical *Via Doloroso* for musicians who perished in the Shoah such as Leon Borunsk (1909-1942), one of Poland's most gifted pianists and accompanists. We may also witness the musicians who survived but who can no longer play as their nervous systems, arms, fingers, or even their memories, which for years had been finely trained in order to play and bring the meaning of music to many, are now irreparably damaged by the experiences of the Shoah. Their music can no longer be made.

Just as Bak mixes colors, motifs of the Shoah, themes from the Torah, as well as his own world of experience to create his own representation of the irreparable, so Messiaen abandoned classical harmonic and rhythmic structures and formulated a new musical language mixing Greek and Hindu rhythms, Christian apocalyptic symbolism, and tone clusters to create what he calls the "charm of impossibilities."[26] As Messiaen writes in the preface to his *Quatuor pour la Fin du Temps (Quartet for the End of Time):*

> My musical language is essentially immaterial, spiritual, and catholic. Here, modes that achieve a kind of tonal ubiquity, melodically and harmonically draw the listener towards eternity in space or the infinite. Special rhythms, beyond meter, contribute powerfully in dismissing the temporal.[27]

Thus, the Levinasian concept of the infinite nature of alterity present in the face of the Other is suggested in Bak's portrayal of silence and is likewise scored through Messiaen's musical language. Although it was not Messiaen's intent to produce a musical commentary on the book of Revelation, Messiaen's Quartet was nonetheless inspired by the first six verses of the tenth chapter of the Apocalypse, with the last portion of the sixth verse being the touchtone for the entire work. Messiaen's inscription reads:

> En hommage a l'Ange de l'Apocalypse, qui lève la main vers le ciel en disant: 'Il n'y aura plus de Temps'. [To the angel of the Apocalypse who raises his hand toward heaven saying: 'There will be no more Time.'][28]

Messiaen intended to create a work which would celebrate the "eternal freedom of the spirit over the temporal captivity of the body." By titling his work *Quartet for the End of Time,* his purpose was not to comment on the length of his internment in the Stalag but rather through the experience of the Stalag to explore the phenomenon of leaving the human realm with its cyclical dimension to rejoin with eternity where countable time is no longer. Messiaen's interest in composing the *Quartet for the End of Time* was thus bound up in the philosophical questions of Time. For a composer, expressions of time are found in rhythmic structures. In Messiaen's words,

> Rhythm is, in essence, alteration and division. To study alteration and division is to study Time. Time—measured, relative, physiological, and psychological—is divided in a thousand ways of which the most immediate for us is a perpetual conversion of the future into the past. In eternity, these things no longer exist.[29]

In composing the Quartet, Messiaen made use of thirteenth-century Hindu rhythms, notably the *ragavardhana.*[30] As suggested by these Hindu rhythms, Messiaen developed a non-retrogradable rhythm,[31] a musical palindrome, where a grouping of rhythmical values could be read identically from right to left or left to right. Such was the key metaphor for the portrayal of infinity:

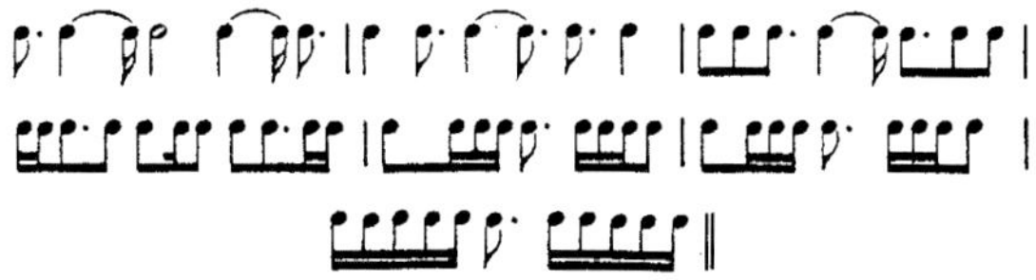

These rhythms, as Messiaen wrote in the preface to the Quartet, were independent of conventional meter and were developed as a means to create the effect of banishing the temporal.[32] For Messiaen, time was the starting point of all creation and certainly the start of the creative impulse for the Quartet. As Susan Rischin observes in her analysis of the Quartet, through non-retrogradable rhythms, Messiaen overcame traditional rhythm and meter, ushering in a type of "musical apocalypse."

The sixth movement of the Quartet, "The Dance of Fury for the Seven Trumpets," employs non-retrograde rhythms throughout as all four instruments play in unison. In the introductory comments to the work, Messiaen notes that this movement is: "Music of stone, tremendous ringing granite; perpetual motion of steel, of enormous blacks of purple fury, of frozen intoxication."[33]

Transcending conventional harmonies sound the sheer magnitude of eternity as all instruments play in unison. The music is frozen. Again, while Messiaen drew inspiration from Revelation's angel who announces the end of time, the point is not to paint a musical picture of the events of the apocalypse but to draw attention to the announcement of cessation of Time, the end of an era in human history.

With Messiaen's music now bringing us to *hear* the infinite, what do we *see?* In the image of granite, both Bak and Messiaen come together. Messiaen has composed what Bak has painted—the *alterity of the infinite.* Yet, as we look into such an infinite, non-reducible alterity, we realize that the works of these two artists, Bak and Messiaen, exist in counterpoint to each other as they move us to respond to a world of the irreparable. As we move forward into the future, Bak and Messiaen will take us in different directions. Of necessity, a new artistic language for both image and rhythm is required, whose relationship to former methods of understanding and interpretation will be ambiguous at best. Such rhythms, or images, must be facile enough to express the gain of historical honesty along with the loss of naiveté regarding any simplistic promise of a better tomorrow. In developing new language specific to their mediums of artistic expression, Bak and Messiaen give way neither to a simplistic construction of hope nor to a self-indulgent despair. As Langer puts it, Bak reflects an art that "oscillates between expectation and dismay."[34] However, while Messiaen's work is ultimately rooted in the book of the Apocalypse interpreted as a reflection of an assured eternal hope in Christ, Bak's work is far less certain about any such ubiquitous hope. Bak asks Messiaen's work to consider the limits of divine potency as his musicians sit as stones, like muted, weakened Apocalyptic Horsemen, playing from a crumbling score that falls to the ground like the Vilna Ghetto. Is any future hope in and of itself reductive with respect to senseless suffering? Furthermore, do notions of divine rescue bypass core issues of theodicy and fail to take seriously the millions of innocent victims, not the least of which were children, whose cries for mercy failed, move a divine delivering arm? On the other hand, Messiaen[35] inquires of Bak's work whether or not, within the realm of the infinite nature of divine alterity, there cannot yet be an act of redemption for humanity even more powerful than that of the Shoah's destruction.

In this respect, the backdrop for the quartet's music in *Sounds of Silence* creates a dark commentary on the silent, frozen, stony, steely, blocks of sound in Messiaen's *Dance of Fury for the Seven Trumpets* and the final movement of the Quartet. Messiaen's inclusion of an eighth movement in his *Quartet For The End of Time* is intended to convey the sense of endlessness. He writes of this movement:

> This Quartet comprises eight movements. Why? Seven is the perfect number, the Creation in six days sanctified by the divine Sabbath; the seventh day of this repose extends into eternity and becomes the eighth day of eternal light, of unalterable peace.[36]

Further, the point is made that what is generally regarded as a conclusion of a piece is not necessarily the end. The eighth movement signifies what is beyond the traditional marking of the conclusion of creation by the Sabbath. And at the end of Time there is an eternity with which we must reckon, a transcendent reality. But is this transcendent reality one of resolution or one of an eternal rest or peace? Or would Bak inform us that such peace is fundamentally found in a responsibility to serve the *Other?*

While for Messiaen the music of stone represents an end of temporal Time, a musical sound-painting of infinity, bathed in an apocalyptic hope (intended or not), Bak's stone scrutinizes and critiques the nature of such an eternity. There is no confidence of a better tomorrow in the dilapidated angelic wings attached to the violinist. As Lawrence Langer comments, there are no flames from memorial candles to be lit or Star of David to reassure.[37] Whatever Messiaen's music may wish to explore concerning a coming period where Time is no more, and for whatever notions of infinity Messiaen sets forth in music that evokes "granite," Bak's granite or stone comprises remnants of chimneys and smokestacks that prod the musicians to toll the bells in a *Funerailles* for the thousands of dead from villages such as Vilna, the dead who must sing their own funeral processionals and herald the corteges of their friends. As the sheet music for the Quartet falls to the feet of the musicians in shapes of the village of Vilna, flanked by hoses and canisters of Xylon B Gas from the extermination chambers, Bak reminds us there is no "last movement"; there is no final piece of music wherein the overwhelming loss, grieving, and mourning is resolved. Such a summarizing "last movement" would be an act of violence with respect to the unresolved suffering of many. In his memoir *Painted in Words,* Bak writes:

> We survivors were badly equipped to deal with loss and mourning. Even where we were certain of the fate of our loved ones, as in the case of those murdered at Ponar, the setting evoked such horror that it offered no place to commune with the dead or search for solace. As there were no funerals and no rituals that could put things in place, our mourning had to go on for years.[38]

In the end, we are forced to reckon with the grim reality of that which is eternally broken, eternally beyond repair, eternally enigmatic, eternally devastated. Just as Messiaen portrays in his "last movement" an eighth day wherein the Sabbath merges into an eternity of light where there is no final "end," Bak's crumbling musicians rise from a stony yet verdant landscape, on the one hand refusing to allow their melodies be silenced, and on the other holding the ultimate success of such a protest, or the assurance of any idyllic peace, in abeyance.

How can Bak's musicians play Messiaen's music? Both Bak and Messiaen point us towards the alterity of the infinite. As I believe Levinas might suggest, the relationship between Bak's quartet series and Messiaen's music is ultimately suggestive of a face-to-face relationship. Both Bak and Messiaen working together form the basis for an ethical call to face the *Other.* While Messiaen's music drives us toward a state where temporal time is no longer, Bak's representation of infinity, through the suggestion of an eternal silence, calls us to observe the faces of the suffering—the call to serve the *Other.* The space of silence, which prepares us for the future, finally prepares us to face the one who is *Other.* As Levinas asserts in *Time and the Other:*

The future is what is not grasped, what befalls us and lays hold of us. The other is the future. The very relationship with the other is the relationship with the future.[39]

As such, the *sound* of silence, if it is to be finally *sounded out,* is the sound of the announcement "Here I Am," the presentation of the subject to the *Other* in a face-to-face relationship, a call to ethical action toward those in proximity to us who have experienced unimaginable personal loss,and whose worlds have been so completely shattered so as to be beyond repair. Further, the responsibility to the *Other,* the state of time itself, is suggested in the very idea of a quartet-music played together with others. Rebecca Rischin notes in her analysis of Messiaen's *Quartet,* "the piece illustrates how captivity paradoxically set free a work that became a testament to creativity."[40] It is as well a work that in itself not only represents the power of art, but the art of relating one to another as a means of surviving in the most horrific of circumstances. And what is the nature of such a relation? As Richard Cohen observes, it is very simply this: *serving others.* "All other significations, in all other registers, derive from this deepest or highest significance."[41]

We have been brought via Bak's musicians and Messiaen's music to a place where we are invited to listen not to music as we have conventionally heard it, but to new musical language that calls us into a relationship with the *Other.* As we sit in silence, we can remember the music we heard in the rhythm of temporal time and in melodic lines that fit well within our "sameness." Yet Messiaen's music, now played by Bak's suffering musicians, is played in a new key and in a new rhythm that is outside of temporality, played in the language of infinity, the very essence of relationship of the subject to the *Other.* Bak's musicians evoke the uncontainable alterity of the *Other,* the unexplainable nature of suffering and grief which has no temporal end, but which finds its solace, such as it is to be had, in being available to serve the *Other.*

---

1 "Meditation" in *Gates of Prayer* (New York: Central Conference of American Rabbis, 1975), 587.

2 Josef Lhevinne, *Basic Principles of Pianoforte Playing* (New York: Dover, 1972), 3. Josef and Rosina Lhevinne are perhaps two of the most noted piano teachers of the last century. Russian by birth and training, they taught for many years at the Julliard School in New York City, where they became noted for their development for some of the greatest pianistic talent of the century. Josef Lhevinne was considered one of the great "modern" masters of the piano along with Rachmaninoff, Schnable, and Hoffmann.

3 Lhevinne, 3-4.

4 Herbert Henck, *Notes on Klavierstucke I-XI* (Mainz: Ergo Music, 1987), 14. Klavierstucke IV and X demonstrate the effect of higher pitches fading sooner than lower pitches, thereby offering an immediate analysis of the sound spectrum. A good interpretation involves the sensitivity of the performer to allow for sufficient time after the production of sound to allow the full body of color to be perceived. The silence following the "death" of sound allows the listener to reflect upon the full range of sound.

5 Lawrence Langer, *Preempting the Holocaust* (New London: Yale University Press, 1998), 118.

6 Jean-Jacques Eigeldinger, *Chopin: Pianist and Teacher as Seen By His Pupils* (Cambridge: Cambridge University Press, 1986), 42.

7 On the phrase "useless suffering" see Emmanuel Levinas, "Useless Suffering," in *Entre Nous: On Thinking-of-the-Other,* trans. Michael B. Smith and Barbara Harshav (New York: Columbia University Press, 1998), 91-101.

8 My recasting of Psalm 137 in light of Bak's irreparable musical landscape.

9 Langer, 117.

10 Langer, 119-20.

11 See Jer 31:15, and Emil Fackenheim, "The Children of Rachel, of Haman, of Job: Post-Holocaust Possibilities of a Fraternal Jewish-Christian Reading of the Book Belonging to Both," in *The Jewish Bible after the Holocaust: A Re-reading* (Manchester: Manchester University Press, 1990), 71-99.

12 See Isa 1:23. "They do not judge the case of the orphan, and the widow's cause never reaches them" (JPS TANAKH).

13 Richard Cohen, *Ethics, Exegesis and Philosophy: Interpretation after Levinas* (Cambridge: Cambridge University Press, 2000), 13.

14 Emmanuel Levinas, "A Religion for Adults," in *Difficult Freedom,* trans. Sean Hand (Baltimore: Johns Hopkins University Press, 1990), 19.

15 Emmanuel Levinas, "The Temptation of Temptation" in *Nine Talmudic Readings,* trans. Annette Aronowicz (Bloomington: Indiana University Press, 1990), 41-43.

16 Robert Gibbs, *Why Ethics? Signs of Responsibilities* (Princeton: Princeton University Press, 2000), 358-59. Gibbs comments, "The Sabbath is a socially institutionalized reflection upon labor that makes labor into labor by organizing the collective moment of rest."

17 Emmanuel Levinas, *Ethics and Infinity,* trans. Richard A. Cohen (Pittsburgh: Duquesne University Press, 1985), 97. In conversation with Philippe Nemo, Levinas says "To say: here I am *[me voici]*...is to do something for the Other. To give. To be human spirit, that's it....I analyze the inter-human relationship as if, in proximity with the Other—beyond the image I myself make of the other man—his face, the expressive in the Other, (and the whole human body is in this sense more of less face), were what *ordains* me to serve him."

18 See Tod Linafelt, *Strange Fire: Reading the Bible after the Holocaust* (New York: New York University Press, 2002), 15-17.

19 See Josh 10:12-15. Read literally, verse 13 claims that the sun was silent. "YHWH has heard the voice of humankind as on the day of Joshua when the sun was silent."

20 Exod 20:1-17.

21 Emmanuel Levinas, *Time and the Other,* trans. Richard A. Cohen (Pittsburgh: Duquesne University Press, 1987), 42.

22 Rebecca Rischin, *For the End of Time: The Story of the Messiaen Quartet* (Ithaca: Cornell University Press, 2003), 7.

23 Rischin, 62. It has been touted that upwards of 5,000 people could have been in attendance, but that would have been impossible given the size of any room sufficient to hold that many people in Gorlitz.

24 Samuel Bak related the influence of Arno Nadel on his artistic journey in personal correspondence with me after the Society of Biblical Literature conference in Philadelphia in November, 2005. Friedhelm Kemp's exhaustive article and bibliography in the book of Nadel's poetry: *Der Weissagende Dionysos; Gedichtwerk. Mit einem Nachwort von Friedhelm.* Veröffentlichungen der Deutschen Akademie für Sprache und Dichtung Darmstadt, 16. (Heidelberg: Lambert Schneider Verlag, 1959) provides additional background on the life and work of Arno Nadel.

25 See the Terezin Chamber Music Foundation website: http://www.terezinmusic.org/templates. The Hawthorne Quartet, based in Boston, champions the works of those musicians who were persecuted and executed by the Nazi's, such as Pavel Haas. The prisoners of Theresienstadt were forced to produce and participate in a Nazi propaganda film depicting the Theresienstadt concentration camp as a kind of "paradise ghetto." Upon the completion of the film, many of the artists in the film perished in Auschwitz. Samuel Bak mentioned during his response to this essay at the 2005 SBL Conference in Philadelphia that the Hawthorne Quartet was used as a visual reference point in his painting of the musicians in the quartet series.

26 Olivier Messiaen, *The Technique of My Musical Language* (Paris: Edition Musicales, 1944; English Trans., 1966), 8, 18.

27 Olivier Messiaen, Preface of *Quatuor Pour La Fin Du Temps,* trans. Danna Nolan Fewell (Paris: Durand, 1942), i.

28 Messiaen, *Quatuor pour la Fin du Temps,* title page.

29 Rischin, 52.

30 Messiaen, *The Technique of My Musical Language,* 9.

31 In music, retrograde is the reversal of reading a rhythm (reading right to left, what is written left to right), and the ensuing change of rhythmical values. A non-retrogradable rhythm is one which has no change of value when reading either right to left, or left to right.

32 Messiaen, *Quatuor pour la Fin du Temps,* i.

33 Messiaen, *Quatuor pour la Fin du Temps,* ii.

34 Langer, 82.

35 Messiaen's work is fundamentally rooted in Catholic mysticism.

36 Messiaen, *Quatuor pour la Fin du Temps,* i.

37 Langer, 119.

38 Samuel Bak, *Painted in Words*, a Memoir (Bloomington: Indiana University Press, 2001), 374.

39 Levinas, *Time and the Other,* 79.

40 Rischin, 6.

41 Cohen, 17.

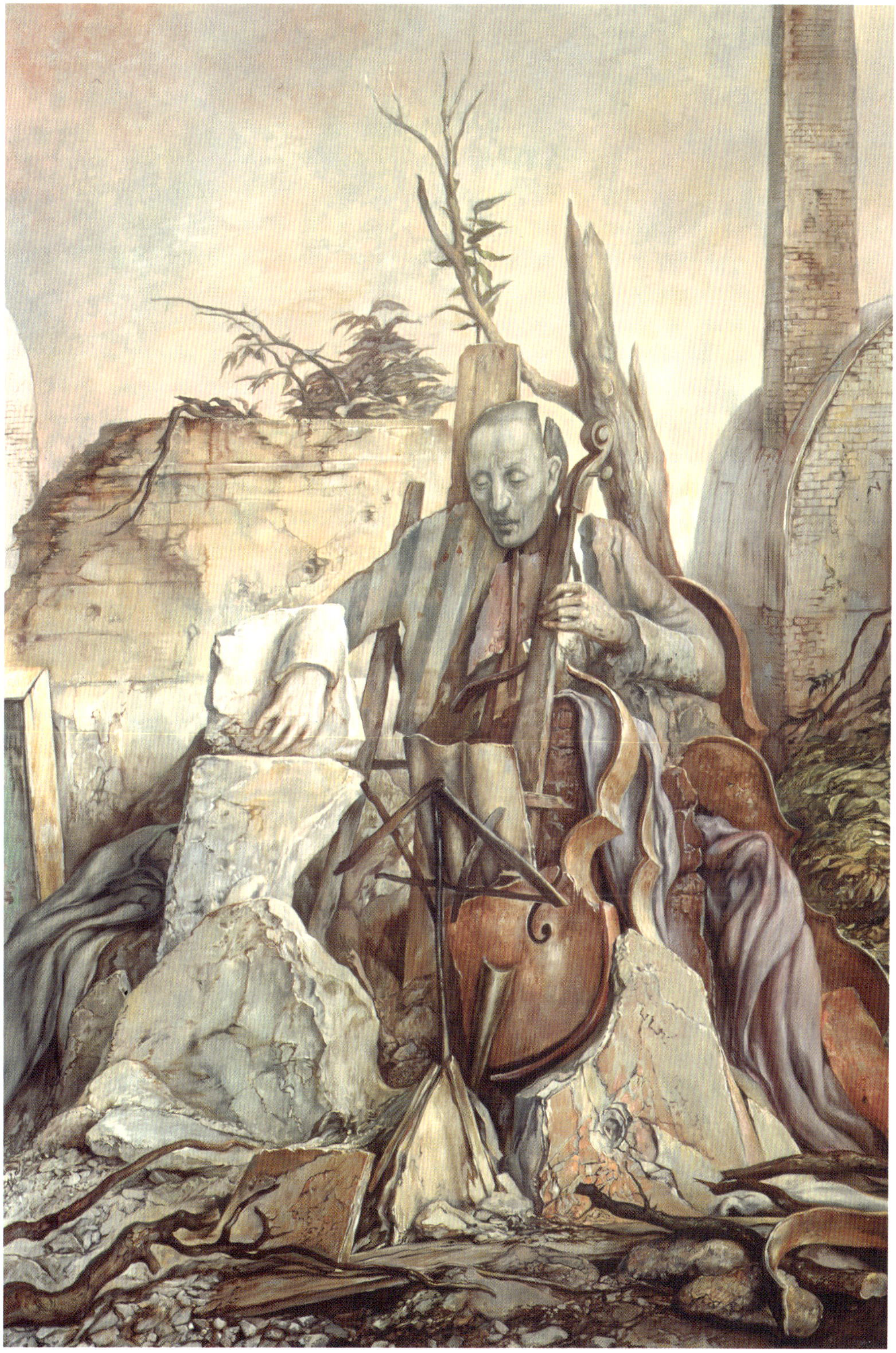

Solo, 1996
Oil on Canvas, 50 x 34"

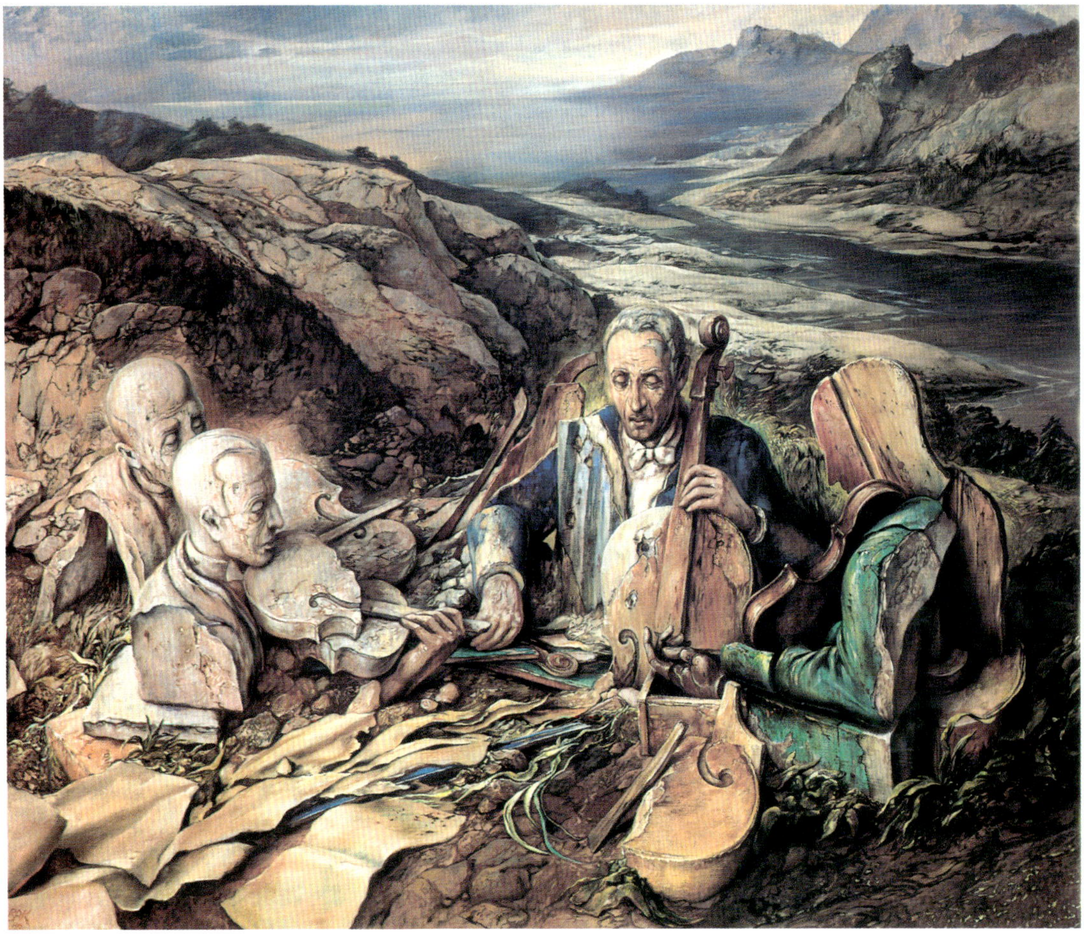

For the End of Time, 1996
Oil on Linen, 32 x 39"

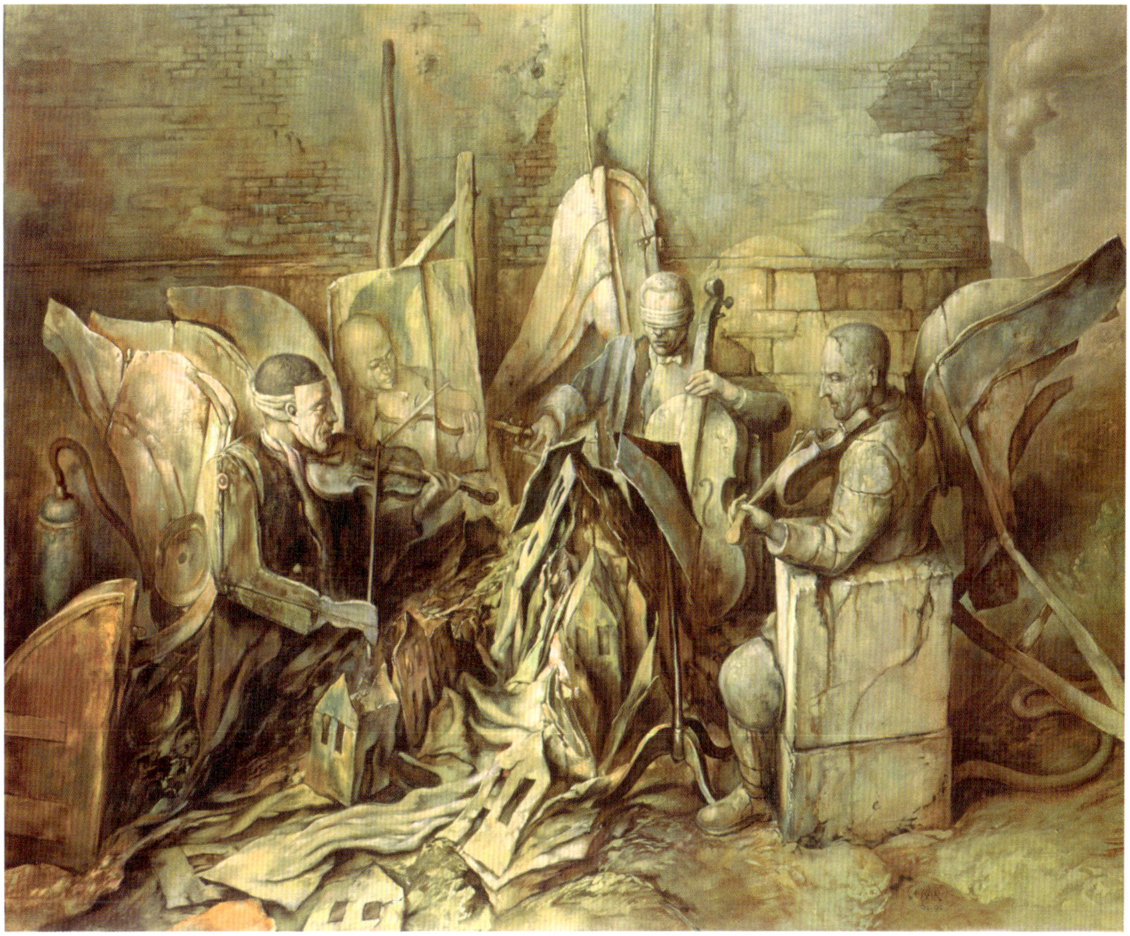

Elegy for a Town, 1995
Oil on Linen, 32 x 40"

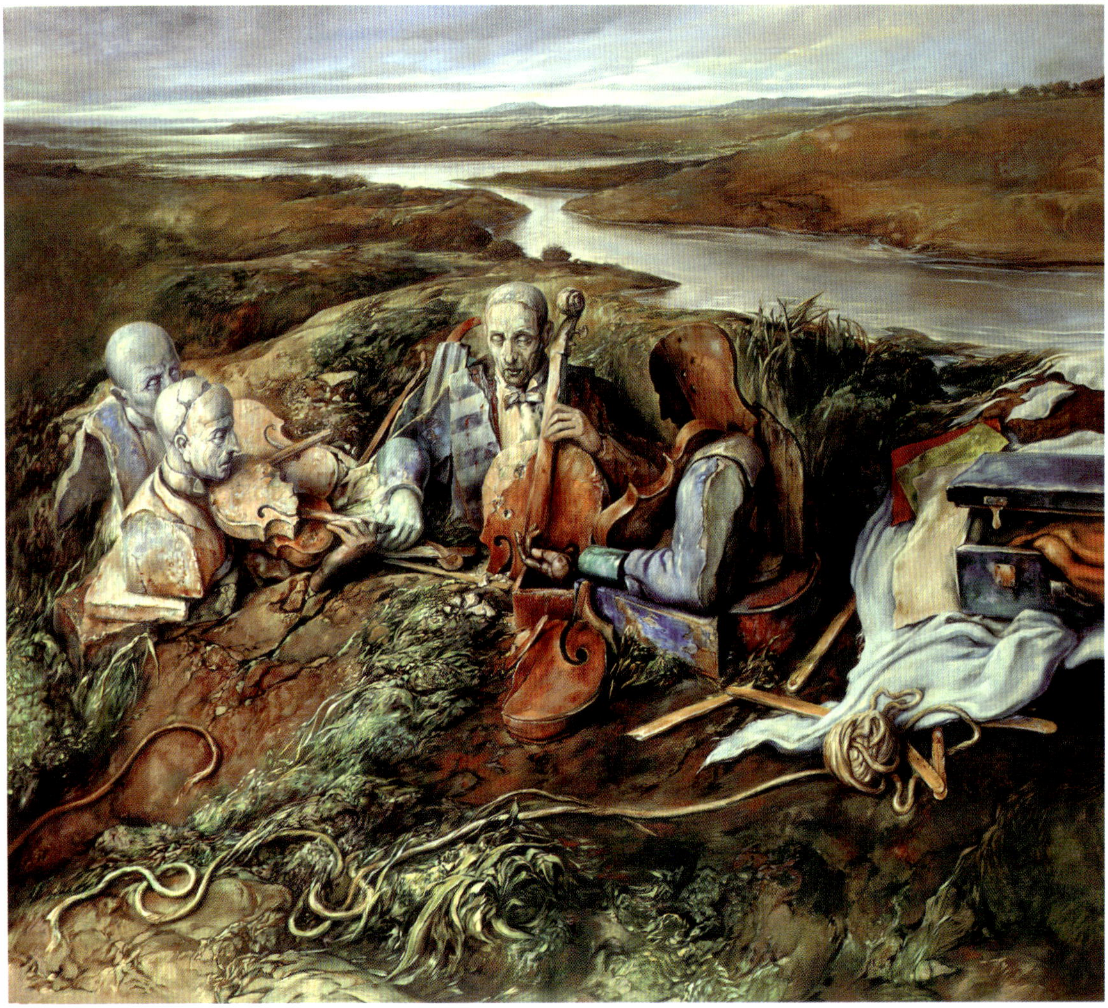

Quartet for the End of Time, 1995
Oil on Canvas, 19 3/4 x 51 1/4"

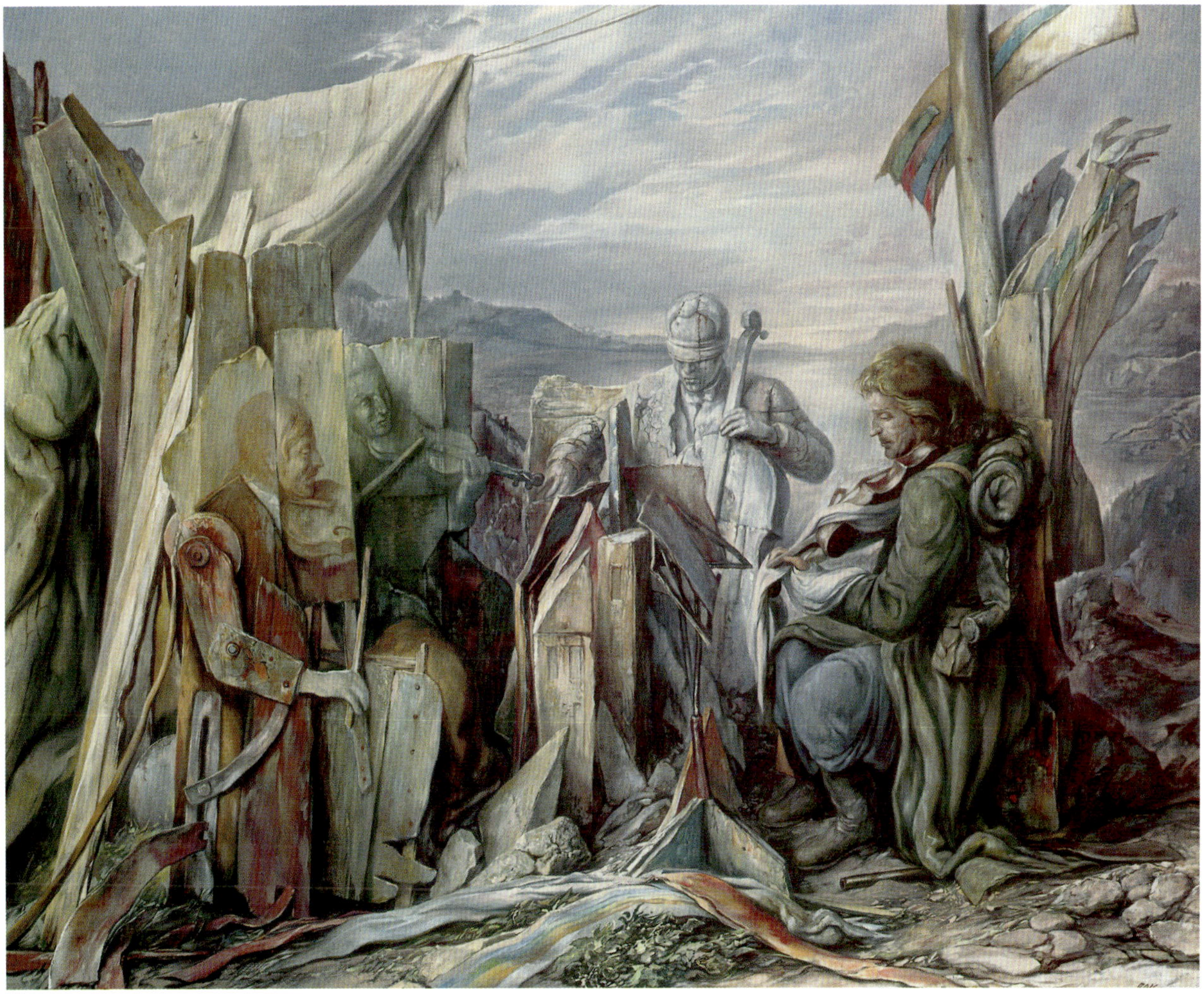

Rainbow Suite, 1996
Oil on Canvas, 32 x 39 1/2"

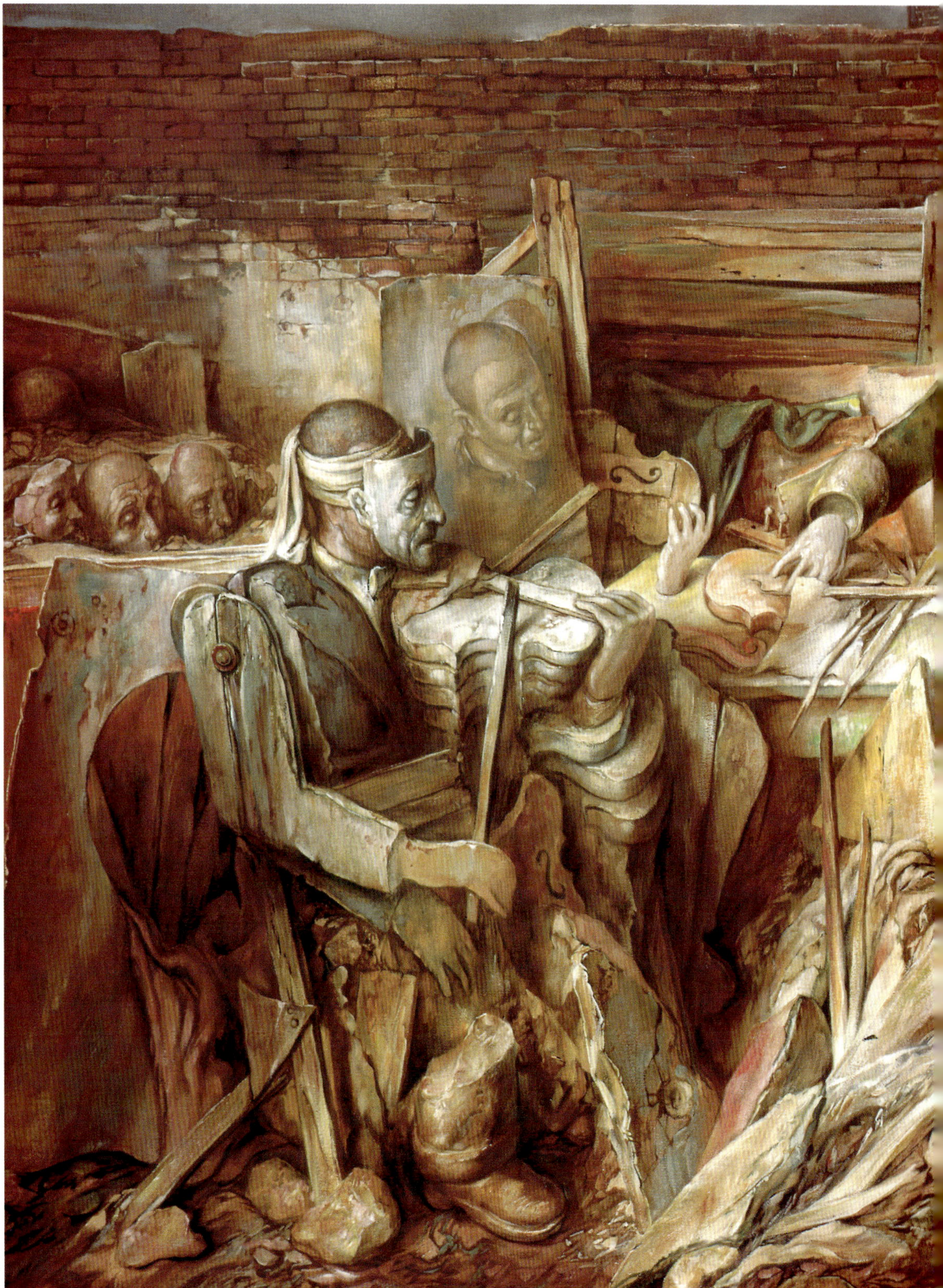

Multiple Voices, 1996
Oil on Canvas
34 1/4 x 50"

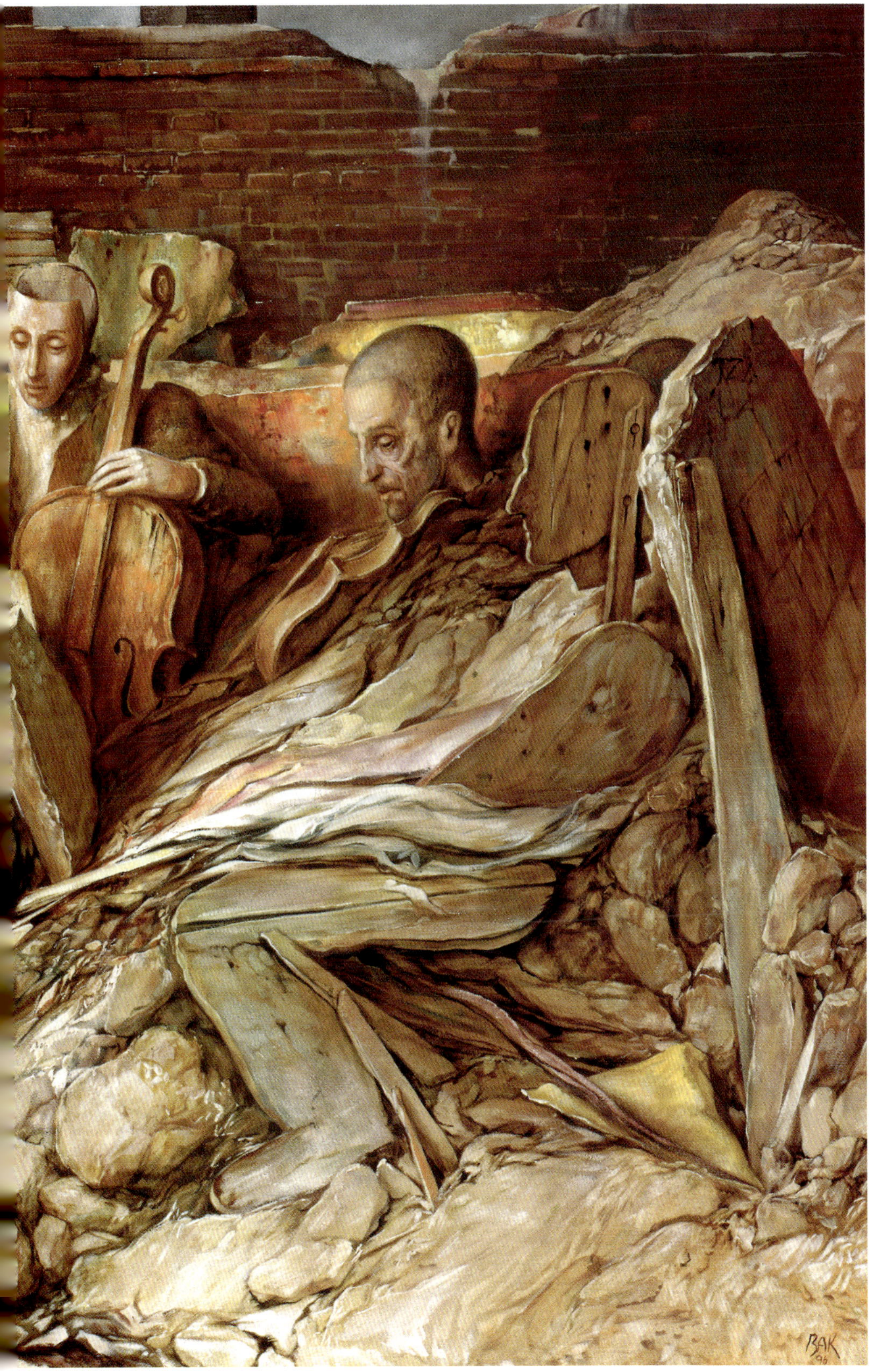
BAK

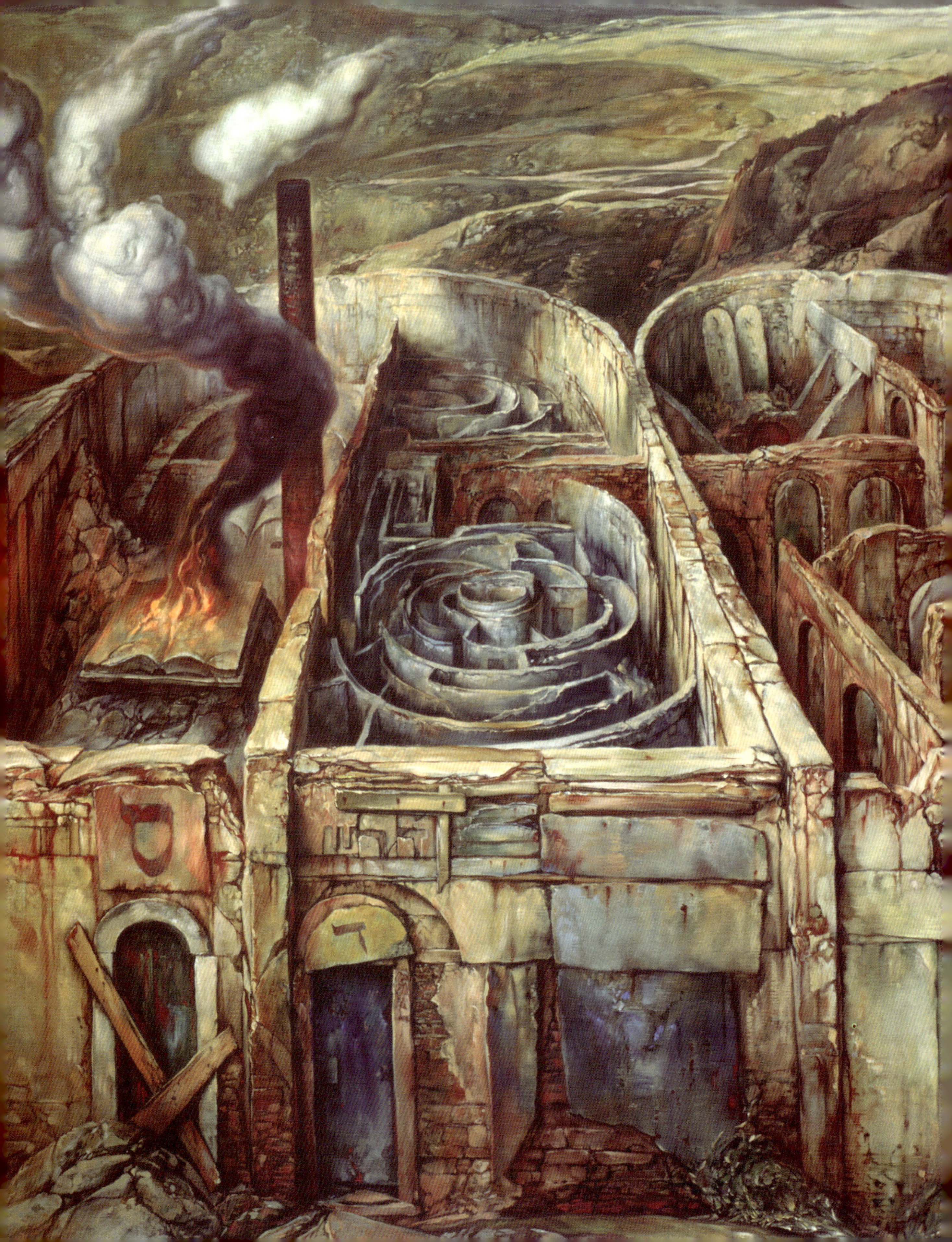

Labyrinths: A Response

SAMUEL BAK

Sitting in front of a screen that displayed digital images of my paintings, placed in a packed Philadelphia meeting room at the Annual Meeting of the American Academy of Religion/Society of Biblical Literature (2005), I carefully listened to the learned scholars who spoke of my art. Their erudite presentations were lively, insightful, and well-structured. Laying no claim to objectivity, I found their papers so captivating that gradually my admiration for the excellence of their work turned into pure amazement. Incredible. How did these literary scholars, seemingly new to the world of art-appreciation and art-history, get all that? Much of what my creative process keeps hidden from my own eyes, and whose real meanings I only grasp at the concluding phases of my work, to them looked self-evident. I felt that very few artists could ever have known a pleasure as profound as mine on that day.

Each of the talks aroused memories and associations, sometimes painful, mostly gratifying. All were intimately entwined with my art. Let me mention a few.

Danna Nolan Fewell and Gary Phillips spoke of the ties that connect me to Albrecht Dürer, and their words brought to my mind Dürer's juvenile self-portrait of 1493. Lurking behind this portrait was a piercing memory from my own faraway past—Vilna in 1941, the Nazi occupation. A little boy of eight, I was being marched through drenching rain towards the newly established ghetto for the Jews. Dragging my wet feet through the city's flooded gutters, I clutched in my hands a rain-soaked pillow that I had brought from home and would soon be forced to abandon. A few years later, freshly arrived in 1945 at a Displaced Persons camp in postwar Bavaria, while browsing through some old and half-torn art books, I first discovered a reproduction of Dürer's earliest self-portrait. Besides sketching his own young face, this precocious artist had on the same paper sketched his left hand and also two mysterious pillows in whose folds I thought I could trace two imaginary faces. No wonder Dürer's strangely foreboding study gripped my young imagination. Dürer and Bak. Here were two pillows, ominously signaling to each other over a chasm of centuries, religions, and wars.

Detail of *Pardes II*, 1994
Oil on Canvas, 51 1/4 x 77 1/4"

Charles Rix dedicated his paper to one of my canvases that depicts musicians and is entitled *Sounds of Silence.* Focusing on its images and iconography, he spoke of the composer Olivier Messiaen, and in particular of his *Quatuor pour la fin du temps.* Indeed, Rix's view of what I tried to say propelled my thoughts to the "end of time," to that mysterious domain that is both limited and boundless. In a sense all my art tackles the problems of what and how we remember and of how vulnerable are memory's configurations. Pondering all that I recall how, in the Paris of the late 1950's, I discovered Messiaen's inspiring *Quartet for the End of Time,* a work of mesmerizing beauty composed in the darkest of times, in a camp for prisoners of war.

Then a student at the *Ecole des Beaux Arts,* I often tuned in to the programs of *France Musique,* on which Messiaen was a frequent guest, and I loved to listen to his comments. When Rix played for our audience a recorded extract of Messiaens' *End of Time,* it at once transported me to my dim room in the ancient rue de Verneuil, to my shaky easel that I had found at the Marché aux Puces and to the blank canvases on which my youthful search for the "deep, deep meaning of my soul" created all sorts of visual confusions. At that time I did not yet know how to express my sense of loss. But by the time of the painting Rix points to, I had discovered my mature visual vocabulary. For me, those musicians do indeed play in, come from, and belong to the end of time.

Yvonne Sherwood's paper pointed to the many signs and signals imbedded in my *Akedah* paintings and spoke of how my cherished and most important teachers, the old masters, helped me to define and refine my painterly discourse. She mentioned the irony and the dark humor present in many of my most somber works. Irony and humor are not the same thing, but both offer forms of critique based on seeing an object or event from two quite different perspectives. When as a child I was told about Abraham and Isaac, I knew of course that this was a revered story about obedience to God. But instinctively I read it in a different way: "Daddy would never, never have done this to me!" In my art work, irony and even humor are never lighthearted devices. Rather, they are essential tools for the achievement of distance, of moral and emotional perspective. I cannot attribute this sense of double vision to that child. But in the artist that he became, it is active all the time.

Alicia Ostriker chose several of my *Genesis* paintings that depict the ambivalent region of dreaming, or being dreamt about, and navigated among their multiple complexities. At her mention of Percy Bysshe Shelley's poem *Ozymandias,* I leapt. Unexpected, but very much to the point, her words returned me to the Israel of 1949, when I finally began my formal high school education in Tel Aviv's most demanding school. Embarking upon four years of hard academic labor, the child-survivor in me had to absorb a lot. He was learning new languages—English, Hebrew—as well as the Hebrew Bible. Shelley's poem, hauntingly powerful, was my initiation into English:

> *"Two vast and trunkless legs of stone stand in the desert.*
> *Near them on the sand, half sunk, a shattered visage lies…"*

As Ostriker intuited, key images in many of my future paintings were inspired by its famous lines.

Dan Mathewson's presentation dealt with Job's rebellious spirit, which in his view is always present in my art. He finds it even in those paintings that deal with the game of chess, a subject that would seem to be far removed from any Biblical inspiration. According to Mathewson, my works depict Job's protest against a world of broken rules, questioning the senseless tragedies that pervade our human existence. Mathewson could not have known of my interminable disputes, many years ago in my Israeli high school, with Dr. Benedict, my beloved Bible teacher. Deeply religious, she couldn't accept my revolt against God's "unjust games," the unfairness of His "tests," and the mass *Akedah* of Job's innocent children. And I was infuriated by what was in my eyes the colossal inadequacy of God's answer to Job. These heated discussions made my classmates sign a petition asking Dr. Benedict and me to stop our arguments and proceed with normal learning.

Lawrence Langer has already published several books and catalogues and many articles on my art; he is one of its chief connoisseurs. His vision of how my works deal with the subject of the Holocaust deeply resonates with my own view, and I am flattered, now as always, by his wonderfully perceptive attention to my work.

Two important essays, by Michael Fishbane and S. Brent Rodríguez Plate, have been added to the present collection. The first was already well known to me; the second provided a revelation. Together they touch on what is a sensitive and important point. Art lives by communicating, and I love being intellectually and emotionally moved by works of art, from the very ancient to the most contemporary. And naturally, I always strive to understand how their effects were achieved. But at the same time, I feel that we can not elucidate all the mysteries of artistic creation, and I think that is a good thing. A painter's overly intellectualized self-awareness might lead to an overdose of artistic scheming and manipulation. Thus, though I am delighted when someone surprises me by taking my hand and leading me to an unexpected and enlightening new reading of my own work, as Plate so beautifully does when speaking of the Kabalistic resonance of my allegories, there always remain strata of my work that I prefer be hidden—some from the public eye, some doubtless from myself. This perception brings me to Michael Fishbane's essay, "Myth, Midrash, and Mysticism," which he wrote for the catalogue of my exhibition at the Spertus Museum in Chicago in 1994. Fishbane speaks of how I imbue old Jewish icons with new identities, and he concludes his introduction with the description of one of my works. It depicts a labyrinth that is set in a vast landscape and can be entered through four different doors, separately marked as P. R. D. S. The doors represent four distinct systems of Kabalistic analysis of the Holy Scriptures, from the simplest, P *(pshat),* to S *(sod),* the most secretive.

For me, this famous PaRDeS of Biblical interpretation offers a parallel, personal meaning. I see in it a metaphor for the paths I take when reaching out to any work of art. Hungry for what it has to offer, I ask myself many questions. How may I widen and deepen my perception of this work? How far can I go? What are its limitations? What are my limitations?

Let me explain. In my work I offer specific objects, figures, and landscapes as allegories of ideas, reflections, and feelings. These visions come to me directly from my familiarity with art history as well as from some strata of my subconscious. My paintings depict alternate realities, yet though they are consciously and carefully composed, certain aspects of them remain obscure. Even to myself. What have I tried to reveal? To conceal? Often I perceive myself outside the walls of this complex labyrinth of interpretations. Deep in my heart I fear being totally unmasked... and, thus, beset by contradictions, I sometimes pray that the doors of my imagined labyrinth might remain locked. Is it an admission of my difficulty in understanding my own self and purposes? Or is it simply an artist's hubris?

On this occasion, however, I am more than grateful for all the new keys that have been handed me. I look forward to moving through the doors they have opened.

—Philadelphia, PA, 2005

Samuel Bak Biography

1933	Born 12 August in Vilna, Poland
1940-41	Under Soviet occupation
1941-44	Under German occupation: ghetto, work-camp, refuge in a monastery
1942	First exhibition of drawings in the ghetto Vilna
1945-48	Displaced Persons camps in Germany; studied painting in Munich
1948	Emigrated to Israel
1952	Studied at the Bezalel Art School in Jerusalem
1953-56	Israeli army service
1956	Received the First Prize of the American-Israeli Cultural Foundation
1956-59	Lived in Paris and studied at the *Ecole des Beaux-Arts*
1959-93	1959-66 lived in Rome; 1966-74 in Israel; 1974-77 in New York City; 1977-80 in Israel; 1980-84 in Paris; 1984-93 in Switzerland
1993	Moved to Weston, Massachusetts

SELECTED SOLO GALLERY EXHIBITIONS

Galleria Schneider, Rome, Italy - 1959, 1961, 1965, 1966
Alwin Gallery, London, United Kingdom - 1965
L'Angle Aigu, Brussels, Belgium - 1965
Gordon Gallery, Tel Aviv, Israel - 1966
Roma Gallery, Chicago, IL - 1967
Pucker Safrai Gallery, Boston, MA - 1969, 1972, 1975, 1979, 1985, 1987, 1989, 1991
Hadassah "K" Gallery, Tel Aviv, Israel - 1971, 1973, 1978
Aberbach Fine Art, New York, NY - 1974, 1975, 1978
Ketterer Gallery, Munich, Germany - 1977
Amstutz Gallery, Zurich, Switzerland - 1978
Goldman Gallery, Haifa, Israel - 1978

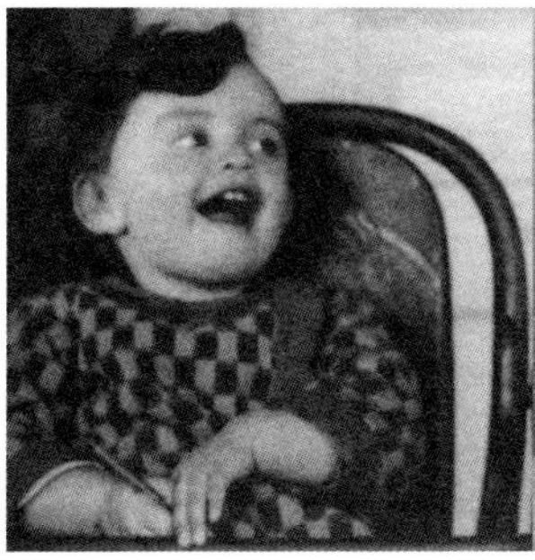

1936

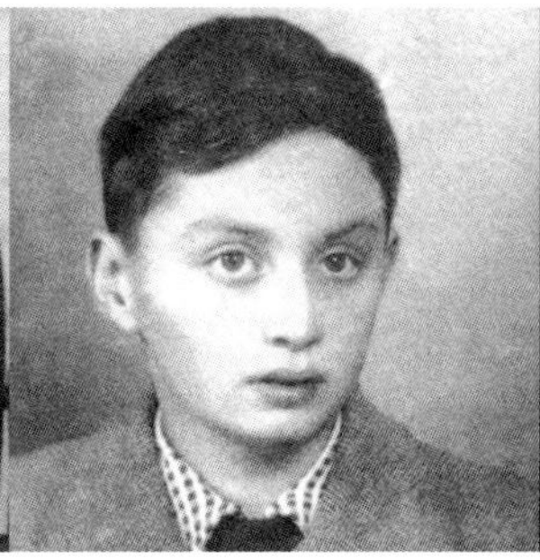

1944

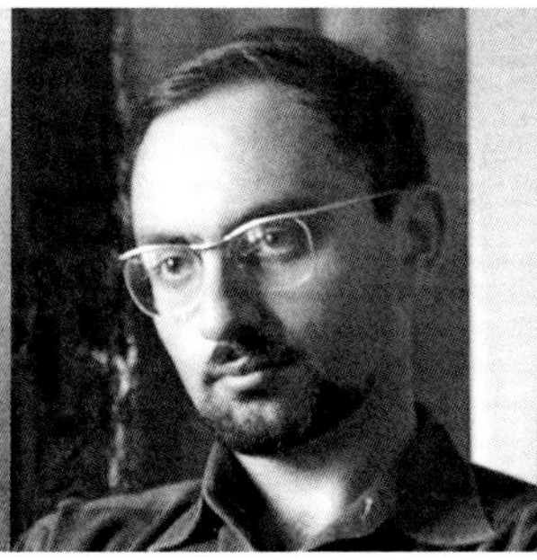

1959

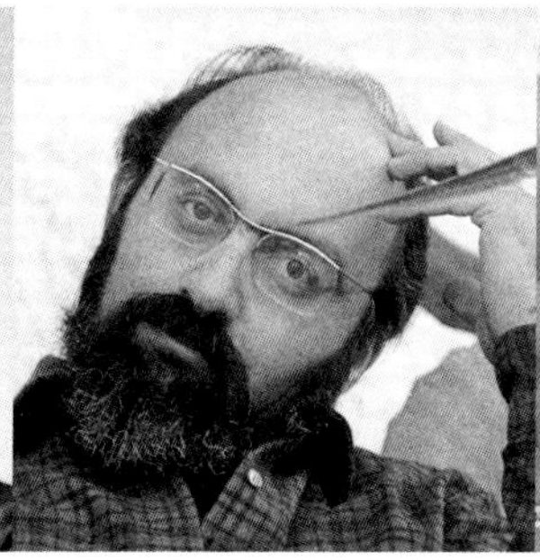

1973

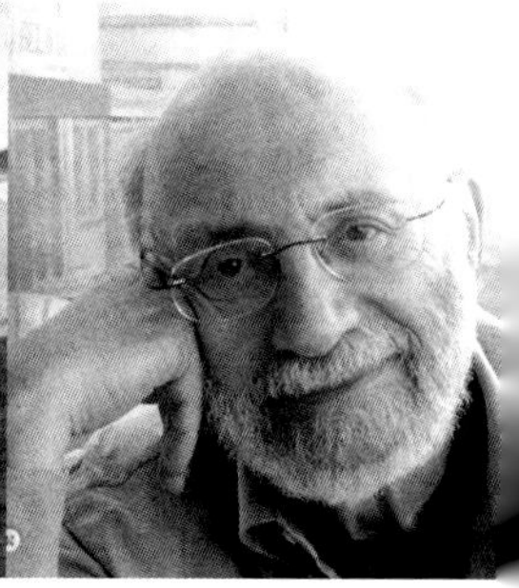

2006

Vonderbank Gallery, Frankfurt, Germany - 1978
DeBel Gallery, Jerusalem, Israel - 1978, 1980
Thorens Fine Art, Basel, Switzerland - 1981
Kallenbach Fine Art, Munich, Germany - 1981, 1983, 1984, 1987
Soufer Gallery, New York, NY - 1986, 1988, 1990, 1992, 1997, 2006
Galerie Ludwig Lange, Berlin, Germany - 1987
Galerie Carpentier, Paris, France - 1988
Galerie Marc Richard, Zurich, Switzerland - 1990
Galerie de la Cathedrale, Fribourg, Switzerland - 1991, 1992
Galerie Picpus, Montreux, Switzerland - 1991, 1992
Pucker Gallery, Boston, MA - 1993, 1995, 1996, 1998, 2000, 2002, 2003, 2004, 2006, 2008
George Krevsky Fine Art, San Francisco, CA - 1998
Beaver Country Day School, Chestnut Hill, MA - 2004
Finegood Gallery, Milken Jewish Center, Los Angeles, CA - 2004
St. Botolph Club, Boston, MA - 2004
Laurie M. Tisch Gallery, Jewish Community Center, Manhattan, NY - 2006

SELECTED MUSEUM EXHIBITIONS

Bezalel Museum, Jerusalem, Israel - 1963
Tel Aviv Museum, Tel Aviv, Israel - 1963
Rose Museum, Brandeis University, Waltham, MA - 1976
Germanisches National Museum, Nuremberg, Germany - 1977
Heidelberg Museum, Heidelberg, Germany - 1977
Haifa University, Haifa, Israel - 1978
Kunstmuseum, Düsseldorf, Germany - 1978
Rheinisches Landesmuseum, Bonn, Germany - 1978
Kunstmuseum, Wiesbaden, Germany - 1979
Stadtgalerie Bamberg, Villa Dessauer, Germany - 1988
Koffler Gallery, Toronto, Canada - 1990
Dürer Museum, Nuremberg, Germany - 1991
Temple Judea Museum, Philadelphia, PA - 1991
Jüdisches Museum, Stadt Frankfurt am Main, Germany - 1993
Hebrew Union College, Jewish Institute of Religion, New York, NY - 1994
Janice Charach Epstein Museum and Gallery, West Bloomfield, MI - 1994
National Catholic Center for Holocaust Education, Seton Hall College, Greensburg, PA - 1995
Spertus Museum, Chicago, IL - 1995
B'Nai B'Rith Klutznick National Jewish Museum, Washington, DC - 1997
Holocaust Museum Houston, Houston, TX - 1997
Lamont Gallery, Phillips Exeter Academy, Exeter, NH - 1997
Panorama Museum, Bad Frankenhausen, Germany - 1998
National Museum of Lithuania, Vilnius, Lithuania - 2001

Snite Museum of Art, Notre Dame University, Notre Dame, IN - 2001
Florida Holocaust Museum, Saint Petersburg, FL - 2001, 2007
Canton Museum of Art, Canton, OH - 2002
Clark University, Worcester, MA - 2002
Neues Stadtmuseum, Landsberg am Lech, Germany - 2002
92nd Street Y, New York, NY - 2002
Jewish Community Center, Memphis, TN - 2003
University of Scranton, Scranton, PA - 2003
City Hall Gallery, Orlando, FL - 2004
Texas Tech University, Lubbock, TX - 2004
Tweed Museum of Art, University of Minnesota, Duluth, MN - 2004
Felix Nussbaum Haus, Osnabrueck, Germany - 2006
University of New Hampshire, Durham, NH - 2006
Yad Vashem Museum, Jerusalem, Israel - 2006

SELECTED GROUP EXHIBITIONS

Image and Imagination, Tel Aviv Museum, Israel - 1967
Jewish Experience in the Art of the Twentieth Century, Jewish Museum, New York, NY - 1975
International Art Fair, Basel, Switzerland - 1979, 1981, 1982, 1984, 1986
Nachbilder, Kunsthalle, Hannover, Germany - 1979
Bilder Sind Nicht Verboten, Städtische Kunsthalle, Düsseldorf, Germany - 1982
Still Life, Tel Aviv Museum, Israel - 1984
Chagall to Kitaj, Barbican Art Center, London, United Kingdom - 1990
Witness and Legacy, Traveling Group Exhibition in North America - 1995

PUBLIC COLLECTIONS

Aidekman Arts Center, Tufts University, Medford, MA
Bard College, Annandale-on-Hudson, NY
Ben Uri Gallery, London, United Kingdom
Beth Israel Deaconess Medical Center, Brookline, MA
Boston Public Library, Boston, MA
Constitutional Court of South Africa, Braamfontein, South Africa
Davis Museum and Cultural Center, Wellesley College, Wellesley, MA
DeCordova Museum, Lincoln, MA
Dürer House, Nuremberg, Germany
Felix Nussbaum Haus, Osnabrueck, Germany
Facing History and Ourselves, Boston, MA
Florida Holocaust Museum, St. Petersburg, FL
Germanisches National Museum, Nuremberg, Germany
German Parliament, Bonn, Germany
Hillel Foundation, Washington, DC

Hobart and William Smith College, Geneva, NY
Holocaust Museum Houston, Houston, TX
Hood Museum of Art, Dartmouth College, Hanover, NH
Imperial War Museum, London, United Kingdom
Israel Museum, Jerusalem, Israel
Jewish Museum, New York, NY
Jüdisches Museum, Stadt Frankfurt am Main, Germany
Kunstmuseum, Bamberg, Germany
McMullen Museum, Boston College, Chestnut Hill, MA
Municipality of Nuremberg, Nuremberg, Germany
Museum of Modern Art, San Francisco, CA
National Gallery of Canada, Ottawa, Canada
National Museum of Lithuania, Vilnius, Lithuania
Panorama Museum, Bad Frankenhausen, Germany
Philips-Exeter Academy, Exeter, NH
Rose Museum, Brandeis University, Waltham, MA
Royal Ontario Museum, Toronto, Canada
Simmons College, Boston, MA
Snite Museum of Art, Notre Dame University, South Bend, IN
Springfield Museum of Fine Art, Springfield, MA
Tel Aviv Museum of Art, Tel Aviv, Israel
Tweed Art Museum, University of Minnesota, Duluth, MN
Haifa University, Haifa, Israel
University of Scranton, Scranton, PA
Williams College Museum of Art, Williamstown, MA
Yad Vashem Museum, Jerusalem, Israel

PUBLICATIONS AND FILMS

Samuel Bak, Paintings of the Last Decade, A. Kaufman and Paul T. Nagano. Aberbach, New York, 1974.

Samuel Bak, Monuments to Our Dreams, Rolf Kallenbach. Limes Verlag, Weisbaden & Munich, 1977.

Samuel Bak, The Past Continues, Samuel Bak and Paul T. Nagano. David R. Godine, Boston, 1988.

Chess as Metaphor in the Art of Samuel Bak, Jean Louis Cornuz. Pucker Art Publications, Boston & C.A. Olsommer, Montreux, 1991.

Ewiges Licht (Landsberg: A Memoir 1944-1948), Samuel Bak. Jewish Museum, Frankfurt, Germany, 1996.

Landscapes of Jewish Experience, Lawrence Langer. Pucker Art Publications, Boston & University Press of New England, Hanover, 1997.

Samuel Bak - Retrospective, Bad Frankenhausen Museum, Bad Frankenhausen, Germany, 1998.

The Game Continues: Chess in the Art of Samuel Bak, Pucker Art Publications, Boston & Indiana University Press, Bloomington, 2000.

In A Different Light: The Book of Genesis in the Art of Samuel Bak, Lawrence Langer. Pucker Art Publications, Boston & University of Washington Press, Seattle, 2001.

The Art of Speaking About the Unspeakable, TV Film by Rob Cooper and Pucker Art Publications, Boston, 2001.

Between Worlds: Paintings and Drawings by Samuel Bak from 1946-2001, Pucker Art Publications, Boston, 2002.

Painted in Words: A Memoir, Samuel Bak. Pucker Art Publications, Boston & Indiana University Press, Bloomington, 2002.

Samuel Bak: Painter of Questions, TV Film by Christa Singer, Toronto, Canada, 2003.

New Perceptions of Old Appearances in the Art of Samuel Bak, Lawrence Langer. Pucker Art Publications, Boston & Syracuse University Press, Syracuse, 2005.

Samuel Bak: Leben danach, Life Thereafter, Eva Atlan and Peter Junk. Felix Nussbaum Haus & Rasch, Verlag, Bramsche, Osnabrueck, Germany, 2006.

Return to Vilna in the Art of Samuel Bak, Lawrence Langer. Pucker Art Publications, Boston & Syracuse University Press, Syracuse, 2007.

Representing the Irreparable: The Shoah, the Bible, and the Art of Samuel Bak, Danna Nolan Fewell, Gary A. Phillips, and Yvonne Sherwood, Eds. Pucker Art Publications, Boston & Syracuse University Press, Syracuse, 2008.

Remembering Angels: Paintings by Samuel Bak. A calendar. January 2008-June 2009. With interpretive essay "Remembering Angels: The Memory Work of Samuel Bak," Danna Nolan Fewell and Gary A. Phillips.

Representing the Irreparable

Author Biographies

DANNA NOLAN FEWELL is Professor of Hebrew Bible at Drew University in Madison, New Jersey. Her published works include: *The Children of Israel: Reading the Bible for the Sake of Our Children* (Abingdon, 2003), *Circle of Sovereignty: Plotting Politics in the Book of Daniel* (Abingdon, 1991) with David M. Gunn, *Compromising Redemption: Relating Characters in the Book of Ruth* (Westminster/John Knox Press, 1990); *Narrative in the Hebrew Bible* (Oxford University Press, 1993), *Gender, Power, and Promise: The Subject of the Bible's First Story* (Abingdon, 1993). She is the editor of *Reading Between Texts: Intertextuality and the Hebrew Bible* (Westminster/John Knox Press, 1992), and co-editor with Gary Phillips of *Bible and Ethics of Reading* (*Semeia* 77; Society of Biblical Literature, 1997).

MICHAEL FISHBANE is the Nathan Cummings Professor of Jewish Studies in the Divinity School at the University of Chicago. He was trained in Semitic languages, biblical studies, and Judaica. His writings span from the ancient Near East and biblical studies to rabbinics, the history of Jewish interpretation, Jewish mysticism, and modern Jewish thought. Among his many publications are a commentary on the prophetic lectionary (Haftarot) in Judaism (Jewish Publication Society Bible Commentary, 2002), and the book *Biblical Myth and Rabbinic Mythmaking* (Oxford University Press, 2003). Professor Fishbane is a member of the American Academy of Jewish Research and was awarded a Lifetime Achievement in Textual Studies by the National Foundation of Jewish Culture.

LAWRENCE L. LANGER was born in New York City and educated at City College of New York and Harvard University. He is Professor of English Emeritus at Simmons College in Boston, Massachusetts. Among his books are *The Holocaust and The Literary Imagination, Holocaust Testimonies: The Ruins of Memory,* which won the National Book Critics Circle Award for Criticism in 1991, *Art from the Ashes: A Holocaust Anthology, Preempting the Holocaust,* and most recently *Using and Abusing the Holocaust.* He has also collaborated with Samuel Bak on five volumes of the artist's work, for which he wrote critical introductions and commentaries.

DAN MATHEWSON is Assistant Professor of Religion at Wofford College in Spartanburg, South Carolina. In 2004 he was a Fellow at the Center for Humanistic Inquiry at Emory University.

He has published and presented papers that examine biblical texts, American Evangelicalism, psychoanalysis, and trauma. His monograph, *Death and Survival in the Book of Job: Desymbolization and Traumatic Experience,* was published in 2006 (T and T Clark).

ALICIA OSTRIKER is a poet, critic, and midrashist. Her most recent volume of poetry is *No Heaven,* her most recent prose volume is *For the Love of God: The Bible as an Open Book.* She is Professor of English Emerita at Rutgers University and teaches in the low-residency Poetry MFA Program of New England College.

GARY A. PHILLIPS is Dean of the College and Professor of Religion at Wabash College in Crawfordsville, Indiana. His published works include the co-authored (with the Bible and Culture Collective) *The Postmodern Bible* (Yale University Press, 1995), and several edited and co-edited volumes: *Poststructural Criticism and the Bible: Text/History/Discourse* (*Semeia* 51; Scholars Press, 1990), *Intertextuality and Reading the Bible* with George Aichele (*Semeia* 69/70; Scholars Press, 1996), *Bible and Ethics of Reading* with Danna Nolan Fewell (*Semeia* 77; Society of Biblical Literature, 1997), *Reading Community Reading Scripture* with Nicole Duran (Trinity Press International, 2002), *Levinas and Biblical Studies* with David Jobling and Tamara Eskenazi (Society of Biblical Literature, 2003). Phillips's research and teaching are focused on ethical and theological questions related to the reading of the Bible arising from the Shoah.

S. BRENT RODRIGUEZ PLATE is Assistant Professor of Religion and the Visual Arts at Texas Christian University in Fort Worth, Texas. He has published several books and numerous articles, essays, and reviews on topics relating to religion and visual culture, including the books, *Blasphemy: Art that Offends, Walter Benjamin: Religion, and Aesthetics, Representing Religion in World Cinema,* and *Religion, Art, and Visual Culture.* He is managing editor of *Material Religion: The Journal of Objects, Art, and Belief.*

BERNARD H. PUCKER is the Founder, Owner, and Director of Pucker Gallery in Boston, Massachusetts. He studied History and English Literature at Columbia University and received a Master of Arts degree in Modern Jewish History from Brandeis University. Mr. Pucker is a Trustee of Facing History and Ourselves, a member of the Board of Directors of the Jewish Publication Society, an Advisory Board member of the Terezin Chamber Music Foundation, a member of the Board of Directors of the Boston Center for Jewish Heritage, and a member of the Arts and Letters Council of The David S. Wyman Institute for Holocaust Studies. Pucker Gallery was founded in 1967 in Boston's Back Bay neighborhood and has represented the art of Samuel Bak since 1969.

CHARLES M. RIX is a PhD candidate in Hebrew Bible at Drew University specializing in ethical aspects of narrative as informed by the phenomenology of Emmanuel Levinas. Rix is an ordained minister and a concert pianist whose performances and master classes have explored the use of Biblical themes in the piano works of Messiaen and Liszt. Rix holds an MA in Old Testament from New Brunswick Theological Seminary as well as a Masters of International Management from the Thunderbird Business School in Glendale, Arizona. He has previously worked internationally for ExxonMobil and presently serves on the Board of Trustees for the Graduate School of Theology at Abilene Christian University in Texas.

YVONNE SHERWOOD is Senior Lecturer in Old Testament/Tanakh and Judaism at the University of Glasgow, Scotland. Her previous publications include *The Prostitute and the Prophet* (T and T Clark, 1996; reprinted in 2004), *A Biblical Text and Its Afterlives: The Survival of Jonah in Western Culture* (Cambridge, 2000), *Derrida and Religion: Other Testaments* (Routledge, 2004, co-edited with Kevin Hart), and *Derrida's Bible* (ed; Palgrave, 2004). She is currently working on a cultural history of the sacrifice of Isaac/the Akedah.

Bibliography

Alter, Robert. *Genesis: Translation and Commentary.* New York/London: W.W. Norton, 1996.

Amishai-Maisels, Ziva. "The Jewish Jesus." *Journal of Jewish Art* 9 (1982): 84-104.

Baigell, Matthew. *Jewish-American Artists and the Holocaust.* New Brunswick, NJ: Rutgers University Press, 1997.

Bak, Samuel. *Bak: Oils, Watercolors, Drawings, 1972-1974.* New York: Aberbach Fine Art, October-November 1974.

———. "Dürer and I." In *Between Worlds: The Paintings and Drawings of Samuel Bak from 1946 to 2001.* Edited by Irene Taylor, 270-95. Boston: Pucker Art Publications, 2002.

———. "The Ghetto Boy." In Tayler, *Between Worlds,* 296-307.

———. *Painted in Words: A Memoir.* Bloomington: Indiana University Press; Boston: Pucker Art Publications, 2001.

———. "Winged Figures." In Tayler, *Between Worlds,* 154-59.

Bak, Samuel, and Lawrence L. Langer. *Landscapes of Jewish Experience.* The Tauber Institute for the Study of European Jewry 25. Boston: Pucker Gallery and Brandeis University Press, 1997.

Bakhtin, Mikhail. *The Dialogic Imagination: Four Essays.* Edited by Michael Holquist. Translated by Caryl Emerson and Michael Holquist. Austin: University of Texas Press, 1981.

Bartheleme, Donald. *Sixty Stories.* New York: Penguin, 1982.

Bartlett, Anthony W. *Cross Purposes: The Violent Grammar of Christian Atonement.* Harrisburg, PA: Trinity Press International, 2001.

Baxandall, Michael. *Painting and Experience in Fifteenth Century Italy: A Primer in the Social History of Pictorial Style.* Oxford: Clarendon Press, 1972.

Bellow, Saul. *Mr. Sammler's Planet.* New York: Penguin, 1995.

Benjamin, Walter. *The Origin of German Tragic Drama.* Translated by John Osborne. London: NLB, 1977.

———. *Walter Benjamin: Selected Writings, Volume 4, 1938-1940.* Edited by Howard Eiland and Michael W. Jennings. Cambridge, MA: Belknap Press of Harvard University Press, 2003.

———. *The Work of Art in the Age of Mechanical Reproduction.* Transcribed by Andy Blunden. UCLA School of Theater, Film, and Television, 1998. Proofed and corrected February 2005.

Bergen, Doris L. "Old Testament, New Hatreds: The Hebrew Bible and Antisemitism in Nazi Germany." In *Sacred Text, Secular Times: The Hebrew Bible in the Modern World.* Edited by Leonard Jay Greenspoon and Bryan F. Le Beau, 35-46. Studies in Jewish Civilization 10. Omaha, NE: Creighton University Press, 2000.

———. *Twisted Cross: The German Christian Movement in the Third Reich.* Chapel Hill: University of North Carolina Press, 1996.

Berkovits, Eliezer. *With God in Hell: Judaism in the Ghettos and Deathcamps.* New York: Sanhedrin Press, 1979.

Blake, William. "To the Accuser Who Is the God of This World." Epilogue to *For the Sexes: The Gates of Paradise.* London: Frederick Hollyer, 1925.

Bloom, Harold. *The Anxiety of Influence: A Theory of Poetry.* London; New York: Oxford University Press, 1975.

Brock, Rita Nakashima, and Rebecca Ann Parker. *Proverbs of Ashes: Violence, Redemptive Suffering, and the Search for What Saves Us.* Boston: Beacon Press, 2001.

Brueggemann, Walter. *Genesis.* Atlanta: John Knox Press, 1982.

Bruns, Gerald L. "Midrash and Allegory: The Beginning of Scriptural Interpretation." In *The Literary Guide to the Bible.* Edited by Robert Alter and Frank Kermode, 625-46. Cambridge, MA: Belknap Press of Harvard University Press, 1987.

Bryson, Norman. *Looking at the Overlooked: Four Essays on Still Life Painting.* London: Reaktion Books, 1990.

Callaway, Mary. *Sing, O Barren One: A Study in Comparative Midrash.* Atlanta: Scholars Press, 1986.

Caputo, John D. *Against Ethics: Contributions to a Poetics of Obligation with Constant Reference to Deconstruction.* Bloomington: Indiana University Press, 1993.

Caruth, Cathy. Introduction to *Trauma: Explorations in Memory.* Edited by Cathy Caruth. Baltimore: Johns Hopkins University Press, 1995.

Chan, C. W. "The Butterfly Dream." *The Philosopher: The Journal of the Philosophical Society of England* 83.2 (Autumn 1995). http://atschool.eduweb.co.uk/cite/staff/philosopher/butter.htm.

Cixous, Hélène. *"Coming to Writing" and Other Essays.* Edited by Deborah Jenson. Translated by Sarah Cornell et al. Cambridge, MA: Harvard University Press, 1991.

Cohen, Arthur. *The Tremendum: A Theological Interpretation of the Holocaust.* New York: Crossroad, 1981.

Cohen, Richard A. *Ethics, Exegesis and Philosophy: Interpretation after Levinas.* Cambridge: Cambridge University Press, 2000.

Delaney, Carol. *Abraham on Trial: The Social Legacy of Biblical Myth.* Princeton, NJ: Princeton University Press, 1998.

Drucker, Johanna. *The Alphabetic Labyrinth: The Letters in History and Imagination.* New York: Thames and Hudson, 1995.

Dürer, Albrecht. *Dürer: Schriftlicher Nachlaß.* Edited by Hans Rupprecht. 3 vols. Berlin: Deutscher Verein für Kunstgeschichte, 1956.

Eagleton, Terry. *Ideology of the Aesthetic.* Oxford; Cambridge, MA: Blackwell, 1990.

Eigeldinger, Jean-Jacques, ed. *Chopin: Pianist and Teacher as Seen By His Pupils.* Translated by Naomi Shohet, Krysia Osostowicz, and Roy Howat. Cambridge: Cambridge University Press, 1986.

Erasmus to Hochstraten on August 11, 1519. *Opus Epistolarum Des. Erasmi.* Edited by P. S. Allen et al, 4:46 (no. 1006). 8 vols. Oxford University Press, 1906-58.

Fackenheim, Emil L. *God's Presence in History: Jewish Affirmations and Philosophical Reflections.* New York: New York University Press, 1970.

———. *The Jewish Bible after the Holocaust: A Re-reading.* Sherman Studies of Judaism in Modern Times. Manchester: Manchester University Press; Bloomington: Indiana University Press, 1990.

Feinstein, Stephen. "'This is not a Pear': Reflections on Samuel Bak's Pear Paintings." In *New Perceptions of Old Appearances in the Art of Samuel Bak,* by Lawrence L. Langer, 1-7. Boston: Pucker Art Publications and Syracuse University Press, 2005.

———. "Witness and Legacy." http://sunsite.utk.edu/neighborhoods/witness/essays/feinstein/feinstein.html.

Feld, Merle. "Across the Jordan." In *Making a Scene: The Contemporary Drama of Jewish-American Women.* Edited by Sarah B. Cohen. Syracuse, NY: Syracuse University Press, 1997.

Felman, Shoshana, and Dori Laub. *Testimony: Crises of Witnessing in Literature, Psychoanalysis, and History.* New York; London: Routledge, 1992.

Fewell, Danna Nolan. *The Children of Israel: Reading the Bible for the Sake of Our Children.* Nashville: Abingdon Press, 2003.

Fewell, Danna Nolan and Gary A. Phillips. "Remembering Angels: The Memory Work of Samuel Bak." *Remembering Angels: Paintings by Samuel Bak.* A calender. January 2008 - June 2009. Pucker Art Publications. Boston, 2008.

Fortunoff Video Archive for Holocaust Testimonies at Yale University. *Tape HVT-618.* Cited in Lawrence Langer, "The Holocaust Theme in the Paintings of Samuel Bak." *Samuel Bak Retrospecktive: 1946-1997.* Catalogue. Bad Frankenhausen, Germany: Panorama Museum, 1998.

Foucault, Michel. *The Order of Things.* Translated by Alan Sheridan. New York: Random House, 1970.

———. *This Is Not a Pipe.* Edited and translated by James Harkness. Berkeley, CA: University of California Press, 1982.

Fox, Everett. *The Five Books of Moses: Genesis, Exodus, Leviticus, Numbers, and Deuteronomy. A New Translation with Introductions, Commentary, and Notes.* New York: Schocken Books, 1995.

Fox, Michael V. *Proverbs 1-9: A New Translation with Introduction and Commentary.* AB 18a. New York: Doubleday, 2000.

Freud, Sigmund. "Mourning and Melancholia." *In General Psychological Theory.* Edited by Philip Rieff, 164-79. New York: Collier, 1963.

Friedman, Maurice. *Problematic Rebel: Melville, Dostoievsky, Kafka, Camus.* Rev. ed. Chicago: University of Chicago Press, 1970.

———. *To Deny Our Nothingness: Contemporary Images of Man.* Chicago: University of Chicago Press, 1978. Reprint, Chicago: Midway, 1984.

Garber, Zev, and Bruce Zuckerman. "Why Do We Call the Holocaust 'the Holocaust'? An Enquiry into the Psychology of Labels." In *Remembering for the Future: Working Papers and Addenda.* Edited by Yehuda Bauer et al, 1879-92. Oxford: Pergamon Press, 1989.

Gibbs, Robert. *Why Ethics? Signs of Responsibilities.* Princeton, NJ: Princeton University Press, 2000.

———. "Unjustifiable Suffering." In *Suffering Religion.* Edited by Robert Gibbs and Elliott R. Wolfson, 13-35. London; New York: Routledge, 2002.

Gilboa, Amir. "Yizhak." In *Modern Hebrew Poetry.* Edited by Ruth Finer Mintz. Berkeley, CA: University of California Press, 1968.

Gorringe, Timothy. *God's Just Vengeance: Crime, Violence and the Rhetoric of Salvation.* Cambridge Studies in Ideology and Religion 9. Cambridge: Cambridge University Press, 1996.

Greenberg, Gershon. "The Death of History and the Life of Akeda: Voices from War." In *The Death of God Movement and the Holocaust: Radical Theology Encounters the Shoah.* Edited by Stephen R. Haynes and John K. Roth, 99-109. Contributions to the Study of Religion 55. Westport, CT: Greenwood Press, 1999.

Greenberg, Irving. "Cloud of Smoke, Pillar of Fire." In *Auschwitz: Beginning of a New Era?* Edited by Eva Fleischner, 7-55. New York: KTAV, 1977.

Gushee, David P. *The Righteous Gentiles of the Holocaust: A Christian Interpretation.* Philadelphia: Fortress, 1994.

Habel, Norman C. "Symbolism of Wisdom in Proverbs 1-9." *Interpretation* 26 (1972): 131-57.

Handelman, Susan. *Fragments of Redemption: Jewish Thought and Literary Theory in Benjamin, Scholem, and Levinas.* Bloomington: Indiana University Press, 1991.

Hanna, Thomas L. "Albert Camus and the Christian Faith." In *Camus: A Collection of Critical Essays.* Edited by Germain Brée, 48-55. Englewood Cliffs, NJ: Prentice Hall, 1962.

Hartman, Geoffrey H., and Sanford Budick, eds. *Midrash and Literature.* New Haven: Yale University Press, 1986.

Hatley, James. *Suffering Witness: The Quandary of Responsibility after the Irreparable.* Albany, NY: State University of New York Press, 2000.

Heidegger, Martin. "The Origin of the Work of Art." In *Basic Writings.* Edited by David Farrell Krell, 139-76. Translated by Albert Hofstader. New York: HarperCollins, 1993.

Henck, Herbert. *Notes on Klavierstucke I-XI.* Mainz: Wergo Music, 1987.

Hitler, Adolph. *Mein Kampf.* Edited by Ralph Mannheim. New York: Mariner Books, 1999.

Hitler, Adolph. *Mein Kampf.* Vol. 1, chap. 11. Cited in http://www.hitler.org/writings/Mein—Kampf/mkv1ch11.html.

Huneke, Douglas. "Glimpses of Light in a Vast Darkness: A Study in the Moral and Spiritual Development of Nazi Era Rescuers." In *Remembering for the Future,* vol. 1. Edited by A. Roy Eckardt and Alice Eckardt, 486-92. New York: Pergamon Press, 1989.

Hutchison, Jane Campbell. *Albrecht Dürer: A Biography.* Princeton, NJ: Princeton University Press, 1990.

Kafka, Franz. *The Sons: The Metamorphosis, The Judgment, The Stoker, and Letter to His Father.* Translated by Edwin and Willa Muir. New York: Schocken Books, 1989.

Katz, Stephen T. *Post-Holocaust Dialogues: Critical Studies in Modern Jewish Thought.* New York; London: New York University Press, 1983.

Kepnes, Steven. "Job and Post-Holocaust Theodicy." In *Strange Fire: Reading the Bible After the Holocaust.* Edited by Tod Linafelt, 252-66. New York: New York University Press, 2000.

Kierkegaard, Søren. *Fear and Trembling; Repetition.* Edited and translated by Howard V. Hong and Edna H. Hong. Kierkegaard's Writings 6. Princeton, NJ: Princeton University Press, 1983.

Koerner, Joseph Leo. *The Moment of Self-Portraiture in German Renaissance Art.* Chicago: University of Chicago Press, 1993.

Kristeva, Julia. *Black Sun: Depression and Melancholia.* Translated by Leon S. Roudiez. New York: Columbia University Press, 1989.

Langer, Lawrence L. "The Holocaust Theme in the Paintings of Samuel Bak." *Samuel Bak Retrospektive: 1946-1997.* Catalog. Bad Frankenhausen, Germany: Panorama Museum, 1998.

———. *In a Different Light: The Book of Genesis in the Art of Samuel Bak.* Boston: Pucker Art Publications; Seattle: University of Washington Press, 2001.

———. *Preempting the Holocaust.* New Haven: Yale University Press, 1998.

Latour, Bruno, and Peter Weibel, eds. *Iconoclash: Beyond the Image Wars in Science, Religion and Art.* Karlsruhe, Germany: ZKM, Centre for Art and Media; Cambridge, MA: MIT Press, 2002.

Levi, Primo. *Survival in Auschwitz: The Nazi Assault on Humanity.* Translated by Stuart Woolf. New York: Collier Books; Simon & Schuster, 1986.

Levinas, Emmanuel. *Difficult Freedom: Essays on Judaism.* Translated by Seán Hand. Baltimore: Johns Hopkins University Press. 1990.

———. *Ethics and Infinity. Conversations with Philippe Nemo.* Translated by Richard A. Cohen. Pittsburgh, PA: Duquesne University Press, 1985.

———. *Nine Talmudic Readings.* Translated by Annette Aronowicz. Bloomington: Indiana University Press,1990.

———. *Proper Names.* Translated by Michael B. Smith. Stanford, CA: Stanford University Press, 1996.

———. "Reality and Its Shadow." In *Collected Philosophical Paper.* Translated by Alphonso Lingis, 1-13. Dordrecht: Martinus Nijhoff, 1987.

———. *Time and the Other and Additional Essays.* Translated by Richard A. Cohen. Pittsburgh, PA: Duquesne University Press, 1987.

———. "Useless Suffering." In *Entre Nous: On Thinking-of-the-Other.* Translated by Michael B. Smith and Barbara Harshav, 91-101. New York: Columbia University Press, 1998.

Lhevinne, Josef. *Basic Principles in Pianoforte Playing.* Philadelphia: Theodore Presser, 1924. Reprint, New York: Dover, 1972.

Lifton, Robert Jay. *The Life of the Self: Toward a New Psychology.* New York: Simon & Schuster, 1976.

———. *The Protean Self: Human Resilience in an Age of Fragmentation.* New York: BasicBooks, 1993.

Limburg, James. *Jonah: A Commentary.* London: SCM Press, 1993.

Linafelt, Tod, ed. *Strange Fire: Reading the Bible after the Holocaust.* New York: New York University Press, 2000.

Littell, Franklin H. *The Crucifixion of the Jews. The Failure of Christians to Understand the Jewish Experience.* Macon, GA: Mercer University Press, 1996.

Lowenthal, David. *The Past is a Foreign Country.* Cambridge: Cambridge University Press, 1985.

Lyotard, Jean-François. *The Differend: Phrases in Dispute.* Translated by George Van Den Abbeele. Minneapolis, MN: University of Minnesota Press, 1988.

———. "The Survivor." In *Toward the Postmodern.* Edited by Robert Harvey and Mark S. Roberts, 144-63. Atlantic Highlands, NJ: Humanities Press, 1993.

Magonet, Jonathan. *A Rabbi Reads the Bible.* London: SCM Press, 1991, 2004.

Maybaum, Ignaz. "The Binding of Isaac" and "Moriah, Massada, Golgotha." In *Ignaz Maybaum: A Reader.* Edited by Nicholas de Lange, 78-80. European Judaism 3. New York; Oxford: Berghahn Books, 2001.

Messiaen, Olivier. *Quatuor Pour La Fin Du Temps.* Bryn Mawr: Theodore Presser, 1944.

———. *The Technique of My Musical Language.* Paris: Édition Musicales, 1944.

Moxley, Keith. "Impossible Distance: Past and Present in the Study of Dürer and Grunewald." *Art Bulletin,* 86.4 (December 2004):750-63.

Nadel, Arno. *Der Weissagende Dionysos. Gedichtwerk. Mit einem Nachwort von Friedhelm Kemp.* Veröffentlichungen der Deutschen Akademie für Sprache und Dichtung Darmstadt, 16. Epilogue by Friedhelm Kemp. Heidelberg: Lambert Schneider Verlag, 1959.

Neher, André. *The Exile of the Word: From the Silence of the Bible to the Silence of Auschwitz.* Translated by David Maisel. Philadelphia: Jewish Publication Society of America, 1981.

Olin, Margaret. "Graven Images on Video? The Second Commandment and Jewish Identity." In *Complex Identities: Jewish Consciousness and Modern Art.* Edited by Matthew Baigell and Milly Heyd, 34-50. New Brunswick, NJ: Rutgers University Press, 2001.

Ostriker, Alicia. "The Bosom of Abraham," "Sarah, or Defiance," "Isaac, or Laughter," and "The Opinion of the Ram." In *The Nakedness of the Fathers: Biblical Visions and Revisions,* 49-66, 67-72, 81-88, 89-90. New Brunswick, NJ: Rutgers University Press, 1994.

———. "A Triple Hermeneutic: Scripture and Revisionist Women's Poetry," In *A Feminist Companion to Reading the Bible: Approaches, Methods and Strategies.* Edited by Athalya Brenner and Carol Fontaine, 164-89. Sheffield: Sheffield Press, 1997.

———. "A Word Made Flesh: The Bible and Women's Poetry." In *Feminist Revision and the Bible,* 56-91. Oxford; Cambridge, MA: Blackwell Publishers, 1993.

Ouaknin, Marc-Alain. *Mysteries of the Kabbalah.* Translated by Josephine Bacon. New York: Abbeville Press, 2000.

Oz, Amos. Foreword. "Painted in Words, Narrated in Colors and Light." In *Painted in Words: A Memoir,* by Samuel Bak, vii-ix. Bloomington: Indiana University Press; Boston: Pucker Gallery Publications, 2001.

Pagis, Dan. "Draft of a Reparations Agreement." *The Selected Poetry of Dan Pagis.* Translated by Stephen Mitchell. Oxford: Carcanet Press, 1972.

Panofsky, Erwin. *The Life and Art of Albrecht Dürer.* Princeton, NJ: Princeton University Press, 1955. Originally published as *Albrecht Dürer,* 1943-48.

Phillips, Gary. "Emmanuel Levinas." In *A Handbook for Postmodern Biblical Interpretation.* Edited by A.K.M. Adam, 154-59. St. Louis, MO: Chalice Press, 2000.

Plank, Karl A. "Broken Continuities: 'Night' and 'White Crucifixion'." Originally published in *Christian Century,* November 4, 1987, 963. http://www.religion-online.org/showarticle.asp?title=1069.

Plate, S. Brent. *Religion, Art and Visual Culture: A Cross-Cultural Reader.* New York: Palgrave, 2002.

———. *Walter Benjamin, Religion, and Aesthetics: Rethinking Religion through the Arts.* New York: Routledge, 2004.

Plath, Sylvia. *The Collected Poems.* Edited by Ted Hughes. New York: Harper & Row, 1981.

Potok, Chaim. *My Name is Asher Lev.* New York; London: Penguin, 1972.

Price, David Hotchkiss. *Albrecht Dürer's Renaissance: Humanism, Reformation, and the Art of Faith.* Ann Arbor, MI: University of Michigan Press, 2003.

Raskin, Richard. *A Child at Gunpoint: A Case Study on the Life of a Photo.* Aarhus, Denmark: Aarhus University Press, 2004.

Read, John. "Albrecht Dürer's Melencolia." http://www.alchemylab.com/melancholia.htm.

Revel-Neher, Elisha. "'With Wisdom and Knowledge of Workmanship': Jewish Art Without a Question Mark." In *Complex Identities: Jewish Consciousness and Modern Art.* Edited by Matthew Baigell and Milly Heyd, 12-33. New Brunswick, NJ: Rutgers University Press, 2001.

Rilke, Rainer Maria. *Letters to a Young Poet.* Translated by Stephen Mitchell. New York: Random House, 1984.

Rischin, Rebecca. *For the End of Time: The Story of the Messiaen Quartet.* Ithaca, NY: Cornell University Press, 2003.

Rosenfeld, Alvin H. "Reflections on Isaac." *Holocaust and Genocide Studies* 1.2 (1986): 242-48.

Rosenzweig, Franz. *The Star of Redemption.* Translated by Barbara E. Galli. Madison, WI: University of Wisconsin Press, 2005.

Roskies, David. *Against the Apocalypse: Responses to Catastrophe in Modern Jewish Culture.* Cambridge, MA: Harvard University Press, 1984.

Rubenstein, Richard L. "Job and Auschwitz." In Linafelt, *Strange Fire,* 233-51.

"Saint Veronica." Wikipedia. http://en.wikipedia.org/wiki/Saint_Veronica.

Sarna, Nahum. *Genesis.* Philadelphia: Jewish Publication Society, 1989.

Scarry, Elaine. *The Body in Pain: The Making and Unmaking of the World.* Oxford: Oxford University Press, 1985.

Schlovsky, Victor. "Art as Technique" and "Sterne's Tristram Shandy: Stylistic Commentary." In *Russian Formalist Criticism: Four Essays.* Edited by Lee T. Lemon and Marion J. Reis, 3-57. Lincoln NE: University of Nebraska Press, 1965.

Scholem, Gershom. *Origins of the Kabbalah.* Edited by R. J. Zwi Werblowsky. Translated by Allan Arkush. Philadelphia: Jewish Publication Society; Princeton, NJ: Princeton University Press, 1987.

Serres, Michel. *Statues: Le second livre des fondations.* Paris: Éditions F. Bourin, 1987.

Shaw, W. David. *Elegy and Paradox. Testing the Conventions.* Baltimore, MD: Johns Hopkins University Press, 1994.

Sherwood, Yvonne. *A Biblical Text and Its Afterlives: The Survival of Jonah in Western Culture.* Cambridge: Cambridge University Press, 2000.

———. "Textual Carcasses and Isaac's Scar, or What Jewish Interpretation Makes of the Violence that Almost Takes Place on Mount Moriah." In *Sanctified Aggression: Legacies of Biblical and Post-Biblical Vocabularies of Violence.* Edited by Jonneke Bekkenkamp and Yvonne Sherwood, 22-43. London; New York: Continuum; T & T Clark International, 2003.

Shokek, Shimon. *Kabbalah and the Art of Being.* London: Routledge, 2001.

Singer, Christa. *Samuel Bak: Painter of Questions.* Video. Toronto, Canada, 2003.

Solomon-Godeau, Abigail. "Living with Contradictions. Critical Practices in the Age of Supply-Side Aesthetics." In *The Critical Image: Essays on Contemporary Photography.* Edited by Carol Squiers, 59-79. Seattle, WA: Bay Press, 1990.

Speiser, E. A. *Genesis.* Garden City, NY: Doubleday, 1964, 1980.

Spiegel, Shalom. *The Last Trial: On the Legends and Lore of the Command to Abraham to Offer Isaac as a Sacrifice.* Woodstock, VT: Jewish Lights, 1993.

Steigmann-Gall, Richard. *The Holy Reich: Nazi Conceptions of Christianity.* New York: Cambridge University Press, 2003.

Steiner, George. "A Conversation Piece." *Granta* 15 (Spring 1985; reprinted 1986): 166-78.

Stern, Chaim. *Gates of Prayer.* New York: Central Conference of American Rabbis, 1975.

Strauss, Walter L., ed. *The Intaglio Prints of Albrecht Dürer: Engravings, Etchings, and Dry-Points.* New York: Kennedy Galleries and Abaris Books, 1976.

Sutzkever, Abraham. *Burnt Pearls: Ghetto Poems of Abraham Sutzkever.* Translated from the Yiddish by Seymour Mayne; introduction by Ruth R. Wisse. Oakville, Ont.: Mosaic Press, 1981.

Tayler, Irene, ed. *Between Worlds: The Paintings and Drawings of Samuel Bak from 1946 to 2001.* Boston: Pucker Art Publications, 2002.

———. "Shards of Time: Samuel Bak and the Art of Memory." In Tayler, *Between Worlds,* 1-20.

Tayler, Mark C. *Disfiguring: Art, Architecture, and Religion.* Chicago: University of Chicago Press, 1992.

Trial of the Major War Criminals before the International Military Tribunal. Vol. 2. Nuremberg, 1945. Cited in Jim Walker, "Quotes from Hitler's Henchmen and Nazi Sympathizers." http://www.nobeliefs.com/henchmen.htm.

Touster, Saul. "In and Out of Surrealism: Placing Samuel Bak." In Tayler, *Between Worlds,* 39-56.

Vawter, Bruce. *On Genesis: A New Reading.* Garden City, NY: Doubleday, 1977.

von Rad, Gerhard. *Genesis.* Translated by John H. Marks. Philadelphia: Westminster Press, 1973.

Whiteley, Nigel. "Readers of the Lost Art: Visuality and Particularity in Art Criticism." In *Interpreting Visual Culture: Explorations in the Hermeneutics of the Visual.* Edited by Ian Heywood and Barry Sandywell, 99-122. London; New York: Routledge, 1999.

Wiesel, Elie. "Art and the Holocaust: Trivializing Memory." *New York Times,* sec. 2, June 11, 1989.

———. *Messengers of God: Biblical Portraits and Legends.* Translated by Marion Wiesel. New York: Summit Books, 1976.

———. *Night.* Translated by Stella Rodway. Penguin: London, 1981.

———. *Sarah's Choice.* Chicago: University of Chicago Press, 1989.

———. *The Trial of God (As It Was Held on February 25, 1649, in Shamgorod): A Play.* Translated by Marion Wiesel. New York: Schocken Books, 1979, 1995.

Wollaston, Isabel. "Traditions of Remembrance: Post-Holocaust Interpretations of Genesis 22." In *Words Remembered, Texts Renewed: Essays in Honour of John F. A. Sawyer.* Edited by John Davies, Graham Harvey, and Wilfred G.E. Watson, 41-51. JSOTSups 195. Sheffield: Sheffield Academic Press, 1995.

Yehoshua, A. B. "Mr. Mani and the Akedah." *Judaism* (Winter 2001): 61-65.

Young, James. *The Texture of Memory: Holocaust Memorials and Meaning.* New Haven, CT: Yale University Press, 1993.

Zabel, James A. *Nazism and the Pastors. A Study of the Ideas of Three Deutsche Christen Groups.* AAR Dissertation Series 14. Missoula, MT: Scholars Press, 1976.

Index